Vietnam from Cease-Fire to Capitulation

Col. William E. Le Gro

U.S. ARMY CENTER OF MILITARY HISTORY

WASHINGTON, D.C.

Vietnam from Cease-Fire to Capitulation

For sale by the Superintendent of Documents, U.S. Government Printing Office
Washington, D.C. 20402

with enduring respect to all the fighting men of South Vietnam, especially the infantry, rangers, airborne troops, and marines. May this book preserve at least a partial record of those who fought long, bravely, and under great handicaps and hardships to preserve individual freedom in their country.

Library of Congress Cataloging in Publication Data

Le Gro, William E
   Vietnam from cease-fire to capitulation.

   1. Vietnamese Conflict, 1961–1975. I. Title
DS557.7.L44   959.704'3   80-607143

This book is not copyrighted and may be reproduced in whole or in part without consulting the publisher.

Second printing 1985—CMH Pub 90-29

Contents

Foreword / Introduction   1   2

Chapter 1
Before the Cease-Fire   5

The Nguyen Hue Offensive / The Counteroffensive / The Military Balance, December 1972: Military Region 1; Military Region 2; Military Region 3; Military Region 4 / Note on Sources

Chapter 2
U.S. Organization for the Cease-Fire   17

Enhance and Enhance Plus / Missions / The Defense Attache Office / Note on Sources

Chapter 3
Landgrab 73   21

Military Region 1 / Military Region 2 / Military Region 3 / Military Region 4 / Relative Strength, 31 January 1973 / The Balance Sheet / Note on Sources

Chapter 4
Consolidating and Rebuilding   33

Political Strategy / Preparing for the Military Option / Note on Sources

Chapter 5
The Third Indochina War: First Half-Year   41

Cease-Fire Violations / The Threat to Saigon / The Cambodian Connection / Sparring in the Highlands / Logistics and Infiltration / The SA-7 "Strella" / Note on Sources

Chapter 6
Cease-Fire II in MR 1 and 2   50

June–August / Early Assessments / Trung Nghia / Plei Djereng–Le Minh / Quang Duc / Military Region 1 / Note on Sources

Chapter 7
Cease-Fire II in MR 3 and 4   65

The Delta Rice War / Tri Phap / RVNAF Delta Dispositions / RVNAF Economics and Morale / Ranger Reorganization / Military Region 3 / Cease-Fire Anniversary / Note on Sources

Chapter 8
The Decline of U.S. Support   80

Military Assistance, FY 1974 / Military Assistance, FY 1975 / Note on Sources

Chapter 9
1974, Year of Decision   88

Estimates and Plans / The Tri Phap Campaign / Elephant's Foot and Angel's Wing / Note on Sources

Chapter 10
Strategic Raids   96

Chi Linh / Tong Le Chon / Binh Duong / The Iron Triangle Attack / An Dien Counterattack / Base 82 / Return to Rach Bap / Phu Giao / Bien Hoa / Xuan Loc / Bao Binh and Rung La / Tay Ninh / Note on Sources

Chapter 11
The Highlands to the Hai Van   110

Quang Tin / Dak Pek / Tieu Atar / Quang Nam / Da Trach and Duc Duc / Thuong Duc / Mang Buk / Plei Me / Duc Duc and Que Son / Hill 1062 / Kontum / Chuong Nghia / Quang Ngai / Note on Sources

Chapter 12
The Ring Tightens Around Hue   125

Nui Mo Tau, Nui Bong, and Hill 350 / Order of Battle / The Railroad / Naval Engagement off Quang Tri / An Assist from the Hungarians / Infiltration into the Thua Thien Lowlands / The Hills of Phu Loc and Nam Hoa / Note on Sources

Chapter 13
The Last Christmas: Phuoc Long   132

Phuoc Long—the Setting / Diversions / Binh Tuy–Long Khanh / Tay Ninh / The Last Days of Phuoc Long / Note on Sources

Chapter 14
On the Second Anniversary of the Cease-Fire   138

Reaction to the NVA's Winter Campaign / Military Region 1 / Military Region 2 / Military Region 3 / Military Region 4 / Congressional Visitors / Note on Sources

Chapter 15
The Central Highlands, March 1975   147

Isolating the Battlefield / Darlac and Quang Duc / Exodus from the Highlands

Chapter 16
The Final Offensive in the North   155

The Offensive North of Binh Dinh / Binh Dinh / Kanh Hoa— the End in MR 2

Chapter 17
The Last Act in the South   165

Tri Tam and Tay Ninh / Long An / The Eastern Front / Tay Ninh / Binh Long / Washington / Reorganization and Redeployment / Xuan Loc / The Last Week / Note on Sources, Chapters 15–17

Chapter 18
Was Defeat Inevitable?   179

MAPS

1 The Military Balance, MR 1, Dec 1972	7
2 The Military Balance, MR 2, Dec 1972	10
3 The Military Balance, MR 3, Dec 1972	12
4 The Military Balance, MR 4, Dec 1972	14
5 Landgrab 73	22
6 Ho Chi Minh Trail Network	37
7 Hong Ngu, Mar–Apr 1973	45

Contents

8 The Highlands, 4 Aug—22 Sep 1973	46
9 The Highlands, Oct 1973	53
10 Quang Duc Campaign, 30 Oct—10 Dec 1973	57
11 Tay Ninh–Saigon Corridor, 1973	74
12 Tri Phap Operation, 12-19 Feb 1974	89
13 Svay Rieng Operations, 27 Apr—2 May 1974	92
14 Strategic Raids, MR 3, Summer–Fall 1974	97
15 Iron Triangle Attack, 16 May—7 Jun 1974	100
16 Strategic Raids, Highlands–Hai Van, May–Sep 1974	111
17 Mo Tau–Bong, Defense of Hue, 28 Aug 1974	126
18 Battle of Phuoc Long, Dec 1974—Jan 1975	134
19 The Fall of MR 2, 8 Mar—2 Apr 1975	148
20 Tay Ninh–Tri Tam Battles, 11-26 Mar 1975	166
21 Battle of Xuan Loc, 17 Mar—15 Apr 1975	168
22 Saigon Defenses, Apr 1975	176

TABLES

1 Relative Strength, Late Jan 1973	28
2 Major RVNAF Units, Jan 1973	29
3 Enemy Order of Battle, Late Jan 1973	29
4 Combat Level Indicators, Jun 1973	51
5 Ranger Deployment, 31 Dec 1973	73
6 VNAF Strikes, Oct–Dec 1973	77

Foreword

An infantryman, Colonel William E. Le Gro, USA (Ret.), fought in New Guinea and the Philippines in 1944 and 1945. Subsequent service included troop and staff duty in Germany and Korea and graduation from the Army War College. As a graduate student at American University in 1963 and 1964, the author specialized in East and Southeast Asia. He was also concerned with Southeast Asia while assigned to the office of the Army's Deputy Chief of Staff for Operations in 1964 and 1965. Colonel Le Gro served in Vietnam in 1966 and 1967 as G-2, 1st Infantry Division, and was Director of Asian Studies at the Army War College from 1969 to 1971. From December 1972 until 29 April 1975, he was a senior staff officer with the U.S. Military Assistance Command, Vietnam, and its successor agency, the U.S. Defense Attache Office, Saigon.

The views, evaluations, and conclusions presented here are those of the author and not necessarily those of the Department of the Army, the Department of Defense, or the Department of State. Faculty and students at service schools will find the book useful, however, and it will be a valuable source for historians.

DOUGLAS KINNARD
Brigadier General, USA (Ret.)
Chief of Military History

Introduction

The final declaration of the Geneva Conference on the problems of restoring peace in Indochina was dated 21 July 1954. The second war in Indochina began two years later as the deadline passed for reunification elections and ended on 27 January 1973 as "The Agreement on Ending the War and Restoring Peace in Vietnam" took effect. But the two-year respite that followed the Geneva Conference of 1954 was not to be repeated. What could be called a third Indochina war began immediately after the 1973 agreement.

Although some traces of the Viet Cong (VC) guerrilla forces remained, as well as a few unconvincing contrivances intended to demonstrate the legitimacy of the Provisional Revolutionary Government (PRG) of South Vietnam, the third Indochina conflict quickly assumed the character of conventional war between regular ground forces. Irregulars played an insignificant role in the final outcome. The war's central characteristic was an invasion across well-defined frontiers. With a secure base in the north and a large army already positioned in South Vietnam, the Democratic Republic of Vietnam (DRV) systematically rebuilt and reinforced its expeditionary force without any effective interference until the South Vietnamese ground forces, short of essential resources and demoralized, abandoned entire provinces to concentrate their battered defenders and then collapsed. What follows is the story of that final Indochina struggle and of the eventual and tragic collapse of the South Vietnamese.

The United States in August 1969 entered secret negotiations to end the war in Indochina. Three and a half years later the final agreement was signed in Paris. In a speech to the nation on 25 January 1972 (text in State Dept. *Bulletin,* 14 Feb. 72.), President Richard M. Nixon made the negotiations public and stressed the urgency the United States attached to disengaging from the war and exchanging prisoners of war. The final agreement required major concessions on the part of the Government of the Republic of Vietnam (GVN) and only required the DRV to return prisoners of war and account for soldiers missing in action.

In the final agreement the United States was allowed only 60 days to remove its remaining forces from South Vietnam. On the other hand, the agreement was silent on the presence of North Vietnamese forces in South Vietnam. In a news conference (24 January 1973) announcing the agreement, The Special Assistant to the President for National Security Affairs, Henry A. Kissinger, responded to a related question:

Our estimate of the number of North Vietnamese troops in the South is approximately 145,000. . . . nothing in the agreement establishes the right of North Vietnamese to be in the South. . . . The North Vietnamese have never claimed that they have a right to have troops in the South . . . The North Vietnamese troops in the South should, over a period of time, be subject to considerable reduction. [State Dept. *Bulletin,* 12 Feb. 73.]

Intelligence suggested that Dr. Kissinger's estimate of the strength of the North Vietnamese Army (NVA) in South Vietnam was on the low side. With 13 division headquarters and 75 regiments, the North Vietnamese could have had as many as 160,000 soldiers in the south, an expeditionary force backed up, supplied, and trained from secure bases in the north and in Laos.

No similar advantage accrued to the South Vietnamese. Their logistical and training bases and lines of communication remained vulnerable to infiltration, sabotage, and attack. The South Vietnamese had never been able to carry the attack to North Vietnam, and the agreement provided that "the United States will stop all its military activities against the territory of the Democratic Republic of Vietnam." Although the United States kept forces in Thailand and in the South China Sea and remained capable of either attacking North Vietnam or supporting the South Vietnamese, that proscription in the words of the agreement remained "durable and without limit of time." (Text in State Dept. *Bulletin,* 12 Feb. 73.)

As time passed, the NVA invasion and attacks grew in boldness and scope without attracting any significant response from the United States. After the final bombing halt following the B-52 raids of Christmas 1972, the North Vietnamese probably never again seriously considered that the United States could be provoked into new reprisals. Even if they had been reluctant to violate the agreement in a brazen manner for fear of American reaction, their inhibitions must have been greatly diminished by the congressional prohibition of 15 August 1973 on further bombing of Cambodia and dissipated entirely during the North Vietnamese conquest of Phuoc Long Province in December 1974. Although conclusive evidence is lacking, the Phuoc Long campaign was probably undertaken, in part at least, to test the American response. Since the United States did not respond, the final offensive could proceed as planned without concern for the high costs that would attend a resumption of American bombing of North Vietnam.

In Article 7, the agreement states that

The two South Vietnamese parties shall not accept the introduction of troops, military advisers, and military personnel including technical military personnel, armaments, munitions, and war material into South Vietnam. The two South Vietnamese parties shall be permitted to make periodic replacement of armaments, munitions and war material which have been destroyed, damaged, worn out or used up after the cease-fire, on the basis of piece-for-piece, of the same characteristics and properties ... .

Those restrictions, however, did not apply to military assistance provided North Vietnam by the Soviet bloc and China. Military equipment, supplies, technicians, and advisers continued to flow into Hanoi after the cease-fire. The agreement, moreover, did not specify how the restrictions would be enforced with regard to the NVA forces already in South Vietnam. Responding to a question about this at the news conference of 24 January 1973, Dr. Kissinger said that it was "not inconceivable that the agreement will not in all respects be lived up to. In that case, adding another clause that will not be lived up to, specifically requiring it, would not change the situation." That appraisal proved to be an understatement, for the restrictions had no apparent effect on North Vietnam's rebuilding and reinforcing its expeditionary force. On the other hand, American shipments to South Vietnam after the cease-fire were meticulously accounted for as replacements for similar supplies and for equipment lost, used up, or evacuated.

The temporary partition of Vietnam by the Accords of 1954 was continued in the Paris Agreement. That was done, according to Dr. Kissinger (press conference, 24 January), because "the provisions of the agreement with respect to infiltration, with respect to replacement, with respect to any of the military provisions, would have made no sense whatsoever if there was not some demarcation line defining where South Vietnam began." But the true demarcation was 30 kilometers south of the 17th parallel on the Thach Han River where South Vietnamese marines held on to the rubble of Quang Tri City. The North Vietnamese maintained the fiction of the Demilitarized Zone (DMZ) by locating a customs post on the south bank of the Ben Hai River. Meanwhile, the most extensive NVA logistic base in South Vietnam was constructed from the DMZ through Dong Ha and west along Highway 9 to Khe Sanh. Dong Ha became a major port of entry for military supplies, and the traffic across the DMZ soon surpassed anything seen in the years before the cease-fire.

Ever since the North Vietnamese began major military operations against South Vietnam, they used the Ho Chi Minh Trail in southern Laos and eastern Cambodia as their principal logistical corridor. By January 1973 about 70,000 NVA regulars were in Laos, mainly in the logistical corridor, and about 30,000 were in Cambodia. In Dr. Kissinger's words:

... there is a flat prohibition against the use of base areas in Laos and Cambodia. There is a flat prohibition against the use of Laos and Cambodia for infiltration into Vietnam ... there is a requirement that all foreign troops be withdrawn from Laos and Cambodia, and it is clearly understood that North Vietnamese troops are considered foreign with respect to Laos and Cambodia. .... It is our firm expectation that within a short period of time there will be a formal cease-fire in Laos which in turn will lead to a withdrawal of all foreign forces from Laos and, of course, to the end of the use of Laos as a corridor of infiltration. [Press Conference of 24 Jan., State Dept. *Bulletin*, 12 Feb. 73.]

That withdrawal failed to materialize. There was little reason to think that it would, considering the entrenched position of the North Vietnamese in southern Laos, their reliance on the logistical network established there, and their record of violating the agreements of 1954 and 1962. In the two years after the 1973 cease-fire, the NVA shifted sizeable logistical units from Laos into South Vietnam as it developed the Route 14 corridor south from Khe Sanh. It also moved its 968th Infantry Division from Laos into the Kontum-Pleiku area. But it did not stop using the corridor. On the contrary, it built macadam roads and added concrete culverts and bridges, and infiltration continued. During 1973 over 75,000 replacements entered South Vietnam, mostly through Laos. South Vietnam lacked the means to cope with that flagrant breach of the agreement, and although the United States was concerned, U.S. reconnaissance over the corridor was greatly reduced and what remained did not reveal the destination of some major NVA reinforcements moving south in late 1974 and early 1975.

Another important provision in the agreement established an International Commission of Control and Supervision (ICCS). The ICCS was supposed to detect and investigate violations, control entry into South Vietnam, and generally supervise the cease-fire. Unfortunately for South Vietnam, two of the four members of the commission, Poland and Hungary, were not impartial. They did not man the entry points into South Vietnam, except those used by the United States, and failed to inhibit in any way the movement of men, supplies, and weapons from North Vietnam. One member, Canada, quickly became disenchanted with the frustrations of dealing with an uncontrollable situation and resigned. Replacing Canada, Iran experienced the same frustrations but persisted in trying to give some balance to the reporting and some meaning to the cease-fire. In the face of the North Vietnamese invasion, however, and opposed at every turn by the decidedly hostile Poles and Hungarians, the other commission members could not have changed the outcome of the conflict, no matter how dedicated they were to fairness, law, and peace.

Domestic politics forced the United States to observe the agreement even while the North Vietnamese blatently violated it. Domestic politics also prevented adequate U.S. support in arms, ammunition, and equipment. Thus the military balance shifted in favor of the invader as the capabilities of the South Vietnamese armed forces declined until they were unable to withstand the final NVA offensive.

1

Before the Cease-Fire

The Nguyen Hue Offensive

The Nguyen Hue offensive of 1972 left both sides exhausted and depleted in manpower, supplies, and equipment. The offensive began on 30 March and ran its course by the end of June. There were three arenas of heavy action. Below the Demilitarized Zone, the North Vietnamese Army (NVA) committed three divisions, several separate regiments, and tanks and heavy artillery to seize its principal objectives, Quang Tri Province and Hue. In the Central Highlands, a force of two divisions with tanks and heavy artillery struck at Kontum. In the south, between Saigon and the Cambodian border, three NVA divisions, also with tanks and heavy artillery, attacked out of Cambodian sanctuaries toward Saigon.

By summer, casualties had amounted to thousands and considerable territory had changed hands. The new dispositions were later to provide decisive advantages to the invader. The 17th parallel was eliminated as the division between North and South Vietnam, and the North Vietnamese Army was free to develop a line of communication from Dong Hoi in Quang Binh Province to Dong Ha and the logistical complex along Highway QL-9 from Dong Ha to Khe Sanh. Western Quang Tri was cleared for the construction of an alternate corridor from Khe Sanh to the B-3 Front in Kontum. (The B-3 Front was the NVA command in the Central Highlands.)

Successes in the Kontum battles removed South Vietnamese influence north and west of Kontum City. The development of a logistical complex at Duc Co and the extension of the alternate corridor south to Binh Long Province became possible, although the Army of the Republic of Vietnam (ARVN), in heavy fighting, managed to delay progress until the end of 1972.

As the campaign in South Vietnam's Military Region 3 (MR 3) ended in the seige of An Loc, only 90 kilometers north of Saigon, the NVA controlled all of Binh Long Province except the province capital and the small garrison at Chon Thanh on Highway QL-13. Only a major effort could keep Highway 13 open north of the ARVN 5th Division base at Lai Khe, and An Loc and Chon Thanh soon became entirely dependent on air resupply. Similarly, the NVA was in position to control land access to Phuoc Binh (Song Be), the capital of Phuoc Long Province. That advantage was to be used with decisive effect in the NVA's conquest of Phuoc Long in December 1974.

The enemy's objectives for the Nguyen Hue offensive in the Mekong Delta, South Vietnam's Military Region 4, lacked the focus that characterized the fighting in other military regions. Communist strategy in that densely populated rice bowl was to attack on a broad front, blanketing the region in order to gain control over as much land and population as possible. Intending to destroy or immobilize the ARVN and overrun province and district capitals, the North Vietnamese launched major, successive attacks by large, main force formations. The South Vietnamese used infantry divisions, ranger groups, and armored cavalry squadrons to engage the NVA's main force, while territorials handled hundreds of local threats.

The Counteroffensive

The plans of the Central Office for South Vietnam (COSVN), the North Vietnamese Army's headquarters in the southern part of South Vietnam, called for seizing An Loc before advancing southward into Bing Duong Province and Saigon. Supported by U.S. bombers, which proved to be crucial, the South Vietnamese fought heroically and denied the enemy An Loc but achieved little else. By the end of 1972, the North Vietnamese still held every important objective they had seized during the campaign. At that time South Vietnam's line of relatively secure control in Military Region 3—that is, bases that could be supported by lines of communication and secured through minor operations—ran from the Cambodian border west of Tay Ninh City, generally east to Dau Tieng on the Saigon River, down to Bau Bang, north of Lai Khe, over to Phuoc Vinh (Phu Giao) on Highway LTL-1A, and along the Song Be and the Dong Nai River to north of Xuan Loc in Long Khanh Province. Highway QL-20 was open from Xuan Loc to Dalat, but local Route 2 south to Baria in Phuoc Tuy Province was hazardous. Highway QL-1 was open to Nha Trang.

Despite staggering losses—the Kontum campaign cost the enemy 4,000 lives—the North Vietnamese in the Nguyen Hue offensive secured a lodgment inside Kontum City, although by mid-June of 1972 the city was again under South Vietnamese control. In tough fighting the ARVN cleared Highway QL-14 from Kontum to Pleiku by early July and opened it to civilian traffic. Enemy interdictions, however, continued to close it periodically until the end of the year. Operations north on Highway QL-14 were less successful, and the enemy retained control from Vo Dinh all the way to Dak Pek. Highway QL-19 remained open to Binh Dinh, although subjected to periodic interdictions, and the situation was tenuous along Highway QL-1 running through the province.

The enemy's main effort in the Nguyen Hue offensive in the Mekong Delta began when the NVA 1st Division moved from its Cambodian base into the Seven Mountains of Chau Doc Province. Losses were heavy on both sides during the last week of March, and the 1st Division managed to retain a foothold in the craggy peaks. Another surge of attacks hit mostly in Chuong Thien and southern Kien Giang Provinces in the second week of April, and by the time the ARVN had reasserted its dominance, nearly 400 of its soldiers had died while another 700 or more had been wounded. During late May and early June, the NVA launched a fresh campaign against Kien Luong District in Kien Giang Province, using the 1st Division to spearhead the drive, but ARVN rangers of the 44th Special Tactical Zone drove most of the 1st Division back to Cambodia. Meanwhile, the NVA 5th Division pulled away from the Binh Long battlefield, moved across Prey Veng Province in Cambodia, and attacked Moc Hoa, the capital of Kien Tuong Province, and Tuyen Binh District town. Badly mauled, the 5th Division, by mid-June, withdrew into Cambodia, followed by the ARVN 7th Division.

The next sharp upsurge occurred on 4 July 1972 when two ARVN battalions were decimated in an ambush in the northern part of the Mekong Delta. Meanwhile, activity increased in and around Base Area 470 where five enemy regiments operated, threatening Highway QL-4 as well as Route 29 between Moc Hoa and Cai Lay. Anticipating a cease-fire, during October many enemy main force units split into small groups to spread control over vast reaches of the delta. They were methodically and thoroughly defeated. The action was punctuated by two high points: one from 2 to 9 October against Highway QL-4 between Can Tho and Saigon; the other beginning on 26 October and much more widespread throughout the delta. When October's fighting had subsided, no major changes in territorial control had taken place, but the NVA's strength in the delta was significantly diminished.

The South Vietnamese counteroffensive in Military Region 1 achieved significant territorial gains. The attack to retake Quang Tri City jumped off on 28 June 1972. Eighty grueling, hard-fought days later, on 15 September, South Vietnamese marines recaptured the Citadel and the rubble that once was the city of Quang Tri.

By the end of the year, the marines had pushed north along the coast to the Thach Han River. The western-most thrust of the counteroffensive ended at Fire Support Base (FSB) Anne, while the security of Hue was improved by recapturing FSB Bastogne. The Hai Van Pass was secure, but only a narrow coastal strip along Highway QL-1 remained in South Vietnamese control south to the Binh Dinh border. (National Route 1 climbs over Hai Van ridge on the boundary of Quang Nam and Thua Thien Provinces. The ridge juts into the sea to form the northern enclosure of Da Nang Bay and separates the northern and southern sectors of MR 1.)

The Military Balance, December 1972

MILITARY REGION 1

Military Region 1, the responsibility of ARVN's I Corps, encompassed the five northern provinces. North of the Hai Van Pass in Quang Tri and Thua Thien were the 1st Division and the Marine and Airborne divisions. Enemy forces in those provinces operated under control of Military Region Tri-Thien-Hue (MRTTH) and the B-5 Front. South of the pass, enemy forces were commanded by North Vietnam's Military Region 5, while two ARVN divisions, the 3d in Quang Nam and northern Quang Tin Provinces and the 2d in Quang Tin and Quang Ngai Provinces, were controlled by I Corps Headquarters at Da Nang. (Map 1)

The NVA began the Nguyen Hue offensive in South Vietnam's Military Region 1 with three divisions, but by the end of the offensive had employed eight divisions, five independent infantry regiments, probably three armor regiments, and six or seven artillery regiments. There were in addition several sapper regiments, perhaps 4, and up to 33 independent local battalions of infantry, field artillery, antiaircraft artillery, reconnaissance troops, and sappers. (Sapper regiments in the NVA were similar to what other armies would call assault or shock infantry, and to the U.S. Army Ranger Battalions of World War II. They were specially trained in employing mines and demolitions and neutralizing and breaching minefields and fortifications. Elements of sapper regiments often preceded regular infantry in the assault of defensive positions. The NVA had also specialized sapper units, smaller than regiments, such as water sappers, trained in swimming and underwater demolitions.)

That formidable force was opposed by five South Vietnamese divisions, a ranger group, some ranger border defense battalions, and the territorial forces of the provinces. (South Vietnamese ranger groups had three battalions, lighter than the regular infantry, authorized 661 men each. A ranger border defense battalion, designed to defend an isolated,

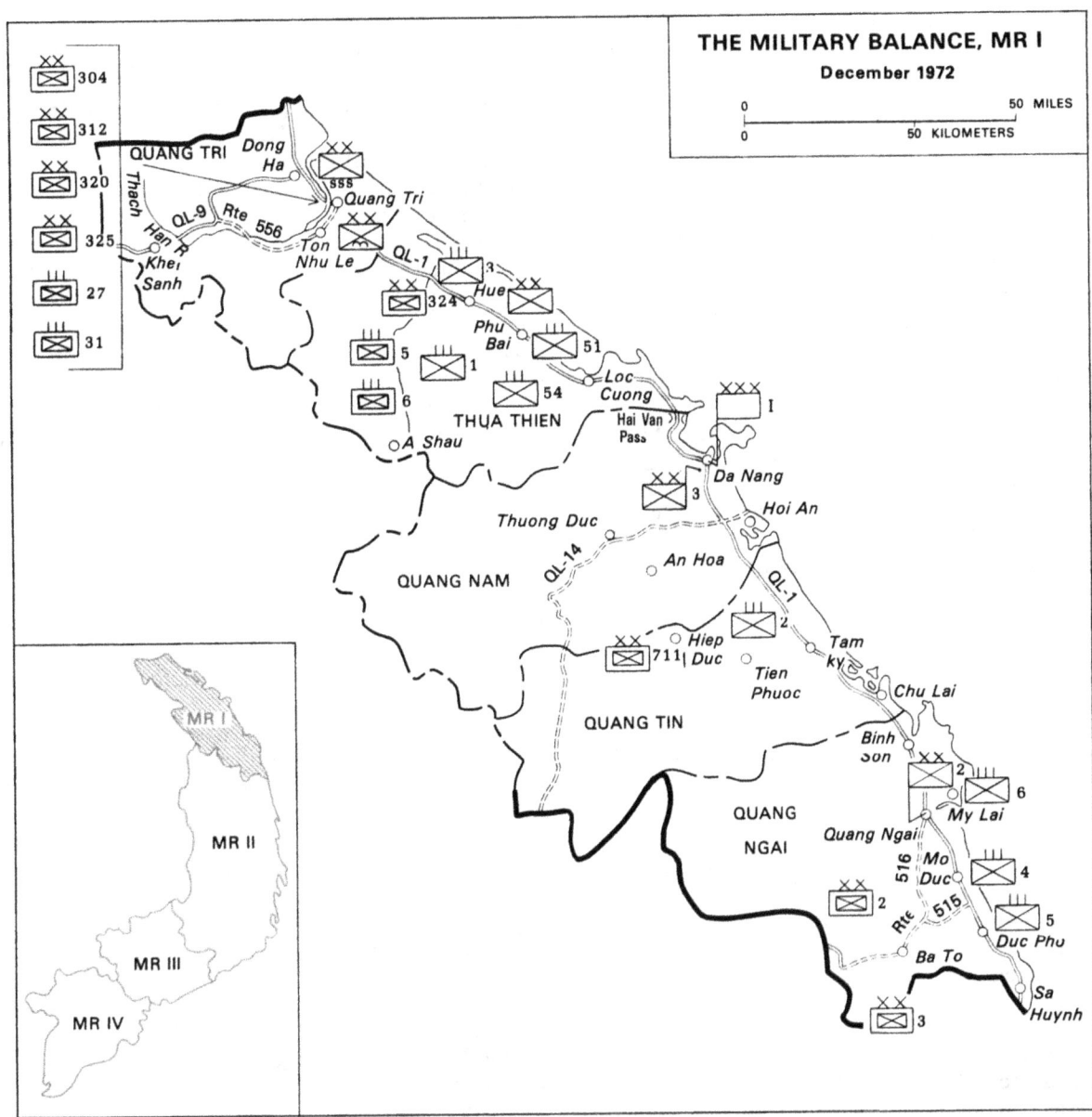

Map 1

forward operating base, was authorized only 461. The territorial forces were composed of Regional Forces [RF] and Popular Forces [PF]. Regional Forces were organized into companies and battalions and were controlled by province chiefs; Popular Forces were organized into platoons and were commanded by village and hamlet chiefs.)

During November 1972, two South Vietnamese marine brigades supported by B-52s and U.S. naval gunfire, attacked north along the coast east of Provincial Route 560 in Quang Tri Province, to seize the south bank of the Cua Viet River. Hampered by stiff resistance and heavy December rains, the marines were in defensive positions by the end of the year, still short of their objective. They were opposed by elements of the NVA 325th Division, prinicipally the 101st Regiment, and the 48th Regiment of the 320th Division, both regiments supported by the 164th Artillery Regiment of the B-5 Front. The 164th was equipped with Soviet 130-mm. field guns. Between the 101st Regiment, operating along the coast, and Quang Tri City, the NVA employed the 27th and 31st Regiments of the B-5 Front, as well as the 18th Regiment, 325th Division. (The practice of assigning the same numerical designation to more than one unit was not unusual in the NVA. The 101st Regiment, 325th Division, was distinct from the 101st Regiment that operated in Tay Ninh and Hau Nghia Provinces under the control of the Central Office for South Vietnam—

COSVN. The 165th Infantry Regiment of the 312th Division was in Quang Tri Province, and another 165th Infantry Regiment of the 7th Division was in Binh Duong Province. Still more confusing for order-of-battle analysts, those two divisions each had 141st and 209th Regiments, while NVA 2d Division in Quang Ngai Province also had a 141st.)

While the marines held Quang Tri City, the Airborne Division was defending the hills south and southwest of the city and attacking toward the line of the Thach Han River. The attacks reached Route 556 between Nhu Le and Quang Tri, and Fire Support Bases Anne and Barbara in the Hai Lang forest were recaptured by airborne troops in November, using tactical air and B-52 strikes with good effect. Activity declined, however, in December because of monsoon rains and flooding. Elements of the NVA 312th Division and the 95th Regiment, 325th Division, opposed the airborne troops south of Quang Tri City. As the year ended, the 95th Regiment was defending on the south bank of the Thach Han from Quang Tri to positions north of FSB Anne. On that regiment's right, northwest of FSB Anne, was the 209th Regiment, 312th Division. The headquarters of the 312th Division was probably located about six kilometers west of FSB Anne with its 165th Regiment in the vicinity. Just to the southwest was the 66th Regiment of the 304th Division. No fewer than four NVA divisions and two B-5 Front regiments were defending the Cua Viet–Thach Han line in Quang Tri: the 304th, 312th, 320th, and 325th Divisions and the 27th and 31st Regiments. The other NVA division that had fought in Quang Tri during the Nguyen Hue offensive, the 308th, was by this time on its way back to North Vietnam to recuperate and rejoin the general reserve.

Besides the Marine and Airborne Divisions, the only other ARVN division north of the Hai Van Pass was the 1st Division. Like the 22d Division in II Corps, the 1st was a heavy division. It had four regiments—the 1st, 3d, 51st, and 54th—and each regiment had four battalions. The 1st Division was responsible for defending from the Song Bo corridor through the Hai Van Pass, for supporting the territorial forces in the defense of Hue, and for securing the line of communication. Opposing the 1st were three regiments of the 324th Division—the 29th, 803d, and 812th—which were generally deployed opposite Hue, the 5th and 6th independent regiments in the hills southwest of Hue, and local main force battalions south of Phu Loc. At year's end, the 3d Regiment of the 1st Division held positions, including FSB T-Bone, south and east of the Song Bo. To its south, the 1st Regiment held FSB Veghel and FSB Bastogne controlling the approach to Hue along Route 547. With headquarters in Phu Bai, the 51st Regiment was patrolling Highway 1 south to the Hai Van Pass. The 54th Regiment was in the hills south and southwest of Phu Bai and Phu Loc.

The ARVN 3d Division had been shattered in Quang Tri during the Nguyen Hue offensive. Although it was still rebuilding and retraining, it was responsible for the important southwestern approaches to Da Nang: Duc Duc District and the Que Son Valley, scenes of some of the heaviest fighting in 1972. Enemy advances in this area inevitably led to the rocketing of Da Nang Airbase, as happened on 26 December. Even more threatening was the possibility of the enemy bringing his field guns within range of the city and the airbase. The ARVN could give up very little more terrain before that threat would become a reality. NVA formations opposing the 3d Division in Quang Nam and northern Quang Tin were the 711th Division with its three regiments—the 31st, 38th, and 270th—and the 572d Tank-Artillery Regiment of the enemy's Military Region 5. A sapper regiment, the 5th, which operated in Quang Nam and Quang Tin Provinces, had been broken in heavy combat during the year and was disbanded in December. Its understrength battalions were assigned to MR 5 and the 711th Division.

The ARVN 3d Division straddled the boundary between Quang Nam and Quang Tin Provinces, which bisected the Que Son Valley. Although the division was able to hold Fire Support Base Ross in the valley's center, it could not reach Hiep Duc. From a base behind Hiep Duc, the 711th Division deployed its regiments forward into the valley and on the ridges above. As the end of the year approached, the division's 31st Regiment had elements southwest of FSB Ross, and its 270th Regiment (also known as the 9th) had elements near Route 536 where it crossed the ridge west of the base and on the Nui Ong Gai ridge to the south. The ARVN 2d Regiment, 3d Division, was in contact on Nui Ong Gai.

Reports from prisoners of war and deserters alluded to serious morale problems in the 711th Division. Malaria and battle casualties had taken a heavy toll, and battalions, particularly those in the 270th Regiment, were below 200 men. The reports gained added credence in the summer of 1973 when the 711th was redesignated the 2d Division and the 270th Regiment was disbanded entirely. The weakness of the 711th gave the aggressive commander of the newly reorganized 3d ARVN Division, Brig. Gen. Nguyen Duy Hinh, the opportunity to move his battalions out of the rocket belt around Da Nang westward into Quang Nam Province and the Que Son Valley.

The ARVN 2d Division fought heavy actions in southern Quang Tin and Quang Ngai Provinces in the fall and winter of 1972. In late September, its 5th

Regiment and the 77th Ranger Battalion failed in a tardy effort to save Tien Phuoc District Town in Quang Tin Province, but the town was subsequently recaptured by the 2d Regiment, 3d Division. Meanwhile, reinforced by the 4th Tank Battalion, the 78th Ranger Battalion, and the 2d Ranger Group, the 2d Division's 4th and 5th Regiments cleared the enemy's 52d Regiment, 2d Division, and elements of the NVA 3d Division from Mo Duc and Duc Pho, two important towns on Highway 1(QL-1). After participating in the Tien Phuoc success, the 6th Regiment returned from the 3d Division to the 2d Division and, with the 1st Ranger Group, operated east of Highway 1 in the Batangan Peninsula and around My Lai. An attempt by the ARVN 5th Regiment to retake the highland district town, Ba To, was unsuccessful. Opposing the 2d Division in Quang Ngai were the 1st, 52d, and 141st Regiments of the NVA 3d Division from its bases in northern Binh Dinh Province.

The NVA 2d Division was in poor condition. It had moved to Quang Ngai Province in June 1972 after incurring heavy losses at Kontum in April and May. It was probably at no more than half-strength when it arrived in Quang Ngai, and it soon lost another third to B-52 raids and ARVN operations. Although the division received some replacements, morale and combat effectiveness in the weeks before the cease-fire were low. NVA objectives in southern Quang Ngai were to block Highway 1 and seize the small port of Sa Huynh. Despite its weakened condition, the 2d Division was going to be handed the mission of achieving those objectives, and as the year ended it was preparing to attack while the South Vietnamese in southern Quang Ngai retained a precarious hold on Highway 1.

Military Region 2

Military Region 2, largest of the four South Vietnamese regions, included all of the provinces of the Central Highlands and the long coastline from Binh Dinh Province south to the northern border of Binh Tuy Province, only 60 miles east of Saigon. At year's end the enemy had three regular divisions and numerous independent regiments and battalions opposing the ARVN's 22d and 23d Divisions, 21st Medium Tank Battalion, and three ranger groups and the Republic of Korea (ROK) Tiger Division. Two of the NVA divisions were in the highlands, the 10th (first organized in December) in Kontum and the 320th in Pleiku. The NVA 3d Division was in Binh Dinh. (Map 2)

The appearance of military balance in Military Region 2—three divisions opposed by three divisions—was deceptive, for the ROK Tiger Division had all but withdrawn from action following hard fighting in April in the An Khe Pass. For that matter, until forced into responding at An Khe when the enemy overran its outposts, the Tiger Division had been quiescent for about three years.

Although the ARVN 22d Division had incurred heavy losses during the Nguyen Hue offensive, the division was somewhat aggressive in moving against enemy bases in Binh Dinh Province and in securing the most important lines of communication, Highway 1 (QL-1) along the coast, and Highway 19 (QL-19), which climbs westward over the Annamite range to Pleiku. Security on the latter route, whose steep grades, blind curves, defiles, and many bridges created ideal opportunities for ambush, was being provided by the 3d and 19th Armored Cavalry Squadrons. The 22d Division had four regiments: the 40th was in northern Binh Dinh in the area of the Bong Son Pass; the 41st was in Tam Quan, the northernmost district of Binh Dinh; the 42d was in reserve in Hoai An District; and the 47th was providing security around Phu Cu on Highway 1. Reinforcing the 22d Division in Binh Dinh were the 14th Armored Cavalry Squadron in Bong Son and two regiments of ARVN rangers—the 4th Ranger Group east of Tam Quan, and the 6th east of Phu Cu.

With the NVA 3d Division recuperating in the An Lao Valley and the ARVN 22d Division exerting pressure on the exits from the valley, the situation had stabilized in northern Binh Dinh Province. Estimates at the time placed the 3d Division at less than 40 percent of authorized strength. Its three regiments—the 2d, 12th, and 21st—were operating with fewer than 800 men each. To the south in Phu Yen, Khanh Hoa, and Binh Thuan Provinces, local security along Highway 1 was adequate to keep traffic moving. In the Central Highlands, meanwhile, South Vietnamese objectives were to drive the enemy from positions around Vo Dinh, north of Kontum City, and to push west in Thanh An District of Pleiku Province to drive the NVA 320th Division from Duc Co.

Kontum City is located near the northern end of a high, rolling plateau with the airfield on the north side of the city at an elevation of over 1800 feet. The land begins to rise abruptly to the east and north where steep, jungle-covered ridges reach an elevation of 2700 feet within 10 kilometers of the city. This arc of hills was defended by the ARVN, but the density of the forest, the steepness of the terrain, and the absence of roads eliminated the area as an avenue for large or mechanized enemy forces.

Although Kontum was the last major city north of Pleiku in the western highlands, Highway 14 (QL-14) continued as an improved road as far as the ARVN outpost at Dak To, about 40 kilometers north of Kontum. The highway was the main route to Kontum from the north. The NVA had used it to enter Kontum in the Nguyen Hue offensive, and although the ARVN had eventually cleared the

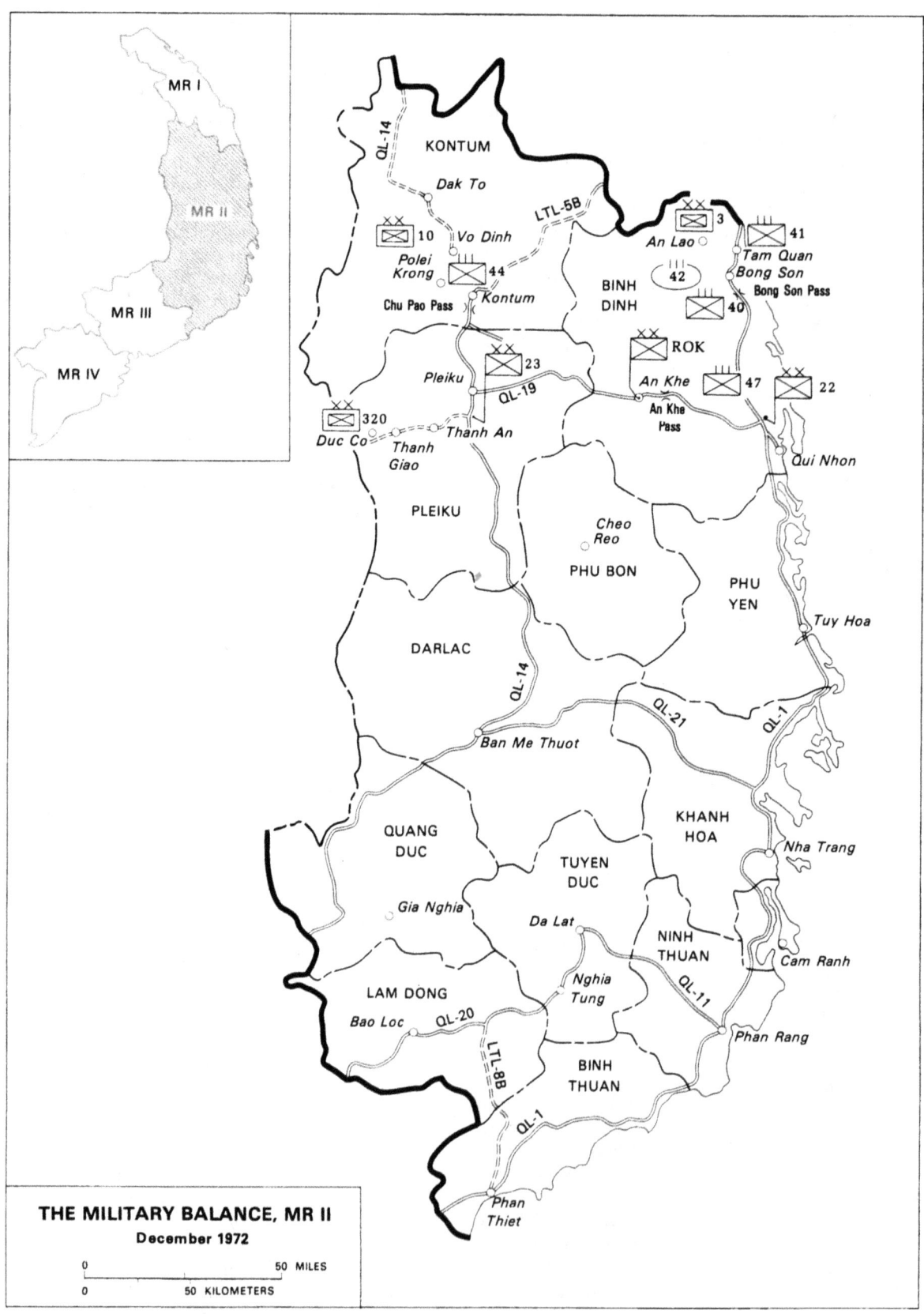

Map 2

city, a number of attempts to push the NVA beyond Vo Dinh, north of Kontum, had failed. The forward ARVN defenses northwest of Kontum were manned by the 44th Regiment, 23d Division at Base N, a strongpoint constructed behind the Dak La Stream and on Eo Gio hill, astride Highway 14 north of Base N, near the Kontum airfield. Strongpont R, south of N, gave some depth to the defense.

The Dak Bla River looped around the city on the south and meandered westward to join the Poko River near Trung Nghia village. The Montagnard hamlet of Polei Krong was on the Poko, just north of the confluence. With the 85th Ranger Border Defense Battalion at Polei Krong, the ARVN held Trung Nghia with Kontum Regional Forces.

The enemy's 10th Division was responsible for control of the area north and west of Kontum City. Its 28th Regiment was probably in the vicinity of the Ngok Bay ridge, a spine-like chain 2,000 feet high that American troops had named Rocket Ridge because the enemy had long used it as a base for firing rockets on Kontum. The 66th Regiment was in the vicinity of Dak To, while on the last day of December 1972, the 95B Regiment, forcing a withdrawal by the 44th ARVN Regiment of the 23d Division, managed to secure a lodgment in the Chu Pao Pass where Highway 14 curves between 3,000-foot peaks south of Kontum City. All three NVA regiments had incurred heavy losses during the Nguyen Hue offensive and were considered to have only about 25 percent of authorized strength. A fourth regiment, the 24B Independent Regiment of the B-3 Front, was located west of the Chu Pao Pass. That regiment was probably at less than 40 percent of authorized strength.

The 320th NVA Division, at about 60 percent of authorized strength, was in Base Area 701 in the vicinity of Duc Co. Its 48th Regiment was near Thanh Giao in western Pleiku Province, and its 64th Regiment was probably close to Thanh An District town. The division had only two infantry regiments at the time, having transferred its 52d Regiment to the NVA 2d Division during August 1972 where it operated in Quang Nam and Quang Tin Provinces. The division's 54th Artillery Regiment was providing support from the vicinity of Thanh An.

Thirty days before the cease-fire, the military balance in the Central Highlands was precarious. The NVA 10th Division had two regiments concentrated north and west of Kontum City and had a third interdicting Highway 14 in the Chu Pao Pass. Although the enemy was unable to keep the road closed, he could interdict the road any time he wished to pay the price. The ARVN was unable to extend its defenses as far as Vo Dinh or beyond Polei Krong in the west. The enemy had the capability of bombarding Kontum and its outskirts by rocket whenever he chose. Although the ARVN was capable of keeping open the line of communication from Kontum to Pleiku to Binh Dinh Province, the enemy could interdict it for short periods of time.

As the year ended, the ARVN 23d Division after heavy fighting was in possession of the border camp at Duc Co. The 23d owed much of its success at Duc Co and in Thanh An District to heavy U.S. B-52 support and to the attached 41st Regiment of the 22d Division, which had taken Duc Co after elements of the 23d had failed. The defense of Duc Co was then turned over to the 73d Ranger Border Defense Battalion. Although events proved that the ARVN could not hold Duc Co indefinitely, it was strong enough to prevent any significant enemy gains elsewhere in Thanh An District. For either side to make any significant tactical gains in the Central Highlands, reinforcements would have to be added to the equation.

MILITARY REGION 3

Military Region 3 contained not only the seat of the government of South Vietnam and its financial and commercial center, but also all of the most important operational, logistic, and training bases of the armed forces. The Joint General Staff (JGS) was in a compound adjacent to Tan Son Nhut Airbase on the northwestern edge of the city of Saigon. Tan Son Nhut itself was the hub of international and domestic air traffic, the headquarters of the Vietnamese Air Force and the 5th Air Division, and the home base of the ARVN Airborne Division. Most seaborne commerce steamed through the ship channels of the Rung Sat south of Saigon and passed through the city's docks on the Saigon River. The headquarters of the Vietnamese Navy was also on the Saigon River, near the major military terminal, Newport, and the largest petroleum storage terminal in the country was a few miles south of Saigon, also on the river, at Nha Be. (Map 3)

Major military training installations were the Quang Trung National Training Center, just north of Saigon, the Thu Duc Training Center, site of the Infantry and Armor Schools until they were moved to Bear Cat, near Bien Hoa, and the Marine Corps Center at Di An, north of Saigon. The ARVN Arsenal was also on the northern edge of the city. Northeast, across the broad Dong Nai River, was the sprawling military complex of Bien Hoa-Long Binh. A modern four-lane highway and the national railway linked Saigon with Bien Hoa. At Bien Hoa were the logistical headquarters of the South Vietnamese Air Force and the 3d Air Division, which contained, except for one squadron at Da Nang, the entire F-5 force. Long Binh, the former logistical center of the U.S. Army in Vietnam, housed the 1st

Map 3

ARVN Associated Depot and later the Command and General Staff College.

The flat rice-lands of the Mekong Delta lay a few miles west of Saigon's city limits with the rice-rich province of Long An to the south. The brushlands of southern Tay Ninh and Binh Duong Provinces started only 25 kilometers north of the city and gave way to the vast jungle of the Dong Nai Terrace, which stretched to the Cambodian border.

Saigon was the focus of five first-class national highways. National Route 1 (QL-1) came from Phnom Penh and traversed Svay Rieng Province before entering Vietnam in Tay Ninh Province west of Go Dau Ha. Highway 1 then passed through Saigon and continued through Bien Hoa and Xuan Loc on its way up the coast. Three major north and northeast routes began in or north of the city. Highway 13 (QL-13), sometimes called Thunder Road for the many ambushes that had taken place along its jungled length, ran north through Lai Khe and An Loc and crossed into Cambodia north of Loc Ninh. Route 1A (LTL-1A) branched off Highway 13 in Phu Cuong, about twenty kilometers north of Saigon, crossed the Song Be, and climbed through the jungles of War Zone D to Don Luan where it joined Route 14. Highway 14 (QL-14) continued on to Ban Me Thuot and points north, but left Military Region 3 at the Quang Duc border.

One of the most secure major roads in Vietnam was Highway 20 (QL-20), which left Route 1 east of Bien Hoa and reached Dalat, 230 kilometers by air from Tan Son Nhut. When Highway 1 was interdicted, Highway 20 was a good alternate route to

Nha Trang. Another secure route and perhaps the most heavily travelled in the country, was Highway 4 (QL-4) to the Mekong Delta. It was vital to Saigon's rice supply, and its several major bridges and thousands of culverts required constant vigilance against sabotage.

By the end of December 1972, both South and North Vietnam had made adjustments in their forces in Military Region 3. The seige of An Loc was over, and only one NVA regiment, 95C, remained in the vicinity. The ARVN 18th Division had turned over the defense of An Loc to the MR 3 Ranger Command with eight ranger battalions. One of the battalions, the 92d, was defending the outpost at Tong Le Chon. The NVA 9th Division (the old 9th Viet Cong Division), leaving its 95C Regiment to prevent any ARVN land movement in or out of An Loc, had shifted its 272d Regiment to the vicinity of Bo Duc in northwestern Phuoc Long Province for rest and refitting. The 271st Regiment of the 9th Division was northeast of Chon Thanh in southern Binh Long Province in position to block the ARVN from using Highway 13 between Chon Thanh and An Loc and to threaten South Vietnamese posts at Chi Linh and Don Luan (also known as Dong Xoai).

Don Luan, in Phuoc Long Province, and Chi Linh, in Binh Long Province, were defended by Regional Forces and were customarily resupplied by air. Chi Linh was beyond the range of secured roads, and all travel was by helicopter. On the other hand, Route 1A connected Don Luan to Phu Giao where the South Vietnamese 7th Regiment, 5th Division, was stationed. In early January 1973, the 7th cleared the highway permitting a convoy to reach Don Luan. North of Don Luan, Highway 14 was interdicted, and much of the logistical support beyond that point was by air. The base at Phuoc Long Province headquarters in Phuoc Binh was resupplied by fixed-wing aircraft and by road via Quang Duc. Just south of Phuoc Binh was the landing strip and village of Song Be, and forces there were within supporting range of those at Phuoc Binh. A transplanted community, New Bo Duc, was constructed south of Song Be; the population consisted of refugees from a village in northern Phuoc Long Province taken over by the North Vietnamese. In northern MR 3, the South Vietnamese controlled only the capitals of Binh Long and Phuoc Long Provinces and Highway 14 as far as the western border of Quang Duc Province. The rest of the territory, which was largely forest and rubber plantations, was controlled by enemy units or was unoccupied by either side.

The ARVN 5th Division had placed its headquarters at Lai Khe in Binh Duong Province, with one regiment usually based at Phu Giao. The NVA 205th Regiment, which had been operating under the control of the NVA 7th Division, was opposing the ARVN 5th in eastern Binh Duong. Concern for the security of Phuoc Long had prompted the stationing of the 9th Regiment, 5th Division, at Phuoc Binh. At the same time, the NVA 7th Division was operating from a base east of Highway 13 between Chon Thanh and Bau Bang.

The ARVN 18th Division was headquartered at Xuan Loc, the capital of Long Khanh Province. It usually kept one regiment based in Bien Hoa and one in southern Binh Duong. The NVA 33d Regiment was in its normal area of operations in Long Khanh Province. The D10 Sapper Battlion was in the Rung Sat south of Saigon. At year's end, the 274th Regiment was believed to be in its traditional jungle base area, the Hat Dich Secret Zone, on the border between southern Bien Hoa Province and Long Khanh.

In western Military Region 3, the ARVN 25th Division was in its base at Cu Chi in Hau Nghia Province, just south of the Saigon River and the Ho Bo Woods. It kept one regiment at Cu Chi, one around Khiem Hanh north of Cu Chi, and one in Tay Ninh at the airstrip west of the province capital. Two battlions of the 50th Regiment, 25th Division, were in the Dau Tieng area of Binh Duong; one battalion was in Tri Tam, and the other was on the west, and opposite, side of the Saigon River. The NVA 101st Regiment was in the vicinity, probably in the Boi Loi Woods east of Khiem Hanh. The NVA 271st Independent Regiment was probably close to the Vam Co Dong River south of Go Dau Ha in Hau Nghia Province, posing a threat to Highways 1 and 22, the line of communication between Saigon and Tay Ninh.

As December came to a close, the 5th and 25th Divisions attacked north into the Saigon River corridor. Three battalions of the 5th moved into the Iron Triangle, while on the west side of the river four battalions of the 25th entered the Ho Bo Woods. Resistance was weak and casualties light.

During the Nguyen Hue offensive in MR 3, the North Vietnamese suffered much more severely than the forces of South Vietnam. Enemy units were dispersed thoughout the northern part of the region, and his local forces were in disarray. NVA units were estimated to be less than 30 percent of normal strength, and local forces were even lower. The NVA nevertheless held the important village of Loc Ninh in northern Binh Long Province and was using it as a political center for the region, and other political centers were being established in northern Tay Ninh Province.

Although the ARVN was conducting some modest offensive operations, it seldom ranged far from established bases, and heavy reliance would have to be placed upon aerial supply of the isolated bases of An Loc and Song Be. The enemy nevethe-

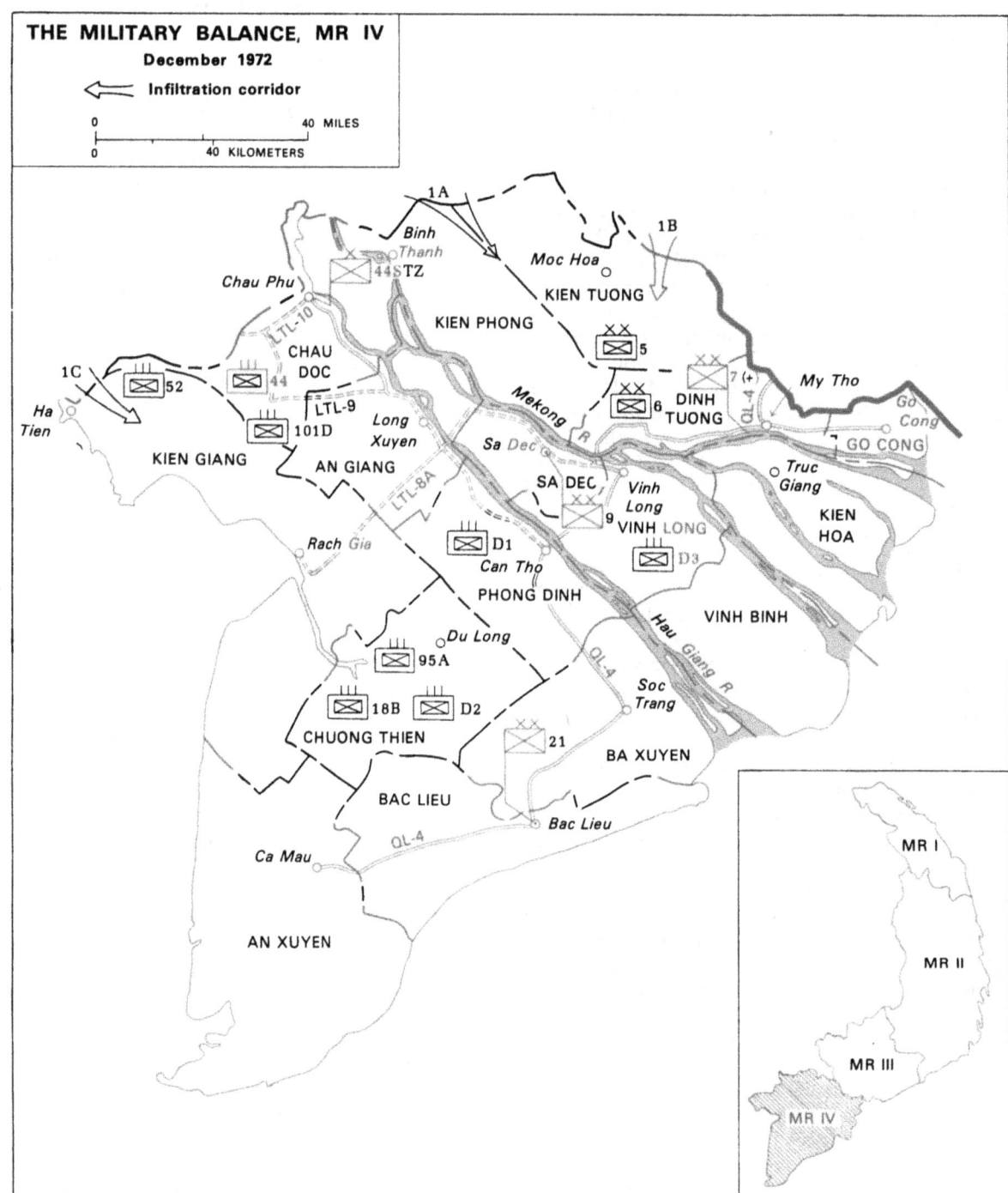

Map 4

less posed no serious offensive threat to friendly forces or population centers in MR 3.

Military Region 4

South Vietnam's Military Region 4 contained 16 of the nation's 44 provinces, more than half of the cultivated land, most of which was devoted to rice, and more than half of the country's population. The region was the broad, tropical, fertile delta of the great Mekong River. Its geographic, demographic, and economic characteristics dictated a war of predominantly small unit actions or attacks by fire and without armor or heavy artillery support. Much of the tactical and logistical movement was by waterway, and many of the battles were fought for control of canals. (Map 4)

By the end of December 1972, the ARVN had three divisions stationed in MR 4. The 7th Division, with headquarters near My Tho, was responsible for Kien Phong, Kien Tuong, Dinh Tuong, and Go Cong Provinces. A major problem facing the 7th was security in densely populated Dinh Tuong. That province was the key to control of Highway 4 (QL-4), the important line of communication leading to Saigon, and it contained the major city of My Tho. It was also the focus of two major enemy infiltration corridors from Cambodia. One, Corridor 1A, generally paralleled the boundary between Kien Phong and Kien Tuong Provinces into the key enemy base, the Tri Phap, at the junction of Kien Phong, Kien Tuong, and Dinh Tuong Provinces. The other, Corridor 1B, came out of Cambodia's Svay Rieng Province and entered Dinh Tuong Province and the Tri Phap through the Plain of Reeds in Kien Tuong Province.

Two enemy divisions opposed the ARVN 7th Division in MR 4. The NVA 5th Division with three regiments, the 275th, the 174th, and the E6, had fought in the Nguyen Hue campaign in the Binh Long battles of April through June 1972, then moved to the Mekong Delta and campaigned in Kien Tuong, Kien Phong, and Dinh Tuong Provinces. The 6th NVA Division was in central Dinh Tuong. Its 24th Regiment was probably located east of My Tho close to the border of Go Cong Province; the 207th Regiment was in northern Kien Phong Province; and the 320th Regiment, which was probably operating as part of the 6th Division, was in southern Kien Phong. The ARVN 7th Division, with an attached regiment of the ARVN 9th Division, had to cope with two independent regiments, the 88th and the DT1, controlled by VC Military Region 2. Although the 7th as the year ended had secured the vital line of communication to Saigon and the enemy's actions were limited to attacks by fire against outposts and populated areas, it had an imposing assignment.

The ARVN 9th Division was responsible for Sa Dec, Vinh Long, Vinh Binh, and Kien Hoa Provinces. The 9th was opposed by only one main force regiment, D3, under the command of VC Military Region 3. One of only two main force regiments in South Vietnam still considered to be predominantly Viet Cong, the D3 Regiment was probably operating in southeastern Vinh Long.

The ARVN 21st Division was responsible for the southwestern delta with an area of operations including Phong Dinh, Ba Xuyen, Bac Lieu, An Xuyen, and Chuong Thien Provinces and the southern half of Kien Giang, including the province capital, Rach Gia. Controlled by MR 3, four enemy regiments operated against the ARVN 21st Division: the VC D1 Regiment in Phong Dinh; and the NVA D2, the 95A Sapper, and the NVA 18B Regiments in Chuong Thien.

ARVN military operations and security in the northwestern delta were the responsibility of the 44th Special Tactical Zone. In December 1972 the 44th consisted of the 4th Armor Brigade and three ranger groups, each with three battalions. The armor brigade had five armored cavalry squadrons equipped with armored personnel carriers. There were no tanks in the delta. Although the headquarters of the NVA 1st Division was located in Cambodia, three of its regiments operated in the border area of Chau Doc Province and northern Kien Giang Province against the 44th Special Tactical Zone. The 1st Division's 101D and 44th Regiments held strongly fortified caves in the Seven Mountains of Chau Doc, while its 52d Regiment operated along infiltration corridor 1C in Kien Giang. Despite the presence of those major enemy forces, it was still possible during daylight to travel by road almost anywhere in the 44th Special Tactical Zone. The NVA 1st Division, the weakest enemy division, was in poor condition and was preoccupied with hostile Cambodian Communist units that raided the division's logistical installations and impeded the flow of replacements.

The enemy in the delta sustained very heavy casualties during the 1972 offensive, estimates for main force units ranging from 15 to 26 percent of authorized strength. During October alone, the enemy probably lost more than 5,000 soldiers, many of whom came from his best forces in the delta. As of the end of the year, few replacements had been received to make up for those losses, and ammunition stocks were probably very low, both factors contributing to the decline in enemy activity during the last part of December.

As the year ended, the situation in Military Region 4 seemed to favor the South Vietnamese. The major route from the lower delta to Saigon was open to commercial and military traffic, the rice harvest was good, ARVN units were in fair condition in spite of heavy combat, and enemy units were greatly understrength, short of ammunition, and in some cases demoralized. The South Vietnamese controlled most of the commerce of the delta, most of the important lines of communication, and all of the important population centers. During the two years following the cease-fire, major battles were to take place in MR 4, and the ARVN would win them all. The outcome of the war, however, was not to be decided in the Mekong Delta.

Note on Sources

The major source of the pre-cease-fire situation was the MACV Official History, Volumes 1 and 2. Order-of-battle information was checked and in some cases provided by ARVN officers who were there at the time. MR 1 information was checked by Lt. Gen. Ngo Quang Truong, ex-commander of I Corps, and Maj. Gen. Nguyen Duy Hinh, ex-commander ARVN 3d Division; Maj. Gen. Phan Dinh Niem, who had commanded the ARVN 22d Division, assisted with II Corps; Lt. Gen. Nguyen Van Minh provided information concerning ARVN disposition in MR 3. Col. Hoang Ngoc Lung, ex-J2/JGS, checked all order-of-battle. The author also consulted his own notes and files derived from documents collected and preserved by Intelligence Branch, DAO Saigon.

2

U.S. Organization for the Cease-Fire

Enhance and Enhance Plus

Projects ENHANCE and ENHANCE PLUS were undertaken in 1972 to accelerate the delivery of equipment and improve the combat capabilities of South Vietnam's armed forces (RVNAF), but the force structure basis for those projects was developed four years earlier. In May 1968 the Military Assistance Command, Vietnam (MACV) submitted a plan to Commander in Chief, Pacific (CINCPAC) for the Consolidated RVNAF Improvement and Modernization Program (CRIMP). CRIMP was intended to provide an improved balance in the combat forces and increase the fire power, mobility, and logistics of RVNAF. It came to be the basis for later force structure changes and Vietnamization.

The RVNAF force structure subsequently approved by the Secretary of Defense under CRIMP called for just over a million men in the armed forces in fiscal year 1971, for about 1,090,000 in fiscal year 1972, and for 1,100,000 in fiscal year 1973. In October 1971 CINCPAC directed a review of the fiscal year 1973 force structure. MACV's review resulted in a plan approved by CINCPAC and the Joint Chiefs of Staff in February 1972. The most important capabilities added to the RVNAF were the new 3d Infantry Division and the 20th Tank Regiment for Military Region 1.

Project ENHANCE was undertaken following the Nguyen Hue offensive to compensate for the heavy materiel losses during that campaign and to deliver replacements before expected cease-fire conditions might curtail the deliveries. In essence, ENHANCE was undertaken to accelerate programs already planned under CRIMP. It provided new units and equipment for the Army, Air Force, and Navy. The following lists summarize the major items of equipment delivered under ENHANCE.

Army: 3 artillery battalions, 175-mm. gun; 2 tank battalions, 90-mm., M48; 2 air defense artillery battalions, .50-caliber and 40-mm.; 100 TOW (tube launched, optically tracked, wire guided) antitank weapons, to be provided to 26 infantry regiments, 3 airborne brigades, 3 Marine brigades, and 7 Ranger groups.

Air Force: 32 UH-1 helicopters; 5 F-5A fighters; 2 A-37 squadrons (Light Bombers); 12 RC-47 photo-reconnaissance airplanes; 1 AC-119K squadron (gunships); 1 C-7 squadron (cargo airplane); 1 C-119G squadron (maritime patrol); 2 CG-47 squadrons (cargo airplane).

Navy: 3 high endurance cutters (WHEC).

ENHANCE was designed to bring the force structure up to planned levels before the cease-fire. In summary, by January 1973 the structure for the ARVN, supported by the ENHANCE shipments, was as follows: 11 infantry divisions (35 regiments, 105 battalions): 1 airborne division (3 regiments, 9 battalions); 7 Ranger groups (21 battalions); 7 armored cavalry squadrons (nondivisional); 3 M-48 tank squadrons (1 deployed, 2 in training); 33 border defense Ranger battalions; 41 105-mm. artillery battalions (36 divisional, 5 nondivisional); 15 155-mm. artillery battalions (11 divisional, 4 nondivisional); 204 105-mm. artillery platoons (2 howitzers each); 4 air defense artillery battalions (1 deployed, 1 in training, and 2 to be activated); 17 miscellaneous battalions (military police, engineers, reconnaissance, etc.).

ENHANCE PLUS was a program to augment and modernize the Vietnamese Air Force (VNAF). ENHANCE PLUS provided the following additional aircraft and units: 2 additional CH-47 squadrons to provide medium helicopter lift for each of the four military regions; 3 additional A-37 squadrons; 2 additional F-5A squadrons; the early activation of 3 F-5E squadrons; 3 additional UH-1 squadrons to bring the total to 19 squadrons and increase the size of the existing squadrons; 10 additional EC-47 airplanes (electronic reconnaissance); 35 0-2 aircraft to replace the existing 0-1's; 2 squadrons of C-130 cargo airplanes to replace the C-123's; 1 additional AC-119K squadron.

ENHANCE and ENHANCE PLUS provided additional aircraft to VNAF as follows: UH-1 (286); CH-47 (23); AC-119K (22); A-1 (28); C-130A (32, resulted in turn-in of all C-123, C-47, and C-119K); A-37 (90, brought total strength up to 249); C-7 (4); F-5A and B (118 brought total strength to 153); EC-47 (23 added to 10 already in service); T-37 (24); 0-2 (35, 1 for 1 exchange with 0-1's.

Shipments under ENHANCE PLUS were made by sea and air. The first cargo aircraft arrived at Tan Son Nhut Airbase on 23 October 1972, and the last shipment arrived at Newport, near Saigon, on 12 December. Nearly 5,000 short tons came by air and 100,000 short tons by sea. Not part of either ENHANCE or ENHANCE PLUS were 31 amphibious vehicles delivered to the Vietnamese Marine Corps in November.

While the United States was rushing equipment to Vietnam to avoid the constraints expected to be imposed by the cease-fire agreement, the Communists were also shoving great quantities of materiel including field guns, tanks, and antiaircraft weapons down the roads into South Vietnam, including SA-2 air defense missiles on their way to Khe Sanh in Quang Tri Province. As later demonstrated, the Communists were not concerned about any restrictions a cease-fire might impose on shipments to South Vietnam; the surge of shipments was instead in response to the heavy losses the NVA suffered during the Nguyen Hue offensive and the ARVN counteroffensive.

Based upon clearly reliable data, MACV estimated that North Vietnam sent nearly 148,000 replacements into South Vietnam during 1972. This estimate included individual replacements to make up for the staggering losses incurred during the campaign but not the organized divisions, regiments, and battalions sent to join the offensive. Although the estimates of enemy losses are based on less reliable information, the NVA probably lost over 190,000 men during 1972. Of these about 132,000 were killed in action, another 46,000 probably died of wounds or were permanently disabled, 2,500 were prisoners of war, and 10,000 turned themselves in to South Vietnamese authorities as ralliers. As was the case with materiel shipments, the North Vietnamese showed no urgency in transporting replacements prior to the cease-fire. Those replacements methodically crossed the border from Laos and the Demilitarized Zone (DMZ) without inspection or control, a condition that persisted until the end.

Missions

Planning for the coming cease-fire at the headquarters of Military Assistance Command, Vietnam, involved consideration of at least seven distinct functions, and new organizations had to be devised to accomplish some of them. First, MACV and all American and third country forces had to be withdrawn within 60 days of the cease-fire. Second, a small U.S. military headquarters was needed to continue the military assistance program for the RVNAF and supervise the technical assistance still required to complete the goals of Vietnamization. This headquarters was to become the Defense Attache Office, Saigon. Third, that headquarters was also to report operational and military intelligence through military channels to U.S. National Command authorities. Fourth, an organization was required to plan for the application of U.S. air and naval power into North or South Vietnam, Cambodia, or Laos, should either be required and ordered. Called the United States Support Activities Group & Seventh Air Force (USSAG/7th AF), it was located at Nakhon Phanom in northeast Thailand. In this regard United States air support operations into Cambodia continued until the autumn of 1973. Fifth, a United States delegation to a Four-Party Joint Military Commission (US, SVN, DRV, PRG) had to be organized. The commission was to serve as a forum for communication among the Four Parties, assist in the implementation of the agreement, and help verify compliance with the agreement. Sixth, planning for the support of the International Commission of Control and Supervision had to be accomplished. And seventh, efforts to recover Americans still missing in action had to continue. For that purpose, the Joint Casualty Resolution Center was established as a successor to MACV's Personnel Recovery Center.

Since the purpose here is to examine the North Vietnamese invasion, the South Vietnamese response, and the United States reaction to the invasion, organizations not directly connected with the events or outcome of the third Indochina war will be mentioned only in passing.

The Defense Attache Office

DAO (Defense Attache Office) Saigon was organized according to requirements established by the Joint Chiefs of Staff, CINCPAC, and Military Assistance Command, Vietnam, and was activated on 28 January 1973 by Maj. Gen. John E. Murray. DAO Saigon was a unique organization. It performed the traditional functions of a defense attache, managed American military affairs in Vietnam after the cease-fire including the programs for the support of South Vietnam's armed forces, administered procurement contracts in support of the RVNAF, and furnished housekeeping support to Americans remaining in Vietnam after the cease-fire. Aside from the support of the RVNAF, it reported on operational matters, such as violations of the cease-fire, and produced intelligence information on which subsequent decisions concerning the Military Assistance Program and American interests in Southeast Asia could be based. The DAO occupied the offices turned over to it by the MACV at Tan Son Nhut Air Base, outside of Saigon, and most of its employees and officials conducted their work from those offices. Small field offices were located in Da Nang, Pleiku, Qui Nhon, Nha Trang, Bien Hoa, Long Binh, Nha Be, Dong Tam, Binh Thuy, and Can Tho.

To perform the traditional representational and information-collecting functions of military attaches, five professional attaches—two Army, two Air Force, and one Navy—were assigned to the

DAO with offices in the American Embassy in Saigon. The senior member of this group was the assistant defense attache, an Army colonel who relieved General Murray of much of his representational functions and who reported to the Defense Intelligence Agency in Washington through attache channels. The attaches made frequent visits to the field where they observed RVNAF units and activities and reported those observations to the defense attache and to Washington.

The deputy defense attache was Brig. Gen. Ralph J. Maglione, U.S. Air Force, previously the MACV J-1. General Maglione was also chief of the Operations and Plans Division, DAO. In addition to having a small plans branch to perform customary military planning functions, Operations and Plans Division had an operations branch that manned the Operations Center and conducted liaison with the RVNAF Joint General Staff and with Headquarters, USSAG, on operational and reporting matters. The training section of the Operations Branch was responsible for training provided to the RVNAF under the Military Assistance Program.

The largest element in the Operations and Plans Division was the Intelligence Branch. The Chief of the Intelligence Branch was responsible for American military intelligence activities in the Republic of Vietnam. He reported directly to the ambassador and the defense attache, coordinated with RVNAF intelligence agencies and other U.S. intelligence activities in South Vietnam, and, in intelligence channels, reported simultaneously on most matters to USSAG, CINCPAC, and the Defense Intelligence Agency. Because DAO Saigon was subordinate to USSAG in operational and intelligence fields, the normal flow of tasking and reporting was through USSAG to CINCPAC and the JCS in Washington.

The Communications and Electronics Division had functions which, like those of the Operations and Plans Division, included support of U.S. military activities as well as continued military assistance to RVNAF. The Communications and Electronics Division supervised a contract which provided communications for DAO, the American Embassy, and other U.S. agencies. The division also gave technical support, through contractors, to RVNAF military communications systems. It also provided liaison and assistance to the RVNAF Joint General Staff and the ARVN Signal Department.

Three divisions within DAO managed the complex military assistance programs for the ARVN, the VNAF, and the Vietnamese Navy: the Army, Air Force, and Navy Divisions.

Despite its broad responsibilities, DAO was authorized only 50 military and 1,200 civilians. It was also told to plan for an early reduction in strength and disestablishment, the latter expected to occur within a year.

To accomplish its mission while planning on phasing out, DAO had to employ contractors to perform many functions. The contracts, however, were also to be reduced in number and scope throughout the year. When DAO Saigon became operational upon the disestablishment of MACV in late January, no fewer than 383 separate contracts were on the books with a total value of $255 million. Slightly fewer than 250 of these were performed in South Vietnam; the others were off-shore. In January 1973, over 23,000 people were employed by contractors in South Vietnam, of whom over 5,000 were Americans, 16,000 were Vietnamese, and the remainder were third-country nationals. By mid-year of 1973 the total was reduced by half.

More than half the American contract employees were involved in training programs for the RVNAF. Of these, more than half were involved in aircraft maintenance, another large group was in communications and electronics, and the rest worked in technical fields ranging from vehicle repair and overhaul to ship overhaul and maintenance. Although most contract employees were located in the Saigon region, sizable groups were at the air bases at Da Nang, in Military Region 2 at Pleiku, Phu Cat, and Phan Rang, and at Binh Thuy, the VNAF air base near Can Tho in MR 4. Two years later, as the final Communist offensive gained momentum, the safety of those Americans in the outlying bases became a matter of major concern, even though their numbers by that time were greatly reduced.

The cease-fire agreement in Vietnam signaled the end of the American advisory effort in that country. The senior officials of DAO scrupulously avoided any offer of operational advice to the Vietnamese with whom they worked intimately and continuously. The technical assistance provided by the military and senior civilian officials of DAO and by the contractors was essential to the RVNAF's modernization and expansion, but the South Vietnamese military would get no advice on military operations, tactics, or techniques of employment. The war belonged to the Vietnamese, and they were going to fight it. The RVNAF knew what to do but had to be provided the means. What they could not control was the steady buildup of North Vietnamese military power within their borders, a buildup which culminated in the final offensive of 1975.

Note on Sources

The MACV Official History was consulted for information concerning ENHANCE and ENHANCE PLUS as were messages sent by MACV to CINCPAC recovered from Defense archives. Concerning the organization and functions of DAO Saigon, the major sources consulted were the MACV Official History, Volumes I and II, and DAO Saigon's Quarterly Review and Analysis, 1st Quarter, FY 74. The author, who was present during the final days of MACV and participated in organizing DAO, has also referred to his own notes and recollections.

3

Landgrab 73

The Paris discussions to end the war had resumed on 19 June 1972. On 8 October, the DRV announced a new proposal that led to "acceleration" in the talks and gave rise to speculation concerning an imminent cease-fire. It is beyond the scope of this work to examine the negotiating issues involved; suffice it to say that the DRV insisted that its new proposal was contingent upon an agreed solution to end the war by 31 October. The United States responded with a pledge to try and reach an agreement by that date. Anticipating success in negotiating, the NVA in mid-October began widespread pre-cease-fire attacks to gain land and population. By the end of the month, ARVN counterattacks had nullified nearly all NVA gains, and discussions in Paris again broke down. (See Department of State *Bulletin*, 13 November 1972, for a report on the October discussions.)

The situation was similar at the beginning of 1973. From information available at the time and from intelligence subsequently gathered through the interrogation of prisoners of war and the exploitation of captured documents, MACV learned that the NVA again planned general attacks throughout most of South Vietnam to take place immediately before the expected date of the cease-fire. These attacks, known as LANDGRAB 73, occurred essentially between 23 January and 3 February 1973. There was, however, a lack of uniformity in local objectives and in the manner in which the local attacks took place.

Military Region 1

In the northern part of South Vietnam, Military Region 1, the NVA B5 Front was in no condition to launch anything but local attacks, as NVA leadership apparently recognized. On the other hand, the B5 Front had no intention of giving up any of the terrain in northern Quang Tri Province for which it had paid so dearly during 1972. Throughout January it vigorously opposed with heavy artillery bombardments attempts by the South Vietnamese marines to advance along the coast toward the Cua Viet. Likewise, south and west of Quang Tri City, the B5 Front forces prevented any expansion of the Airborne Division's positions into the hills south of the Thach Han River and against the Thach Han River line itself.

The enemy continued to reinforce his defenses in the highlands north of the Thach Han River and west of Quang Tri City. Elements of the NVA 304th Division were shifted to this sector, and additional antiaircraft units were brought into the B5 Front, so that by the end of January elements of at least 11 antiaircraft regiments were deployed in northeastern Quang Tri Province. An additional tank battalion from North Vietnam evidently entered the Quang Tri Front on the Cua Viet during January and was probably used in countering the South Vietnamese marines on the 26th. Despite very heavy artillery fire and tank reinforcements, the marines succeeded in temporarily establishing a lodgment at the mouth of the Cua Viet on 28 January.

South of the B5 Front, in the area of operations controlled by MRTTH (MR Tri-Thien-Hue), the situation called for a different approach. The populated lowlands along the coast seemed to the North Vietnamese to invite infiltration and occupation. If a political presence could be established there, post-cease-fire evidence of the legitimacy of the NLF could be offered. Therefore, military operations by the main forces of MRTTH were designed to support infiltration.

Elements of the 803d Regiment, 324B Division, had moved into the lowlands south of Camp Evans, and regular forces were moving toward the lowlands north of Hue on 24 January. The next day, artillery and ground attacks increased against RVNAF positions north, west, and south of Hue. Between 27 January and 3 February, elements of the 803d attempted to interdict Highway 1 in the vicinity of the An Lo bridge. In this area alone, the enemy lost approximately 200 killed in fierce fighting in which the North Vietnamese captured a number of hamlets before being ejected. South of Hue, the NVA 5th and 6th Regiments, attacking in the lowlands around Phu Bai, penetrated several hamlets, although most of the infiltrators were intercepted before reaching the populated areas. About 175 enemy soldiers died in the fighting south of Hue. Although the enemy in MRTTH was partially successful over the eight-day period in establishing some control, ARVN forces subsequently drove the infiltrators out. Undoubtedly contributing to the enemy's failure and the South Vietnamese successes was the general antipathy of the population for the Communist forces. The people recalled the massacres of Tet 1968.

South of the Hai Van Pass, NVA operations to seize land and people prior to the cease-fire were

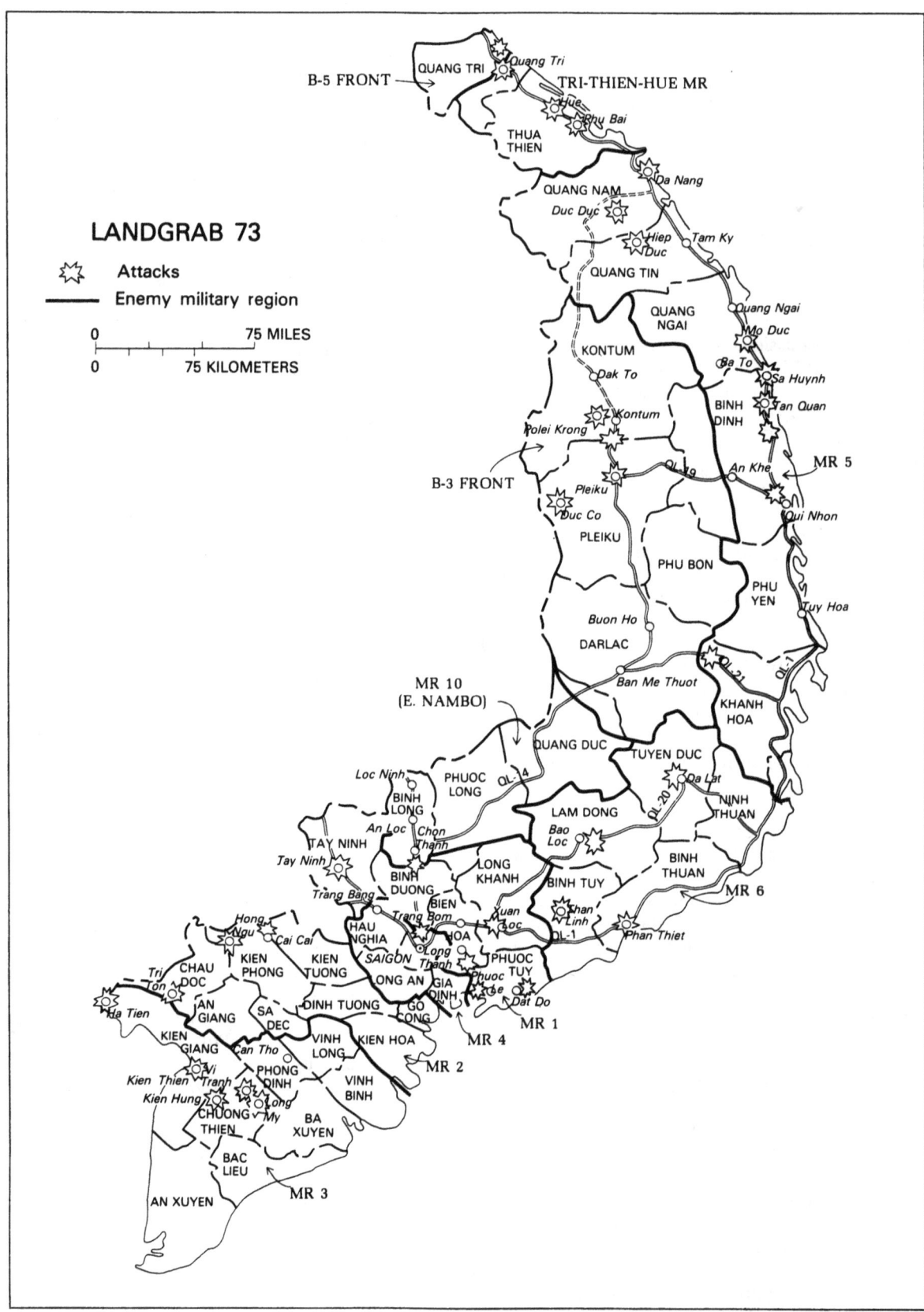

Map 5

under the control of NVA Military Region 5. Intelligence available at the time revealed that officials of MR 5 mistakenly believed that teams of the International Commission for Control and Supervision (ICCS) would be in position at the time the cease-fire became effective. Although the North Vietnamese seized some hamlets and villages, ARVN counterattacks soon drove most of the local and NVA forces out. Both the NVA and the local forces overextended themselves in the brief campaign and could not secure their gains.

Intelligence sources revealed that the NVA expected its main forces to be able to contain the ARVN in its bases and thereby permit local forces to invest the hamlets and villages. The basic assumption was that even though the cease-fire might stop all military activity, local forces would be able to conduct political and propaganda activities without interruption. As it turned out, ICCS teams were not available or deployed to prevent ARVN countermoves, and it is doubtful, even had they been in place, whether they would have had any appreciable influence on military operations.

In northern MR 5, NVA attacks were heaviest in three areas: Front-4 operations were conducted in Quang Nam; the 711th Division operated to contain the ARVN in the Que Son Valley and prevented the ARVN from advancing into the important enemy logistical base in the Hiep Duc region; and provincial and local forces operated in northern and central Quang Ngai, while the NVA 2d Division attacked in the southern district of the province.

In Quang Nam Province, Front-4 had completed its preparations for the attacks by 22 January 1973, including having the 575th Artillery Battalion move rockets into four firing positions for attacks against Da Nang. Fighting began on the morning of 26 January with a ground attack against Duc Duc and a rocket attack against Da Nang.

Numerous attacks by fire and infantry assault were simultaneously conducted against South Vietnamese positions and lines of communication throughout the province, and all district headquarters in Quang Nam Province were hit. Da Nang received rocket attacks for three consecutive days. Coincident with the attacks on the major headquarters and district capitals, the NVA supported the local forces infiltrating the hamlets and villages. NLF flags were sighted in the hamlets of western Hieu Duc District, southern and western Dai Loc, Dien Ban, northeastern Duc Duc, western Duy Xuyen, and parts of northern Que Son District. Subsequent ARVN operations recovered some of these outlying villages and hamlets; the final result probably correctly reflected the relative military balance and political influence in the area.

Southwest of Que Son, just across the province boundary in Quang Tin Province, was the important NVA logistical area centered at Hiep Duc. The 711th Division was committed to defending this vital area and thus played no offensive role in LANDGRAB. Two days after Christmas 1972, the ARVN 3d Division launched a strong, fast-moving spoiling attack aimed at tearing up the enemy's Hiep Duc base. Deep penetrations were made in the first few days, and the I Corps Commander, Lt. Gen. Ngo Quang Truong, sought to exploit the early success by detaching the 51st Infantry Regiment from the 1st Division and, on 3 January, sending it to reinforce the advancing 3d Division. Maj. Gen. Nguyen Duy Hinh, commanding the 3d, committed the 51st Regiment on the night of 16 January to continue the attack to seize Fire Support Base (FSB) West, a strongly fortified position defended by elements of the NVA 711th Division on Hill 1460 guarding the eastern approach to Hiep Duc. The 51st was able to advance only part way up the slopes of Hill 1460 and could not dislodge the enemy infantry holding the crest. Meanwhile, elements of the 3d Division's 2d Regiment were across the Que Son Valley and had seized the hill above Chau Son, thus controlling Route 534 into Hiep Duc. On 24 January, the 3d Division's attack continued; the objective was FSB O'Connor on high ground just east of Hiep Duc. Two days later, with the cease-fire imminent and the local enemy forces moving into the populated lowlands of Quang Nam, the 3d Division had to terminate its attack barely short of its final objective. A strong counterattack by the 711th Division forces still on FSB West prevented the 3d Division's infantry from gaining FSB O'Connor, but the heavy casualties sustained by the 711th demoralized and weakened it severly. By the end of January, 3d Division troops were busy clearing local forces from the hamlets west and southwest of Da Nang, and by the end of the month only one hamlet remained under enemy influence in Dai Loc District.

Between 23 and 26 January, enemy local forces in Quang Ngai Province infiltrated into assembly areas in the lowlands and on 27 January attacked throughout the lowlands, rocketing the provincial and district capitals and interdicting Highway 1 (QL-1) in a number of places. Several RF and PF posts were overrun. In southern Quang Ngai, the 52d Regiment, NVA 2d Division, established defenses around the district town of Ba To, which it had controlled since the fall of 1972. Rather than challenge this position, the ARVN deployed to prevent the 52d from moving toward the lowlands.

Holding its 1st Regiment in reserve, the NVA 2d Division used one battalion to support local forces in Mo Duc, kept one battalion in the base area, and deployed the third to support the attack of the 141st Regiment in Duc Tho District. It was in Duc Tho that the greatest threat to ARVN security occurred.

On 27 January the 141st's attack reached Highway 1 south of Duc Tho and secured the rest of the district south to the border of Binh Dinh Province. The area captured included the small fishing and salt-making port of Sa Huynh, in which two battalions of the NVA 12th Regiment, 3d Division, supported the attack of the 2d Division. Since the NVA had blocked the only north-south line of communication and had secured a seaport, however small and undeveloped, in the center of the country, the South Vietnamese could hardly permit this situation to go unchallenged. Vigorous counterattacks succeeded in driving the enemy from Sa Huynh by 16 February. Enemy losses in the fighting may have exceeded 600 men, but probably of greater importance was the psychological and political impact of the defeat. Despite having seized Sa Huynh only the day before the cease-fire, the Communists were outraged at being ejected from lands they "legitimately" occupied at the moment of cease-fire. Sa Huynh became a Communist cause and plans for its recapture appeared regularly in intelligence reports until the final days of the Republic.

Military Region 2

The southern part of Communist Military Region 5 included Binh Dinh, Phu Yen, and Khanh Hoa Provinces. Intelligence collected before the cease-fire provided an accurate preview of what could be expected there. The enemy's objectives were to isolate the northern districts of Binh Dinh, hold the ARVN 22d Division in its bases, cut Highway 1 (the only north-south route of any importance under South Vietnamese control), and gather to the NLF as much land and as many people as possible. From the NVA point of view, the prospects for success seemed good, for large segments of the population in the coastal areas of Binh Dinh and Phu Yen had long been sympathetic to the VC, and the ARVN 22d Division had yet to establish any reputation for excellence in battle. Since the area along Highway 1 was fairly densely populated, it would provide a significant population base.

Fighting started in northeast Binh Dinh when, by 23 January 1973, elements of the 12th Regiment, NVA 3d Division, moved from bases in the An Lao valley toward the Tam Quan lowlands. Beginning on the 24th and lasting until the 28th, the attacks were designed to fix the ARVN 41st Regiment in its bases and support the attack of the NVA 2d Division just to the north at Sa Huynh.

South of the Lai Giang River, in Hoai An District, the rest of the NVA 3d Division attacked government posts and attempted to prevent the deployment of the 22d Division. On 28 January, the local forces began their attacks along Highway 1 and in the hamlets and villages, successfully cutting the highway just south of the Bong Son pass and in several places in Phu Yen Province. Farther south, in Khanh Hoa, other attempts to cut Highway 1 were unsuccessful. Although contacts were light and scattered in Khanh Hoa Province, the enemy succeeded in interdicting Highway 21 (QL-21), temporarily isolating Ban Me Thuot from the coast. By the day after cease-fire, a number of hamlets in Phu Yen were under Communist control, but hard fighting by RF and PF succeeded by 2 February in eliminating Communist control in all but two hamlets. By the 5th all of Highway 1 was back under government control, although the route remained closed to traffic until all destroyed bridges were repaired.

Although the enemy seemed to enjoy great chances for success in Binh Dinh and Phu Yen Provinces, it was clear by the first week of February that he had failed to achieve any significant gains. Highway 1 was open from Khanh Hoa Province to the Quang Ngai border, the towns and villages were in South Vietnamese hands, and the local enemy forces had incurred extremely heavy losses.

The NVA's B3 Front included Kontum, Pleiku, Phu Bon, and Darlac Provinces, part of Quang Duc, and western districts of Binh Dinh. Objectives assigned to enemy forces in B3 Front were similar to those in southern MR 5: to hold the ARVN 23d Division in place, isolate the cities of Kontum, Pleiku, and Ban Me Thuot, and interdict the main highways. Attaining these objectives would effectively extend control over the population of the highlands. Although the objectives were in no important way different from those assigned in the attacks which preceded the aborted cease-fire in October 1972, the enemy apparently had learned one important lesson in the October fiasco: it was fatal to begin the attack two weeks before the effective date of the cease-fire. This time the North Vietnamese waited until the night of 26 January to make their moves into the hamlets and villages, and not until the morning of the cease-fire did the attacks reach full intensity. The timing meant that the ARVN would have to conduct its counterattacks after the cease-fire and thus—so the theory had it—be subject to ICCS observation and control.

Preparations for occupying the villages and hamlets in the highlands began on 20 and 21 January when elements of both enemy divisions, the 10th and 320th, began attacks to tie down ARVN defenders. Employing the 24th and 28th Regiments, the 10th Division on 27 January attacked Polei Krong and Trung Nghia, forcing the ARVN 85th Ranger Border Defense Battalion to withdraw from Polei Krong on the 28th. The 320th meanwhile attacked Duc Co on the 20th and the next day gained control of the camp.

Route interdictions began later. On 26 January, in coordination with the Polei Krong and Trung Nghia attack, the 95B Regiment, 10th Division, seized Highway 14 (QL-14) where it traversed the Chu Pao Pass and held on until 10 February. Farther south, in Darlac Province, a bridge on Highway 14 near Buon Ho was destroyed and several hamlets infiltrated. Contact with Ban Me Thuot by way of Highway 14 was interrupted until about 14 February. The enemy's Gia Lai Provincial Unit closed Highway 19 (QL-19) at the Pleiku–Binh Dinh border and maintained the block until 4 February. South of Pleiku City, elements of the 320th Division were successful in closing Highway 14 temporarily. Pleiku City itself received repeated attacks by 122-mm. rockets on 28 January, but damage was light.

Although the enemy's main forces in the highlands achieved their initial objectives in the LANDGRAB campaign, their ultimate failure can be attributed to the weakness of local forces. Not only did they fail to hold occupied villages, but also they sustained heavy losses and the military effectiveness of their units decreased significantly. The most important gain was the recapture of Duc Co in time to receive the ICCS, yet this achievement was caused more by ARVN overextension than by 320th Division strength. By mid-February the military balance in the highlands was generally the same as it had been at the end of December 1972.

NVA Military Region 6 included five South Vietnamese provinces, the beautiful mountain provinces of Tuyen Duc and Lam Dong and the coastal provinces of Ninh Thuan, Binh Thuan, and Binh Tuy. This was a sparsely populated region and relatively isolated from the war. The ARVN had no regular forces deployed there, and the RF and PF maintained effective control.

The enemy in MR 6 had only four NVA infantry battalions, one NVA artillery battalion, and two VC infantry battalions, all of them weak and understrength. Action began on the night of 26 January with an attack on a hamlet north of Dalat, the capital of Tuyen Duc. Another enemy force attempted unsuccessfully to enter a hamlet north of Phan Thiet in Binh Thuan. Although local forces interdicted Highway 20 (QL-20) east of Bao Loc in Lam Dong Province, the RVNAF cleared the route by 30 January. Another thrust was repulsed with heavy losses at Tanh Linh district town in Binh Tuy on 27 January. On the morning of the 28th, the day the cease-fire was to become effective, the number of hamlets entered increased significantly, especially in Binh Thuan, but an NVA battalion entering a suburb of Dalat was quickly ejected.

The LANDGRAB campaign in MR 6 was clearly a failure. The RF and PF performed capably, and by the end of January the situation was clearly under South Vietnamese control. Highway 1 through the coastal provinces was never successfully cut, and the only lasting result of the campaign was the serious depletion of the enemy's local force battalions.

Military Region 3

The enemy's Eastern Nam Bo Region was roughly the same as South Vietnam's Military Region 3 (Binh Tuy, Gia Dinh, Hau Nghia, and Long An Provinces were excluded). In addition to scheduling attacks close to the cease-fire date, the NVA in October 1972 had also learned that it lacked the strength to infiltrate the Saigon area with main forces. Thus LANDGRAB 73 in Eastern Nam Bo did not begin until a few days before the cease-fire was to become effective, and Saigon was not an objective.

As in other populated areas of South Vietnam, the enemy's objective just before cease-fire was to extend the area under Communist control and gather more people to the National Liberation Front, but in the Eastern Nam Bo region a second objective applied: to establish a suitable capital for the NLF in South Vietnam. Intelligence collected in the weeks before cease-fire appeared to indicate that Tay Ninh City, the capital of Tay Ninh Province, had been selected; but for reasons not fully clear, the Communists failed to allocate sufficient forces to capture the city. ARVN preemptive operations in January 1973 most likely eliminated the enemy's capability to assign main forces to a Tay Ninh campaign. As a result, only relatively weak, local forces were available, and the campaign failed.

At the end of the first two weeks in January, ARVN III Corps began an attack into the Saigon River corridor and advanced all the way to Tri Tam in the Michelin plantation. Enemy losses were estimated in excess of 400 killed. The damage and disruption caused in enemy bases in the Long Nguyen Secret Zone and the Boi Loi woods were extensive. Heavily supported by B-52's, the ARVN disrupted the enemy's plans for pre-cease-fire operations. The NVA 7th Division was forced to deploy in the Michelin plantation, and the ARVN contained it there during this critical time. The Michelin operation also impelled the NVA to keep major elements of the 9th Division in defensive positions around An Loc and Loc Ninh in Binh Long Province. Intelligence reports had indicated that the 9th was to play an important role in the Tay Ninh attacks.

The number and intensity of attacks by fire significantly increased from 23 through 25 January. Widespread attacks by fire and assault began on the 26th and 27th against ARVN and RF-PF outposts, mostly on those located in defense of major lines of communication. Among those hit were Trang Bang on Highway 1, the vicinity of Trang Bom in Bien Hoa Province, the junction of Highways 1 and 20 in Long Khanh Province, Highway 13 south of Chon Thanh and north of Lai Thieu in Binh Duong Province, Highway 15 south of Long Thanh and north of Phuoc Le, and Highway 23 in southern Phuoc Tuy Province near Dat Do. Enemy casualties were fairly heavy, especially along Highway 13 south of Chon Thanh, where the Communists lost over 120 killed.

The Communists attained some short-term successes, for about 144 hamlets were reported contested at one time or another during the period 23-29 January 1973. (During the October 1972 attacks, only 96 hamlets were contested.) Nevertheless, by 3 February only 14 hamlets remained under enemy control, and four days later all hamlets in the region were back under control of South Vietnamese forces. The line-of-communication interdictions were also short lived; all major roads were open by 1 February.

In keeping with the Communist goal of political control, terrorist attacks during the brief campaign were few, apparently on the theory that widespread terrorism would antagonize the people. As it was, in most instances the people would leave their hamlets as the enemy forces entered and return only when government forces had ejected the Communists. The enemy's political objectives were not achieved, the attempt to seize Tay Ninh City never approached success, and territorial forces were able to clear the enemy from outlying hamlets with only minimal assistance from the ARVN. The cost of the campaign for the enemy was heavy: over 2,000 Communist troops were killed and 41 captured. A large proportion of the casualties occurred in local forces; they were weak at the beginning and weaker still at the end. They never recovered.

Military Region 4

Just as the ARVN preempted enemy operations in Military Region 3 so it did also in the Mekong Delta. In a delta-wide operation known as DONG KHOI, the ARVN and territorials planned to attack for six days beginning on 15 January, but so spectacular were the early successes that the operation was extended for six more days. Losses of over 2,000 killed and disruptions in deployment and logistical activity, coming just before LANDGRAB, seriously affected the enemy's ability to launch a significant offensive.

The areas the Communists planned to capture in the delta were those having the greatest potential for subsequent exploitation and expansion. In the northern delta, they considered the border area with Cambodia from Ha Tien in the west to the Parrot's Beak in the east to be most important, to include northern Kien Giang, Chau Doc, Kien Phong, Kien Tuong, and Long An Provinces. Western Hau Nghia Province also had high priority as did central Dinh Tuong Province. Highway 4 from the southwestern delta to Saigon crossed the center of Dinh Tuong, and the area around My Tho, the capital, was densely populated. The Communists also wanted to extend their control in Chuong Thien Province. Having already established control in the U Minh Forest, they could anchor the terminus of infiltration cooridor 1C from Cambodia through Kien Giang into the lower delta. But because of the South Vietnamese DONG KHOI operation, none of these goals was destined to be realized.

Communist Military Region 2 included eight of the delta provinces: in the north, Chau Doc, which contained the enemy base in the Seven Mountains on the Cambodian border; to the east, Kien Phong and Kien Tuong, with the vast marshy area of the Plain of Reeds; to the south of these three border provinces, the central Mekong provinces of An Giang and Sa Dec, whose dense populations were under relatively strong South Vietnamese influence and control, and the vital, populous province of Dinh Tuong; and in the far south, the coastal provinces of Kien Hoa and Go Cong.

LANDGRAB 73 in Communist MR 2 appeared to begin on 23 January 1973 when two battalions of the NVA 207th Regiment crossed the Cambodian border into northern Kien Phong Province. This invasion coincided with at least 13 light attacks by fire and ground probes. Two Communist soldiers captured that day revealed that the NVA's intention was to capture the district town of Hong Ngu, destroy all government posts along the border, intercept RVNAF relief columns, and then extend the attack southward deep into Kien Phong Province. Attacks were recorded along the entire border. In one of many sharp engagements northeast of Cai Cai, RVNAF casualties were light but the enemy lost 32 killed and two prisoners. In heavy fighting on the 25th, the ARVN again incurred light casualties but killed 47 of the enemy. Enemy losses in less than three days exceeded 100 killed in exchange for only minor ground advances. Following this flurry of attacks, the fighting in Kien Phong Province abated and remained so until the eve of the cease-fire. South Vietnamese bases were subjected only to sporadic light attacks by fire.

In Dinh Tuong, despite a heavy concentration of enemy main force units in the center of the province (the 5th and 6th Divisions, the E1, 6th, DT1, and 320th Regiments, and possibly elements of the 174th Regiment), the level of activity was surprisingly low. Even on 28 and 29 January, when the number of attacks approximately doubled, the weight of the attacks remained low. Although ground contact was made with elements of the 174th Regiment in the area known as Tri Phap, these contacts subsided after the cease-fire, probably attributable to the enemy's high casualties.

In eastern Dinh Tuong and Go Cong Provinces a prisoner reported that main forces, including the NVA 88th and 24th Regiments, were to break down into small units and conduct political activity among the population. This tactic was to create the impression that the local forces were everywhere throughout the delta and would support Communist political activity. The troops had instructions to limit the use of heavy weapons and thus gain more credibility as local guerrillas. Local South Vietnamese forces responded effectively to this campaign, and the Communists achieved no significant gains.

The NVA's Military Region 3 included the nine provinces of the lower delta. Kien Giang, on the Cambodian border, was the northernmost. The delta capital and the headquarters for the ARVN IV Corps was at Can Tho in the central Mekong province of Phong Dinh. The Communists' only relatively secure and uncontested base area in the delta was in MR 3, the U Minh Forest, a vast mangrove swamp and forest extending across the border of Kien Giang and An Xuyen Provinces on the coast of the Gulf of Thailand.

As elsewhere in the delta, activity in MR 3 increased sharply on 23 January. Well over half of the incidents reported were harassments and attacks by fire against South Vietnamese posts. In the northwest, the NVA 1st Division sent troops across the frontier from Cambodia with the apparent purpose of having them in position for the kickoff of operations at the time of the cease-fire. Documents captured in sharp fighting near Ha Tien village in northwestern Kien Giang were identified as belonging to a battalion of the 52d Regiment, 1st Division, and subsequent interrogation of a captured prisoner confirmed the battalion's presence as well as those of the regimental headquarters and a second battalion. The prisoner also gave evidence of the regiment's low morale; many of the soldiers had recently been released from miltiary hospitals, and the general health of the unit was low. The regiment's mission was to occupy the Ha Tien area and show the VC flag prior to the cease-fire. Combined RVNAF operations, employing the Air Force and the Rangers, pushed the 52d back into Cambodia. Air strikes killed more than 70 soldiers of the 52d, and ground fighting accounted for at least 15 more.

The enemy's 44th Sapper Regiment, also subordinate to the 1st Division, began operations in the Seven Mountains of Chau Doc on 15 January with attacks by fire against South Vietnamese posts. The 44th moved into the Seven Mountains near Tri Ton on 23 January to occupy as much territory and gain control of as much population as possible, but ARVN counteroperations again prevented any significant successes. The third element of the NVA 1st Division, the 101D Regiment, apparently remained in its base in the Seven Mountains and contributed to LANDGRAB only with attacks by fire.

The highest level of enemy activity in NVA Military Region 3 occurred in Chuong Thien Province. No fewer than four NVA regiments were available to converge on the province capital, Vi Thanh. The NVA 18B Regiment was to the northwest, the 95A Sapper Regiment was south along with elements of the D2 Regiment, and part of the D1 Regiment was in eastern Chuong Thien near the Phong Dinh Province border. The headquarters for MR 3 was in the center of the province.

The number and intensity of attacks increased sharply on 26 January, including a series of mortar and rocket attacks, some with 120-mm. mortars, southwest of Y Tang. The activity increased again on 27 January and a number of outposts and district towns experienced ground attacks and attacks by fire. Contingents of the D2 Regiment penetrated the district town of Long My as far as the marketplace before they could be driven out. On the same day Kien Thien received a heavy bombardment followed by a ground attack by elements of the 95A Sapper Regiment. This attack was also repelled. At Kien Hung, through the nights of 27 and 28 January the 18B Regiment conducted attacks by fire. By the morning of 28 January the town was surrounded by enemy troops, but South Vietnamse forces successfully held. The province capital, Vi Thanh, received sporadic attacks by fire, but casualties and damage were light.

Attacks were widespread to the far south, primarily against territorial force outposts and district towns; but in no case did the situation change markedly from that before the LANDGRAB campaign got under way. The activity appeared to crest by midday on 28 January, and a general uneasy quiet followed. During LANDGRAB in MR 2 and 3, at least 125 hamlets came under Communist attack, but no more than 20 were ever being contested at any one time. No main lines of communication were ever threatened, and all major roads and canals remained open to traffic. Assassinations and other terrorism lagged. Nowhere in the Mekong Delta did the Communists make any significant or lasting gain. In the face of the highly successful South Vietnamese-DONG KHOI campaign, the enemy apparently realized that major territorial acquisitions were impossible.

Relative Strength, 31 January 1973

There are countless ways to display order of battle comparisons. All can be misleading if they are used to form judgments regarding relative strengths and capabilities without reference to other factors

TABLE 1: RELATIVE STRENGTH, LATE JAN. 1973

	MR 1	MR 2	MR 3	MR 4	Total
RVNAF: Ground combat troops (thousands)	145-170	143-146	155-175	246-257	689-748
In Regular units (thousands)	75-90	27-29	50-60	40-50	192-229
Regional and Popular Forces (thousands)	70-80	116-117	105-115	206-207	497-519
Trainees, Admn. and service troops, and casuals (thousands)	---	---	---	---	c.200
Divisions	5	2	3	3	13
Regiments and brigades*	16	7	9	9	48#
Regular battalions*	95	50	64	55	264
Enemy: Troops (thousands**)	96	42	41	40	219
Combat troops (thousands**)	71	25	25	27	148
NVA regulars	68	19	20	16	123
Viet Cong	3	6	5	11	25
Admn. and service troops (thousands**)	25	17	16	13	71
NVA regulars	19	9	5	1	34
Viet Cong	6	8	11	12	37
Divisions	8##	3	2	3	16
Regimental Hq.*	54	11	13	16	94
Battalion Hq.*	195	73	77	79	424

*Includes independent regiments and battalions.
#Total includes 7 Ranger groups.
**In most cases, figures have been rounded down rather than up.
##Includes an air defense division.

such as training, battle experience, weaponry, tactics and techniques of employment, missions, morale, and mobility. Showing the opposing forces that appeared on the South Vietnam battlefields as the final two years began is nevertheless useful in understanding later developments.

Table 1 shows the number of troops and units. The figures for the enemy were compiled by experienced analysts from intelligence gathered from many sources over a number of years; although estimates, these figures are reasonably reliable.

Table 2 shows the deployment of RVNAF divisions, and Table 3 gives the order of battle of NVA and VC forces.

TABLE 2
MAJOR RVNAF UNITS, JAN. 1973

Military Region 1

1st Div, Regts: 1, 3, 51, 54; 2d Div, Regts: 4, 5, 6; 3d Div, Regts: 2, 56, 57; Airborne Div, Brigades: 1, 2, 3; Marine Div: Brigades, 147, 258, 369.

Military Region 2

22d Div, Regts: 40, 41, 42, 47; 23d Div, Regts: 44, 45, 53.

Military Region 3

5th Div, Regts: 7, 8, 9; 18th Div, Regts: 43, 48, 52; 25th Div, Regts: 46, 49, 50.

Military Region 4

7th Div, Regts: 10, 11, 12; 9th Div, Regts: 14, 15, 16; 21st Div, Regts: 31, 32, 33.

TABLE 3
ENEMY ORDER OF BATTLE, LATE JAN. 1973

S. Vietnam MR 1 (71,350 troops)

NVA B-5 Front, Quang Tri Province (47,200 troops)

Divisions 325th (5,000) Regts: 18, 95, 101; 320B (3,500) Regts: 48B, 64B; 312th (6,000) Regts: 141, 165, 209; 304th (5,000) Regts: 9, 24B, 66.

Regts, Inf and Sapper: 27B (1,000); 31st (500); 126th Naval Sapper Gp (500); 270B (1,000); DMZ Sapper Gp (5 Bns, 1,500).

Regts, Armor: 202d (4 Bns, 500); 203d (4 Bns, 500).

Regts, Arty: 45th (1,000); 58th (1,000); 68th (1,000); 84th (1,000); 164th (1,000); 166th (500).

Misc Bns: 15th Sapper (150); 47th Inf (300); 75th AAA (150).

NVA Military Region Tri-Thien (8,600 troops)

324B Division (Thua Thien—5,000) Regts: 29, 803, 812.

Regts, Inf (Thua Thien): 5th (1,000); 6th (1,000).

675B Arty Regt (Quang Tri—500)

Misc Bns (Thua Thien): 7th Sapper (200); 11th Rcn (200); 35th Rocket (200); 582d Inf (300); Phu Loc Inf (200).

NVA Front-7, Quang Tri Province (750 troops)

Battalions: 808th Inf (250); 810th Sapper (250); 814th Inf (250).

NVA MR 5, Quang Nam and Quang Tin Provinces (9,800 troops)

Divisions: 711th (3,500), Regts: 31, 38, 270; 2d (4,000) Regts: 1, 52, 141.

Regts, Sapper: 45th (550); 5th (1,000).

572d Tank/Arty Gp (500).

Misc Bns (Quang Tin): 32 Rcn (150); 120th VC Montagnard Inf (100).

NVA Front-4 (3,300 troops)

Quang Nam, Misc Bns: 1st NVA Inf (200); 2d NVA Inf (150); 42d VC Rcn (150); 80th NVA Inf (150); 83d NVA Inf (150); 86th NVA Inf (150); 89th NVA Sapper (200); 91st NVA Sapper (200); 471st NVA Sapper (150); 575th NVA Arty (250); 577th NVA Arty (250).

Quang Tin, Inf Bns: 11th NVA (150); 70th NVA (150); 72d NVA (150); 74th VC (150).

Quang Ngai, Misc Bns: 38th NVA Inf (150); 48th NVA Inf (150); 70th VC Sapper (150); 107th Rocket (NVA, 100); 145th VC Inf (150).

Separate Combat Platoons, all MR 1 (1,700).

S. Vietnam MR 2 (25,550 troops)

NVA B-3 Front (12,350 troops)

Divisions: 320th (3,000) Regts: 48, 64; 10th (3,800) Regts: 28, 66, 95B.

Regiments: 24C Inf (800); 40th Arty (1,100); 400th Sapper (800).

Misc Bns: 2d NVA Inf (200); 5th NVA Inf (200); 28th NVA Rcn (250); 297B NVA Armor (200); 631st NVA Inf (250); unidentified Arty (200).

Kontum (P) Bns: 304th NVA Inf (250); 406th NVA Sapper (150).

Gia Lai (P) Bns: 2d NVA Inf (250); 45th VC Inf (150); 67th VC Inf (200); 408th VC Sapper (200).

Darlac (P) Bns: 301st NVA Inf (200); 401st NVA Sapper (200).

NVA MR 5 (6,800 troops)

3d Division (3,500), Regts: 2, 12, 21.

405th NVA Sapper Bn (150).

Binh Dinh (P) NVA Inf Bns: 50th (200); 52d (200); 53d (150); 54th (200); 55th (200); 56th (200).

Phu Yen (P) NVA Bns: 9th Inf (150); 13th Inf (150); 14th Sap (150); 96th Inf (150).

Khanh Hoa (P) Bns: 7th NVA Sap (200); 12th NVA Inf (200); 407th NVA Sap (200); 460th NVA Inf (200); 470th NVA Inf (200); 480th NVA Inf (200); Khanh Hoa VC Sap (200).

VC MR 6 (1,250 troops)

Misc Bns: 130th NVA Arty (150); 186th NVA Inf (200); 240th NVA Inf (150); 481st VC Inf (200); 482d VC Inf (150); 810th NVA Inf (250); 840th NVA Inf (150).

VC MR 10: 251st VC Inf Bn (150).

Separate Combat Platoons, all MR 2 (5,000).

S. Vietnam MR 3 (24,600 troops, all under COSVN)

Divisions: 7th (4,100) Regts: 141, 165, 209; 9th (4,100) Regts: 95C, 271, 272.

Regts, Inf: 201st (600); 205th (1,200); 271st (1,200); 101st (1,100); 33d (1,200); 274th (900).

429th Sapper Cmd Hq (400); 29th Sapper Regt (600); Sapper Bns: 7, 8, 9, 10, 11, 12, 16 (1,400).

Separate Sapper Bns, NVA: 89th (150); 268th (150); 4th (150); 6th (150); 7th (150); 211th (150).

Separate Sapper Bns, VC: 10th (100); 12th (150).

Armor Bns: 3d (200); 5th (200).

Arty Bns: 35th Bn, 96th Arty Regt, NVA (250); 2d NVA (150); 74A NVA Rocket (150); 3d NVA (150); 8th VC (150); 74B NVA Rocket (150).

Inf Bns, VC: 168th (150); 368th (150); 1st (Tay Ninh) (150); 6th (150); 20th (150); 445th (150); 9th (150); 269th (150); 508th (150).

Inf Bns, NVA: 14th (200); 1st (250); 2d (100); 4th (150); 267th (250); 506th (150).

Separate Combat Platoons, all MR 3 (2,800).

S. Vietnam MR 4 (27,050 troops)

COSVN (11,700 TROOPS)

Divisions: 1st (3,400) Regts: 44 Sap, 52, 101D; 6th (2,300) Regts: 24, 207; 5th (3,900) Regts: 275, 6, 174.

Regts, Inf: Z-15 (900); Z-18 (700).

Arty Bns: Bn/96th NVA Arty Regt (250); Bn/208th NVA Arty Regt (250).

VC MR 2 (3,800 TROOPS)

DT-1 Regt (600).

Misc Bns: 504th NVA Inf (200); 207th VC Sapper (100); 309th VC Arty (150).

NVA Sapper Bns: 267B (100); 281st (200).

VC Inf Bns: 209th (100); 268C (150); 271st (150); 278th (150); 279th (200); 295th (300); 310th (200); 512th (300); 516A (200); 516B (150); 590th (150); 502d (200); 514C (200).

VC MR 3 (5,750 TROOPS)

Regiments: VC D-1 (600); NVA D-2 (900); VC D-3 (1,000); NVA 18B (900); NVA 95th (900).

962d NVA Inf Bn (100).

VC Sapper Bns: 2012d (150); 2014th (150).

VC Arty Bns: 2311th (100); 2315th (100).

VC Inf Bns: Tay Do (100); U Minh 10th (250); U Minh 2d (100); 764th (150); 501st (150); 857th (100).

SEPARATE COMBAT PLATOONS, ALL MR 4 (5,800)

At the end of January 1973 the ARVN had an assigned strength of about 450,000 men. Of this strength about 152,000 were in the infantry divisions and another 10,000 in the Ranger groups. A small number was assigned to the separate nondivisional artillery, cavalry, and tank units. The remainder was to be found in training, logistical, and other service and administrative support organizations and in hospitals. South Vietnam also had a Navy of about 42,000 and an Air Force over 54,000. It had in addition about 325,000 in the Regional Forces, some 200,000 in the Popular Forces, and over 4,000 in the Women's Armed Forces Corps, for a total authorized strength of close to 1.1 million. Actual strength was probably less than a million, however.

In contrast, the North Vietnamese at the time of the cease-fire had about 148,000 combat troops in South Vietnam, including slightly over 16,000 assigned to 15 antiaircraft artillery regiments. Supporting this force in South Vietnam were some 71,000 administrative and logistical troops.

These gross figures—1.1 million South Vietnamese versus 219,000 Communists in South Vietnam—tell little about relative combat power, however. A closer look at the combat force structures and the missions of the opposing armies gives one a somewhat clearer understanding. For example, the North Vietnamese combat strength in South Vietnam included 15 infantry divisions. These were opposed by 13 RVNAF divisions. As another example, the Communists fielded 27 separate infantry and sapper regiments, whereas the only roughly comparable units in the RVNAF were 7 Ranger groups.

At this point, attempts at comparing combat units begin to break down. This is because of the entirely different missions the opposing armies had. Communist combat strength in the South was devoted almost entirely to offensive operations against fixed government bases, hamlets and villages, and lines of communication, while the separate RVNAF battalions were assigned almost exclusively to fixed defensive missions. Thus, comparing some 140 separate Communist battalions of infantry, sapper, reconnaissance, tank, and artillery to the 54 ARVN Ranger battalions and 300 or more regional force battalions is rather meaningless.

Any consideration of North Vietnamese strength should also take into account a large administrative and logistical support force within North Vietnam similar to South Vietnamese backup forces. North Vietnam also had the distinct advantage of not having to defend lines of communication or base areas in North Vietnam from ground attack. It did, however, have to use significant numbers to defend against air attack in North Vietnam and small numbers to protect lines of communication through Laos and Cambodia.

The Communists normally maintained five training divisions in North Vietnam: 304B, 320B, 330th, 338th, and the 350th. In January 1973, however, elements of only two NVA regular infantry divisions, the 308th and 308B, were in North Vietnam.

Two more divisions were soon to return to North Vietnam from Quang Tri Province, the 312th and 320B, and later the 316th Division came back from Laos. The 341st Division was re-created in the southern part of North Vietnam, and the 338th was converted to a regular line infantry division. In addition to having a sizable training base and strategic reserve, the North Vietnamese maintained in each of the seventeen provinces a provincial unit of about regimental size. They also had a militia estimated at 1,600,000, many of whom were employed in air and coastal defense and in logistical and engineering work. A regional force was drawn from the best of the militia, contained men only, and had an estimated strength of 51,000. Exclusive of the militia, the North Vietnamese in January 1973 had an army between 500,000 and 570,000, of which about 290,000 were in North Vietnam, 65,000 to 70,000 in Laos, 25,000 in Cambodia, and the rest in South Vietnam.

The North Vietnamese Army thus contained about 100,000 men more than that of South Vietnam. It also contained more infantry divisions, a reserve (which the ARVN could not afford), far more antiaircraft artillery and air defense missiles (of which the ARVN had none), and a larger tank force.

The North Vietnamese, on the other hand, had only a small navy of about 3,000 men, limited to close-in security of territorial waters. They had one KOMAR guided missile boat, but failed to deploy it southward. The North Vietnamese Air Force was small but contained some modern air-to-air fighters that had earlier proved their capability against U.S. fighter-bombers. In January 1973, about 10,000 men were assigned to the North Vietnamese Air Force, operating about 300 aircraft including slightly over 200 jets, a few turboprops and helicopters, and some 60 assorted propeller airplanes. The air force was light in transport aircraft, and its jets were devoted entirely to air defense. South Vietnam's air force, in comparison, was well-balanced. Although its pilots had no experience in air-to-air combat, they had developed a high degree of skill in ground support, reconnaissance, and transport roles. As events developed, the two opposing air forces were never to be employed against each other.

One of the most spectacular developments during the cease-fire period was the rapid increase and sophistication in the air defense system the North Vietnamese moved into South Vietnam. Sometime in January 1973 and probably not later than the 27th, elements of the 263d NVA SAM Regiment, equipped with SA-2 missiles, deployed to Khe Sanh in Quang Tri Province. The regiment had four firing battalions and one support battalion, each firing battalion having four to six launchers and occupying one firing site. Aerial photography disclosed the construction of three sites in the Khe Sanh area during February, and a fourth battalion moved into a site in April. (In a television appearance on Face the Nation on 11 March, Secretary of State Rogers was "pleased to report here this morning that the missile site has been removed from Khe Sanh."—Department of State *Bulletin*, 2 Apr. 73. p. 373. The Secretary was misled by a preliminary report from Saigon; the launchers did disappear from one of the sites, but they reappeared within a few days. Launchers, missiles, and related equipment were periodically shifted from site to site around the Khe Sanh complex.)

The SA-2, a Soviet missile similar to the U.S. NIKE, had a range in distance and altitude of about 19 nautical miles and 85,000 feet. Its location in the Khe Sanh area provided protection to the important logistical complex the North Vietnamese were constructing in Quang Tri Province along Highway 9 and at the junction of that route and Highway 14. One air defense division, the 377th, was deployed to South Vietnam, while in North Vietnam there were over thirty automatic weapons regiments, more than ten SAM regiments, and from time to time up to nine air defense divisions. The ARVN, on the other hand, had four battalions of antiaircraft, but only two of these were operational.

The Balance Sheet

The operations of late January and early February 1973 followed the patterns established in October 1972 when a cease-fire had appeared imminent, except that the enemy waited until much closer to the date of the cease-fire to start the campaign. Otherwise, the objectives and techniques were substantially the same. Main force units generally defended the territory already under control and attacked to fix ARVN regulars in their bases while local NVA and VC units entered the hamlets. Throughout South Vietnam, the campaign between 28 January and 9 February cost the Communists over 5,000 killed in exchange for little alteration in the situation that existed in mid-January. By 9 February, only 23 of more than 400 hamlets attacked were still reported as contested.

U.S. observers at MACV in Saigon attributed the enemy's failures to errors on his part, the limited capabilities of the local forces, and an outstanding performance by the RVNAF. The enemy had obviously erred in delaying his pre-cease-fire operations in the expectation that the RVNAF would be deterred in counterattacking by the presence of ICCS teams.

The Communists committed their other important strategic mistake by breaking down the local forces into small units and attacking at so many places, thereby reducing the staying capacity of any local unit. The ARVN and local RF and PF were able to react deliberately against these hamlet challenges and to eliminate them one by one. The enemy's local forces were decimated and never recovered. South Vietnamese forces had clearly learned much of the enemy's strategy and objectives from the preview in October and had planned accordingly.

LANDGRAB 73 spanned the end of the second Indochina war and the beginning of the third. It demonstrated that South Vietnam's armed forces could probably hold their own against the force the North had at that time on the southern battlefields. It also demonstrated that the military balance in South Vietnam was close to even.

Note on Sources

Two principal sources were used: The MACV Official History and a MACV study "LANDGRAB 73." Order of battle information was derived largely from Defense studies and estimates retained by DAO Saigon Intelligence Branch. More details on deployments were obtained from American Embassy reports, extracted from DAO files, as well as from notes retained by the author. Deployments and other order of battle information were checked by the Vietnamese officers mentioned in the "Note on Sources," Chapter 1. Much of the information on Sa Huynh was from a Fact Sheet, prepared from MACV records, by DAO Intelligence Branch in May 1973.

4

Consolidating and Rebuilding

Political Strategy

In anticipation of the cease-fire, the North Vietnamese developed a strategy consisting of two parallel elements: political and military. Although this strategy was no departure from the fundamental theory that guided the prosecution of the war from its beginning, its restatement contributes to an understanding of subsequent events. Recognition of the endurance of this strategy and its ultimate objective, the conquest of South Vietnam, provides a frame of reference in which the tactics of the post–cease-fire period can be examined.

The political was the public element of Communist strategy. As the element that the North Vietnamese propagandized worldwide and used in exhortations to the troops, it first became apparent on the eve of the January cease-fire in a replay of the events preceding the aborted cease-fire of October 1972. Its supporting military activity was to capture as much populated area as possible just before the cease-fire, show the flag, and rely on the NVA main forces to contain the RVNAF while local forces entered the hamlets and villages. There the Communists would await the arrival of the teams of the International Commission for Control and Supervision to declare and guarantee their legitimacy in newly won areas. The success of this tactic depended on the local forces to gain access to the population and subsequently to win, through the gamut of persuasions from propaganda lectures to kidnapping and assassinations, allegiance from the South Vietnamese and defections from their forces. But the LANDGRAB campaign failed.

Much was learned about the political element of Communist strategy through the exploitation of captured documents and interrogation of prisoners of war and ralliers to the South Vietnamese side. One such document was Directive No. 2/73, issued by the enemy's Central Office for South Vietnam (COSVN) in late January to coincide with the signing of the cease-fire agreement. Enunciating the guidelines for activity during and after the cease-fire, this document was explained to all Communist forces in South Vietnam. It announced the beginning of a new political struggle in which military units were to play a secondary role in support of the political efforts of the cadre. They were to help the VC with its proselyting role, harrass the RVNAF, defend the "liberated" areas, conduct terrorist campaigns, protect "mass movements," and secure the resettlement areas within the Communist-controlled regions of the country. Essentially, this document contained the rationale for the campaign.

Although disappointed by the failures of January and February, the Communists did not abandon the political offensive. COSVN Directive No. 2/73 called upon the Viet Cong's infrastructure, or political arm, to accomplish five tasks sequentially: (1) motivate the population; (2) develop mass movements; (3) reform the infrastructure and local armed forces to suit prevailing conditions and to mirror the governmental structure of South Vietnam; (4) strengthen the infrastructure, the revolutionary government, and its armed forces; and (5) adapt operational procedures to new situations and missions. Although the guidance was admittedly vague, it was to be executed with readily definable programs. The COSVN directive applied only to COSVN forces in the southern part of South Vietnam, but it was based on high-level guidance from Hanoi and had its counterparts in the other military regions and fronts.

One of the major components of the political offensive was propaganda. There were three broad targets for it: "world opinion," in which were included, with different objectives, both the United States and North Vietnam's allies; the citizens and armed forces of South Vietnam; and the Communists' own people and soldiers.

The principal thrust of the propaganda message to the world was that the Communists were scrupulously observing the terms of the cease-fire in the face of constant, aggressive violations by the other side. The only offensive operations undertaken by the Communist forces were to punish the "Thieu puppets" and promote peace. This line persisted until its credibility was worn irreparably thin by the NVA's conquest of Phuoc Long Province in December 1974. Although its effectiveness cannot be objectively measured, Soviet and Chinese military and economic assistance to North Vietnam increased after the cease-fire, while American help tapered off. An estimate based on information available in early 1975 showed that North Vietnam received from its Communist allies a record 2.8 million metric tons of imported commodities during 1973. This volume was over 50 percent greater than that received during 1972 and more than 10 percent higher than the previous record set in 1971. The trend continued throughout 1974, when more than 3.5 million tons were received.

That the propaganda to encourage desertion and disaffection among RVNAF troops failed is shown in desertion statistics. For example, in the first half of 1973, desertions among territorials, the most vulnerable to Communist propaganda, remained relatively constant, declining slightly from a high in February. Desertions in the ARVN declined sharply from February to June, the period of most intensive Communist proselyting activity. Almost without exception the desertions were simply desertions and not defections to the Communist side.

The third target of the propaganda campaign, the NVA, was especially important because its soldiers were anticipating a real peace and an early return to their northern homeland. With inconsequential exceptions, the only NVA soldiers who went home were the severely wounded and sick, essentially those who could never be returned to battle. Even ex-prisoners of war, unless they were in poor physical condition, were assembled in retraining camps in the South and reassigned to combat units. Many Communist PWs released by the South Vietnamese after the cease-fire rallied or were captured again.

The first former Viet Cong PW to rally in Phu Yen Province turned himself in on 10 June 1973 to Dong Xuan Disrict. His testimony was typical. He said that a thousand PWs were released in Binh Dinh Province on 10 and 11 March 1973. Their first formal activity was so-called political training during a 10-day period of reorientation and rest. Next they were told that they would have to spend another period of time, unspecified, working for the revolution and for ultimate victory. About 700 of the prisoners, men not over 30 years old, were assigned to military units in Communist MR5; about 300 who were over 30 were sent back to their home provinces to be assigned to VC Province Party Committees.

The heavy fighting of 1972, the high casualties and little evidence of accomplishment, combined with the profound disappointment on being ordered to remain in the southern battlefields, had lowered morale in many units. The failure of the cease-fire to bring peace had to be rationalized and attributed to the perfidy of the South Vietnamese.

Another tactic included in the political strategy was resettlement of the "liberated" areas. In some parts of the country, this involved moving civilians from North Vietnam down Laotian trails into the wooded, primitive areas of the Central Highlands. In other cases such as in South Vietnam's Military Region 3, it involved bringing in not only Northerners, but also Southerners who had fled their homes in Tay Ninh and Binh Long for the relative safety of Cambodia.

One example of this program was described in the interrogation of a soldier who had been in the 12th Artillery Battalion of the 711th NVA Division before defecting on 22 June 1973 in Que Son District, Quang Nam Province. This rallier described a speech, made at the hospital in which he was a patient, by To Huu, who was introduced as the Secretary of the Central Headquarters of the North Vietnamese Labor Party. Huu had traveled from Hanoi on an inspection trip with other members of the Government. According to the rallier, Huu said that if the South did not strictly observe the cease-fire agreement, the Armed Forces of the North would "deal heavy blows" to the enemy in the South. In the meantime the Army's missions would be to promote self-sufficiency in producing food and to train to improve combat skills and be always ready to fight. He added that many youths, including young women, were being bought from North Vietnam to construct roads and installations in the base areas and that when a true peace was achieved, they would be employed in civil enterprises and agriculture in the "liberated" areas.

The world wide propaganda campaign was launched soon after the agreement was signed. On 30 January 1973, Hanoi Radio said that the United States and South Vietnam must "bear full responsibility" for cease-fire violations and demanded that Saigon "immediately withdraw" its forces from "areas under Provisional Revolutionary Government, Republic of South Vietnam control." The broadcast blasted President Thieu's 28 January speech, which, it claimed, proved his intention "to sabotage the agreement right at the outset." It also charged that Deputy Assistant Secretary of State William Sullivan sought "to cover up these violations" and had "hinted at the possibility of resuming United States military intervention, which makes one question the United States attitude toward seriously implementing the agreement."

Meanwhile, Le Duc Tho and Foreign Minister Nguyen Duy Trinh were attending a banquet hosted by top Russian officials in Moscow. This visit ostensibly was to brief the Soviet leadership on the final round of talks in Paris. In Hanoi, the North Vietnamese Central Committee convened a special conference on 29 January to hear government leaders report on the Paris Agreement. Truong Chinh, Chairman of the National Assembly's Standing Committee, urged the audience to propagandize "deeply and widely" the "great victory of the agreement on ending the war."

To administer the areas in which new settlers were being established, immediately after the cease-fire and perhaps before, the North Vietnamese began sending in large numbers of bureaucrats. By mid-May more than 3,000 were on their way to South Vietnam, their functions covering the full spectrum of government and public administration. By far the largest enemy-controlled population in South Vietnam, possibly as many as 180,000 people, was in northern and western Quang Tri Province, spreading southward into western Quang Tin and Quang Ngai, as well as western Quang Nam. Many of the people were Montagnards who had fled to Laos but had returned to their homes after the cease-fire. In northern Quang Tri, which was under exclusive North Vietnamese control as far south as the Thach Han River, a provincial government, integrated into the North Vietnamese system, developed gradually, probably beginning in the winter of 1972, and by the time of the cease-fire the process was virtually complete. Local offices of the Departments of Communications and Transportation, Culture, Education, Finance, and Public Health were established while the Lao Dong (Communist) Party of North Vietnam began operating in Quang Tri, co-located with government headquarters in Dong Ha.

Farther south, in South Vietnam's Military Region 2, Communist administration in the villages was on a much smaller scale and vulnerable to interference. A survey in early May 1973 in Phu My District in the center of the coastal plain of Binh Dinh Province disclosed that about 25,000 of the district's 100,000 people were under Communist control. According to the survey, since the cease-fire the Communists had established resident Village Administrative Committees in 13 of the 15 government-recognized villages of Phu My. In 9 of the villages the Communists had constructed permanent, publicly identified village offices, usually of palm leaves and thatch, and some displayed the Provisional Revolutionary Government (PRG) flag. In the other 4 villages, they used private homes for offices. In My Chanh, the village office was within 500 meters of and plainly visible from the South Vietnamese village office. In order to fill some of the vacant positions in the village administration in Phu My, the VC demobilized some of the military cadre and brought them back to perform administrative duties. The Communists constructed fences around sections of villages and hamlets and told the people that those areas would be defended if the South Vietnamese government tried to interfere. They also began confiscating South Vietnamese identification cards, replacing them with Communist documents. When an individual wanted to leave the area, he would call at the village office and obtain his South Vietnamese identification card, which he needed for travel in areas controlled by the RVNAF. Upon returning to the village, he would turn in his South Vietnamese card and pick up his Communist card.

Preparations for issuing identification cards were discovered soon after the cease-fire throughout Vietnam. Notes made in a book belonging to an unidentified cadre from Communist Military Region 5 (Quang Da Special Zone Party Committee) disclosed that 50,000 identification cards were available for distribution some time after 25 December 1972. Other notes revealed that 165,000 identification cards would be issued following the cease-fire but would be back-dated beginning in February 1970 in order to create the impression that the bearer had been under the control of the Communist government since the date of issue of the card.

An example of how a local VC political unit interpreted and determined to execute COSVN Directive No. 2/73 was contained in a report from a member of the VC Can Tho Province Committee. On 19 February 1973, the Committee issued a directive entitled "Indoctrination Document for Can Tho Province Unit." The mission of the Communist Armed Forces, as described in this directive, was to support the political struggle through violence and bloodshed although this did not mean, the directive insisted, that they would conduct attacks that "clearly violated" the cease-fire. On the other hand, it did not mean that they would cease hostile action. This sort of rationalization was fairly typical of the guidance given to local units during this period. The Communist military force in Can Tho Province was expected to occupy and control all rural areas so that the political and administrative organizations could establish jurisdiction. They were not to use firepower to overwhelm the RVNAF but only to protect their political forces from attack. The directive went on to say that the combat units were to protect VC "controlled territory" so that VC organizations in "liberated" areas could be developed. They were also to eliminate South Vietnamese officials in the villages and hamlets, surround government outposts with mines and booby traps, increase guerrilla warfare by harassing the RVNAF with small-scale attacks and ambushes, capture weapons, and organize indoctrination sessions "to develop the spirit of leadership." Coincident with these low-level military operations, armed propaganda units had two primary missions: to enter South Vietnamese-controlled territory and recruit in the vicinity of the outposts manned by territorial forces; to move among the population, propagandizing, recruiting soldiers, and collecting taxes. During the months following the cease-fire, Communist activities in the delta generally followed the patterns suggested by this directive.

The guidance for military-supported political activities in Can Tho Province was similar to that issued in Tay Ninh Province. In late April 1973, COSVN conducted a meeting concerning proselyting among the Cao Dai, a religious sect centered in Tay Ninh City. At this meeting, the Lao Dong Party Committee advised that the time had come to concentrate on developing the "liberated" areas and not to be concerned with launching military campaigns. Political capabilities and local infrastructures would be expanded. The NVA had paid a high price to achieve the cease-fire agreement, and it behooved the VC leadership to operate within the framework of the agreement to recover its political, economic, and military strength. In Tay Ninh Province, the Thien Ngon and Xa Mat areas would be developed into political and economic resettlement areas. (Thien Ngon was in north-central Tay Ninh Province, and Xa Mat was north of it on the Cambodian border. This was the area in which contingents of COSVN Headquarters had been located before most of them slipped across the border during the Cambodian incursion of 1970.)

The Northern leadership expected more of the Southern cadres than they were able to deliver. One of the Southerners at the meeting said that one of the greatest problems they faced was the lack of success in recruiting new party cadre at local levels. The problems arose, they said, from the gradual isolation of the cadre from the people and local units and because the political cadre had suffered greatly during the 1972 campaign and LANDGRAB 73.

Preparing for the Military Option

Even as the political offensive was being conducted internationally and locally, supported by relatively minor military operations, unprecedented preparations for new main force warfare were under way in North Vietnam and along the lines of communication into South Vietnam. Anxious to deny observation of these preparations, the NVA provided protection for them by deploying new antiaircraft systems into South Vietnam. Although the North Vietnamese were largely successful in denying VNAF visual or photo reconnaissance over sensitive areas, they were not successful in preventing U.S. reconnaissance drones from photographing the buildup.

Attempts by the ICCS, which was supposed to monitor shipments of all war materials into South Vietnam, to deploy to the border crossing points were effectively thwarted by the Communists. One such effort ended in tragedy on 7 April 1973 when two ICCS helicopters, flown under contract by Air America, were shot down along Route 9 in Quang Tri Province, en route to Lao Bao on the Laos frontier. One was hit by an SA-7 heat-seeking antiaircraft missile and crashed in the forest killing all nine passengers and crew, including a North Vietnamese officer who was suppose to be guiding the flight over an approved course to Lao Bao. The other helicopter, hit by small arms and machine gun fire, made an emergency landing without casualties.

Attempts to establish an effective ICCS post at Duc Co, the proposed entry point into Pleiku Province, also failed. Because of inadequate health protection and sanitation facilities provided by the Communists, all ICCS members became ill with malaria, dysentery, or other ailments. The post was abandoned in May 1973, although the closing was of little consequence, because while in Duc Co, the team was never permitted outside its compound without Communist escort and was not allowed to observe any traffic or military activity.

As mentioned earlier, the North Vietnamese were receiving ample shipments of military assistance from Communist allies, principally the Soviet Union and China. The problem facing the NVA was not the quantity of material coming into North Vietnam but rather transportation of the equipment into South Vietnam, storing it, and distributing it to the combat units. Nevertheless, over the years, even in the face of intensive U.S. air attacks, the NVA had developed a complex and remarkably efficient system for the movement of supplies into South Vietnam (Map 6).

With the advent of the cease-fire, the system was streamlined and expanded. Unfettered by American air attacks in North Vietnam, Laos, or South Vietnam, the system was soon able to handle increasingly large tonnages of ammunition, tanks, and other heavy equipment and at the same time transport to South Vietnam the thousands of replacements required by the NVA.

In a strategic sense, this logistics system provided the North Vietnamese with the military option of renewing the main force war if the political offensive failed to achieve its objective. Signs that the political offensive might fail must have been apparent to the North Vietnamese leadership early in 1973, for it was then that a new surge of replacements and heavy equipment began to move south. In a remarkably short time, the NVA established in the South its strongest military position during the course of the entire war.

The organization responsible for the movement of all personnel and materiel into South Vietnam was the Headquarters, General Directorate for Rear Services. Located in Hanoi, the headquarters directly controlled the operations of all support units in North Vietnam, Northern Laos, and Military Region 559, the latter controlling operations of logistics groups in southern Laos, the Republic of Vietnam, and Cambodia. In December 1972, there were five logistical groups subordinate to MR 559: Group 470 had jurisdiction generally in the triborder area of Laos, Cambodia, and South Vietnam and southward into the mountain provinces of South Vietnam; Group 471 controlled activities north of Group 470 and into the A Shau Valley of Vietnam's Thua Thien Province; Group 473's area

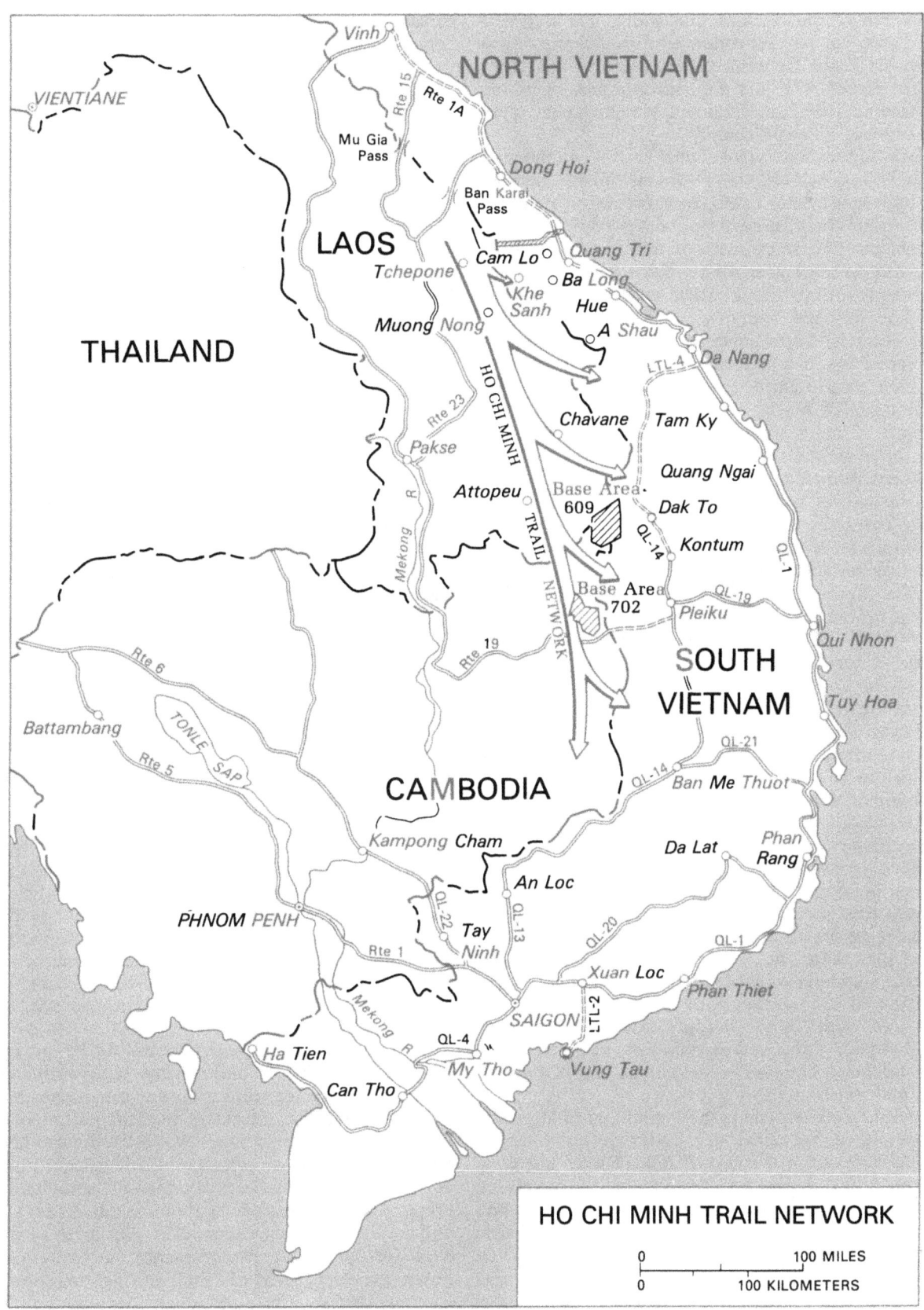

Map 6

was north of the A Shau and ended just south of Khe Sanh, but also extended into the Muong Nong region of Laos; Southern Laos was the operating area of Group 472; and the southern part of North Vietnam and the Ban Karai and Mu Gia passes were the responsibility of Group 571.

Each group had subordinate to it a number of Binh Trams, which were administrative, tactical, and logistical headquarters, responsible for all activities within their respective areas of operation. In December 1972, there were 45 Binh Trams with an approximate total strength of 75,000 men. The composition of a Binh Tram varied with the scope of its activities and the region in which it was located. Binh Tram 35, for example, in Saravane Province of southern Laos, had a headquarters and staff of about 450 men, two infantry companies of about 125 men each, two NVA engineer battalions with a total strength of about 500, a transportation truck battalion, three antiaircraft artillery battalions, and two communications-liaison battalions. Binh Tram 37 was located farther south in Laos in Attopoeu and had a strength of about 3,400 men. Its additional strength was accounted for by four standard transportation battalions and a river transportation battalion. As the year ended, about 19 of the 45 Binh Trams in the system were operating in southern Laos from the Mu Gia Pass to the Cambodian border. Considerably mobile, Binh Trams were observed moving from Laos into South Vietnam during the 1972 offensive to provide better support for heavily engaged combat forces. Although Binh Trams suffered severely from American bombing during the 1972 campaign, their recovery after the cessation of the bombing was rapid.

The headquarters for MR 559 was located in the southern part of North Vietnam. In addition to the engineer, transportation, and communications battalions operating under the control of the Binh Trams, the 559th directly controlled up to four engineer regiments and the equivalent of a transportation battalion. In addition to the Binh Tram system, a number of other North Vietnamese forces contributed to the security of the lines of communication through Laos. Among these were the NVA 968th Infantry Division in Saravane Province, several independent infantry battalions, and a number of antiaircraft artillery regiments.

As long as American planes continued to interdict the supply corridors through Laos, the NVA had to maintain the large number of Binh Trams and way stations along the routes. Trucks could run only at night or under other conditions of reduced visibility. Replacements had to march on foot from North Vietnam to their final destinations in South Vietnam. This required stations for rest, rations, and medical attention. When the bombing stopped, the roads could be improved and used around the clock. March distances were increased and troops began making the journey by truck rather than on foot, freeing a number of Binh Tram soldiers for employment elsewhere.

The Intelligence Branch of DAO Saigon took note of these new developments and recommended that new travel times be used in estimating the arrival of NVA replacements. Subsequent interrogation of prisoners and ralliers confirmed the validity of this new estimating policy. The distance from Vinh, for example, where one of the first Binh Trams was located, to the DMZ was about 300 kilometers. This was a 20-day march, while by vehicle it took only two days. A replacement destined for COSVN, having to travel 1,250 kilometers from Vinh, was on the trail for about 100 days, while DAO Saigon estimated the travel time by vehicle to be about 25 days. This was in April 1973; by the winter of 1974, travel time to COSVN had been reduced to under 20 days.

Several categories of troops used the NVA transportation network. First, and the largest proportion, were combat replacements moving south. Movements of this category began slowly, but by the end of 1973 more than 75,000 individual replacements had moved into South Vietnam. A much smaller category was composed of military and civilian cadre who had been on missions in the North and were returning South, or who were replacing cadre in Southern assignments. A third category were civilian settlers to populate the "liberated" areas; this group was also proportionately small. The fourth category consisted of organized units such as antiaircraft regiments and tank battalions. There were also large numbers of trucks in convoys moving ammunition, supplies, and equipment for replacing losses and equipping new units. In the absence of American air interdiction of the roads in Laos and North Vietnam, the NVA for the first time in the war was able to move badly wounded soldiers out of primitive hospitals in South Vietnam to better treatment in North Vietnam. Limited numbers of released PWs were also moved north on trucks that had discharged their cargoes and were returning for new loads.

By comparing the experiences of the previous years, analysts were able to draw conclusions concerning enemy capabilities and intentions based upon the intensity and size of the infiltration and the logistical movements. The NVA would periodically conduct so-called transportation offensives to deliver surges of supplies and equipment, sometimes in preparation for major operations, at other times only to replace depleted stocks. The greatest numbers of individual replacements normally came down the Ho Chi Minh Trail during the southern Laotian dry season, December through July. An exception occurred during 1968 when trail activity remained high throughout the year to replace the heavy losses incurred during the Tet offensive early in the year. A record number of over 235,000 men probably made the arduous trek to the southern battlefields that year. Something over 25,000 were destined for the B-3 Front; the balance was more or less evenly divided among the DMZ-MRTTH area, Military Region 5, and COSVN.

The heavy replacement flow continued into the summer of 1969 so that by the end of that year over 100,000 more fresh troops had arrived in South Vietnam. The effort tapered off after June 1969 and remained at a relatively low level until preparations for the 1972 Nguyen Hue offensive placed new demands on the replacement system. In December 1971 a fresh surge of infiltration began, continuing for about 12 months. By the end of the year over 150,000 recruits had been outfitted, trained, and marched south.

The year 1972 thus was second only to 1968 in numbers arriving in the South. Individual replacements only were normally considered in these estimates, although in 1968 about 30,000 troops belonging to tactical units were also included. In 1972 elements of the six NVA divisions participating in the Nguyen Hue offensive, over 40,000 men, were not included in the estimate. About 20 percent of the individual replacements went to the B-3 Front because of the heavy losses experienced there, a significant departure from the 1968 experience. NVA forces in Quang Tri and Thua Thien Provinces got over 40 percent, while COSVN took about 25 percent. MR 5, because of its lower requirements, received the remainder. The 1972 replacement program began to slacken in September, but continued at a fairly respectable rate into February 1973. At the same time elements of three exhausted, understrengh divisions—the 304th, 308th, and 312th—were pulled out of Quang Tri Province into North Vietnam to refit and retrain for at least six months.

In mid-March the NVA began a transportation offensive that was to last almost to the end of the dry season in southern Laos. Convoys of unprecendented size—as many as 300 trucks in each—were seen heading south through Laos. Large quantities of food and ammunition were being received in storage areas in Quang Tri Province. In addition to streamlining the Binh Tram system, at least seven Binh Trams were converted to antiaircraft artillery, infantry, or engineer regiments. Photography in April disclosed improvement on four major routes from the DMZ into Quang Tri and Thua Thien Provinces. Heavy traffic was seen on Route 534 from Laos to Hiep Duc in Quang Tin Province, and extensive roadwork was observed on several roads into the B-3 Front's area. Road improvement appeared intended to link the NVA units operating on the edge of the coastal lowlands with Base Areas 609 and 702 in the Central Highlands. (Base Area 609 was in the triborder area in western Kontum Province and in Attopeu and Ratanakiri Provinces of Laos and Cambodia respectively, while Base Area 702 was next to Route 19 in Ratanakiri Province, Cambodia, and just north of Duc Co in Pleiku Province.) Similar route improvement activities were noted in photographs of Tay Ninh Province.

The force the North Vietnamese were constructing, reinforcing, and supplying in the south was a modern, mechanized army that moved on wheels and tracks and required a steady supply of fuel. The old way of moving tons of gasoline and diesel fuel through Laos in drums would no longer suffice. A system of pipelines was the only feasible way to satisfy increasing demands and prepare for a new general offensive. For several years, North Vietnam had received its petroleum fuels via pipelines from China and ship-to-shore lines (Soviet tankers at the port of Bai Chay) north of Haiphong. A four-inch pipeline brought the fuel south to Vinh. Construction of a main line south of Vinh was started in 1968 and completed across the Mu Gia Pass into the Muong Nong base area in Laos in February 1969. By February 1973 the main line had been extended to the Chavane area of Laos, while since early 1972 a major branch had been supplying the A Shau area in Thua Thien Province. Another spur line was built off the main line to the Laotian-South Vietnamese border in early 1973 where it appeared to serve Routes 966, 14, and 534. By April 1972 another pipeline had been constructed generally following Route 101 from the Thu Thu petroleum storage site north of Bat Lake into the DMZ. This line branched off the main Vinh-Mu Gia line and served NVA divisions in Quang Tri and Thua Thien Provinces during the Nguyen Hue offensive. A major fuel storage area was built at Cam Lo in Quang Tri Province, and a line was extended south of Ba Long. By September 1973, new pipeline construction was seen 14 miles south of Ba Long to a new storage site at A Luoi in the A Shau Valley.

During January 1973 and immediately following the cease-fire, the NVA took advantage of the halt in American air interdiction of the Ho Chi Minh Trail to reinforce its tank and artillery strength in South Vietnam. Attrition during the Nguyen Hue offensive had reduced the tank force to an estimated 100 vehicles, but by the end of April, estimated tank strength was close to 500. Many of the tanks were seen and photographed on the improved roads in southern Laos.

The principal medium artillery pieces of the NVA were Soviet 122-mm. howitzers and 122- and 130-mm. guns. They outranged the American-supplied 105- and 155-mm. howitzers of the ARVN and were more accurate at long range than the few U.S.

175-mm. guns in the ARVN corps artillery. (The ARVN had five battalions of 175s, each with 12 guns. Three battalions were deployed in MR 1 and one each in MR 2 and 3. The gun had a maximum effective range of 32,000 meters. The 105-mm. and 155-mm. howitzers had maximum effective ranges of 11,000 and 15,000 meters respectively. Ranged against these weapons were the 122- and 130-mm. Soviet field guns with ranges of 23,000 meters and 26,000 meters respectively. The Soviet 122-mm. howitzer had a range comparable to the U.S. 105-mm. howitzer, many of which were also in the NVA artillery force.)

By the end of April the NVA had increased its artillery strength in South Vietnam by the introduction of at least 170 more 122- and 130-mm. guns, bringing the total to over 250. As was the case with replacement soldiers, no accounting was made to the ICCS, but the ICCS teams nevertheless kept close track of U.S. shipments into Bien Hoa, Da Nang, and other ports of entry.

Of particular concern to the South Vietnamese as well as to American officers responsible for planning for renewed U.S. air operations, should they be ordered, was a rapid and significant increase in the NVA's air defense forces in northern Quang Tri Province. Order-of-battle experts had evidence that elements of 10 NVA antiaircraft regiments were operating in Quang Tri Province at the end of 1972. By the end of January 1973, two more regiments had joined this force and by the end of April, the count had risen to 13, even after two of the Quang Tri regiments had shifted into Laos. These antiaircraft regiments were equipped with cannon ranging from the automatic 20-mm. to 100-mm. They also had 12.7 and 14.5-mm. antiaircraft machine guns, and many of their 57-mm. cannon were radar-controlled. Furthermore they had the SA-7 "Strella" Soviet hand-held, heat-seeking missile, and early in 1973 evidence began to accumulate that at least some of the SA-7s were an improved version. Also early in 1973 the 263d SAM Regiment moved into Quang Tri Province and set up near Khe Sanh. By the end of April this regiment had constructed eight SA-2 sites around Khe Sanh and had placed weapons in four of them. Although it would have been prudent for the South Vietnamese to have destroyed the sites before they became operational, the VNAF lacked the sophisticated ordnance, the radar jamming gear, and the navigational aids required for such a mission. Even had it been possible politically for American planes to do the job, significant losses would have been expected. While ominous for the future, Communist reinforcement of its expeditionary army in South Vietnam was consistent with the political offensive enunciated in the strategy directives.

Note on Sources

The section on North Vietnamese post-cease-fire strategy was derived largely from documents captured by the ARVN, translated at the J2/JGS Document Exploitation Center, and furnished to DAO Saigon. Principal among these documents was a copy of COSVN Directive 2/73. Interpretations of this and other documents, as well as reports of interrogations of prisoners of war and ralliers, were found in DAO reports, studies, and estimates and in reports originated by the U.S. Embassy, Saigon.

Strength and other personnel reports, prepared by the RVNAF J-1, and furnished to DAO Saigon, provided information on RVNAF desertion and absentee rates.

Unclassified reports by the Foreign Broadcast Information Service (FBIS) provided quotations from the Hanoi press and radio.

Reports, appraisals, estimates and fact sheets prepared by the Defense Intelligence Agency and DAO Saigon were used as the basis for information concerning the NVA logistical and tactical buildup in South Vietnam. Finally, translated editions of the J2/JGS Daily Intelligence Summary and notes retained by the author were used to describe certain aspects of the enemy strategy and general situation.

5

The Third Indochina War: The First Half-Year

Cease-fire Violations

As the post-cease-fire flurry subsided, activities in the four military regions began to develop patterns that persisted through the summer of 1973. As has been said so many times, there were four wars in South Vietnam, a different one in each military region.

In Military Region 1 both sides avoided serious contact as the NVA continued to consolidate and defend its positions and to construct its major logistical bases in northern Quang Tri and western Thua Thien Province. The South Vietnamese meanwhile used artillery sparingly and air power not at all in defending military posts and lines of communication along the coast.

In Military Region 2 the opposing sides developed strong positions around Kontum City. While the ARVN sought to keep NVA forces out of rocket range of the city and its airfield and to keep open Route 14 south to Pleiku, the NVA's new 10th Division pressed against the city's defenses to the north and west. Another area of contention developed around the westernmost ARVN outposts of Plei Mrong and Plei Djereng. The latter was destined not to survive because it was much too close to Duc Co, the major NVA logistical base in the highlands. The Communists also worked to improve their north-south logistical route from the vicinity of Dak To southward through the Plei Trap Valley of western Kontum Province. Combat in the eastern part of MR 2 centered primarily in Binh Dinh Province, where the NVA constantly harassed South Vietnamese posts, in the populated areas and along lines of communication. The ARVN responded with sorties into NVA areas in order to deny the enemy easy access to the coastal lowlands.

In Military Region 3 the NVA concentrated against Tong Le Chon, an isolated ARVN post deep in Communist-controlled northern Tay Ninh Province, located close to the Song Saigon, where the river was still a quiet stream winding through dense jungle on its way to the South China Sea. Existence of the post had forced the enemy to detour from preferred logistical corridors from Tay Ninh into Binh Long Province and southward along the Saigon River to Binh Duong. The NVA in March 1973 began a siege of the post destined to last for a full year. Although action elsewhere in the region was relatively light, harassment of outlying hamlets and resettlement areas was constant.

In Military Region 4 the heaviest action centered in the Seven Mountains area of Chau Doc Province, where ARVN Rangers were undertaking a slow and costly campaign to destroy the remaining elements of the NVA's 1st Division in that mountain stronghold. Other intense combat occurred in the Hong Ngu region along the border close to where the Mekong River enters South Vietnam from Cambodia. The rest of the region experienced relatively persistent harassment of Regional and Popular Forces outposts and of populated areas.

Relying on information supplied by the RVNAF Joint General Staff (JGS), DAO Saigon began reporting statistical and descriptive information on cease-fire violations. Arbitrary definitions were established in order to categorize hostile action. For example, a "minor attack by fire" was one in which 20 or fewer high explosive rounds hit a friendly position or populated area and in which casualties were five or less. For attacks of more than 20 rounds or five casualties, the category was a "major attack by fire." Contacts between ground troops were similarly defined as "minor" if ARVN casualties did not exceed five; as "major," if casualties were six or more. RVNAF ground operations resulting in combat were not reported as South Vietnamese cease-fire violations. The attitude taken by reporting officials in the JGS seemed to be that the RVNAF had the right to be in the particular area in which the conflict took place, and any resulting firefight was a violation attributed to enemy encroachment on South Vietnamese territory. Similarly, RVNAF artillery firings into suspected or known enemy locations were not reported as violations. The rationale was that the firing was defensive and in response to a clear threat or to a prior violation by Communist forces. Even though a certain amount of distortion thus crept into the reporting system and inaccuracies were doubtless present, the statistics on cease-fire violations provided a general idea of trends and patterns.

A look at Military Region 1 reports, probably the most accurate of those submitted from the field, shows a pattern of minor activity so characteristic of I Corps. In the three weeks immediately following the cease-fire, during the final phase of LAND-GRAB 73, there were 58 major contacts between opposing forces, but in the fourth week, 18–24 February 1973, there were only 3. In the 20 weeks from 18 February until 5 July 1973, the weekly average for major contacts in the region was only 1.25. Minor contacts were also at the lowest level in the country, with 517 reported between the start of the cease-fire and 17 February. After that date a downward trend began, so that by the first week of July, the rate was down to 20 per week. The total in the 20-week period was only 1,107, a weekly average of 55.

The record in Military Region 1 becomes remarkable when compared with other regions, particularly the delta. Over 800 minor contacts occurred in Military Region 4 in the three weeks following the cease-fire. By July, the weekly rate was still in the 90's; the total for the 20 week period was 2,652, for a weekly average of over 130. Major contacts also maintained a high level in the delta; during the same period, the average was over 5.3 per week.

Casualties naturally followed a similar trend. In the three weeks following the cease-fire, about 500 ARVN soldiers died in combat in MR 1, compared to about 300 in the delta. The casualties then began to taper off in MR 1 until by July only 15 to 20 were killed in action each week, while the rate remained high in MR 4 with a weekly total of 80 or more.

The frequency of ground combat in Military Region 2 was between the low of MR 1 and the high experienced in the delta. Three weeks after the cease-fire and up until 5 July, the average frequency of major contacts had fallen to 3.25 per week; the number of minor contacts during this period was 1,205, an average of 60 per week. III Corps forces had more minor contacts (1,341), but major contacts were at the same low level as in MR 1, 1.25 per week.

The record of attacks by fire was also illustrative of the general situation and reflected the order of battle and the diversity among the four regions. In the delta, for example, enemy attacks by fire were frequent, though the rate remained fairly constant for the first five months after the cease-fire. This high rate reflected the large number of isolated outposts manned by South Vietnamese territorials which seemed to draw fire as candle flames attract moths. Since ARVN artillery was deployed throughout the delta, the customary response to an enemy mortar or rocket attack (the enemy had no field guns or howitzers in the delta), was counterbattery fire. From the cease-fire to 5 July, the JGS reported over 3,900 attacks by fire in Military Region 4, 46 percent of the country-wide total. ARVN artillery expenditures, partly in response to enemy fire, also remained fairly constant after the cease-fire, except for the first three weeks when South Vietnamese gunners fired about 190,000 rounds (105-mm. and 155-mm. howitzer). By the first week in July, IV Corps forces in the delta had expended almost 555,000 rounds, a modest 21 percent of the country-wide total.

By disregarding the first three weeks of the cease-fire, when expenditures were extremely heavy in Military Region 1, a more meaningful representation of ammunition usage appears. Over 25 percent of the artillery ammunition used after 17 February was fired in the delta. The consistency of the delta war is even more dramatically shown by ammunition figures after 29 April, when the heavy expenditures in MR 1 were sharply reduced. About one-third of the ammunition fired from 29 April to 5 July was expended in the delta.

As alluded to earlier, the high level of combat during LANDGRAB 73 in MR 1 was revealed in the statistics on attacks by fire and ammunition expenditure. In the first three weeks following the cease-fire, more than 46 percent of the enemy's attacks by fire were directed at targets in MR 1. Although the rate remained fairly high (second in the country) for the rest of the period, the share of attacks by fire in the region's I Corps had dropped by 5 July to 30 percent. A much more striking decline occurred in RVNAF artillery usage; in the three weeks following the cease-fire, nearly 670,000 rounds were fired by I Corps forces, almost 50 percent of the country total; but after 29 April, I Corps' ammunition usage accounted for only 18 percent of that fired country wide.

Attacks by fire in Military Region 2 were the lowest in the country. During the period under discussion, only 800 attacks by fire were directed at II Corps forces in the region, 9 percent of the total; 20 percent of these were launched in the first three weeks of the cease-fire. Ammunition usage was also the lowest, 430,000 rounds, or 16 percent of the total. This percentage would have been even lower had it not been for the heavy fires in support of attempts to retake Polei Krong and Trung Nghia in western Kontum Province in June. ARVN artillery fired 62,000 rounds in the four weeks of this action.

Attacks by fire in Military Region 3 were also relatively low, only 15 percent of the country total. Ammunition expenditures reflected that figure: 450,000 rounds for the period, or about 17 percent of the total. During a brief two-week period, (3-15 June), however, the region's gunners fired 87,000 rounds supporting an unsuccessful attack to open Route 13 from Lai Khe to Chon Thanh. This represented 57 percent of the shells fired from 29 April to 5 July.

The Threat to Saigon

The attempt in June 1973 to open Route 13 was symptomatic of a strategic malady from which the ARVN in Military Region 3 suffered throughout the months following the Nguyen Hue offensive up until the final capitulation. In an attempt to get more depth in the defense, the ARVN had maintained positions and outposts deep in territories which, if not under firm enemy control, were nevertheless subject to easy enemy interdiction with minimum forces. In strong positions guarding the western, northern, and eastern approaches to Saigon, the ARVN held in good order and in strength sufficient to repel any enemy offensive, assuming no significant reinforcement of Communist forces. The southern approaches were adequately protected by the dispositions of IV Corps around My Tho, and no sizable threat could develop in the Rung Sat, the extensive mud and mangrove delta of the Saigon and Dong Nai Rivers.

The defensive arc was nevertheless quite close to the capital. In the northwestern sector at Cu Chi the 25th ARVN Division was only 25 kilometers from Tan Son Nhut airbase. Although only one regiment was usually kept in the Cu Chi area, substantial territorial forces gave density and depth to the defenses there. Since this was perhaps the most likely approach to Saigon for armor, extensive antitank ditches were dug near strong points. The 25th kept one regiment at Tay Ninh West and the other in the Khiem Hanh–Tri Tam–Boi Loi triangle. Although inside contested territory, these dispositions afforded essential depth to the defense. The trouble was that the enemy often exercised his capability to interdict the tenuously held routes to the outposts, so that major operations were frequently required to run the resupply convoys, and increasingly heavy burdens were placed on aerial resupply.

The enemy crowded the ARVN defenses with local battalions, as well as main force regiments. Contact was virtually constant in the Ho Bo and Boi Loi areas north of Cu Chi, but an even more serious threat developed in the Long Nguyen, a heavily wooded, long-time enemy base area in the gap between Cu Chi and the 5th ARVN Division at Lai Khe. The 9th NVA Division pushed into this area from its bases in the Michelin and Minh Thanh plantations and was soon threatening lightly held territorial positions on the northern leg of the so-called Iron Triangle: Rach Bap, Base 82, and An Dien.

An appreciation of the seriousness with which an enemy salient in the Iron Triangle had to be viewed can be gained from the following: First, the southern vertex of the Triangle, opposite the village of Phu Hoa and at the confluence of the Saigon and Thi Thien Rivers, is only 26,500 meters from the runways of Tan Son Nhut and Bien Hoa airbases, and maximum range of the 130-mm. field gun is 26,700 meters. Second, a successful crossing of the Thi Thien River below Ben Cat would isolate the 5th Division at Lai Khe, probably result in eliminating the defenses in front of the Binh Duong Province seat at Phu Cuong, and place enemy forces in a position for a rapid move into Saigon.

The lack of contiguous depth to the defense was much more apparent and had more immediate and serious consequences in the center sector where the NVA in the Nguyen Hue offensive had taken Loc Ninh, the district town north of the Binh Long Province seat of An Loc. Although the garrison at An Loc withstood the seige, destroying dozens of tanks and entire battalions in the process, eliminating the immediate threat to Binh Duong Province and Saigon, and providing a much needed psychological boost, the South Vietnamese were left with a large, critical base that could be supplied only by helicopter.

A similar problem existed southwest of the An Loc perimeter where at Tong Le Chon the enemy's siege by 25 March had begun in earnest. Soon after that date all resupply had to be parachuted, evacuation became almost impossible, and bombardment was almost continuous. Helicopters could not land without prohibitive risk, and the NVA antiaircraft positions around the camp became so dense that even approach by helicopter became almost impossible. In a 16-week period beginning on 25 March, the NVA conducted almost 300 attacks by fire against the camp, expending over 13,000 mortar, rocket, and artillery rounds. There were also 11 ground attacks and at least 9 attempts by sappers to infiltrate defenses. The NVA supported the attacks with psychological bombardments, promising over loud-speakers to afford the defenders safe passage out of the camp and appealing to the camp commander to lead his men out.

As of the first week in July, the total strength of the 92d Ranger Battalion inside the camp and two close-in outposts was 224 officers and men, of whom 34 were out of action because of wounds or illness. Total casualties for the period were 16 killed, 4 seriously wounded, and 192 lightly wounded or sick, including some with beri beri and malaria. Despite isolation and deteriorating morale, the ranger battalion nevertheless held fast and during those 16 weeks counted 86 enemy soldiers killed and 10 individual weapons captured, including an antiaircraft machine gun, and claimed destruction of one enemy 105-mm. howitzer.

During the 16-week period, the VNAF flew over 3,000 sorties supporting this little camp. The planes dropped more than three hundred 400-pound bundles of food and other supplies, of which 134 were recovered by the defenders while the remainder fell into enemy hands.

The besieging force consisted at first of a battalion of the 271st Regiment, 9th NVA Division, later replaced by a battalion of the 201st Independent NVA Regiment. Also included in the forces surrounding Tong Le Chon were a battalion each of the 42d and 271st NVA Antiaircraft Regiments of the 69th Artillery Group and firing batteries of the 28th NVA Artillery Battalion, the latter equipped with 130-mm. field guns.

South of the An Loc perimeter on National Route 13, was another isolated garrison at Chon Thanh. Although regiments of the 5th ARVN Division were rotated in and out of Chon Thanh, the basic defense was the responsibility of territorials and rangers. A sortie out of the camp in early June by the 7th Infantry, 5th ARVN Division, progressed only five or six kilometers before being stopped with moderate casualties. This was an unsuccessful attempt to link up with the 8th Infantry attacking north out of the advanced base at Bau Bang, north of Lai Khe. Chon Thanh remained cut off for the rest of the war. An outpost at Chi Linh, southeast of the An Loc perimeter on the Song Be River, also required helicopter resupply.

Northeast of An Loc, a jungle-cloaked peak rises 700 meters out of the rolling woods, plantations, and farms of the Dong Nai terrace. Its beautiful, symmetrical cone shading Phuoc Binh, provincial seat of Phuoc Long Province, can be seen on clear days from Saigon. On some maps Phuoc Binh is labeled Song Be for the swift-flowing river that curves around the north base of the mountain. A military garrison was located at an airstrip near Phuoc Binh. This province headquarters was in no way integral to the defenses of Saigon; its importance was exclusively political in that throughout the war, the South Vietnamese could still claim possession of all province capitals.

Until the NVA Phuoc Long offensive of December 1974, Phuoc Binh could be reached by road from Kien Duc, in Quang Duc Province to the northeast, although the route was long and circuitous: from Nha Trang to Ban Me Thuot, thence to Gia Nghia and over to Kien Duc, then west to Phuoc Binh. Route 14 was kept open by troops posted at Duc Phong, about half the distance between Kien Duc and Phuoc Binh. Road travel was also possible with some risk south from Duc Phong to a small outpost at the Bunard plantation, but not beyond. The ARVN was unable to open Route 14 north of Don Luan (also known as Dong Xoai) after mid-March, although one convoy managed to get through an ambush on Route 1A and make it to Song Be. Even when interdictions of Route 1A south of the regimental base camp at Phuoc Vinh (called Phu Giao by the ARVN) became common, the ARVN managed to keep 1A open to Phuoc Vinh most of the time, but not to Don Luan, which became totally dependent on aerial resupply.

The situation in the eastern sector was different, there being no isolated areas dependent on airlift for supply or evacuation and all major roads being open. Civilian and commercial as well as military traffic moved without escort on Route 20 to and from the mountain resort and gardens of Dalat. National Route 1 was open for all traffic to the coastal town of Phan Thiet, and Highway 15 was open to the beaches at Vung Tau. The 18th ARVN Division, with territorials in support, had no serious difficulties with the NVA's 33d and 274th Regiments in Long Khanh and Phuoc Tuy Provinces, although these main forces and some local units made travel hazardous on Interprovincial Route 2 from Xuan Loc to Ba Ria. Constant patrolling was also necessary to protect traffic on Interprovincial Route 23 between Dat Do and Xuyen Moc in southern Phuoc Tuy.

The Cambodian Connection

The main ship channel of the great Mekong River empties into the South China Sea opposite the port city of Vung Tau. Convoys of tugs and barges for Phnom Penh marshalled there for the slow tow to Tam Chau, 150 miles up the brown river, just short of the crossing into Cambodia. All of the heavy tonnage comprising U.S. assistance to Cambodia—mostly ammunition, fuels, and rice—had to go this way since the Communists had closed off Phnom Penh from Cambodian ocean ports. The border areas of South Vietnam's Kien Phong, Chau Doc, and Kien Giang Provinces, as well as the southern reaches of the adjacent Cambodian Provinces of Prey Veng, Kandal, Takeo and Kampot, had long been used by the NVA and VC for base areas and lines of communication. The NVA in early 1973 had up to 11 regiments in Cambodia, all used in South Vietnam except for 3 or 4 deployed against Cambodian Government forces.

The situation that developed in this border area was unique and was due to the interaction of a number of factors: American efforts to keep the convoys moving; the NVA's attempts to stop them; the ARVN's support of the convoy effort as well as its determination to prevent Communist main force incursions and infiltration of supplies and men into Vietnam; the NVA's persistent commitment to keep the lines of communication open through Cambodia into South Vietnam; and finally, the peculiar harassment the Cambodian Communist units inflicted on the supply lines and depots of their NVA allies. While this last factor appeared to have little lasting effect on NVA effectiveness in South Vietnam, there was evidence of serious incidents which doubtless required the NVA to divert troops that could otherwise have been devoted to more productive activity.

The river town of Hong Ngu, where the Hong Ngu tributary flows into the Mekong, became the focal point of the NVA's attacks to clear impedi-

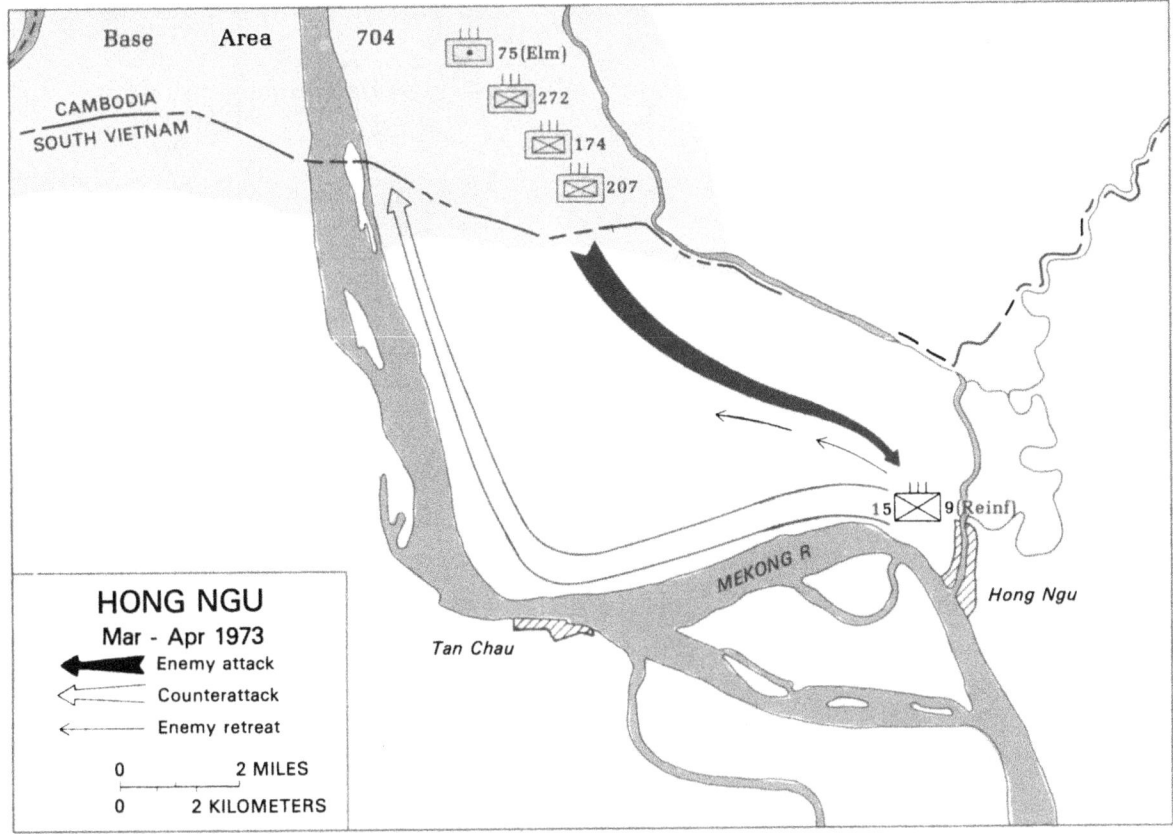

Map 7

ments to infiltration and interdict the Mekong convoys as they moored at the Vietnamese Navy Base of Tan Chau before churning on into Cambodia. In March, the NVA concentrated above Hong Ngu in Cambodia the 207th Regiment, 6th NVA Division; the 174th Regiment, 5th NVA Division; the 272d Regiment (detached from the 9th NVA Division, which remained in the area of Minh Thanh and Michelin plantation of South Vietnam's Military Region 3); and elements of the 75th Artillery Group. With the 207th leading, supported by artillery, the North Vietnamese attacked from Prey Veng Province, Cambodia—NVA base area 704—toward Hong Ngu. Not only did they meet immediate heavy resistance, but their rear area was pounded by B-52's and tactical bombers. The U.S. air effort in support of the Cambodian campaign to clear the Mekong banks from the Vietnam border to Phnom Penh was in full swing. (Map 7)

Benefits to the ARVN defense of Hong Ngu and Tan Chau were substantial. Several reliable reports told of heavy casualties and damage to the NVA's storage areas. One B-52 strike on 23 April 1973 north of the border between the Mekong and the Hong Ngu stream probably caught a large portion of the attacking force. Survivors reported seeing impressed civilians carrying the bodies of more than 100 NVA soldiers from the area. Many bunkers were destroyed, and the scent of death was heavy in the air.

In mid-April, the ARVN 15th Infantry, 9th Division, together with the 2d Armored Cavalry Squadron and a Regional Forces Group, counterattacked. Although casualties were heavy, excellent VNAF and Vietnamese Navy support helped enable the ARVN troops to clear the east bank of the Mekong from Hong Ngu to the Cambodian frontier. Not only was control of this stretch of the river never again seriously threatened, but also the thrust inflicted heavy casualties and dealt a damaging blow to enemy morale. By the end of May, one battalion of the 207th NVA Regiment had only 100 men. By the 4th of May, when the Hong Ngu fighting had wound down to intermittent small contacts and light shellings, 422 enemy dead had been counted, while ARVN casualties were 94 killed, 743 wounded, and 36 missing.

Civilian casualties in the action were by far the highest since the cease-fire, over 300, of which 80 were killed by NVA artillery. Almost 300 houses were destroyed by enemy fire. In the second week of April alone 123 high-explosive 122-mm. rockets slammed into Hong Ngu.

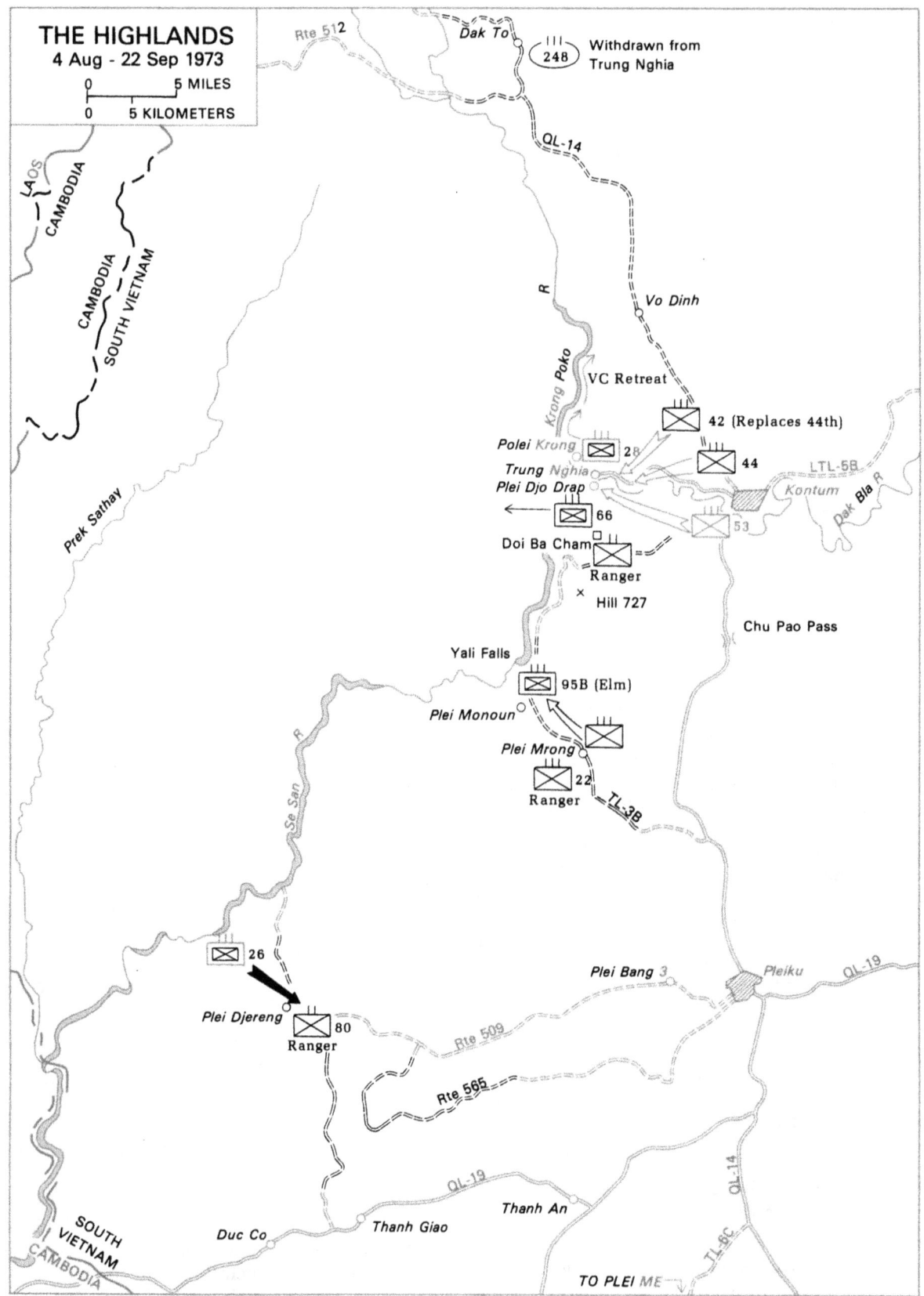

Map 8

Sparring in the Highlands

The situation in regard to isolated outposts was much the same in Military Region 2 as in Military Region 3. There was a deep but fragile arc of outposts manned by ranger border defense battalions and territorials extending north from Kontum City, and one isolated border camp, Plei Djereng, west of Pleiku. All had to be supplied by air.

Mang Buc, just inside Kontum Province on the border with Quang Ngai Province, was north of Kontum with no usable road in-between. Southwest of Mang Buc, over ridges rising to 2,100 meters, was Dak To, the only remaining position along Route 14 north of Kontum still held by the RVNAF, and Dak To itself was of little concern to the North Vietnamese because they were building a new highway that would bypass the camp on the west. South of Mang Buc and northeast of Kontum was the isolated camp of Chuong Nghia (also known as Plateau Gi). It too posed no particular problem for the North Vietnamese since they built a road bypassing it. (Map 8)

West of Pleiku, on the slopes of the high plateau above the valley of the Se San River, was Camp Le Minh at the village of Plei Djereng. This post posed a different problem for the NVA. It was on the edge of a base area being expanded from Duc Co. It was also on Route 509 leading directly to Pleiku. And it was astride the Route 14 complex that was under construction and would eventually link Khe Sanh in Quang Tri Province with the Bu Dop–Loc Ninh logistical center north of Saigon. For the ARVN the problem was familiar: only a major operation could open Route 509 from Pleiku to Plei Djereng, and the forces for that were not available. Thus Le Minh had to be supplied by air.

The most important ARVN tasks in the Kontum-Pleiku defense were to keep the enemy from closing Highway 14 between the two cities, prevent NVA artillery from interdicting Pleiku Air Base or hitting the military logistical centers in the area, and keep Highway 14 open to Ban Me Thuot and Highway 19 open through the Mang Yang Pass. The western trace of the defense, which left much of the terrain uncovered, was anchored in Thanh An District on Highway 19 about midway between the junction of Highways 19 and 14 and the NVA's base at Duc Co. From Thanh An, the trace went north bending in toward Highway 14.

The forward positions west of Kontum were just east of Polei Krong and the adjacent village of Trung Nghia near the confluence of the Dak Bla and Krong Poko rivers. The NVA had attacked Polei Krong and Trung Nghia during the cease-fire landgrab and still occupied Polei Krong, which it appeared determined to hold, not only to provide a good point of departure for an attack on Kontum but also because Polei Krong was astride one of the best north-south lines of communication. This area became the scene of some of the heaviest fighting in Military Region 2 during the summer and early autumn of 1973. Southwest of Kontum, on Three Points Mountain (Hill 700) overlooking Provincial Route 3B and the Dak Bla River, was the isolated outpost of Doi Ba Cham, accessible only by helicopter.

In mid-May, VNAF aerial observers saw two 130-mm. guns being moved into position northwest of Kontum. Primarily through agent reports, ARVN intelligence officers learned of NVA plans to use artillery against ARVN artillery batteries in the Kontum City area. Shortly afterwards, heavy attacks by fire hit the ARVN fire bases and positions of the 53d Infantry Regiment, 23d ARVN Division, northwest of the city on Eo Gio Hill and Bases N and R. Two NVA ground attacks against Doi Ba Cham were repulsed. Artillery bombardments by the NVA's 40th Artillery Regiment, employing 130-mm. gun and 122-mm. rocket fire, continued against forward ARVN positions and artillery batteries during the first week of June, while elements of the 10th NVA Division conducted ground probes against three forward ARVN positions. On 7 June, a major attack by battalions of the 66th Regiment, 10th NVA Division, and the 24th Independent NVA Regiment, supported by at least 10 T-54 tanks and by fire from 130-mm. guns and 122-mm. rockets, struck ARVN positions at Trung Nghia and Polei Krong. The attack drove a regional force battalion and elements of the 44th ARVN Regiment from their positions, affording the NVA control of positions 17 kilometers west of Kontum City.

Even as the 10th NVA Division was pressing hard against the Kontum perimeter, the 320th NVA Division was trying to force contraction of the ARVN defenses west of Pleiku as well as those protecting Highway 14 north of the city. In early May, ARVN intelligence learned that at least one battalion of the 95-B Regiment, 10th NVA Division, had moved out of the Chu Pao Pass area and into a base near Plei Monoun, just south of the Yali Falls, there to prepare for attacks on the ARVN ranger base at Plei Mrong.

In late March a more serious situation was developing in Thanh An district on Highway 19 where elements of the 320th Division began moving from Duc Co toward the ARVN base at Thanh Giao. In the first week of April, the defenders were pounded by 18 separate bombardments and beat off five major ground attacks, although an outer defense perimeter was forced to pull back. Examination of shell fragments disclosed the presence of 130-mm. guns and 120-mm. mortars. It was obvious that the NVA wanted more buffer space east of Duc Co.

VNAF's aerial observers saw a new compound of 34 buildings being erected near the airfield, and photos disclosed extensive new road construction. VNAF bombers attacked a crossing on the Se San River, which forms the Cambodian border at this point, and destroyed 13 medium ferries while ARVN's aggressive defense at Thanh Giao caused the NVA to back off for a few weeks.

By 1 May the 320th Division's 64th Regiment was bivouacked north of Thanh Giao and the 48th remained to the south. Nevertheless, no significant attacks took place, and the ARVN 47th Regiment, 22d Division, having moved from Binh Dinh Province, stiffened the defenses in Thanh An District.

The RVNAF II Corps Commander, Maj. Gen. Nguyen Van Toan, could deploy the 47th Regiment to reinforce Pleiku with confidence that the 22d Division could control the situation in Binh Dinh without it. Over a year having passed since the 22d was badly mauled in Kontum, the division was well on the way to recovery. In northern Binh Dinh the division nibbled at enclaves seized by the Communists in January, finding that the NVA 3d Division was barely effective. The 12th NVA Regiment was in western Tam Quan District, and the 2d and 21st Regiments had pulled out of Hoai Nhon to refit and receive replacements west of the An Lao River in Hoai An District. The fighting strength of the enemy battalions was probably under 200 men each. Having lost heavily in LANDGRAB 73 and in post-cease-fire engagements, the division's morale, as well as its strength, was at a low point, while the ARVN 22d Division was gaining strength and appeared to be imbued with the confidence and drive of its commander, Brig. Gen. Phan Dinh Niem. In any event, with the 6th Ranger Group operating in Tam Quan District, the 40th and 42d Regiments in Hoai Nhon, and the 41st Regiment in Phu My, the 22d ARVN Division as mid-summer approached controlled the main lines of communication and populated coastal regions of Binh Dinh Province.

The South Vietnamese outnumbered the NVA and VC forces in Military Region 2. The ARVN 22d and 23d Divisions had a total of seven regiments in Binh Dinh, Kontum, and Pleiku Province. There were also the 2d Ranger Group, detached from III Corps, and battalions of the 7th Rangers from IV Corps. In all there were 18 Ranger battalions in MR 2 in the summer of 1973. On the other side of the ledger, the enemy had his 3d, 10th, and 320th Divisions, the first two with three regiments and the third with two. The NVA also had four separate regiments and as many as 40 understrength independent battalions but total enemy combat strength in MR 2 was probably under 30,000. The NVA nevertheless demonstrated at Trung Nhia and Polei Krong an ability to concentrate the forces required at a vulnerable objective to achieve temporary success. On the other hand, the enemy failed to concentrate against any decisive objectives in Pleiku or Binh Dinh Provinces, even though the RVNAF was spread thinly throughout the corps area. The activity in MR 2 during the early summer of 1973 illustrated a perennial truth about main force combat success and failure in Vietnam: despite overall numerical and qualitative inferiority, the NVA could concentrate forces, achieve temporary fire and maneuver superiority, attack with some degree of tactical surprise, and overwhelm local RVNAF defenses.

Logistics and Infiltration

By the end of June, at least three NVA transporation regiments were moving supplies along the northern section of Highway 14 from the Khe Sanh area into the A Shau Valley. At least three major storage depots were moved out of Laos into South Vietnam, probably to be located in the new Highway 14 area. As much as 10,000 short tons of supplies were moved into the B-3 front and NVA Military Region 4 during June. This amount was evidently part of the estimated 50,000 short tons which crossed the DMZ into Quang Tri during the first weeks after the cease-fire. The Highway 14 network inside South Vietnam would, when completed, provide an alternate to much of the Ho Chi Minh Trail in Laos. Significantly, when the roads in the southern Laos panhandle were washed out in the southwest monsoon, the Route 14 net in the northern highlands of South Vietnam would be dry and trafficable.

Enemy logistical developments received close attention at DAO and by the J2 of RVNAF. A competent intelligence estimate, employing conservative criteria, concluded that as of the end of May 1973, the NVA had moved supplies into Laos and South Vietnam in sufficient quantities to support offensive operations in South Vietnam at the 1972 (31 March 72–January 73) level for 13 to 18 months and that these supplies would be sufficient to begin a similar offensive by July 1973. Replacements, however, had not yet been received in the numbers required to bring combat units up to the strengths preferred by the NVA for launching an offensive.

From January through June, 65,000 replacements arrived in South Vietnam. This compared to over 92,000 during the same period of 1972. Even when reassigned ex-prisoners of war were added to the totals, a picture of understrength enemy units remained. The RVNAF JGS had estimated enemy casualties during 1972, killed, permanently disabled, or died of wounds, at over 178,000. Even if generous adjustments were made for possible exaggerations, there was no question but that losses were extremely heavy and an estimated 39,000 more enemy soldiers were permanently put out of action during the first six months of 1973. Thus the enemy still had some catching up to do in regard to replacements (RVNAF losses were also heavy in 1972 with over 40,000 killed. Although much lower than those incurred during the Nguyen Hue offensive, casualties in the first half of 1973 were substantial: 15,800 killed, 5,000 dead from non-combat causes, 73,700 wounded in action, and 16,000 injured from noncombat causes.)

Guns and tanks were also moving south. A reasonable estimate, proved accurate by information acquired subsequently, was that the NVA had brought about 140 new 122-mm. and 130-mm. guns into South Vietnam since January 1973, and that about half of these went to COSVN with the rest to Military Region 5 and the B-3 Front. About 250 new tanks also entered the country, also going to COSVN with smaller equal shares to the B-3 Front and MR 5.

The SA-7 "Strella"

Amid the remarkable increase in NVA antiaircraft strength in South Vietnam the gravest threat to VNAF planes, particularly in the southern part of the country, was the SA-7 hand-held missile. From the cease-fire until the end of June, there were 22 reported SA-7 attacks on VNAF aircraft, 8 of which shot down the planes. The following tabulation gives the date / province / aircraft and result:

4 Feb / Quang Tri / A-37, destroyed
25 Feb / Dinh Tuong / UH-1H, missed
3 Mar / Dinh Tuong / A-1H, missed
3 Mar / Dinh Tuong / AC-119, missed
3 Mar / Binh Duong / UH-1, missed
6 Mar / Dinh Tuong / UH-1, missed
20 Mar / Dinh Tuong / A-37, missed
23 Mar / Tay Ninh / CH-47, missed
24 Mar / An Xuyen / UH-1, missed
28 Mar / Binh Long / A-1H, destroyed, pilot missing
28 Mar / Binh Long / AC-119, missed
29 Mar / Binh Long / A-1H, destroyed, pilot missing
29 Mar / Binh Long / F-5A, destroyed, pilot missing
7 Apr / Quang Tri / UH-1 (ICCS), destroyed, 7 killed
16 Apr / Tay Ninh / L-19, missed
20 Apr / Kien Phong / A-1G, destroyed
20 Apr / Kien Hoa / UH-1, destroyed, 1 killed, 3 wounded
29 Apr / Kien Phong / L-19, missed
30 Apr / Kien Phong / L-19, missed
8 May / Tay Ninh / UH-1H, missed
3 Jun / Tay Ninh / CH-47, destroyed, 5 killed
25 Jun / Tay Ninh / UH-1H (two), missed

The concentration of firings and successful attacks in Binh Long Province reflected the intensity of the VNAF air support provided during the effort to relieve the siege of Tong Le Chon. The rather low ratio of successful firings—slightly better than one out of three—was attributable in large degree to effective countermeasures adopted by the VNAF. As the SA-7 was fired, it had a distinctive flash which could often be seen from the air, followed by a characteristic smoke and vapor trail. With attack aircraft flying in pairs, one or the other of the pilots might see the missile coming and take or direct evasive action. High-energy flares were sometimes tossed out or mechanically ejected, frequently causing the missile's heat-seeker to lock on and track the flare and burst a harmless distance from the plane. Helicopter crews were also alert to watch for missiles, and in order to reduce infrared emissions, UH-1 helicopters were modified. The hot-spot on the fuselage below the main rotor was shielded and the exhaust diverted upwards by means of an elbow attached to the tailpipe. But regardless of these moderately effective measures, the result of this contest between air and ground was an environment that forced reconnaissance and attack aircraft above optimum operating altitudes and virtually eliminated the employment of large helicopter formations.

As the NVA was preparing for the assault on Trung Nghia in Kontum, as NVA regiments were making their futile but bloody attempts to continue the attack out of Cambodia into Hong Ngu, and as the ring was being drawn ever more tightly around Tong Le Chon, the diplomats were meeting again in Paris to assert once more the desire of all parties for a real cease-fire and a lasting peace in Vietnam. The communique that issued from the conference marked the beginning of a period which in Saigon was called "Cease-fire II."

Note on Sources

Statistical information on cease-fire violations was principally derived from DAO Saigon Quarterly Assessments, March and June, 1973. The RVNAF/JGS reports on this subject were the primary source used by DAO in publishing its Quarterly Assessments. The general situation prevailing in the country during this period was described with reference to DIA, DAO, Saigon, U.S. Embassy and J2/JGS reports, studies, and assessments. Particularly helpful in this regard were the contributions of Gen. Phan Dinh Niem, commander of the ARVN 22d Infantry Division, who filled in many blanks and corrected some erroneous data concerning the activities and deployment of his division and other forces in the highlands and in Binh Dinh.

6

Cease-Fire II in MR 1 and 2

June–August

The third Indochina war reached a milestone of sorts on 13 June 1973 when the four parties to the original agreement got together in Paris and issued a communique calling upon themselves to observe the provisions of the 28 January cease-fire. The communique was followed by a decline in combat activity that reached the lowest level since the brief hiatus following the LANDGRAB campaign, but this pause was also temporary. The United States then shored up its commitment to Vietnam by assigning one of its toughest, most experienced diplomats, Graham Martin, to be Ambassador in Saigon. Meanwhile, members of the Canadian delegation to the ICCS began making preparations to leave Vietnam, having announced on 29 May that they had come to supervise a cease-fire but instead were observing a war. The Canadians had had no illusions concerning the feasibility of their task. They gave it the best they could, enduring considerable hardships and dangers, and suffering casualties in the bargain.

Dr. Kissinger held a press conference in Paris in which he released the text of the joint communique to take effect at noon on 15 June. His questioners were justifiably skeptical, and Dr. Kissinger barely concealed his own doubts:

What was signed today is an amplification and a consolidation of the original agreement. It is not a new agreement. . . it is our hope that by what has been done today a significant step has been taken in the consolidation of peace in Vietnam and Indochina. . . . the history of Indochina is replete with agreements and joint declarations. I am not naive enough to pretend to you that the mere fact of having again agreed to certain words in itself guarantees peace; but I will also say that since all parties have worked so seriously for the past three weeks, we have every hope that they will match this effort with performance and therefore there is fresh hope, and we hope a new spirit, in the implementation of the agreement, which in itself is maintained. [Department of State *Bulletin*, July 9, 1973, p. 46.]

The communique would have no lasting effect because it had no power of enforcement behind it. It contained no requirement that North Vietnam abandon its fundamental objective; neither did it promise sanctions against any party that chose to ignore its provisions. Perhaps, viewed from Saigon, it provided some reason to hope that South Vietnam could count on enough U.S. support to continue the defense of the country.

There was naturally high interest in Saigon about what effect the communique would have on the level of combat. For the reporting offices of the Defense Attache Office, notably the Operations Division, 15 June marked the beginning of a new reporting period: "Cease-fire II." Based on statistics collected from South Vietnam's JGS and reported as indicators of combat activity, some restraint was imposed by both sides during the first week of Cease-fire II. Table 4 illustrates general declines in activity, comparing the period from 10 June to noon on the 15th (only 5 1/2 days) with the period from noon on the 15th through the 21st.

Fifteen instances of increased activity, indicated by asterisks, occurred in the period following Cease-fire II. Little significance can be attached to any of these instances, except to note that Military Region 1 reported a sharp increase in "incoming artillery" and all regions except Military Region 3 reported an increase in "friendly killed-in-action." There was an abrupt decline in RVNAF offensive indicators in MR 3: "Artillery rounds fired" were 3,712, down from 38,745, and there were no "VNAF sorties flown," compared to 236 the preceding period. Cease-fire II appeared to have the least effect, on both sides, in Military Region 4. Changes were small in most categories.

Early Assessments

The military intelligence community in Vietnam collected considerable information about an enemy buildup but few signs that a major offensive was imminent. Instead, it was faced with contrary, or at least ambivalent, data emphasizing the so-called political struggle and claiming adherence to the cease-fire. At the end of July, the Intelligence Branch of DAO noted that construction on the NVA's new logistical corridor inside South Vietnam, Route 14, was continuing, that the pipeline was being extended, and that ammunition shipments into South Vietnam were at a high level. But these preparations notwithstanding, no new offensive was seen in the offing. The RVNAF J2 had independently reached similar conclusions in a study showing considerable understanding of the situation and of enemy capabilities and intentions.

About a month and a half before Cease-fire II, the President of South Vietnam, Nguyen Van Thieu, discussed his personal estimate with the cabinet. The gist of his remarks, which reached the American Embassy, corresponded to the view held there

TABLE 4: COMBAT LEVEL INDICATORS, JUNE 1973

Indicator	MR 1		MR 2		MR 3		MR 4	
	10-15 Jun	15-21 Jun	10-15 Jun	15-21 Jun	10-15 Jun	15-21 Jun	10-15 Jun	15-21 Jun
Incidents	114	93	99	70	144	97	349	267
Major	16	22*	13	10	10	6	38	25
Minor	59	30	21	16	54	33	178	125
Major contacts	3	1	2	3	0	0	6	2
Minor contacts	36	40*	63	41	80	58	127	115
Incoming arty	1696	2210*	551	528	484	327	1800	1428
Rounds arty fired	12280	5580	14762	11144	38745	3712	22186	22038
VNAF sorties scheduled	132	68	305	232	428	285	76	94*
VNAF sorties flown	14	3	137	49	236	0	44	30
Friendly killed	19	38*	16	18*	41	4	52	70*
Friendly wounded	112	114*	123	123	105	46	275	270
Enemy killed	92	79	173	127	31	31	174	133
Enemy wounded	0	1*	2	1	0	2*	6	0
Civilians killed	8	15*	1	2*	6	2	17	15
Civilians wounded	9	11*	1	1	3	7*	50	12

*Increased activity.

that the Communists were not likely to attack in strength during 1973. Thieu said that the Communists would enjoy the best advantage if they would wait until near the end of President Nixon's term to launch their offensive. He believed they would not move sooner realizing that President Nixon would intervene in the defense of South Vietnam.

The irony of what President Thieu said would not become apparent for many months. He could not have known that two days later Nixon would "accept full responsibility" for the Watergate affair and dismiss his four closest political advisers. Neither could he have predicted that Nixon would leave office 15 months later. The Communists also were undoubtedly surprised by the political turmoil in Washington and would not be quite ready by the time of Nixon's departure in August 1974 to begin the final drive. In the summer of 1973, almost everyone on the scene—Communists, South Vietnamese, and Americans—could agree on three things: the Communists were not ready for a new offensive; they were incapable of resuming guerrilla warfare; and the nature and tempo of military activity in support of the political struggle would remain about the same for the balance of the year. In fact, some analysts were extending their predictions of relative quiescence well into 1974.

Communist resolutions and military directives circulating among troops in South Vietnam in the summer of 1973 reiterated and expanded the general guidance of COSVN Resolutions 2 and 3. As corroborated by the interrogation of ralliers, these documents seemed to direct a holding action in the South while the armed forces were reconstituted and strengthened. They admitted to a present inability to pursue successfully a large-scale offensive, but expressed confidence and pride in the preparations under way—the system of roads, pipelines, airfields, and refurbished main forces—that would offer them this option in the near future. Although their propaganda carried no hint, by late summer the Communists had abandoned the illusion that there could ever be a political settlement, or a tripartite council, or an election that would serve their purposes. The summer of 1973 found the Communist leadership as well as the common soldiers badly demoralized. Peace had not come as promised, the battlefields were still very dangerous, and the RVNAF were showing strength nearly everywhere. Although the South Vietnamese knew the U.S. Congress had voted that American bombing in Cambodia would stop on 15 August, they also heard President Nixon say that on the day the last U.S. bomb fell in Indochina he would "work with the Congress in order to take appropriate action if North Vietnam mounts an offensive which jeopardizes stability in Indochina and threatens to overturn the settlements reached after so much sacrifice by so many for so long." The South Vietnamese, however, could not know that Nixon's vice-president would be forced to resign in disgrace within two months, that Nixon had already lost all his ability to work with the Congress concerning Vietnam, and that he would be out of office himself within a year.

On 4 July 1973 the enemy's South Vietnam Liberation Army issued a directive for the conduct of the struggle in the second half of the year. Signed by Maj. Gen. Tran Do, the army's Deputy Political Officer, it was essentially an exhortation to bolster sagging morale among the cadre. The cadre was told that a great advantage had been won through the terms of the cease-fire but that efforts must be redoubled, particularly in proselyting, if final victory was to be grasped. Furthermore, all cadre would have to work toward modernization of the Liberation Army and correct such tendencies as "pacifism, rightism and passivism." Local military units would be strengthened and their combat efficiency improved. Another order, COSVN Directive 934, turned up in Long An Province in August. Dated the 7th, it recognized the "new opportunities" afforded by the joint communique of 13 June. The United States, according to COSVN, had been forced to abandon its previous policies with regard to Vietnam and would probably not intervene again militarily. Meanwhile, the Liberation Forces would consolidate and rebuild and encircle South Vietnamese controlled areas. These resolutions followed on the heels of To Huu's visit in May during which COSVN's propaganda and training cadre was roundly criticized for inefficiency in carrying out its ideological and educational responsibilities. Thus, following a temporary downturn in activity, a new phase of combat was about to begin.

Trung Nghia

When the ARVN 44th Regiment, 23d Division, was driven out of Trung Nghia by a tank-infantry assault on 8 June 1973 the South Vietnamese immediately tried to retake the position. Casualties mounted on both sides as successive attempts failed to dislodge the deeply entrenched enemy, who enjoyed the advantage of observation from the heights of Ngoc Bay Mountain. In early July, the 44th gained a few meters and dug in on the eastern edge of the village of Ngoc Bay but could move no farther, despite the employment of massive artillery preparations and air strikes. (Map 9)

Stalled in the attempt to take Trung Nghia by frontal assault, General Toan determined that an approach from the south against the positions at Plei Djo Drap, directly across the Dak Bla River from Trung Nghia, would strike the defenses in the flank and force a withdrawal. He therefore directed the

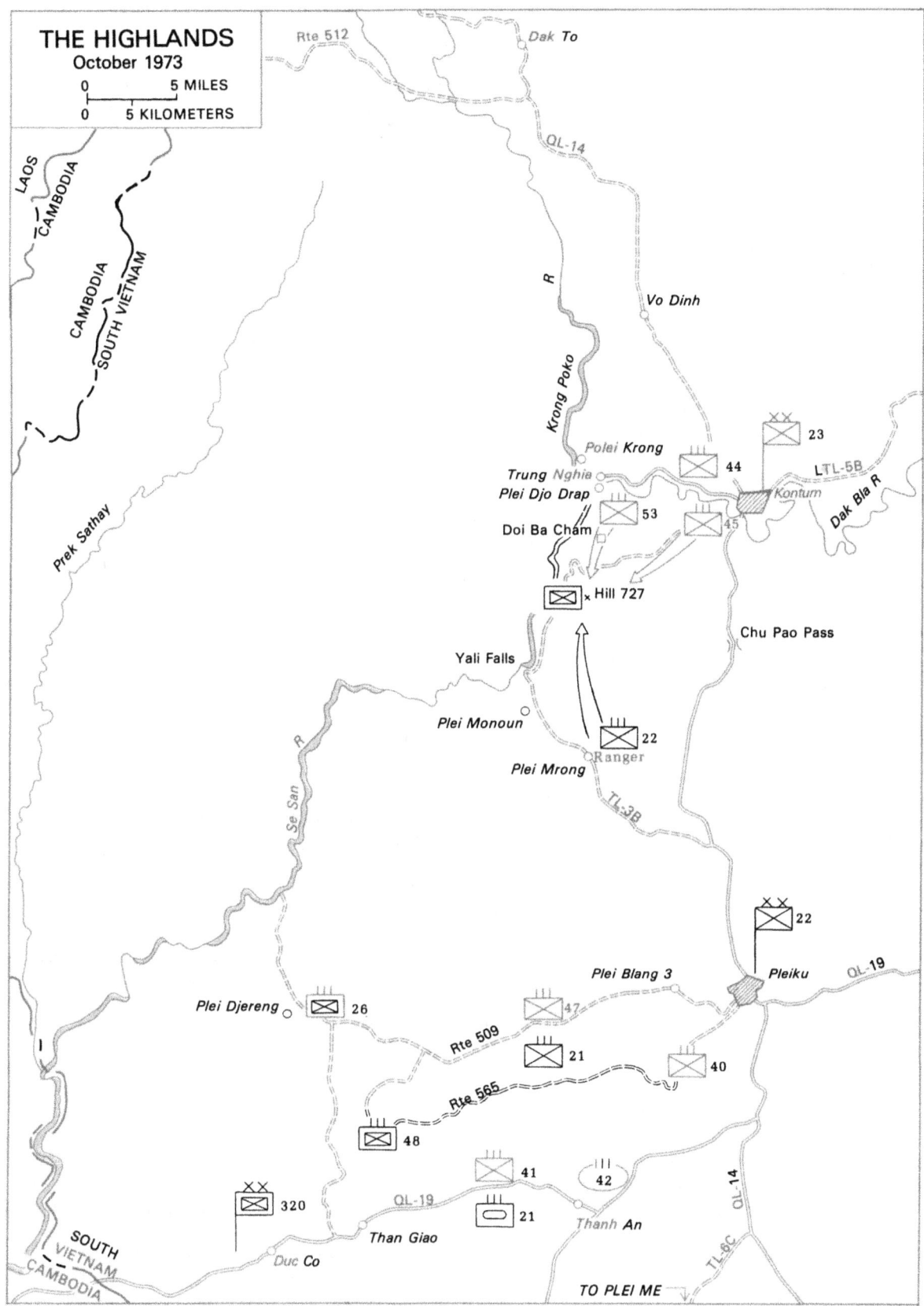

Map 9

23d Division, reinforced with rangers, to attack north from the base at Plei Mrong.

The southwest monsoon, in full force over the western highlands of Pleiku and Kontum Provinces in early August, allowed the NVA to maneuver in daylight since aerial observation was spotty and artillery and air strikes consequently much less effective. Plei Mrong and its camp, called Ly Thai Loi by the ARVN, was situated on Provincial Route 3B south of the Yali Falls of the Krong Bolah and the enemy concentration around Plei Monoun. The ARVN move north caused activity to pick up during the week of 4-10 August when the NVA 28th Reconnaissance-Sapper Battalion of the B3 Front launched seven separate attempts to take the camp, supported by 75-mm. and 130-mm. gunfire. ARVN Ranger units in the field north and south of the camp also came under attack. A few days later a battalion of the 95B Regiment, 10th NVA Division, hit the ARVN 22d Ranger Border Defense Battalion at Doi Ba Cham, just north of Plei Mrong, but was repelled, leaving 150 dead on the battlefield.

Meanwhile, the ARVN 45th Regiment, 23d Division, advancing in the Plei Monoun area to the Krong Bolah River, encountered other elements of the 95B Regiment. Combat with the 95B continued throughout the month in the Plei Mrong sector, and its losses were substantial, probably as many as 200. But despite these losses, the 95B was successful in preventing the ARVN from closing on the Dak Bla River.

The NVA was nevertheless suffering from the bombardment at Trung Nghia. Damage to the NVA 24B Regiment was so severe that it was withdrawn to the Dak To area for recuperation and replaced by elements of the 66th and 28th Regiments, 10th Division. The 28th, recently strengthened by replacements from the North, took up the defense of Trung Nghia while the 66th held Plei Djo Drap. (At this time it became apparent that the 24B Regiment was attached to the 10th Division, while the 95B, the third regiment of the 10th, was taking its direction from B3 Front.) Meanwhile, South Vietnam's tired 44th Regiment was replaced in the attack by the 42d Regiment of the 22d Division, flown to Kontum in C130s from Binh Dinh Province. This fresh regiment, and a small but important change in tactics, made the difference. Rather than engage in large infantry assaults, the 42d methodically eliminated enemy bunkers, one by one, using platoon-sized assaults supported by 81-mm. mortars firing delayed-fuze rounds which blew away overhead cover and killed or exposed the occupants. Prisoners of war later attested to the effectiveness of this technique, particularly the use of delayed fuzes.

On 1 September 1973, the 42d Regiment began the final assault on Trung Nghia, advancing cautiously to find that except for a few isolated riflemen the enemy had withdrawn. The 28th NVA Regiment, depleted by casualties and malaria, limped north along the Poko River. Some of its wounded, left behind and captured, revealed that forces defending Trung Nghia had suffered losses of 30 percent on the whole, and that in some units with considerable sickness casualty rates were as high as 60 percent. On the other hand, the 42d's casualties were light. Furthermore, the ARVN replacement system was working well and in mid-September the two divisions, the 22d and the 23d, were at about 90 and 85 percent strength, respectively.

While the 42d Regiment entered Trung Nghia, the 53d Regiment, 23d ARVN Division, advanced along the south bank of the Dak Bla River and occupied Plei Djo Drap, vacated by the withdrawing 66th NVA Regiment, which crossed the river to recuperate. Trung Nghia was cleared of all enemy by 7 September, and the 42d entered Polei Krong on the 16th. During the rest of the month mopping-up operations cleared enemy remnants from the slopes of Ngoc Bay Mountain, while skirmishing between the ARVN Rangers and elements of the NVA 95B continued around Plei Mrong. But as the success of the 42d Regiment transformed gloom and frustration into euphoria at South Vietnam's II Corps headquarters, a major blow fell on Plei Djereng.

Plei Djereng-Le Minh

One of the few impediments to the steady projection of the NVA's logistical corridor down the length of the western highlands of South Vietnam was an ARVN camp at Plei Djereng, called Le Minh, manned by the 80th Ranger Border Defense Battalion. The position, situated astride Route 613 and blocking free movement from Communist-controlled Plei Trap Valley into the NVA logistical base at Duc Co and east to Pleiku, was an obvious enemy objective. (Map 9)

There was ample warning of an impending attack. A master sergeant from an NVA reconnaissance company turned himself in to Thanh An District, Pleiku, on 16 September and said that the NVA 26th Regiment of the B3 Front would attack Plei Djereng before the end of September. Considerable reliance was attached to the master sergeant's report because his knowledge of the 26th Regiment's order of battle confirmed other information previously collected.

Armed with this intelligence, the battalion commander at Le Minh intensified his security operations around the camp. On 22 September, only one company was inside the camp perimeter together with several families belonging to the battalion; the other two were patrolling outside the wire, although they did not range far from the camp. About noon the 26th NVA Regiment began an assault employing a heavy artillery bombardment including 122-mm. and 130-mm. guns, mortars, and rockets and accompanied by T-54 tanks. As the battle raged through the afternoon, radio contact with the camp was lost, and the battalion commander was mortally wounded. Rain and poor visibility prevented VNAF support. No reinforcement was attempted by the corps commander, although two teams of Loi Ho Rangers (long range reconnaissance patrols) were moved by helicopters into the battle area to reestablish communications and attempt to rally the defenders. In the face of overwhelming NVA strength, this mission had no chance of success. The Rangers reported seeing 6 T-54 tanks, while VNAF pilots after the attack counted 10 and destroyed 3. But this was two days later; rain and poor visibility prevented the VNAF from providing support during the attack. Of 293 men in the 80th Ranger Border Defense Battalion when the battle began, 200 were killed or captured in this short, violent action.

Until the attack on Le Minh, the corps commander, Maj. Gen. Nguyen Van Toan, had enjoyed a deserved reputation as a forceful, if not brilliant, field commander. President Thieu, visiting Pleiku on 1 October along with Chief of the Joint General Staff, General Cao Van Vien, to commemorate the 16th anniversary of II Corps, harshly rebuked General Toan for not reacting to the advance warning of the attack and taking steps to reinforce or at least provide adequate artillery support to the defenders. For General Toan, who some observers felt would be awarded his third star on the occasion of the President's visit, the reprimand was indeed a shattering experience. Although Toan would eventually become a lieutenant general and was to employ his forces with considerable skill during his remaining time in command, of far greater significance than the blow to his ego was the possibility that his lapse at Le Minh (as viewed by President Thieu), may have started a decline of confidence in his ability that culminated in his relief 11 months later.

In any event, Toan seemed to recover rapidly and immediately proposed a plan to retake Le Minh. His subsequent actions revealed, however, that he was less interested in Le Minh than in destroying the NVA 320th Division. President Thieu had directed him to use whatever means necessary to prevent the enemy from concentrating and seriously threatening South Vietnamese forces or territory in Military Region 2. General Toan, with some justification, considered the other NVA division in the highlands, the 10th, to be less than a major menace, having recently experienced heavy casualties in the fighting around Trung Nghia. He therefore decided to concentrate on the 320th, which he believed would be capable of major offensive operations by early 1974, if not crippled in the meantime.

His plan, which he began implementing in mid-October, involved building and occupying strong points along Provincial Route 509 from Pleiku west to Le Minh as bait to entice the 320th into concentrating in the open terrain where Toan could destroy its battalions with air and artillery. He built another strong position where a road used by the NVA into Base Area 701 crossed Provincial Route 6C about 10 kilometers north of and within artillery-supporting range of Plei Me. The position was in relatively open, rolling brush land, and General Toan, whose background was armor, manned it with a task force consisting of a battalion of M-48 tanks, a reconnaissance squadron, a four-gun battery of 155-mm. howitzers, and a regional force battalion, hoping that the 320th would accept the challenge to its line of communication. Instead, however, the 320th kept the pressure on Thanh An District, along Highway 19, and against the ARVN outposts west of Pleiku along Provincial Route 509. Attacks by fire were frequent and heavy, but throughout the summer little ground changed hands and the 320th Division was never seriously hurt. Behind the screen of the 320th, the NVA 470th Logistical Group moved in from Cambodia and set up its headquarters in Duc Co.

By early October, General Toan directed that operations in Binh Dinh be turned over to the province chief and that only one regiment of the 22d Division, the 40th, remain in the coastal province. The fighting commander of the 22d, Brig. Gen. Phan Dinh Niem, who had been wounded more than a dozen times in his long career in battle, had moved his command post to Thanh An District, Pleiku. His 47th Regiment was west of Pleiku with the 21st Ranger Group advancing in the direction of Plei Djereng on Provincial Route 509. In mid-October the 40th was airlifted into Pleiku and assigned to operate west of Pleiku, generally along Provincial Route 565. The 41st Regiment, with the 21st Tank Regiment, was moving on Highway 19 toward Thanh Giao; the 42d Regiment, following its victory at Trung Nghia, was in reserve.

The 23d Division was still responsible for operations in Kontum Province and had its 44th Regiment, supported by territorials, securing the northwestern approaches to the city, while the 45th and 53d Regiments were closing in on Hill 727 west of Kontum City, the last major lodgment of the enemy east of the Krong Bolah River. The 22d Ranger Group at the same time was advancing on Hill 727 from Plei Mrong. Thus, while the victory at Trung Nghia had restored some relative stability to the sector northwest of Kontum and had reduced the threat to the ARVN artillery, logistical and air bases around the city, the situation in western Pleiku

Province was far from settled. Pleiku Airbase and artillery fire bases in the province had been rocketed, and the 320th Division was responding to General Toan's extension of outposts along Provincial Route 509 by moving out from its Plei Djereng base to attempt to force their contraction. To exploit this perceived opportunity to put the 320th out of action, General Toan had the entire 22d Division airlifted by VNAF C130's to Pleiku.

While elements of the 48th Regiment, 320th Division, harassed the ARVN advanced base at Plei Blong 3, near Pleiku, the 2d Bn of the ARVN 40th Regiment fought a fierce engagement with an enemy battalion, supported by five T-54 tanks, southwest of Plei Blong 3 on the afternoon of 23 October. Losses were heavy on both sides. Although other bloody skirmishes followed, none presented General Toan with the opportunities for even gradual attrition such as he enjoyed at Trung Nghia against the NVA 10th Division. In western Pleiku Province, the 320th had room for maneuver and was not committed to defend a small piece of terrain as the 10th was at Trung Nghia. The decision to give up the offensive and pull back to defensible positions in a shallow strip west of Pleiku was, however, forced upon General Toan by the turn of events in Quang Duc.

Quang Duc

Quang Duc, the mountain province where Vietnam bends westward and the Annamite Range begins to slope down to the terrace of the Dong Nai, was important commercially for its vast timber resources and militarily, for both sides, because of the lines of communication that passed through it. After the NVA had closed surface travel from Saigon to Phuoc Long by the direct route through Binh Duong, the only land access available to the South Vietnamese was via Ban Me Thuot and Quang Duc. As far as the NVA was concerned, Quang Duc was pivotal to the extension of its Route 14 out of Mondol Kiri Province, Cambodia, and Darlac Province, South Vietnam.

Because South Vietnamese forces controlled Highway 14 as far south and west from Ban Me Thuot as the Tuy Duc crossroads, the NVA's new Route 14 had to pass through Cambodia and reenter South Vietnam in that salient of Mondol Kiri Province that juts into Quang Duc near a place called Bu Prang. The site of an abandoned U.S. Army Special Forces camp, Bu Prang and its short runway perched atop a high, forested ridge astride National Highway 14 near Tuy Duc crossroads at the Cambodian border. Before reaching the Phuoc Long border of South Vietnam's Military Region 3, Highway 14 was joined at the little hill town of Kien Duc by Local Route 344, coming over from the Quang Duc Province capital of Ghia Nghia. This road junction was vital because its control provided an alternate route from Ban Me Thuot—through Dak Song and Ghia Nghia on Provincial Route 8B. Important as well was the road junction at Dak Song, where Provincial Route 8B left Highway 14. (Map 10)

Until mid-May 1973 when the NVA's projection of its new line of communication reached Bu Prang and while the South Vietnam's access to Phuoc Long through Quang Duc remained unthreatened, neither side paid much attention to Quang Duc. ARVN engineers were working on local roads, primarily to improve access to the timber preserves in the northeast section of the province, and the only enemy activity of any note was mining to harass and delay this project. Only three regional force battalions were located in the province. They were supported by six 105-mm. howitzer platoons (12 guns), which had no occasion to fire since the cease-fire. Additionally, 27 popular force platoons were scattered about the province. These territorials were nearly all Montagnards, and the province population was 60 percent tribal.

Around the beginning of May, a regional force patrol, moving out from its lonely outpost near Bu Prang, made contact with an NVA reconnaissance party and killed four. The rest of May and June were quiet until enemy harassment of the RF positions around Bu Prang began in early July, evidently in response to the unusually aggressive patrolling ordered by Col. Nguyen Hau Thien, Quang Duc's province chief. Mortar attacks, accompanied by some light infantry probes, continued through July, as did RF forays into the "old" Bu Prang positions on the border west of the Tuy Duc crossroads. In the last week of August, Colonel Thien tried a reconnaissance in force with two RF battalions. Both met heavy resistance short of their objectives on the border and returned to camp. This inconclusive skirmishing took on an ominous note in early September when the first evidence appeared disclosing that COSVN had sent two battalions of its 271st Regiment from southwest of Tay Ninh City up to Quang Duc. The presence of an NVA main force regiment was a new and dangerous development in Quang Duc. Colonel Thien asked for reinforcement and was given an RF battalion from Darlac Province. He complained about the poor performance of the Darlac battalion, and General Toan agreed to replace it with another battalion from Khanh Hoa. This gave Colonel Thien a force of four RF battalions, two of his own Quang Duc battalions and two from Khanh Hoa. He located the entire force at the mutually supporting bases of Bu Prang and Bu Bong, each with a platoon of 105-mm. howitzers.

The NVA 271st Independent Regiment had been roughly handled by the ARVN and VNAF in the

Cease-Fire II in MR 1 and 2

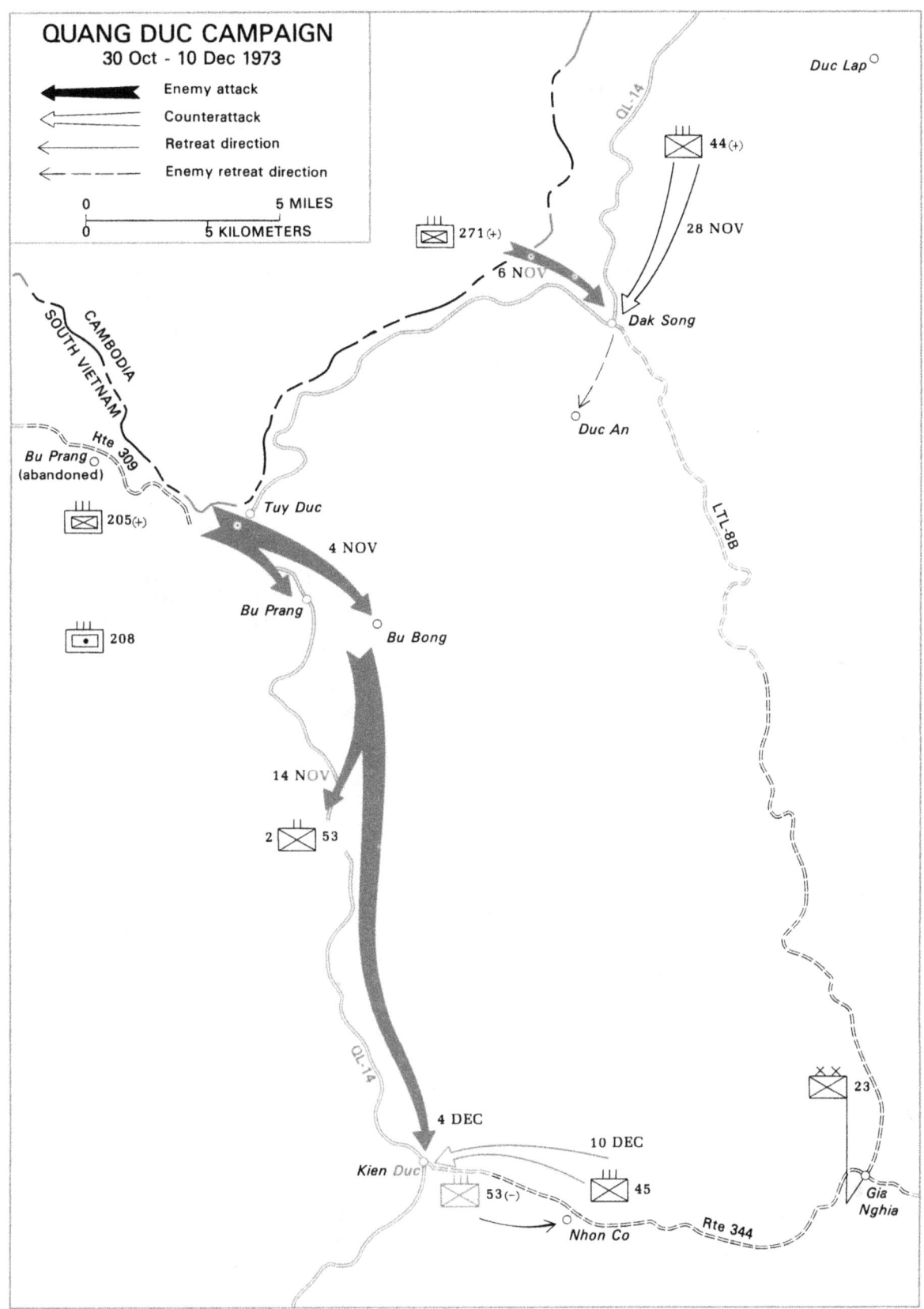

Map 10

early months of 1973 in marsh and ricelands along the Vam Co Dong River and the Cambodian border in Hau Nghia Province and southern Tay Ninh. COSVN had pulled it back to Cambodia in April for reorganization and recuperation. Afterwards the regimental headquarters and two of its battalions, the 8th and 9th, were trucked to Bu Dop in northern Phuoc Long Province, while the other, the 7th, was sent to operate under Long An Province authority. (When the 271st Regiment was committed to battle in Quang Duc, it had three battalions; the third was evidently an infantry battalion from the Tay Ninh-Svay Rieng Military Region (C-50), probably attached to the 271st during the reorganization phase in April.) Leaving Bu Dop, the 271st marched through Bu Gia Map and arrived northwest of Bu Prang in late August, ready to assist in the defense of the new line of communication and to deny the ARVN use of Highway 14 in the border region. Successive attempts by the Quang Duc territorials failed to gain any ground west of the Tuy Duc crossroads, as the rest of Quang Duc Province remained relatively quiet.

Meanwhile, NVA preparations for the Quang Duc campaign continued. A task force headquarters, designated Unit 95, was established at Bu Dop in Phuoc Long Province, and the NVA 205th Independent Regiment was assembled there for movement to Quang Duc. The 205th had been operating since the cease-fire in South Vietnam's Military Region 3, and before moving to Bu Dop it had been in northern Binh Duong Province east of the Michelin plantation. Three more maneuver elements joined the task force at Bu Dop before its composition was complete: the 429th Sapper Regiment, the 46th Reconnaissance Battalion, and a tank battalion (probably the 20th) from the COSVN 26th Armor Group. Artillery support was provided by the 208th Artillery Regiment, 69th Group, COSVN, which had been operating in Binh Long. Antiaircraft artillery, including 23-mm. automatic cannons, joined the force as well as a detachment equipped with SA-7 antiaircraft missiles.

Unit 95 had reached division strength, but this was not yet realized at South Vietnam's II Corps headquarters. Given the meager defenses in Quang Duc, it was surprising that the NVA leadership committed a force of such overwhelming size. The fact that it did so appeared to reflect the inadequacy of NVA tactical intelligence, which had been demonstrated on several occasions, and a respect for RVNAF capabilities. Such a commitment also underscored the importance attached to the principal objective—construction and protection of the line of communication. Much later, after the major engagements were over and the Communist leadership considered the threat to its line of communication significantly diminished, South Vietnamese intelligence officers discovered that continued offensive operations by the enemy's Quang Duc task force were designed to draw RVNAF into the province and keep them occupied, thereby reducing the forces available for employment against the B3 Front. Had the forces been available, General Toan might have accommodated the enemy in this regard. They were not, however, and Quang Duc security had to revert to territorials and Rangers.

By the end of September 1973, reconnaissance and survey parties from the 208th Artillery Regiment had selected firing positions and observation posts near the Tuy Duc crossroads at Bu Prang, Bu Bong, and Kien Duc. Firing batteries moved into Quang Duc by the end of October with their 85- and 122-mm. field guns and 120-mm. mortars. To insure consistency in survey and firing, the only maps authorized for use in the 208th Artillery were the 1:50,000 series printed in Hanoi.

The NVA 205th Infantry Regiment, with the 429th Sapper Regiment attached, arrived in assembly areas near Bu Prang in mid-October, and on 23 October the 208th Artillery began a five-day rehearsal preparatory to the attack. Meanwhile, the NVA 271st Regiment with the 46th Reconnaissance Battalion moved toward Dak Song.

The 208th Artillery began softening up Bu Prang and Bu Bong on 30 October. Each day 122-mm. rockets and mortar and artillery shells fell on the two camps. The camp commander kept his four RF battalions outside the perimeter, patrolling near the Tuy Duc crossroads, and the local defense of the two positions was the responsibility of an RF company, an engineer platoon, and the two platoons of artillery. The attack began just before dawn on 4 November. The NVA 205th Regiment, with the 429th Sappers and two companies of tanks and armored personnel carriers, overran the badly outnumbered and outgunned defenders. They destroyed two ARVN howitzers, towed the other two away, and outside the camps dispersed the four RF battalions. During the assault on Bu Bong, the commander of the NVA 205th was seriously wounded and had to be evacuated.

General Toan responded rapidly to the situation in Quang Duc Province, although he had available only sketchy information concerning the enemy's strength and dispositions. He immediately ordered the ARVN 23d Division to pull the 53d Infantry out of western Kontum and get it started toward Ban Me Thuot. As this order was being executed, a blow fell on Dak Song, the camp controlling access to Route 8B, the only land access to Quang Duc from Ban Me Thuot. The defenses at Dak Song crumbled under assault of the NVA 271st Regiment; Gia Nghia, the province capital, was cut off. But the 53d ARVN Infantry was on the way; by 8 November, its 1st Battalion was approaching Dak Song. The 2d

Battalion, 53d ARVN Infantry, was flown into Nhon Co airfield west of Gia Nghia and began moving north on Highway 14 toward Bu Prang and Bu Bong.

Meanwhile, the NVA 205th Regiment began executing the next phase of its orders: it turned over the defense of the newly won positions at Bu Prang and Bu Bong to another element of the task force and began deploying south generally along Highway 14 from Bu Prang toward the Doan Van bridge. South of Bu Prang it had its first taste of battle with ARVN regulars from the 23d Division. In the early morning of 14 November, the 3d Battalion, NVA 205th Regiment, with a platoon of tanks, smacked into the defensive perimeter of the 2d Battalion, 53d Infantry. The 2d Battalion held, knocked out 2 tanks, and captured 9 crew-served weapons and 27 automatic rifles. The enemy left 100 dead on the field. A second attack was repulsed the next day with moderate losses to the enemy. The 3d Battalion, NVA 205th Regiment, had to be withdrawn; only 100 effective soldiers remained in the ranks.

Despite these serious losses, the 205th continued its advance south toward Kien Duc. With only the 2d and 3d Battalions available (the 1st was still engaged near Dak Song), the ARVN 53d Infantry prepared to defend the Kien Duc road junction. The NVA 205th began probing these defenses on 21 November. On the 23d Communist leaflets were found around Kien Duc, signed by the Commander in Chief, National Liberation Front Forces, advising RVNAF officers and men to stop trying to retake Bu Prang, Bu Bong, and Dak Song and threatening to attack Gia Nghia with tanks if the South Vietnamese persisted. (The NVA, with steadily diminishing justification, still believed strongly in the psychological impact of tanks against the ARVN.)

While skirmishing took place around Bu Prang, Dak Song, and Kien Duc, General Toan continued to send forces to Quang Duc. The 21st Ranger Group and the 44th and 45th Infantry Regiments of the 23d Division began their deployments. In the highlands, the 22d ARVN Division pulled back from western Pleiku in order to assume the defense of Kontum, vacated by the departing 23d Division. On 28 November, the 44th Infantry of the ARVN 23d Division, with a battalion of Rangers, attacked into Dak Song, forcing the withdrawal of the reinforced 271st NVA Regiment, which pulled back toward Duc An, leaving blocking elements on Route 8B.

Its reconnaissance and preparation completed, the 205th NVA Regiment, reinforced with the 429th Sappers and supported by tanks and the 208th Artillery Regiment, attacked the Kien Duc road junction on 4 December, wounding the regimental commander and forcing the elements of the 53d Infantry to withdraw six kilometers east to Nhon Co airfield. Casualties were moderately heavy on both sides; the 53d lost 40 killed, 40 wounded, and 80 missing. The 205th quickly began to replace some of its losses; about 100 fresh troops, lately arrived from North Vietnam, joined the regiment at Kien Duc on 8 December.

Meanwhile, General Toan flew to Saigon to report on the Quang Duc situation to President Thieu and General Vien. The President told him not to be concerned about lost outposts, but to direct his efforts to the destruction of the NVA forces in Quang Duc. These instructions no doubt pleased General Toan. That same day he ordered the 23d Division commander to put his command post in Gia Nghia and to fly his 45th Regiment to Nhon Co. Within hours six C-130's landed elements of the 23d Division at Nhon Co, although the airfield there was under intermittent artillery and rocket attack. That night and the next day, the 21st ARVN Rangers removed the last road blocks on Route 8B south of Dak Song. Casualties were heavy, but the first convoy since September soon rolled into Gia Nghia from Ban Me Thuot.

Although the commander of the 53d Infantry had recovered from his wound and asked for the mission of retaking Kien Duc, Colonel Tuong, commanding the division, assigned the task to the 45th. This regiment was fresh, while the 53d's battalions had been in nearly constant action for a month. Following an intense and effective artillery and air preparation, the 23d Division Reconnaissance Company and the 3d Battalion, 45th Infantry, led the attack into the trenches, bunkers, and rubble at the Kien Duc road junction. The NVA 205th was forced to retire with heavy losses; its 1st Battalion lost 40 percent of its strength at Kien Duc, and its sapper company was so decimated that it was disbanded after the battle. A rallier later reported that the 205th lost more than 200 killed and 400 wounded in its Quang Duc campaign.

The 23d ARVN Division, using its 44th Regiment, continued effective operations during December and early January, primarily in the Bu Prang – Bu Bong area, against the NVA 271st Regiment's forces remaining there. With the route again secured from Ban Me Thuot through Gia Nghia to Phuoc Long, General Toan's responsibilities in the highlands and Binh Dinh demanded that the 23d leave Quang Duc Province to deal with more pressing threats.

In Quang Duc the NVA exploited the benefits of prolonged and detailed preparation and capitalized on its ability to concentrate overwhelming force against lightly defended objectives. Although these factors combined to produce success in the initial battles, the RVNAF, employing with particular skill its newly developed capability of rapid air deployment, its professional application of close air support and artillery fire, and its experienced regular infantry, won the campaign. The NVA was denied the use of Highway 14 through Quang Duc, its line of communications in the border region around the Tuy Duc crossroads remained subject to harassment and interdiction, and the RVNAF were able to regain and keep control of the logistical route to Phuoc Long. Quang Duc proved once again that the South Vietnamese, provided sufficient ammunition, fuel, and maintenance support, could overcome the traditional advantages enjoyed by the attacker.

Military Region 1

For the NVA, the last half of 1973 was a period for rebuilding and expansion. The intense fighting in the B-3 Front area, from Kontum to Quang Duc, was the direct result of the determination of the NVA to expand its logistical system—particularly the Route 14 complex—and prevent RVNAF encroachment into base areas and lines of communication. The level of combat in South Vietnam's Military Region 1 was comparatively low, simply because the NVA's northern Quang Tri and western highland bases and logistical routes were neither seriously threatened nor interfered with. The North Vietnamese continued construction and stockpiling activities in full view of RVNAF positions and made little effort to camouflage. They did attempt to prevent aerial observation and photography, and the density of their antiaircraft defenses denied manned flight over sensitive areas such as Khe Sanh and Cam Lo. Since the enemy required no additional terrain or routes for his logistical activities, there were only minor adjustments in the line of contact.

As Cease-fire II came to MR 1, General Truong, commanding I Corps, made some adjustments in defensive sectors assigned to his divisions north of the Hai Van Pass. The Marine Division retained responsibility for the northern approaches in Quang Tri Province and was given operational control of the 51st Regiment, 1st Infantry Division, which replaced the Airborne Division west of Highway 1. The Airborne Division was assigned the defense of the Co Bi-An Lo Bridge sector, while the 1st Infantry Division was responsible for the western and southern defenses of Hue as far south as Phu Loc District and the Hai Van Pass. South of the Hai Van Pass, the 3d Infantry Division held Quang Nam Province and the northern district of Quang Tin Province, which included the Que Son Valley. The 2d Infantry Division was spread from the valley southward to cover the rest of the region to the boundary of Binh Dinh Province.

The Marine Division's sector was the most stable and least active in the region, if not in the entire country. Opposing riflemen exchanged invectives rather than bullets. The Marine Division commander, Brig. Gen. Bui The Lan, reported in early July that no rifle or artillery fire had been directed against his troops since March. He said that he would respond in kind to any attack against his positions and that one of his targets would be Dong Ha city itself, which was within range of his artillery. The Communists undoubtedly understood the risks associated with any significantly heightened activity in the Quang Tri sector. They were rebuilding Dong Ha, and its small port was rapidly becoming a major storage and transhipment point for military supplies. VC activity in the marine rear was all but wiped out, although fragments of the infrastructure probably still functioned clandestinely among the 27,000 refugees settled in Hai Lang District behind the front. Adding to the strength of the division and its attached 51st Infantry were six RF battalions and 12 PF companies, all from Quang Tri Province. The PF companies and some of the RF companies were integrated with marine companies occupying the same positions. General Lan was quite pleased, saying that the PF companies were the equal of the RF.

He attached two of the RF battalions to marine brigades in the line where they were assigned sectors to defend, while two other battalions, seriously understrength after malaria-ridden tours in the western mountains, were shifted to coastal areas of operations east of Quang Tri City. General Lan also had some armor under his control—the 18th Cavalry Squadron with a troop of M-41 tanks and two troops of armored personnel carriers and a reinforced company of M-48 tanks. Later in the year he was to gain control of a Ranger group, but he had to return the 51st Regiment to the 1st Division west of Hue. The stability of the main front enabled General Lan to keep three battalions in reserve and to rotate battalions to Saigon for two-week periods of rest and family visits. In spite of extended tours in positions face to face with the enemy, morale in the Marine Division was the best in the armed forces.

Meanwhile, the NVA, also taking advantage of the cease-fire in Quang Tri, in December withdrew its 320B Division to Thanh Hoa Province in North Vietnam. Following the 308th and 312th Divisions, the 320B became the third NVA infantry division to deploy home from the Quang Tri front since the 1972 offensive.

The most sensitive part of the Hue defenses was the sector guarding the critical An Lo Bridge. Less than 15 kilometers from the Imperial City, the An Lo Bridge carried Highway 1 across the Song Bo River at the mouth of the Song Bo Valley. Not only was this sector the northwestern gateway to Hue, but its control by the enemy would isolate the Marine Division. The Airborne Division was given the task of its defense, made all the more difficult by Typhoon Opal that hit the northern coast in October. Flooding in the Song Bo Valley forced the Airborne to evacuate several defensive positions in the Co Bi area, and the Communists were able to occupy some of them before the paratroopers could return. Further complicating maneuver and logistics, the An Lo Bridge was washed out, and all traffic had to use a one-way Bailey bridge installed by I Corps Engineers.

Until the typhoon struck, the Airborne Division was making fair progress strengthening the west bank defenses of the Song Bo. Attached to the division were two RF battalions, employed as regular infantry, a tank company, and an armored personnel carrier troop, and the division commander, Brig. Gen. Le Quang Luong, was confident of their ability to accomplish their mission. The Airborne Division had been rushed to Quang Tri and Thua Thien Provinces in May 1972 to turn back the NVA advance, and it was proud of its record there. But its losses had been heavy; from its deployment to Military Region 1 until January 1974, nearly 2,900 airborne officers and soldiers had been killed in action, about 12,000 had been wounded, and 300 were missing in action. For a unit whose organization called for only 13,500, these losses meant that most of its finest leaders and fighters had perished or were out of action, and the ranks were filled with unseasoned replacements. By December 1973, the traditional esprit and its accompanying high morale were significantly weakened under the impact of poverty suffered by soldiers and their families. The quality of replacements declined, and their numbers were not sufficient to compensate for battle losses and desertions. Nevertheless, General Luong, with his division committed on a relatively narrow front, was able to hold a reserve of two battalions and release a regiment for corps reserve.

Although the Airborne Division defenses were dangerously shallow south of the An Lo Bridge, the deeper positions held by the ARVN 1st Division to the southeast were under greater enemy pressure. A small tributary of the Song Bo twisted through the hills and joined the river west of Hue; it was along this stream, the Ngoc Ke Trai, that the forward positions of the ARVN 3d Infantry Regiment, 1st Division, were sited. In the first heavy action in the sector following Cease-fire II, two 3d Infantry positions west of the confluence fell to Communist attack in late July. The pressure continued, and the 3d Infantry gave up four more outposts along the Song Bo in late August. Another series of positions along the Ngoc Ke Trai fell in November as signs of deteriorating morale and weak leadership began to appear in the formerly highly respected 1st Division. Casualties resulting from the enemy assaults were light, and the rapid collapse of the defenses could only be attributed to faltering will and uninspired leadership. At this time Lt. Gen. Lam Quang Thi, I Corps Deputy Commanding General and commander north of the Hai Van Pass, detached a battalion from the 51st Infantry and returned it to the 1st Division to reinforce the Song Bo defenses. The 1st Division Commander, Brig. Gen. Le Van Than, further reinforced the 3d Regiment with a battalion of the 1st Infantry Regiment. The line stabilized toward the end of the year, but not until after General Truong had accomplished the removal of General Than and replaced him with Col. Nguyen Van Diem. Colonel Diem took command of the division on 31 October but could make no noticeable headway in solving the division's tactical and morale problems. These were too much the results of conditions beyond the control of the commander: an extended front under continuous enemy pressure, the debilitating effects of cold, wet, typhoonal weather; inadequate supply to the forward infantry outposts; and the worsening economic straits in which the men found themselves.

If the 3d Infantry's control of the situation in the Song Bo–Ngoc Ke Trai sector was unsettled and worrisome to the 1st Division commander, the 54th Infantry Regiment's hold on the southern approaches to Hue inspired little confidence either. The 54th held Mo Tao Mountain and other key positions in the Song Ta Trach sector. The Ta Trach River, which was the main tributary of the Song Huong—the famous Perfume River that flows through the heart of Hue beneath the walls of the ancient Citadel—formed a natural corridor into the city. Although the forward positions were in contested terrain, the NVA maintained only light pressure throughout the last part of 1973.

The 54th's sector of responsibility was wide; it extended south to Phu Loc District and the northern end of the Hai Van Pass. After winding north through the Pass, Highway 1 in Phu Loc paralleled the railroad along the beach, over numerous culverts and bridges. At Phu Loc a great massif, whose highest peak was Bach Ma at 1448 meters, tumbled down to end abruptly at the bay. Bach Ma was an ideal site for severing Thua Thien and Quang Tri Province from the rest of the country. Neither side occupied it at cease-fire, but the ARVN soon after established an outpost at the summit. The NVA followed suit, and by August 1973 two ARVN RF companies faced a small enemy force less than 100 meters away.

During clear weather, Bach Ma provided good observation of Highway 1 at Phu Loc, but as the rainy season arrived, clouds rested on the summit not only obscuring vision but making resupply of the forces on top virtually impossible by helicopter. Although an informal understanding had been reached with the North Vietnamese—they would stop firing at VNAF helicopters from their positions on the mountain if the VNAF fighter-bombers would stop attacking their positions—the weather closed in by late August, and all resupply had to be carried up the steep mountain trail on foot. It was no surprise, therefore, when the RF on Bach Ma abandoned their positions in the face of a relatively light enemy attack on 12 October. The event was viewed mostly as a psychological setback at I Corps headquarters, and no plans to retake the positions were seriously considered, since Bach Ma's importance as an observation post would be nil until the dry season returned to Thua Thien. Nevertheless, its loss represented another small chink in South Vietnam's armor, one that would go unrepaired until the end.

Given the overwhelming NVA capability for rapid reinforcement from the north, the thin line of shallow positions held by the overextended RVNAF, and the extreme vulnerability of the sector to isolation from the south, it was not surprising that an attitude of gloom pervaded General Thi's headquarters in the months following Ceasefire II. Nor was it surprising that General Thi clung to the belief—or perhaps a hope expressed as a belief—that U.S. B-52's would be decisive in saving Quang Tri and Thua Thien in the event of an NVA offensive. After all, massive U.S. air and naval power was required to turn back the NVA's assault in 1972. And that time the enemy started behind his own goal line; this time he was already on the ARVN 30. Although having scant confidence that U.S. bombing would be resumed, DAO and USSAG planners cooperated with I Corps in keeping target folders current, and direct liaison between I Corps and USSAG was established for this purpose. General Thi had observed that since the NVA had placed thousands of tons of supplies and equipment in open, visible storage throughout northern Quang Tri and Western Thua Thien, the B-52s could wipe them out in 10 days. He added, significantly, that his three divisions could successfully defend the two northern provinces against a determined enemy attack, but only with U.S. air support. This assessment was shared by the chiefs of intelligence and operations branches, DAO.

Cease-fire II began in southern Quang Nam Province on an ominous note scarcely noticed at DAO, or for that matter at South Vietnam's JGS. The ARVN 78th Ranger Battalion received a number of concentrated bombardments on its positions guarding the Thu Bon Valley approach to the flatlands south of Da Nang. One of its companies was forced to abandon its position and rejoin the battalion, which received prompt orders from I Corps to hold its position. Although the attacks subsided, they were an unperceived precursor to violent assaults in 1974. But at the time, the late summer and fall of 1973, the NVA's 711th Division was the only sizeable main force element facing the ARVN 3d Division in Quang Nam and northern Quang Tin, and the 3d, with the help of Rangers and territorials, could deal with this threat adequately.

Meanwhile, as the rice harvest was coming in during September and October, NVA-supported local Communists became active in the hamlets along the coast and in the larger valleys, and security deteriorated in the wake of bridge-minings and assassinations. Still, by the first anniversary of the cease-fire, General Nguyen Duy Hinh, who was proving to be one of the most effective division commanders in the RVNAF, was so much in control of the situation that he could keep an entire regiment, the 2d Infantry, in reserve, and each of the committed regiments, the 56th in southern Dai Loc and northern Duc Duc Districts of Quang Nam, and the 57th in the Que Son Valley, could hold a battalion in reserve. The division's fighting and headquarters positions were dug deeply into hillsides with connecting tunnels, and General Hinh was justified in his confidence that his division could protect Da Nang and the lowlands against the NVA 711th. Five of South Vietnam's district seats of Quang Nam, however, were within range of NVA 130-mm. guns, and their security was questionable. Of these, Thuong Duc and Duc Duc were the most vulnerable.

While the ARVN 3d Division concentrated south and west of Da Nang, the ARVN 2d Division had the formidable task of securing the coastal piedmont and plains from the Binh Dinh boundary north to Tam Ky in Quang Tin Province, a distance of 135 kilometers. Fresh from its victory at Sa Huynh, the 2d Division was to support the territorials in clearing the lowlands west of Highway 1 of the remnants of VC units. By October, the division could claim substantial success in this mission, and the emphasis shifted to continuing the pressure on local VC units until they withdrew into the foothills. The division's battalions, reinforced with Rangers and territorials, pushed into the piedmont to block the enemy's supply lines to the coast, find and destroy supply bases, deny access to the rice harvest, protect refugee villages, and secure Highway 1 against enemy attack. Added to these generalized missions was one very specific requirement, imposed not only by orders from I Corps but compelled by the honor of the division: defend Sa Huynh. The 4th Infantry Regiment was assigned this mission, keeping two battalions entrenched in the hills overlooking the small fishing village. The 4th, with one RF battalion attached and another under the command of the district chief, was responsible for security in Duc Pho District of Quang Ngai, but its control extended scarcely 5,000 meters west of Highway 1.

The 5th Infantry Regiment, 2d ARVN Division, had missions parallel to the 4th, but operated in the central coastal district of Mo Duc. The 5th was reinforced by two RF battalions, but its success in maneuvering west of Highway 1 was also limited, although security along the highway was reasonably well maintained. North of Quang Ngai City, in Son Tinh District, the 11th Ranger Group had the responsibility, but it was probably among the least effective units of this kind. With battalions that could muster only 225 to 300 men for operations, its performance was desultory at best. The group's 68th Battalion typified the general lack of combat efficiency characteristic of the other two battalions, and for that matter, most of the 12 RF battalions in Quang Ngai. The 68th was driven from its dug-in positions on Hill 252—in the important Cong Hoa Valley approach to Quang Ngai City—in October by an inferior VC unit. After stalling in attempts to retake the hill, it was sent—somewhat as punishment for failure—to an active area south of Chu Lai. There, on the night of 17 December, the 95th VC Sapper Company of Binh Son District infiltrated the sleeping battalion command post, caused over 50 casualties including the battalion commander and his deputy, and carried away an 81-mm. mortar, eight PRC-25 radios, 15 M-16 rifles, five .45-caliber pistols, and five binoculars.

The 6th Infantry Regiment of the 2d Division was responsible for the sector from Chu Lai to the division boundary north of Tam Ky and like the other two regiments, engaged in numerous contacts with local VC through the fall and winter of 1973. There were 6 major bridges and at least 25 shorter spans along the stretch of Highway 1 in the 2d Division sector. All had to be protected, and the mission was nearly always assigned to territorials. Enemy water-sappers—underwater demolition teams—got to the Ba Bau Bridge south of Tam Ky the day after Christmas and dropped it in the river. On Christmas, they blew up the Tra Can Bridge in Duc Pho District, right under the noses of an RF Company. Maj. Gen. Tran Van Nhut, the 2d Division Commander, was so incensed at this debacle—the RF Company commander had been warned that a VC unit was seen reconnoitering for the attack—that he slapped the captain in jail. According to General Nhut at the time, at least a part of the problem of territorial ineffectiveness in Quang Ngai Province was traceable to the fact that a very high percentage of the RF, PF, and Peoples' Self-Defense Force troops had relatives in the Communist ranks; family loyalties often took precedence over military orders and duties.

The night after Christmas, VC units entered two resettlement villages across the river from Quang Ngai City, killed a village chief and nine others, and destroyed at least six houses. This attack differed from the routine sapper assaults on RVNAF installations and lines of communication in that it was part of a country-wide Communist campaign to destroy South Vietnam's refugee settlement program, which against formidable obstacles was achieving some success. But the enemy attacks in Quang Ngai against these already tragic figures were particularly brutal.

The campaign against the refugees started in May. The first attack in Quang Ngai Province was described as minor in the sense that there were no reported casualties. The VC had entered a hamlet in Son Tinh District and burned the tents the people were living in while they were working on permanent houses. The Social Welfare Service of Quang Ngai promptly replaced the tents only to have them burned again a few days later. The frequency and intensity of attacks increased in July as the VC moved in with mortars and civilian casualties began to mount. The constant mortaring of two sites in Mo Duc led to their abandonment. Duc Pho resettlement sites not only suffered mortar attacks, but VC sappers infiltrated and destroyed houses with demolitions, some with the occupants still inside. In other hamlets the VC entered at night and sowed footpaths with antipersonnel mines.

The attack on An Tinh Hamlet in Son Tinh District on 6 September was a classic in execution. VC sappers entered at 0300, and after they were inside the fence another VC unit began mortaring the nearby outpost, effectively confining the defenders to their little fortress. As the mortar fire began, the sappers moved methodically through the hamlet, throwing incendiary grenades into the dry, thatch houses and firing B-40 rockets. Because the people had taken cover in their bunkers, only five were seriously wounded, but all 322 houses burned to the ground in a spectacular blaze fed by high winds. The tragedy was visible for miles. But the people of An Tinh were a stubborn lot, and by the end of October they had rebuilt once more.

As the cease-fire anniversary came and went in southern Military Region 1, the situation resembled more than anything else the conditions in the Mekong Delta: ARVN regulars had control of the major population centers and the important lines of communication; the NVA was more or less on the ropes but recovering, rebuilding, and receiving replacements; and South Vietnamese territorials were taking the brunt of the Communist attacks—attacks that eroded morale, exacerbated already strained economic conditions, and contributed to a slow but perceptible decline in the population considered under government influence or control.

Note on Sources

The statistics relating to cease-fire violations before and after the joint communique were derived from the DAO Saigon Quarterly Report, June 1973. The situation prevailing at the time was described with reference to the DAO Saigon Monthly Intelligence Summary and Threat Analysis and the RVNAF J2/JGS Study: "Enemy Situation in RVN 45 Days after the 13 June Joint Communique."

Captured enemy documents and interrogation reports provided by J2/JGS were used in describing enemy plans and activity. Intelligence information reports of DAO, Saigon and offices of the U.S. Embassy, Saigon, were also consulted.

Much of the information concerning Quang Duc came from the author's own notes and recollections of his visit there immediately after the ARVN recaptured Kien Duc.

General Niem was again very helpful in providing information and comments concerning combat actions in Military Region 2. Similarly, Generals Truong and Hinh, commanders respectively of I Corps and the 3d ARVN Division, assisted greatly in assuring accuracy in the description of activity in Military Region 1.

7

Cease-Fire II in MR 3 and 4

The Delta Rice War

While post-cease-fire fighting in the northern and central provinces of South Vietnam alternately surged and subsided as opposing sides grappled for key terrain, the war in the Mekong Delta became a contest for the rice harvest. Nearly 90 percent of Communist rice requirements, to be filled from South Vietnam sources, were requisitioned in the delta.

For the South Vietnamese, the rice war meant that enemy lines of communication had to be interdicted to prevent shipment of rice to delta base areas as well as to collection points in Cambodia where much of it was transshipped to Communist units in South Vietnam's Military Regions 2 and 3. Intelligence efforts were therefore concentrated on rice requisitioning, transport, and storage. The J2 of the Joint General Staff had estimated that some 58,000 metric tons of rice had been collected in the delta during the 1972 harvest, and the object was to cut this drastically in 1973. For the Communists, the rice war meant controlling more rice-producing hamlets, protecting the forays of rice-requisitioning parties, securing canals used for the movement of rice boats, and preventing intrusions by the RVNAF into storage areas.

The South Vietnamese were motivated by more than the simple purpose of denying the rice to the enemy; besides the obvious political imperative to reduce—or at least limit—the enemy's influence over the delta's population and resources, South Vietnam needed the delta's rice to feed its own people and armed forces. By September 1973, a shortage of rice was already developing in Saigon. An early season drought had disrupted planting, and shipments of delta rice for the year were 326,500 metric tons, considerably behind that of 1972 (465,500). Furthermore, raging floods had struck the coastal lowlands of the northern provinces of MR 1 and MR 2, destroying much of the rice crop and stores.

The enemy's rice production in areas under his control in South Vietnam was negligible, and only forces north of COSVN's domain were normally provided any rice from North Vietnam. Consequently, heavy demands were placed on Cambodian and delta rice. All sizeable NVA forces in Cambodia were sustained by Cambodian rice, and much of this rice was also delivered to COSVN forces inside South Vietnam. The Cambodian rebel forces were experiencing shortages of their own and by the fall of 1973 were becoming increasingly reluctant to permit the NVA to fill rice requisitions in Cambodia. Competition for rice resulted in armed clashes between the two Communist allies and increased the importance of South Vietnam's delta rice.

Since the defeat of Cambodia's 32d Brigade at Phnom Penh in May 1973, the entire Cambodian–South Vietnamese border region from the Gulf of Thailand to the eastern edge of South Vietnam's Hong Ngu District in Kien Phong Province was controlled by NVA and Khmer Communist forces. The only Cambodian government presence was at Samma Leu, a small navy river station north of the border. The frontier area, in some places as deep as 35 kilometers into Cambodia, contained major NVA supply routes and rear service centers. The two most significant centers were in the O Mountain complex, opposite the Seven Mountains in South Vietnam's Chau Doc Province. One was the rear base of the NVA 1st Division, the NVA 195th Transportation Group, and the 200th Rear Service Group; the other was NVA Base Area 704, which contained part of the NVA 207th Regiment's supply area.

Near O Mountain was the southern terminus of the Ho Chi Minh trail, the beginning of infiltration corridor 1-C serving Communist units throughout the southwestern delta and providing conduits for illegal commerce in rice and other commodities between South Vietnam's border provinces and the NVA's Cambodian base areas. While markets flourished on the Cambodian side of the border for trade with the NVA forces in contraband rice and other commodities, South Vietnam garrisoned its border, established blocks on the canals, rivers, and trails that crossed the frontier, and patrolled the region vigorously with ARVN and navy units. A major campaign was also started in the summer of 1973 to destroy or force the NVA 1st Division out of its redoubt in the Seven Mountains. Earlier post-cease-fire battles around Hong Ngu had severely damaged NVA forces in this region. Now, as the RVNAF began its offensive against the NVA 1st Division and imposed a well-planned, though indifferently executed, rice blockade, the pinch was felt. As if this were not trouble enough for the Cambodian-based NVA, the Khmer Communists decided to force the NVA to leave the border region entirely.

They prohibited sales of Cambodian rice to NVA and VC units, creating a serious rice shortage.

Consequently, COSVN directed that the required rice be requisitioned from South Vietnam's delta and that the blockade be broken. Information concerning this COSVN directive was obtained from ralliers and captured documents. The main methods to be used: (1) district and province cadre were to bag rice in the hamlets and move it to secure caches; (2) armed units were to secure all routes used for the movement of rice; (3) armed units were to enter South Vietnamese controlled areas and seize rice; (4) Cadre were to negotiate deals with South Vietnamese villagers who would transport purchased rice to Communist areas; (5) all units were to begin farming on land under their control with the aim of self-sufficiency; and (6) women and children living in VC-controlled hamlets were to enter South Vietnamese markets, buy small quantities of rice and bring it to VC areas, making as many trips as possible but keeping each purchase small to reduce the risk of suspicion and discovery.

In the border area the enemy achieved the most success with tactics number four and six and relied on the mechanism of the market itself to provide the rest of the rice requirement. For example, a kilogram of rice in South Vietnam brought 80 piastres in June and 180 piastres in September, while on the border, in the VC market at Ca Sach, a kilogram commanded 115 piastres in June and 250 in September. The price differential offered in the markets in Cambodia was worth the risk to some smugglers and consequently drew significant amounts of rice across the border.

According to estimates, at least 600 tons of rice was smuggled out of the delta each month, August through October, from the Tan Chau market across the Mekong and up the small canals that laced the swamp and paddy fields to the border. The scope of this smuggling operation depended on complicity on the part of local regional and popular forces, as well as on the Vietnamese Navy at Tan Chau. Reliable evidence indicated that some high-level officials were involved and profiting from the trade. Other routes were used to transport clandestine rice in the border area, but the Hong Ngu-Ca Sach arrangement was the largest.

Meanwhile, fears began to mount in Saigon that Communist rice-procuring would lead to runaway inflation in rice and other commodities. Orders went out from Saigon directing province chiefs to crack down on illegal trade and to tighten the blockade. Thereupon, the chiefs of Chau Doc, Kien Giang, and Kien Phong established restricted, controlled, and free trade zones in each province. The entire border was designated a restricted zone, meaning that no commodity could cross legally. Parts of the Seven Mountains and the Tram Forest of western Ha Tien in Kien Giang Province were also declared restricted zones. Controlled zones were established, primarily in Hong Ngu District, in which citizens could legally possess only limited quantities of commodities. Except for a five-kilometer radius around the district town itself, all of Hong Ngu was either restricted or controlled. Those parts of Chau Doc and Ha Tien adjacent to the Seven Mountains and the Tram Forest became controlled zones, while other parts were free trade zones in which goods could move without restrictions.

The blockade was barely under way when Military Region 4, responding to the Saigon rice delivery plan, instituted far more stringent controls. The Saigon plan, aimed at preventing a rice shortage in the capital and the Central Highlands, made it illegal in the border provinces to move rice or paddy (unmilled) rice anywhere without specific permission, except for small amounts for family consumption. Any unauthorized movement, whether across the border or not, was grounds for arrest and confiscation.

Elements of all police and military forces were employed in the blockade and collection plan. Navy and marine police were responsible for stopping and searching all craft on major waterways. Combined checkpoints were manned by RF, PF, National Police, military police, and sector intelligence sections at all major land crossing points. Each village organized a mobile inspection team made up of police, PF, and local officials, while RF and PF established check points on the roads and highways. Airmobile operations, using regular ARVN forces, were conducted regularly against known VC market places. To check on the entire operation, General Nghi, the region commander, assigned police from the Military Region 4 Special Branch to report directly to him on any evidence of corruption in local officials and units. Inefficiency and corruption in the execution of the plan nevertheless continued to undermine the blockade. Even so, there is no doubt that the blockade worsened the existing rice shortage among the enemy forces in Cambodia.

Desertions increased in the Communist ranks as men became progressively more despondent and hungry. Ralliers and prisoners of war told of extremely austere diets and of little hope for relief. Although relatively ineffective in Hong Ngu, the RVNAF blockade in the Seven Mountains of Chau Doc was very tight; the province chief gave it the highest priority and his personal attention. It was in large measure responsible for one of the most resounding RVNAF military victories of the post-cease-fire period: the destruction of the NVA 1st Division.

The attack to drive the 1st NVA Division out of the Seven Mountains was launched in early July

1973 by the 44th Special Tactical Zone, where principal forces consisted of the 7th Ranger Group and the 4th Armor Group (armored personnel carriers). The Seven Mountains was a chain of rugged, forested, cave-pocked peaks stretching in a ragged line from the Cambodian border at Tinh Bien 25 kilometers to below Tri Ton, a district headquarters in the shadow of Nui Co To, the southernmost peak in the chain. Although the tallest of the seven was only 700 feet high, rising as they did from a featureless, often flooded plain, they were spectacular prominences and gave the impression of far greater size.

Just north of the border in the Seven Mountains, Nui O was one of the main bases of the NVA 1st Division, which had moved there from battles around Phnom Penh in the summer of 1972. Establishing defenses as far south as Nui Co To, the 1st Division was primarily responsible for screening and protecting movement along infiltration corridor 1-C, which passed to the west of the mountains. Secondary objectives included protecting rice collection teams, proselyting, and harassing South Vietnamese communities and military installations throughout the region.

As the 44th's offensive began, intelligence revealed that the NVA 1st Division Headquarters had pulled out of the Nui O base and was established in the Cambodian town of Kampong Trach, north of Ha Tien.

The NVA 52d Regiment was operating in Cambodia north of Ha Tien, while the 101D Regiment and most of the 44th Sapper Regiment were in the border region south of Nui O. The attacks by fire conducted by the 101D Regiment in Tinh Bien and Tri Ton increased in late July, and the 44th Special Tactical Zone reacted, not only to reduce the threat to the districts, but also to break the screen protecting infiltration corridor 1-C. In late August, a number of sharp contacts between elements of the 101D and ARVN Rangers resulted. Units from the NVA 1st Division infiltrated into positions in Nui Giai and Nui Co To mountains during September, and a concerted drive was started by the 44th Special Tactical Zone to dig them out. The 101D Regiment received 300 fresh replacements from North Vietnam in August and moved into position on Nui Dai in September. As the Rangers, with up to 10 battalions operating, and territorials maneuvered into the mountain strongholds, casualties mounted and the rocketing and mortaring of populated areas by the NVA continued.

Just as a stalemate seemed to have been reached, casualties and the RVNAF blockade began to weaken the 101D and the other 1st Division units and the enemy began to break. NVA hospital records recovered by RVNAF near Nui Dai disclosed that units of the 1st NVA Division had lost nearly 900 soldiers to sickness and wounds from the cease-fire to 20 September. Captured on 2 October, two prisoners of war from the 101D revealed that the NVA 1st Division had been deactivated. Soldiers from the 44th Sapper and 52d Infantry Regiment were transferred to the 101D, which had only 300 men left. The 101D then became a brigade, assumed control of the artillery and support units of the 1st Division, and began operating directly under NVA Military Region 3.

By the end of October, with its battalions down to less than 200 men each, the 101D withdrew from the Seven Mountains into its Cambodian sanctuary. Although it continued to operate in the border region, it never again presented a serious threat to South Vietnamese forces in Military Region 4. The RVNAF 44th Special Tactical Zone and its 7th Ranger Group had accomplished its mission.

Tri Phap

There was more to the rice war than the illegal trade and skirmishes along the border. And there was more to infiltration in the delta than that which took place in Kien Giang Province along corridor 1-C. Dinh Tuong Province, with its bustling market capital of My Tho, was the key province in the eastern delta. Through My Tho passed Highway 4 to Saigon, a major channel of the the Mekong, and several large canals. One of three principal NVA infiltration routes, corridor 1-A crossed the Cambodian frontier near the border between Kien Phong and Kien Tuong Provinces, traversed the maze of canals through the Plain of Reeds, and ended in the watery wasteland called the Tri Phap (listed as Base Area 470 by allied intelligence) where those provinces join Dinh Tuong. A branch of corridor 1-B from the "Parrot's Beak" of Svay Rieng Province entered the Tri Phap from the northeast. An insurgent base established during the 1945–1954 war, the Tri Phap was partly covered with brush, with little land suitable for cultivation, essentially a swamp that over the years had been laced with permanent fortifications and hidden storage areas. No allied force had succeeded in occupying or inflicting any serious damage to the installations or enemy forces in the Tri Phap. Immediately after the cease-fire, RVNAF units in Dinh Tuong were preoccupied with maintaining security in the central and northern reaches of the province and could not divert the forces necessary to clean out the Tri Phap, even though they were aware of increased enemy activity there.

A document captured on 9 August disclosed that the Z-18 Regiment of NVA Military Region 2 was moving into the Tri Phap from Cai Bay District in northern Dinh Tuong Province and that it would probably be replaced in Cai Bay by the Dong Thap-

1 Regiment. Information in the document pertaining to planned attacks in northern Dinh Tuong was confirmed by attacks on several outposts on 8 August. Furthermore, aerial photography showed that fields north of the Tri Phap had been planted in rice, part of the NVA's effort to become self-sustaining in the delta. With pressure mounting along Highway 4, however, IV Corps could not then challenge the NVA activities in and north of the Tri Phap. Nevertheless, the RVNAF repulsed, with heavy losses to the enemy, numerous battalion-sized attacks against outposts and fire bases in Cay Bay, Cai Be, and Sam Giang Districts during July and August. In the first week of September alone, enemy casualties in the region were 144 killed, while those of the RVNAF were 17 killed and 78 wounded.

The surge in enemy attacks, which continued through November, was motivated in part, as in the border provinces, by the harvest and marked by Communist attempts to gather as much of it as possible. But beyond that, the enemy objectives were to protect the installations in the Tri Phap, expand the base area there, and use the infiltration corridors from Cambodia without interference from the RVNAF. Success in these ventures would force contractions of the RVNAF defenses along Highway 4, demoralize the soldiers of the ARVN 7th Division charged with the resposibility, and support the proselyting campaign among South Vietnamese troops.

As the year wore on, RVNAF units slowly wore down the four main force regiments in NVA Military Region 2—the Z-18th, Z-15th, E-24th, and DT-1. Despite receiving hundreds of fresh replacements from the north, these regiments gradually lost ground to aggressive attacks. The NVA 207th Regiment, which had suffered so badly in its disastrous Hong Ngu campaign, was required to provide soldiers to replace losses in the E-24th Regiment. These demoralized soldiers were intercepted en route to the Tri Phap area in September; their casualties were heavy and 14 were captured. The NVA 6th Division was disbanded that fall, and its depleted regiments were assigned to NVA Military Region 2. The RVNAF Joint Operations Center provided data on casualties in December that showed nearly 40 percent of all enemy killed during the last half of 1973 died in the delta. Although the figures were estimations the ratio was probably very close to reality, supported as it was by weapons captured and corresponding RVNAF casualties.

The year ended in a flurry of Communist activity throughout the delta. Incidents of ground attacks and attacks by fire reached the highest level since the cease-fire. Losses were heavy on both sides, but no significant changes in the tactical situation were apparent. Nevertheless, a steady erosion of security was under way and most evident in Chuong Thien and northern An Xuyen Provinces, where the 21st ARVN Division was only marginally effective against persistent enemy operations to expand control. Four NVA regiments operated in Chuong Thien—the 95A, 18B, D-1 and D-2—and they were adequately supported with weapons, ammunition, and replacements through the Kien Giang corridor, despite the frequent successful RVNAF operations near the Cambodian border against this logistical route.

As the first anniversary of the cease-fire approached, no early decision was foreseeable in the delta. Although harassed by increasingly threatening RVNAF offensives, the NVA still maintained control over major infiltration corridors into the delta and managed to gather enough rice to sustain its forces, though some troops were on short rations. Communist strategy had undergone no great modifications; it still focused on acquiring rice, proselyting, and eroding South Vietnam's territorial and population control. Despite severe personnel losses and a few minor military defeats, the NVA was gaining in the delta.

RVNAF Delta Dispositions

The three ARVN divisions in the delta were reacting differently to the deteriorating situation in Military Region 4. True to their records of past performance and in concert with the nature of the leadership they received, they ranged from highly effective to consistently poor. On the high side was the 7th Division, operating principally in Dinh Tuong. Commanded by spartan and austere Maj. Gen. Nguyen Khoa Nam, who was later to command IV Corps and still later to take his own life after the capitulation, the 7th had become particularly skillful in rapid deployment, netting significant catches along the infiltration corridors. As the year drew to a close however, severe rationing of fuel, imposed to compensate for spiraling costs, drastically limited the division's mobility. The permanent withdrawal of RF and PF from exposed positions balanced this disadvantage somewhat, in that General Nam less frequently had to dispatch troops in what were often futile but costly attempts to rescue beseiged outposts; he could select areas of deployment more likely to result in combat with major units or large infiltrating groups. Employing advantages of surprise, superior mobility, and firepower, including effective coordination with the VNAF, the 7th was usually the clear winner in that kind of encounter. Going to the relief of outposts too often drew the relief force into an ambush in which all advantages lay with the enemy.

Major changes in the 9th Division took place toward the end of the year. Its commander, Maj.

Gen. Tran Ba Di, was replaced by Brig. Gen. Huynh Van Lac. Of more immediate impact was the reorganization which drew all Rangers out of IV Corps and eliminated the 44th Special Tactical Zone. This change required the 9th to assume responsibility for Chau Doc and northern Kien Giang Provinces, as well as Kien Phong. It turned over its two southern provinces of Vinh Long and Vinh Binh to the 7th Division, recovered its 14th Regiment, which had been under the operational control of the 7th, and released its 15th Regiment to the operational control of the ARVN 21st Division in Chuong Thien Province. Thus, with two infantry regiments, General Lac replaced the equivalent of three Ranger regiments in the northern districts of the border provinces. It was feasible only because the enemy main force in the area had been so severely damaged in the Hong Ngu and Chau Doc battles.

In June 1973 the 21st ARVN Division, which deservedly had the worst reputation for discipline and effectiveness among the divisions in the delta, was given a new commander, Brig. Gen. Le Van Hung, who had done well at An Loc. Although General Hung (who was also to die a suicide) had nowhere to bring the division but up, progress was slow. He gradually replaced ineffective subordinates with combat-proven officers, many from airborne and Ranger units, and observers noted some slight improvements in morale and combat effectiveness. General Hung employed the 15th Regiment, under his operational control from the 9th Division, exclusively in Long My District of Chuong Thien, while his three organic regiments, the 31st, 32d, and 33d, operated throughout the rest of Chuong Thien and northern An Xuyen. The 32d and 33d had few contacts with the enemy, other than receiving attacks by fire; but in late December, the 3d Battalion, 31st Infantry, was ambushed while marching to the relief of an RF outpost, and more than 100 of its men were killed. This event illustrated again long-standing defects in leadership and training in this regiment and supported the DAO's year-end assessment that the division was no more than "marginally combat effective."

Because the territorials were raised and stationed in their home provinces and districts, their numerical strength in each military region was largely a function of the local population. With a population of over seven million, Military Region 4 was authorized nearly three times as many territorials as Military Region 1, and twice as many as were authorized Military Regions 2 and 3.

The regional force soldiers in Military Region 4 were assigned to 144 battalions and 125 separate companies and were employed by 18 Sector Tactical Commands. But nearly all units were seriously understrength due to a combination of factors: combat losses, desertions, ineffective recruiting, and the "flower soldier" practice whereby a soldier was carried on the rolls but for a fee paid to the unit commander he was never required to be present for duty. Overall, RF strength in the delta was less than 80 percent of authorized, and NCO strength was even lower. While most of the battalions carried assigned strengths of 350 to 400 men, out of an authorized 561, some, such as those in Ba Xuyen and Chuong Thien Provinces, were down to 300. With such a reduced assigned strength, as few as 150 soldiers would be present for operations in a typical Chuong Thien battalion, a battalion smaller than a company. Quite understandably, as unit strengths declined, so did combat ability and morale, while desertions increased. Remarkably, the territorials in a few sectors, notably Kien Tuong and Go Cong, maintained high assigned strengths, a reflection of inspired leadership. But overall desertions exceeded recruitments, and strengths continued their slow but steady erosion.

Declining strengths influenced another debilitating situation. A well-intentioned unit training program for territorials had been devised by Central Training Command and ordered executed by the JGS, but the demands of combat on the depleted units made it progressively more difficult for the more embattled of the sector commanders to release RF and PF units for training. Combat efficiency in the most active sectors thus declined still further.

In early 1974, General Vien, Chief of the Joint General Staff, ordered the JGS to investigate, study, and report on the territorials of MR 4. The study revealed some interesting facts. During the first three months of 1974, for example, MR 4 territorials lost 8,852 men killed, wounded, or missing during mobile operations away from fixed bases. In these engagements, they accounted for 5,344 enemy killed or captured, a ratio of about 1.6 to every enemy casualty, excluding the uncounted enemy wounded. The relative weapons losses in these operations was also instructive. While the RF and PF lost about 1,600 weapons, they salvaged about 1,800 of the enemy's. But the most revealing and alarming discovery concerned the comparative losses during enemy attacks on territorial outposts. In the same three-month period, RF and PF casualties, including missing, were nearly 1,300, while enemy losses were only 245, a ratio of 5 to 1. Weapons losses in defensive engagements were even worse—1000 lost against 100 recovered. The obvious conclusion was that mobile operations by territorials were immensely more profitable than defense of fixed outposts. But the JGS team also found that only 2,192 out of 22,884 offensive operations involving units of company size and larger resulted in combat with the enemy, a poor record attributed to weaknesses in intelligence, operational planning, and techniques. While this judgment was at least partially valid, benefits were derived even from mobile operations that netted no enemy. The confidence of the population in their local forces was strengthened, and the enemy was often compelled to move or discontinue his activities while the territorials maneuvered through the area.

There were 3,400 outposts, watch towers, and bases to be defended in MR 4. These ranged from large complex positions with supporting artillery to remote mud forts garrisoned by weak, under-strength PF platoons. The futility of attempting to defend the vast delta from isolated posts scattered about the paddies, canals, and swamps had been recognized by General Nghi as well as the JGS, but despite the strong desire to reduce the number of posts, to do so would remove all government presence from many contested villages and hamlets, surrendering the population to the Communists. In 1973, nevertheless, MR 4 withdrew forces from 97 outposts while 193 were lost to enemy attacks. Meanwhile, emphasis on mobile operations was increased. Operating in their home provinces, some RF battalions earned hard-fought reputations for aggressiveness and success. Unfortunately, a battalion's achievement in its native sector often impelled the corps commander to deploy it to another province under the operational control of an ARVN division. As often as not, the division would employ the battalion in a particularly hazardous role and give it inadequate logistical and administrative support. Fresh morale problems would develop and, tragically, superior RF battalions were reduced to the level of the majority.

The Vietnamese Navy in the delta was charged with providing security on the major waterways, patrolling the coastline to prevent enemy supply boats from entering, and supporting ARVN and territorial force operations. Although the Navy could boast of low desertion rates, a generally well-maintained fleet of small craft, and higher morale than in the rest of the armed forces, its performance in the delta was far below what it should have been. In good measure, the reason for its ineffectiveness lay in an aversion to coordinating operations with the other services. Although General Nghi, as region commander, had all the authority he needed to direct coordinated operations involving all forces in the delta, by the time this authority filtered down through the structure it had lost its force. ARVN sector and sub-sector commanders, as well as commanders of tactical units, exercised no authority over naval units and naval commanders consequently remained independent and aloof, often unwilling even to attend sector planning and briefing sessions.

There were, happily, some exceptions to this rule. A case in point was the Navy's role in special operations to interdict the NVA's infiltration route through Kien Giang into Chuong Thien (Infiltration Corridor 1-C). The "brown-water" navy—that is, the shallow draft boats plying the rivers and canals—was especially successful intercepting enemy attempts to cross the Cai Lon River and its tributaries. But while combined operations enjoyed some success interfering with enemy movement along interior routes, the "blue-water" navy failed to intercept the enemy's supply craft sailing down the coast from Cambodia. The blue-water boats were too deep of draft to follow suspicious sampans into the shallow inshore waters, and the brown-water responsibilities ended where the waterways emptied into the Gulf of Thailand.

The blue-water navy in the delta operated from two major bases. The 4th Coastal Flotilla, with 26 patrol craft, was based at An Thoi on Phu Quoc Island and was responsible for coastal waters down to the border of An Xuyen Province. There the 5th Coastal Flotilla assumed responsibility which extended around the Ca Mau and northeast along the coast to the MR 3 boundary. The 5th operated 27 patrol craft from Nam Can, a former $50 million U.S. Navy base with excellent dry dock facilities. The brown-water fleet, with 362 boats, operated from 17 locations throughout the delta.

RVNAF Economics and Morale

A melancholy accompaniment to the slow but steady erosion of government influence in the delta was being heard, not only in the delta, but throughout South Vietnam. The outward appearances of a bustling, growing economy, as seen in the prosperous looking shops and restaurants of Saigon and in the dense, noisy traffic that choked its boulevards, scarcely disguised a stagnant commercial and industrial situation but still misled the casual observer. The truth was that galloping inflation had taken hold, and those that suffered most were those to whom the country owed the most, those upon whose strength and constancy survival depended: the soldiers, airmen, sailors, and officers of the RVNAF. The consumer price index rose 65 percent during 1973, but more devastating to the serviceman and low paid public official, whose incomes were fixed at a bare subsistence level, was the fact that rice doubled in price during the year. An unfortunate combination of international and domestic events was responsible for South Vietnam's worst year economically since 1965-66. In 1972 the NVA offensive and poor weather had reduced the expected rice crop, and that disappointing harvest was followed by an even less productive one in 1973. The deficit had to be compensated for by imports at a time when rice on the world market was soaring. This fact, in combination with the domestic shortage, drove the price to the consumer even higher.

South Vietnam's tough rice control program was doubtless of some benefit, but it could not thoroughly dampen market-driven trends.

Meanwhile, the U.S. aid dollar, as well as other forms of foreign assistance to Vietnam, was declining in value under the influence of worldwide inflation. Imported commodities therefore entered the country at drastically inflated costs. Cooking oil, laundry soap, and brown sugar, for example, were all selling at 200 percent above 1972 prices; driven by the international petroleum crisis of 1973, gasoline rose by 213 percent and kerosene by 196 percent. And while import prices climbed, South Vietnam's opportunities to earn foreign exchange declined with the departure of the U.S. forces. The U.S. withdrawal also aggravated high levels of unemployment. In 1969, about 160,000 Vietnamese were direct employees of the United States; by September 1973, the number had dropped to less than 20,000. This decline was matched by the disappearance of jobs whose functions indirectly depended on the U.S. payroll in Vietnam.

The severe unemployment greatly affected the families of soldiers because a soldier's family could only survive if it had a source of income other than military pay. Disquieting evidence that the depressed economy and inflated market were having deleterious effects on RVNAF morale and effectiveness began to appear in mid-1973. Reports of particularly heinous instances of venality surfaced, sometimes in official channels, but more frequently in private conversations between DAO people and RVNAF officers whose sensibilities were offended by the corrupt practices of their countrymen, even though they understood the conditions that impelled men to seek dishonorable means to supplement their livelihood. And even when corruption was not mentioned, the serious economic plight of officers and soldiers was cited as contributing to defeats and portending future disaster. Here are some examples:

On 15 December the Communists attacked a position in the Song Bo corridor west of Hue defended by a company of the 1st ARVN Division. According to the new 3d Infantry commander, Col. Hoang Mao, the company incurred only light casualties before breaking and running in panic. Similar performances occurred in other regimental positions, and Colonel Mao attributed this conduct to poorly trained draftees with low morale. The regiment had borne the weight of the NVA's attacks that autumn, and its extended period in the line had aggravated its declining morale, but the root cause of the problem was widespread disaffection in the ranks traceable to the growing deprivations suffered by military families.

The Airborne Division was the elite of the ARVN. It could still boast an all-volunteer force and the high esprit that went with special and rigorous training. But even it was not immune to South Vietnam's economic malady. In a despairing interview with a trusted American friend, a young paratrooper captain, battle tested in Cambodia, An Loc, and Quang Tri, told of demoralization in the airborne as largely the result of worsening economic conditions. Another reason for low morale was the continued commitment of the division—trained and psychologically equipped for difficult offensive operations—in a static defensive role in northern MR 1. Add to this the fact that the division bases were at Tan Son Nhut and Bien Hoa and the soldier's families lived on or near them. In any event, this dedicated 29-year-old veteran deplored the decline of discipline in the division, which he said could be traced to the absence of the airborne spirit in leaders who had recently joined the division, a spirit hard to kindle in the bunkers and trenches of Thua Thien Province.

More importantly, he cited the desperate economic conditions among the troopers' families, which the officers and noncommissioned officers were powerless to relieve. As a direct consequence, the empathetic leader was loath to punish severely any soldier whose derelictions were traceable to despair or concern for his suffering family. Absences, even some desertions, went unpunished, and alcoholism and drug addiction increased, as did incidents of "fragging." (Slang for the practice of murdering or attempting to murder officers or noncommissioned officers; derived from fragmentation grenade, the usual weapon of choice.)

The division commander, Brig. Gen. Le Quang Luong, was acutely aware of the problems; his personal leadership and concern for his men no doubt prevented collapse. In fact, the division fought some of its most effective and gallant engagements in the months following.

Illegal trading in fuel used by the South Vietnamese Navy was a favorite means of income augmentation in the delta. An incident in September in southern An Xuyen Province is illustrative. In September near Vam Song Ong Doc, a small fishing port at the mouth of the Ong Doc River, a Navy boat was reportedly sunk by gunfire and three sailors were wounded, apparently in an ambush set by the VC. But the facts were quite different. It seems that Navy vessels regularly sailed up the coast and called at Vam Song Ong Doc to sell diesel fuel, a commodity in great demand by the fishing fleet as well as the Communists, who used it in their boats. The the 412th RF Battalion had been watching this for some time and finally demanded 1,000 piastres (about $2) per 55-gallon drum sold. After the crew refused, reportedly explaining that all the proceeds had to be sent to the Chief of Naval Operations in Saigon, the RF attacked. Some accommodation was apparently arrived at because before long the boats were again engaged in the diesel trade, though the market had been moved upriver. Preoccupation with this illegal operation distracted the Navy from its important mission of intercepting Communist boats that were infiltrating the coast with impunity from the Ong Doc River to An Xuyen's northern border.

There were a few documented cases wherein RVNAF officers and soldiers sold weapons, ammunition, and other military equipment and supplies for cash, knowing full well that they were trading with the enemy. But the most despicable of all cases of venality—and reports of these were widespread and persistent enough to deserve credence—were the demands of VNAF helicopter crews for payment from ground troops for the evacuation of casualties. This is not to say that this practice was the rule, but that it happened at all was a vivid commentary on a pernicious flaw and the conditions which spawned it.

A typical colonel in the RVNAF was paid less than 40,000 piastres per month, the equivalent of about $80.00, this after about 20 years of service, virtually all of it in wartime. Of course he received a few other emoluments, but basically he was supporting a family group of perhaps 10 people on $80 per month. At prices prevalent in the winter of 1973, half of his earnings went for rice. This meant, among other things, that every able person in the family had to bring in some income. Practices ranging from simple nepotism through the entire gamut of activity that well-fed, comfortably-housed Americans might call malfeasance understandably became part of the system. The wonder is that so many honest, devoted officers and public servants managed, through strength of character and with the help of friends and families, not only to survive but also to take care of their less fortunate subordinates.

Ranger Reorganization

In September 1973, a JGS evaluation of the structure and employment of Ranger forces culminated in a recommendation from General Vien to President Thieu. Approved by the President, it was developed by 31 December into a plan of reorganization. Essentially the plan's major purpose was to reconstitute a small strategic reserve for employment by the JGS and small reaction forces for the first three military regions. The planners accepted the unpleasant fact that the two general reserve divisions—the Airborne and Marine—were probably permanently committed in Military Region 1; a Ranger reorganization would result in a slight surplus of uncommitted battalions and help restore some flexibility to the RVNAF as a whole. The planners also took into account the deterioration of South Vietnamese control in the western and Central Highlands but with unwarranted optimism calculated that Rangers would eventually be redeployed to frontier posts in lost or contested sectors. In any event, the fact that Ranger battalions were programmed for deployment on the borders in the indefinite future provided uncommitted battalions for the present for reserve or other missions.

The planners also recognized the unique situation along the Cambodian border in Military Region 4. The Rangers of 44th Special Tactical Zone around the Seven Mountains and the ARVN regulars and territorials in other reaches of the frontier had all but eliminated the enemy main-force threat and were dealing with some success with infiltration. Thus the decision was made to eliminate the 44th Special Tactical Zone and deactivate its nine Ranger battalions, with officers and men reassigned to battalions in the northern part of the country. This made tactical sense, but unfortunately, the delta Ranger battalions had been recruited in the delta, and the soldiers showed their displeasure at being reassigned from their home provinces by deserting in great numbers. By 1 January 1974, the original 54 Ranger battalions had been reorganized into 45, and each belonged to one of 15 Ranger groups (regiments). Rather than having three different types of battalions—organic to regiments, border defense, and separate—all were to follow one table of organization and equipment.

The new concept of operations for Rangers visualized that 27 forward defense bases, mostly along the Laotian and Cambodian borders in Military Regions 1, 2, and 3, would be occupied by a minimum of one Ranger battalion each. At this time, however, only six of these border posts were occupied by Rangers; the others were inaccessible because of enemy operations or were in enemy hands. Each military region was to keep one Ranger group in reserve, dedicated to the reinforcement or rescue of any threatened or besieged Ranger base. A 30-man Ranger headquarters was established in each of the three military regions where Ranger battalions were assigned to oversee training and administrative matters. Its commander was the corps commander's adviser on Ranger employment. At year's end, Ranger deployment and strength was as shown in Table 5.

Military Region 3

RVNAF efforts to open lines of communication to beleaguered bases, interdict NVA logistical routes, and damage enemy base areas and the NVA's response to these actions raised the level of combat in Military Region 3 after Cease-fire II. There were a number of sharp contacts, particularly in Tay Ninh and Binh Duong Provinces, but no

TABLE 5: ARVN RANGER DEPLOYMENT, 31 DEC. 1973

Groups	Strength, 1 Feb. 1974		
MR 1*	1st Bn	2d Bn	3d Bn
11th	384	409	385
12th	382	415	398
14th	489	442	480
15th	530	530	502
MR 2#			
4th	421	457	454
6th	582	575	598
21st	258	377	365
22d	406	412	463
23d	388	372	424
24th	584	371	372
25th	357	327	351
MR 3			
31st	590	572	595
32d	642	662	603
33d	508	710	470
(Reserve)			
7th**	422	452	472

*All MR 1 battalions understrength because of desertions of Rangers transferred from MR 4.

#The 4th and 6th Groups were assigned to the general reserve in the Saigon area but were deployed along Highway 1 in Binh Dinh, under the operational control of MR 2. The MR 2 Groups were understrength because of recruiting difficulties in the highlands where all were deployed.

**The 7th Group was located at the Long Binh Base near Saigon.

Map 11

terrain changed hands. The VNAF carried out heavy raids against NVA bases in Tay Ninh, Binh Long, and Phuoc Long Provinces, and the NVA retaliated with a rocket attack on Bien Hoa on 6 November that destroyed three F-5A fighters and with a sapper raid on the Shell petroleum storage site at Nha Be on 2 December that virtually wiped it out. The Communists also sent water-sapper teams into South Vietnamese Navy docks near Saigon and sank six small craft. Just a few miles southwest of Saigon, on 15 December, they ambushed an unarmed U.S. Joint Casualty Resolution Center Team and killed a U.S. Army captain, the first American serviceman to die by Communist fire after the cease-fire. This incident effectively ended all efforts by U.S. casualty resolution teams to enter areas not considered absolutely immune from enemy intrusion.

Behind the screen of harassing and sometimes destructive attacks, and beyond the range of effective RVNAF interference, Communist forces in Military Region 3 built warehouses, workshops, roads, and antiaircraft positions, receiving new weapons, combat vehicles, and replacements while assembling a logistical and training base that spread across the northern border of MR 3 from Bu Dop in Phuoc Long to Lo Go in Tay Ninh. The Communists were also concentrating freshly arrived battalions of tanks, artillery, and antiaircraft weapons, together with infantry replacements for the divisions that were protecting the buildup. By September they had completed the deployment of the 367th Sapper Group from Phnom Penh to Tay Ninh for further employment in the Saigon area.

The NVA strategy in Tay Ninh called for continuing pressure along lines of contact, preventing the RVNAF from probing too deeply into the base area, and undermining the fragile hold the RVNAF maintained on the vital corridor between Tay Ninh City and Saigon. This pressure was exerted from three directions and spilled over prominently into Hau Nghia Province through which the corridor passed into the northwestern suburbs of Saigon. From the Cambodian salient of Svay Rieng Province, called the Parrot's Beak, NVA forces probed RVNAF outposts along the Vam Co Dong River. The river port of Go Dau Ha was kept under constant threat. Since the port was the junction of National Routes 1 and 22, only 10 kilometers from the Cambodian frontier, its loss would sever Tay Ninh and isolate sizable South Vietnamese forces there. (Map 11)

The NVA prevented any RVNAF forays toward its northern Tay Ninh base along local Route 4 (TL-4); this road led into the NVA's growing headquarters, logistical, and political complex around Lo Go, Thien Ngon, Xa Mat, and Katum. Moving within range of the ARVN's 25th Division forward base at the Tay Ninh airfield, the ARVN outpost and communications relay station on Nui Ba Den mountain, and the RF base at Soui Da, the NVA regularly harassed these positions with artillery, mortar, and rocket fire and made resupply of Nui Ba Den hazardous by frequently directing antiaircraft fire and SA-7 rockets at VNAF helicopters.

The NVA exerted strong pressure against the Tay Ninh-Saigon corridor from its forward combat bases along the Saigon River from the Michelin Plantation to the Ho Bo Woods. The Ho Bo area was flat, almost featureless terrain, laced with trenches and tunnels, deeply pocked with ragged lines of bomb craters left by numberless waves of B-52s, its shattered plantations overgrown with head-high weeds and dense brush. Nearly 10 years of battle litter defaced the countryside, and a tangle of tank-tread marks gave it the appearance of an abandoned armored training ground. Hidden beneath were the bunkers and fighting positions of several NVA main force units, the principal occupant being the 101st Infantry Regiment.

The 101st had entered Nam Bo, the southern battlefield, in 1966 from North Vietnam and had been a more or less constant resident of the Tay Ninh-Hau Nghia-Binh Duong region since its first punishing engagements with the U.S. 1st Infantry Division that year. In the summer and fall of 1973, it was backing up local battalions harassing ARVN territorials and elements of the 25th Infantry Division generally north of Highways 1 and 22.

Principal targets for NVA artillery and mortar attacks were Khiem Hanh, a forward base protecting the northern approach to Go Dau Ha; Trang Bang, a principal town and defensive position astride Highway 1 midway between Tay Ninh City and Saigon; Cu Chi, the main base of the ARVN 25th Infantry Division; and the defensive position at Trung Lap north of Highway 1. Although a night rarely passed without some kind of attack against these or smaller posts, major contacts were infrequent. But in one major engagement in late September, the 2d Battalion, 49th Infantry, 25th Division, was caught in a devastating ambush in a rubber plantation between Highway 22 and Khiem Hahn. More than half the battalion were casualties, including 43 killed, and the battalion lost nearly 150 weapons and 18 field radios. Shortly afterward some command changes were made in the 25th, including the division commander and commanders of the 46th and 49th Regiments. The road to recovery was long and slowly travelled for the 49th Infantry, but on the other hand, the 50th Infantry of the 25th Division, during the last half of 1973, enjoyed more successes than failures in sweep operations around Phu Hoa, and in southeastern Binh Duong and Hau Nghia Provinces.

In the only other major contact in the Tay Ninh-Saigon corridor up to the cease-fire anniversary, a Hau Nghia Regional Force battalion met a battalion of the NVA 101st Regiment, reinforced by a local company, northeast of Trang Bang. When the smoke cleared, the Hau Nghia battalion, among the best RF units in MR 3, collected 32 enemy weapons on the battlefield and buried 56 NVA soldiers. RF casualties were 19 killed and 33 wounded.

In the last half of 1973 in southern Binh Long and western Binh Duong Provinces, very little combat took place. The NVA continued its buildup in the Minh Thanh Plantation and the Lai Khe-Ben Cat area, shifted its artillery southward into the Long Nyugen area from where it increased the weight and frequency of attacks against the ARVN bases. But the only ground engagement of note took place in early January just west of Chon Thanh when the 2d Battalion, 8th Infantry, ARVN 5th Infantry Division, was struck hard by the 7th Battalion, 209th Infantry, NVA 7th Division. Charged with blocking Highway 13 and preventing any ARVN advance toward Minh Thanh, the 7th Battalion killed 36 ARVN soldiers in this engagement, wounded 26 others, and captured 85 weapons.

The most significant action during this period in MR 3 took place along Highway 1A between Song Be and Saigon. Continuing to isolate the Phuoc Long capital of Phuoc Binh, NVA troops used artillery, mortars, rockets, and ground attacks against all RVNAF posts and positions along the 75-kilometer stretch of road between Phu Giao and Song Be. They bombarded the airfield at Song Be and attacked the Don Luan post, but the heaviest action took place south of the Phu Giao base as the NVA 7th Division attempted to block the highway and blow the bridge over the Song Be river. The NVA intention was not only to deny ARVN the use of the road and isolate the garrisons north of the bridge, but also to screen the movement of artillery and supplies south from Bu Dop in northern Phuoc Long to forward combat bases in the dense forests north of Bien Hoa and Xuan Loc. In fact, the NVA itself was using sections of Highway 1A between Bu Dop and Phu Giao for the movement of artillery.

The ARVN 5th Division was roughly handled by the NVA 7th Division between Lai Khe and Phu Giao, and one result of the 5th's consistent failures was the relief of its commander and his replacement in November by Col. Le Nguyen Vy. (Colonel Vy was later to take his own life upon the surrender of his division to the NVA on 30 April 1975.) The 18th ARVN Division fared much better under the leadership of an aggressive commander, Brig. Gen. Le Minh Dao (who was to surrender to the Communists after a gallant defense of Xuan Loc in April 1975), and Highway 1A was kept open as far as Phuoc Vinh. The 18th also saw action around Xuan Loc and in its southern sector of Phuoc Tuy, but nothing decisive was accomplished by either side.

The NVA seige of Tong Le Chon continued through the year, and the 92d Ranger Battalion's defense was rapidly becoming legendary. But the cost was high. After a brief respite following Ceasefire II, the shelling resumed, moderately enough at first, but reached crescendo proportions later in the year as the NVA added 120-mm. and 160-mm. mortars and 122-mm. and 130-mm. howitzers and guns to the batteries ranging on the camp. Antiaircraft artillery, including 37-mm. and 57-mm. guns from the newly formed 377th Antiaircraft Artillery Division at Loc Ninh continued to make supply difficult and evacuation next to impossible.

The NVA 200th Battalion, which had been used in local security missions in the Tay Ninh logistical area, was assigned to the infantry element of the NVA siege force. One of its platoon leaders rallied to the South Vietnamese side in September with some interesting comments on the conduct of the operation. He said that in June the NVA organized a company to collect parachuted supplies that fell outside the Tong Le Chon perimeter, which between April and June amounted to about 80 percent of all supplies dropped. After June, according to this rallier, VNAF techniques had improved to the point where only 10 percent of the drops were recoverable by the company. He asserted that an understanding had been reached between the ARVN Rangers and the NVA whereby the C-130s dropping supplies would not be fired upon so long as the company would not be opposed as it collected the supplies outside the perimeter. This assertation cannot be corroborated, but it fits the general character of the situation at Tong Le Chon.

If there was a tacit withholding of fire against the C-130s at Tong Le Chon, it certainly did not apply to helicopters. Many attempts were made to fly helicopters into Tong Le Chon to evacuate casualties and land replacements. Between late October and the end of January, 1974, 20 helicopters attempted landings; but only 6 managed to land and 3 of these were destroyed by fire upon landing. In the last week of December 1973, a CH-47 Chinook helicopter was destroyed as it landed, the 13th helicopter hit by enemy fire on a Tong Le Chon mission during December alone. Casualties were 9 killed and 36 wounded. Another crashed and burned in January, and as the anniversary of the cease-fire came and went, 12 seriously wounded soldiers of the 92d Ranger Battalion remained in the beleaguered camp.

South Vietnam's leadership was concerned and frustrated over the NVA buildup north of Saigon. Largely beyond reach of ARVN artillery and protected by large and mobile NVA infantry formations, the NVA was openly constructing a modern, mechanized, heavily fortified logistics and communications center. In late October President Thieu decided to attack this enemy complex with air strikes. The concentrated attacks did not begin until 7 November, and South Vietnam made known that they were in response to the NVA's 6 November rocketing of Bien Hoa Air Base, an indication it still felt obliged to rationalize offensive operations in terms of retaliation for NVA cease-fire violations.

Not a part of the concentrated program, a single attack was made in late October against Xa Mat in Tay Ninh Province, a small hamlet on the border with Cambodia which had been named as a "point of entry" in Article 4 of the "Protocol to the Agreement Concerning the International Commission of Control and Supervision," but at which no ICCS team had been posted for the simple reason that the Communists did not want their activities at Xa Mat observed. The only report DAO received concerning the air attack was through an agent who passed through Xa Mat. According to his account, the market, a fuel dump, and about 60 structures were destroyed.

Another separate attack was made on 6 November, the day the NVA rockets destroyed three F-5As at Bien Hoa, when the VNAF made 33 fighter-bomber sorties against NVA concentrations around the ARVN base at Don Luan. Military Region 3 claimed the destruction of numerous fighting positions, about 100 enemy soldiers killed, and four secondary explosions.

From 7 November to 5 December, spotty records revealed about 800 sorties of fighter-bombers, including A-1s, F-5s and A-37s were flown. It began with attacks against Bo Duc and Loc Ninh areas. Although the results of the Bo Duc strike were not reported, Military Region 3 claimed good results against Loc Ninh storage facilities, including fuel, and antiaircraft positions. A contrary version was given by Brig. Gen. Le Trung Truc, a VNAF officer on detached duty in the office of the President. General Truc said that most of the bombs landed miles from the targets, that attacking fighters released at excessively high altitudes to avoid antiaircraft fire, and that poor targeting, poor execution, and low VNAF morale were to blame for the meager results. Criticisms such as these, from RVNAF commanders as well as from U.S. observers, persisted throughout the campaign and certainly had some merit. Even the enemy antiaircraft gunners complained, according to an agent reporting on a Katum strike, that the VNAF flew too high to be reached by their 37-mm. guns.

Lest there be an assumption that VNAF fighter pilots lacked courage to fly through flak, they did habitually assume high risks in attacking enemy forces while in support of ARVN infantry. The inhibition against flying too low through heavy antiaircraft fire stemmed more from the realization that no ARVN unit was in peril and perhaps more cogently that, under the constraints on military assistance, lost airplanes would not be replaced and damaged ones would be grounded for months awaiting repair. On the strikes against Loc Ninh on 30 November and 3 December, pilots reported flak between 4,000 and 12,000 feet and bomb release altitudes were between 7,000 and 10,000 feet. While these release altitudes were too high for precision bombing and rocketing, they did produce some visible results, although VNAF attacks had no lasting effect on the enemy's capabilities.

Attempts by the JGS and Military Region 3 to assess the damage to NVA installations were frustrated by the lack of an aerial photographic system in VNAF as well as by the remoteness of the areas attacked and the dense foliage that concealed many of the targets. Agents filtered back with a few reports, and these were probably accurate as far as they went but were far from comprehensive. Pilot reports were also used to assess bomb damage but these may well have been colored by wishful observations. A brief summary of the campaign is given in Table 6.

TABLE 6
VNAF STRIKES, OCT.–DEC. 1973
(date / location and targets / sorties)

Late Oct / ZA MAT installations / not reported
Market, fuel dump, 60 houses destroyed; 50 civilians killed. Source of report: agent

6 Nov / DON LUAN base area, supplies, artillery position. / 33 fighters
100 soldiers killed; 6 combat positions destroyed; 4 secondary explosions. Source of report: MR 3.

7 Nov / BO DUC tank regiment (3 battalions), weapons, and ammunition storage. / Not reported.
Results not reported.

7Nov / LOC NINH airfield construction, fuel and other military stores, AAA positions. / 36 fighters
1 AAA position, many structures and installations destroyed. Source of report: MR 3. All of the targets were north of Loc Ninh in rubber plantation west of junction of Highways 13 and 14, except for two targets adjacent to Highway 14.

8 Nov / LO GO food storage / not reported
4 motorbikes, 18 bicycles, 4 oxcarts, ammunition, 6,000 kilos of rice and 2,000 liters of gasoline destroyed; many houses and supplies destroyed; many NVA cadre and soldiers killed including 32 from COSVN financial affairs section. Source of report: two separate agents. Likely that this report refers to 10 November strike since MR 3 reported no strike on LO GO on 8 November.

10 Nov / LO GO Hq installations, shop, supplies. / 34 fighters
Large fire, many structures destroyed. Source of report: MR 3.

10 Nov / PHU GIAO positions of Hq 7th NVA Div and 209th NVA Regt; artillery positions. / 40 fighters
Many structures, combat positions, and tunnels destroyed. Source of report: MR 3. Strike was not part of the campaign against the NVA logistical base, but part of support given ARVN defending Highway 1A near Phu Giao.

12 Nov / THIEN NGON Hq installations, artillery, airfield construction, AAA positions, storage. / 53 fighters
11 structures and many combat positions and trenches destroyed; 73 structures damaged. Source of report: MR 3 and VNAF photography.

13 Nov / MINH THANH rice storage and artillery positions. / 18 fighters
15 secondary explosions. Source of report: MR 3. Minh Thanh was not part of the COSVN logistical complex, but was important forward operating base.

14-22 Nov / PHUOC LONG artillery, AAA positions, supplies. / 122 fighters
Damage not reported by MR 3. Strikes were not part of campaign against enemy logistics, but rather in support of Phuoc Long Sector against growing enemy threat at Phuoc Binh–Song Be

17-22 Nov / AN LOC area tanks, bridge, trucks, installations. / 78 fighters
5 tanks, 5 trucks, 2 bridges, 4 AAA positions, 15 structures, and 1 ammunition supply point destroyed. Source of report: MR 3. Strikes were in support of the ARVN Rangers defending AN LOC.

23 Nov / KATUM command posts, barracks, supply points, tracked vehicles, AAA positions, trucks, construction equipment. / 68 A-1s; 44 F-5s.
69 structures, 5 fuel dumps, 1 supply dump, 6 AAA positions, 17 bunkers destroyed or damaged. Source of report: MR 3 and VNAF A2.

27 Nov / LOC NINH structures, tracked vehicle repair shop, 2 bridges, AAA and artillery positions. / 96 planned, about 75 flown; A-37s, A-1s, and F-5's.
106 structures, 6 AAA positions, 1 bridge destroyed; 1 bridge damaged; 1 fuel storage site burned. Source of report: MR 3 and VNAF A2. Strikes were clustered around junction of Highway 13 and local Route 17, about 9 kilometers south of Loc Ninh. They were more important in support of An Loc defense than in connection with campaign against the NVA logistical buildup.

30 Nov / LOC NINH installations, supplies, fuel dumps, AAA positions. / 41 A-1s; 27 F-5s.
167 structures, 9 AAA positions, 6 bunkers destroyed; 16 secondary explosions. Source of report: VNAF A2. Targets were north of Loc Ninh in the plantation and along Highway 14A. Heavy flak was encountered.

30 Nov / MINH THANH and PHU GIAO artillery positions and troop assemblies; logistical sites. / 17 fighters
Results not reported. Strikes in support of ARVN at Phu Giao and Chon Thanh.

5 Dec / BU DOP installations / 23 A-1s, 17 F-5s, 18 A-37s
45 buildings, 2 AAA positions, 1 ammunition storage site destroyed; fuel dump burned; many secondary explosions. Source: VNAF A2.

14, 27, 29, 30, and 31 Dec. / TONG LE CHON area logistic, artillery, and AAA positions. Troops; bridge. / 65 A-1s, 46 F-5s.
1 AAA position, 1 122-mm. rocket site, 3 mortar positions, 3 boats, 95 structures, and 1 supply dump destroyed; 8 secondary explosions and one large fire. Source of report: VNAF A2. Strikes served dual purpose of attacking large logistical complex in the Sroc Con Trang area (called the "Fish Hook" by Americans) and support of Rangers at Tong Le Chon.

Cease-Fire Anniversary

On the first anniversary of the Paris Agreement in early 1974, the Communists issued statements presenting their views on the cease-fire and the situation in South Vietnam. Hanoi published a "White Paper" assailing U.S. and South Vietnamese "provocations." Its charges were accompanied by the rattle and roar of thousands of trucks coursing south across the DMZ and through Laos in a mammoth "transportation offensive" started in December 1973. Thousands of tons of supplies were accumulating in the southern stockpiles, and by the cease-fire anniversary the NVA had sufficient stocks to support an offensive comparable to that of 1972 for over a year. Meanwhile, NVA engineers extended their fuel pipelines into the A Shau Valley in Thua Thien Province, and the Laotian pipeline was passing through the tri-border junction into Kontum Province. During the year following the cease-fire, the NVA increased its artillery and tank strength in the south at least four-fold.

Despite some surges of concentrated effort, such as the MR 3 air campaign of November and the aborted attempts to advance on the NVA logistical base at Duc Co, the RVNAF was unable to interfere significantly with the NVA's steady accumulation of logistical and combat strength. One major inhibiting factor was the growing density of NVA antiaircraft defending the major logistical corridors and troop concentrations. In the year following the cease-fire, the NVA added one air defense division and at least 12 regiments to the expeditionary force so that by the cease-fire anniversary 2 air defense divisions and 26 regiments were deployed in South Vietnam. Included in the force were SA-2 and SA-7 missiles and radar-controlled guns; these, in particular, forced the VNAF, which had none of the sophisticated electronic counter-measures employed by the U.S. Air Force in such a high-threat environment, to operate above effective attack altitudes.

Preparations for resuming the offensive were being made north of the DMZ in concert with the buildup in the South. The NVA strategic reserve was being reconstituted, and most of its fighting elements were being concentrated in Thanh Hoa Province between Hanoi and Vinh. Here the NVA I Corps was organized in the fall of 1973, and the 308th, 312th, and 320B Divisions, having returned from the Quang Tri front, were assigned to it. Adding to reserve strength, the major elements of the 316th Division returned to North Vietnam from northern Laos, and the 341st Division, located immediately north of the DMZ, was reorganized from its territorial status into a deployable infantry division. The sixth major element of the NVA strategic reserve, the 308B Division, was still in garrison in the Hanoi area. Compounding the already tenuous situation facing the RVNAF in Kontum and Pleiku Province, the NVA 968th Division began deploying from southern Laos into the western highlands of

South Vietnam, and by the end of January 1974 its 9th and 19th Regiments were already there.

As the RVNAF leadership and the DAO observers in Saigon viewed the situation, the warning was clear: although there existed a rough parity of military power deployed in the South, considering the obviously heavier requirements on South Vietnam to protect a dispersed population and long lines of communication, the RVNAF could retain not even one division in general reserve. The planned defense possessed no flexibility whatsoever, and adjustments were possible only by giving up terrain and usually population along with it. On the other hand, the NVA not only possessd considerable flexibility in choosing objectives and selecting forces to employ, but it also had six full-strength infantry divisions, adequately supported by artillery, tanks, and supplies, to throw into the battle at the decisive moment. Furthermore, improvements made in roads southward and the absence of U.S. air interdiction reduced North Vietnamese deployment times to the point where a surprise appearance of the NVA reserve became a worrisome possibility.

Note on Sources

References used in describing the situation in the delta during the last half of 1973 included, most importantly, reports and studies made by J2/JGS, translated and retained by DAO Saigon Intelligence Branch; similar reports of rallier interrogations and captured documents; DAO Intelligence Summaries and reports; operational reports and intelligence information from headquarters IV Corps; reports from the U.S. Consul General, Can Tho; a JGS report on the status of territorial forces in Military Region 4; and the author's own notes recorded during meetings with the J2/JGS, and visits to Military Region 4.

The section on morale in the RVNAF was derived largely from reports by U.S. Military Attaches who had regular contact with knowledgeable Vietnamese officers, from DAO Saigon Economic Reports, and from recorded observations made by liaison officers of DAO Intelligence Branch.

Information on the Ranger reorganization came from the DAO Saigon Quarterly Assessment, December 1973, and reports from offices of the U.S. Embassy.

Combat activity and the air campaign in Military Region 3 came from personal observation by the author, reports by the principal liaison officer from DAO Intelligence Branch with the VNAF, and information reports from the Consul General, Bien Hoa, the U.S. Embassy, and DAO Saigon.

8

The Decline of U.S. Support

Military Assistance, Fiscal Year 1974

U.S. military assistance to South Vietnam was "service funded." This meant that, unlike other programs funded by Congress in a military assistance appropriations act, the money for support of the Vietnamese military was contained in the Army, Navy, and Air Force sections of the Department of Defense appropriations bill. A carryover from the days of active U.S. military participation in the war, the Military Assistance Service Funded (MASF) program for Vietnam became obsolete with the departure of American forces from Indochina in January 1973. But months passed before the Defense Department, the Services, and the Congress could adjust to the changed situation with a new military assistance program. In the interim, DAO Saigon requisitioned supplies and equipment for the RVNAF under continuing congressional resolution authority, based on the program of assistance developed jointly with South Vietnam's Defense Ministry and JGS in early 1973 and in anticipation of adequate funds in the Defense Appropriation Act for fiscal year 1974.

The U.S.-funded part of the RVNAF budget for fiscal year 1974 called for expenditures of $1.1 billion. But on 19 December 1973, Rear Adm. T. J. Bigley, Director for East Asia and Pacific Region, International Security Affairs (ISA) Department of Defense, cabled General Murray warning that the Senate committee had reduced service-funded military assistance for Vietnam and Laos to $650 million of new obligational authority in the 1974 Defense Appropriation bill. The House committee had recommended slightly more than $1 billion, and the two committees in conference agreed to $900 million. Admiral Bigley told General Murray that Vietnam's share of the $900 million would be about $813 million. Although the ceiling for Vietnam and Laos spending during the fiscal year was set by the Congress at $1,126 million, General Murray was asked for ideas on how the Vietnam MASF program could be adjusted to the lower limit of FY 74 money. (Msg, Bigley to Murray, 192200Z Dec 73, Log 907-73.)

Meanwhile, Headquarters Department of the Army, taking note of the reduction being contemplated in the Congress, suddenly cut off all operational and maintenance funds for Vietnam for the rest of the fiscal year. When General Murray found out about this, he asked Ambassador Graham Martin for authority to tell Lt. Gen. Dong Van Khuyen, Commanding General of the Central Logistics Command, so that the Vietnamese could adopt some procedures to conserve supplies until the new appropriation made more money available. The Ambassador refused on the grounds that disclosure would be too unsettling politically. (The near disastrous result was that the South Vietnamese continued requisitioning and using up supplies at their usual rate. With a four-month order-to-ship time, the supply line dried up in April and the system was never to recover.)

Less than 24 hours later, Admiral Bigley had General Murray's reply, which was prefaced with the remark that General Murray was not able to discuss the cut with the South Vietnamese authorities because of the political sensitivity. He would leave that onerous task to Ambassador Martin. He also pointed out that Admiral Bigley's request for an immediate response precluded a detailed review of the MASF program; he could offer only rough observations. First, the source of prior year funds—theoretically $313 million which would bring the Laos and Vietnam programs up to the $1,126 million ceiling authorized by Congress—had not yet been identified, and about $723 million of the FY 74 program had already been obligated. This meant that if the true ceiling turned out to be $813 million—that is, if the additional $313 million could not be found—only $90 million remained to carry the Vietnam program for the six months remaining in the fiscal year. Add to this about $200 million worth of unbudgeted critical shortages already identified—shortages that were the result of the unexpectedly heavy combat actions of 1973—and anyone could see that a dangerous situation was developing.

General Murray's list of critical shortages included $180 million for ground ammunition, $5 million for medical supplies, $4.3 million for subsistence, $8 million for air ammunition, and an undetermined sum to buy or operate more landing ships, tank (LST), as a hedge against the enemy's capability to close the land route to Hue. General Murray tentatively identified budgeted savings of $33 million by eliminating the RVNAF dependent shelter program, a project that had high morale value for the armed forces and had been promised by President Nixon. Improvements to lines of communication would also be cut, and spare parts for ships and aircraft reduced to a critical level. Although he offered some other saving alternatives, General Murray admitted that none was feasible. He also noted that the considerable cost of packing, crating, handling, and shipping of military assistance supplies had not been budgeted; these costs would also have to be borne within the ceiling.

The day after Christmas, Ambassador Martin sent his analysis of the military assistance situation to the White House. Trailing General Murray's hurried response by six days, the Ambassador's message contained a more complete review, and the shortfalls in the program had been refined by General Murray and his staff. Consequently, the shortage cited by Ambassador Martin was more than double that earlier anticipated by General Murray. The Ambassador's message is quoted here in full (Msg, Martin to White House, 26 Dec 73, Log 930-73.):

1. It seems quite clear that a new review at the highest levels of the future priorities to be accorded U.S. Military Assistance to the Republic of Vietnam is imperative. Although we tend to concentrate, quite properly, on the still existing deficiencies in the ARVN in order to correct and improve them, such concentration leads us to overlook the inescapable fact that the process of "Vietnamization" so ably implemented by General Abrams with the assistance of all the U.S. Armed Services has, in fact, worked out very well. The ARVN has not only held well, but has up to now kept the other side off balance. If we remain constant in our support, and determined to carry out the commitments we have made at the highest level, we have every right to confidently expect that the GVN can hold without the necessity of U.S. armed intervention. Therefore, the additional resources necessary to discharge the commitments already made will, in reality, return enormous dividends in the achievements of U.S. objectives not only in southeast Asia, but throughout the world.

2. Perhaps it will contribute to perspective to recall that in the last six months we have witnessed an evident consolidation of internal support for President Thieu and his administration; the reorganization of that administration to better cope with the economic realities, and the conclusion of economic agreements with the FRG, France and Japan which will help surmount current problems and act as a catalyst in attracting other donors. The joint GVN and U.S. actions in publicizing massive North Vietnamese violations of the Paris agreements has successfully conditioned world reaction to accept the strong GVN reactions to these DRVN violations as quite proper and natural responses to North Vietnamese aggression. The highest officials of the Polish and Hungarian ICCS Delegation have privately informed us that they estimate the NVN/VC forces control 20 percent less territory than on January 28, 1973. Politically, the NVN/VC proselytizing has clearly been unsuccessful. Obviously, Moscow and Peking have been informed that, both politically and militarily, the initiative is passing to the GVN side.

3. Yet the military capability of NVN forces is now greater than at the time of the Easter 1972 offensive. Whether it will be utilized in another major force offensive or be maintained as a deterrent to GVN elimination of PRG forces is a decision which, I believe, has not yet been taken in Hanoi. It will be greatly influenced on their estimate of the will, the morale, and the military capability of the RVN. This in turn, will be greatly conditioned on the RVN estimate of the present validity of our commitments to them.

4. It is a bit hard here in Saigon to determine the practical effects of the just passed defense appropriation bill on our ability to carry out the commitments made solemnly and unequivocally by the U.S.G. to the GVN. However, we have received some preliminary indications of Washington thinking that trickle half way around the world. If these are only partly true, then we are in considerable danger of very soon being in open, glaringly obvious default of those commitments.

5. The immediate repercussions on the increasingly evident self-confidence and up-beat morale of the GVN and the ARVN, while not possible to calculate with precision, will certainly be adverse and could be more serious. The short range effect on the presently delicate and fragile relationship with the Soviets, the Chinese, the Middle East and even with Europe, should we welsh on our commitments here, can best be determined in the White House. But it seems self-evident that the one most single precious commodity we possess just now is the faith of others in the constancy and reliability of American commitments. The cost of our failure to keep it here, even in dollar terms, will be incalculably greater than the immediate sums that now seem to be in question.

6. I am quite aware that reserves of all the services have been dangerously depleted by the emergency demands of enhance, enhance plus, and the recent emergency requirements for Israel. Nevertheless, I am convinced that the ingenuity and resourcefulness of the armed services can find ways to meet our requirements, if only our civilian leaders will unequivocably establish the overriding national priority that must be accorded meeting these requirements.

7. Before the January agreements, at the time of the January agreements, after the January agreements, again at the time of the June communique, and most especially at the San Clemente meeting in April between President Nixon and President Thieu, we have reiterated the commitment that we will maintain the armament level existing on a one-for-one replacement basis. Yet, almost from the beginning every action we have taken seems, upon review, to have been calculated to convince senior officers of the ARVN that we were not really serious about keeping that pledge. Of the many examples I will mention only two:

8. The fact is that with 52 percent of the VNAF total personnel strength in training, it is understandable that maintenance of VNAF aircraft would constitute a problem. Both the VNAF and we have instituted corrective action with the help of the USAF. Yet when suggestions are received from Washington to add 8 perfectly flyable F5A's to those scheduled to be removed for "corrosion control," and it just so happens that the addition of this particular number coincides with the need perceived in Washington for Iran and Korea repayment, the RVNAF and ARVN quite naturally wonder about the purpose of this kind of game playing. The current end result is that President Thieu has ordered the VNAF to inflict maximum possible damage in retaliatory raids in response to DRVN violations of the ceasefire, but to lose no aircraft in the process since all will be desperately needed when a major force attack is made. Consequently, the VNAF, although willing and able to aggressively press low level attacks, are not permitted to fly low enough over targets to achieve the precision results of which they are capable. If I could inform President Thieu that replacements of F5A's would be automatic, the results would be startling. Under present circumstances I cannot do this, despite the fact that we are committed to do so.

9. The second example is that despite the commitment for one-for-one replacement, despite the pace of the fighting since the "ceasefire" in January and June which has resulted in a greater total of casualties than the total of U.S. casualties during our years of active engagement, USARPAC's tentative ammunition replacement through the balance of this fiscal year would leave a projected balance on 1 July far below the ceasefire level that represents a minimum safety position against both enemy capabilities and also present estimates of their intentions. The following table graphically illustrates the problem. [In thousands. First figure is cease-fire level; second is projected, end June.]

40-mm. HE	c-f 4,093.0
- end June	779.0
60-mm. HE	3,038.0
- end June	248.0
81-mm. Illum.	175.3
- end June	32.0
66-mm. LAW	106.7
- end June	21.0

10. These rounds have been selected as examples because they are unique to ARVN ammunition requirements. As used in the Delta the 40 MM round has effectively increased mobility of ARVN forces in resisting enemy activities. The 60 MM and 81 MM ILLUM are mortar rounds substituting for heavy artillery requirements within the small ARVN defense perimeters. The 66 MM LAW is the main ARVN weapon for defense against the very real enemy tank threat which now exists.

11. These are only two examples, but are enough to underscore the problem. The quickest, easiest and least expensive way to achieve the objectives we have formally set for ourselves is to reaffirm the priorities already established and permit the armed services to proceed with the implementation of the programs they now have before them. Original estimates were made on the assumption that the ceasefire would be reasonably respected by the other side. Given the increased level of military activity throughout South Vietnam we estimate that we will need a minimum of $494.4 million more than the projected $1,126 in FY 74. This is broken down as follows:

$180 for ground ammunition.
$69.7 for equipment not called forward or above program levels.
$200 for priority RVNAF requirement (estimate).
$10 for medical supplies.
$3 to operate additional LST's.
$4.3 for subsistence.
$9 for air munitions.
$18.4 for POL.
$494.4 total.

12. The addition of this total of $494.4 million to the $1.126 billion brings us to the total of $1.62 billion we will need in the fiscal year to reasonably discharge our commitments. I reiterate I am fully aware of the burden this will put on the services but I also reiterate my conviction that, given clear and unequivocal statement of the priorities and goals by the highest levels, their ingenuity and resourcefulness will find the way to implement such decisions.

The next day Admiral Bigley clarified the funding situation somewhat in a message to General Murray. (Msg, Bigley to Murray, 272200Z Dec 73, Log 936-73.) Since $826.5 million had already been obligated, only $300 million remained for both countries for the last half of the fiscal year, despite the fact that $562.1 million of unobligated prior year funds remained.

Meanwhile, General Murray clarified the requirement for funds above the originally budgeted amount and specifically identified the critical need for ammunition funds. (Murray to Brig. Gen. Richard H. Thompson, ODCSLOG, DA, 2 Jan 74, Log 09487.) About $221 million was necessary to build up ammunition stocks and only $43 million remained of unobligated FY 74 funds. General Murray was not a patient man; considerate of others, thoroughly professional, perceptive, and highly skilled in the use of colorful language, but not patient. From Christmas on he had been on the receiving end of a plethora of vague—and sometimes inaccurate—messages from Washington and Honolulu concerning cuts in the MASF program, none of which provided him or the RVNAF staffs the information they required to plan fuel and ammunition usages, flying hours, maintenance or any other budgeted military activity for the next six months. His small capacity for forbearance virtually disappeared by 11 January, and he asked for the answers he had been searching for since first warned of the impending MASF reductions. In a message to CINCPAC and the Department of Defense (ISA), he put it this way (Msg, Murray to Brig. Gen. Charles A. Jackson, CINCPAC/J8, 11 Jan 74, Log 038-74.):

1. During the past month there has been a deluge of front and back channel messages from services and DSAA on FY 74 status and impact of new legislation.

2. Information appreciated but nothing conclusive or consistent enough to lock in on where we actually stand. No two messages cite the same figures, and volume of information has created much concern, many questions and virtually no answers.

3. Cannot determine whether funds here have been cut or, if so, from what to what. Reduction intimated, but nothing concrete. Concerned chiefly that dollar apportionment among RVNAF services may be out of balance before year-end since MILDEPS handle funds separately.

4. Understand FY 74 ceiling for Vietnam and Laos $1,126 million, including $900 million NOA (new obligational authority). Reportedly, $814 million of NOA is Vietnam and $86 million Laos. Do not know Laos and Vietnam breakout of total $1,126 million or significance of $226 million difference above NOA. All this too inconclusive to establish meaningful priorities for requisitioning balance of year or to know to what extent service and country priorities should be inter-related.

5. Basic questions (applicable to Vietnam —not Laos) are:
A. Do we now have FY 74 country dollar ceiling to be managed overall as in regular MAAG, or do our services at Washington still have separate ceilings managed through channels to DAO service divisions?
B. What is country ceiling (or service ceilings)?
C. What are other dollar restrictions, if any, e.g., MPA, PEMA etc,?
D. What is NOA dollar limitation, and what is service breakout of NOA, if service ceilings apply?
E. What is exact significance of difference between NOA and ceiling, and what is service breakout, if service ceilings apply?

6. Propose CINCPAC become focal point for clarifying current funding status and for funneling DSAA and MILDEP funding developments to DAO balance of FY 74. This in consonance with MASF category IV procedures and would eliminate or reduce uncertainties, confusion and message traffic. Also assist in staying within ceiling constraints. With ground ammo alone running at over a million dollars a day, matters can get quickly

askew unless we know that such a pace is within the ceiling and appropriation restraint.

The response he got from Hawaii shed some light—diffused though it was—on the subject. The news was not all comforting.(Msg, Jackson to Murray, 160413Z Jan 74, Log 053-74.) The Defense Department comptroller had determined that Vietnam's share of the new obligational authority would be about $820.5 million rather than the original $813-814 million estimate. But the question regarding the $1,126 million ceiling, and where the money would come from to permit obligations up to it, was not definitely answered. The administration was planning to ask the Congress to raise the authorization to $1.4 billion for FY 74; this, according to CINCPAC would "allow use of all possible dollars, including prior years." CINCPAC reminded General Murray, although General Murray was already painfully aware of it, that much of the $820.5 million of FY 74 money had already been obligated, and the ceiling increase was required to authorize additional obligations, assuming that prior year funds could be found and used.

Answers to General Murray's other questions were deferred for further study. But the most crucial issue, how much total money would be available for the FY 74 program, remained in doubt, although Washington advised General Murray on 20 January that a supplemental increase would be requested of Congress to bring the country program up to $1,054.8 million. (Msg, Maj. Gen. Peter C. Olenchuck, ODCSLOG, DA, to Murray 202208Z Jan 74, Log 066-74.)

This amount would reduce the concern in Saigon substantially, but Congressional response to such a request would most likely be negative. Meanwhile the war continued and supplies dwindled as moratoriums were imposed on requisitioning pending the outcome of the budgetary impasse.

General Murray did not wait for further definitive word from Washington or Hawaii. Early in January he began a series of conferences with the RVNAF logistics staff, principally with General Khuyen and General Cao Van Vien, Chief of the Joint General Staff, to impress upon them the need to conserve supplies, particularly ammunition. Without divulging all that he knew about the FY 74 program, he urged them to apply strict controls against the likelihood of diminished resources. General Vien reacted immediately. New available supply rates (ASR) were applied on all critical ammunition items on 25 February, reducing further the ASRs General Vien had ordered on 25 January.

Meanwhile, General Murray continued to receive new interpretations of the money situation from Washington. The $1,126 million ceiling on obligations during FY 74 for Vietnam and Laos, whether from current or prior year funds, was reiterated.

Against this ceiling, the Department of Defense had allocated $700 million for the Army (of which $301 million was ammunition for Vietnam), $26 million for the Navy, and $400 million for the Air Force. Since $826.5 million had already been obligated as of 30 November 1973, only $229.5 million remained for all services (and this included funds for Laos). In this message, General Murray was advised that the Department of Defense was planning to ask Congress to raise the ceiling to $1.6 billion, rather than to $1.4. (Olenchuck to Murray, ODCSLOG, DA, 0422107Z Feb 74.)

General Murray viewed this information with some skepticism, since he understood the mood of the Congress and the effects of Watergate on President Nixon's Vietnam commitments about as well as anyone did in Washington. The most he could plan on was the Vietnam share of the $1,126 million, which by this time had been refined by the Department of Defense to $1,059 million.

In early February, General Murray tried to explain in a message to CINCPAC and Washington why the ceiling imposed overly severe restrictions on the Vietnam program, how the situation had changed since the program's drafting in early 1973, and the impact of those changes on RVNAF requirements. Since the FY 74 program had been agreed upon, significant price increases had occurred in equipment and fuel and the level of combat anticipated for a cease-fire period did not pertain. Increasing enemy capabilities created a high-threat environment; an inflation rate of 65 percent in South Vietnam drove subsistence costs correspondingly up; the imposition of a ceiling after 75 percent of the funds had been obligated left no flexibility for adjustment of priorities; the inability to identify the status of prior year funds to be applied to the $1,054 million ceiling created the possibility of overcommitment and compelled the suspension of all Army requisitions for the past two months; the apparent inclusion of other unanticipated costs within the ceiling, such as packing, crating, handling, and shipping further reduced the amounts available for RVNAF support; and bookkeeping adjustments had placed considerable FY 73 costs onto FY 74 funds. (Msg, Murray to Lt. Gen. William G. Moore, CofS, CINCPAC, 0910332 Feb 74, Log 130-74.)

Vice Adm. Raymond Peet, Director of Military Assistance in the Department of Defense, appreciated General Murray's lucid assessment and assured him that it would help support the Secretary of Defense's request to raise the congressional ceiling to $1.6 billion. (Msg, Peet to Murray, 222212Z, Feb 74, Log 168-74.)

Formal hearings on appropriations for South Vietnam began in the Senate Armed Services Committee on 12 March 1974. Meanwhile, the severe controls Generals Vien and Khuyen had placed on ammunition expenditures were having some saving results. By mid-April, however, the on-hand stockage of the most critical item of ammunition—105-mm. howitzer, high explosive—was still dangerously low; only about 52 days of supply remained and less than that if high consumption rates required to repel a major offensive were applied.

Aside from the opposition of many influential members of the House and Senate to any sizable assistance for Vietnam, the Department of Defense and the services were further handicapped in their efforts to convince the responsible committees that additional monies should be made available for Vietnam because seemingly no one in any Defense agency knew how much prior year money had been obligated or what supplies and equipment had already been provided. In any case, the Senate Armed Services Committee refused to raise the $1,126 million ceiling on 3 April, responding in large measure to Senator Edward M. Kennedy's leadership. The next day, the House rejected the administration's request to raise the ceiling to $1.6 billion, as well as a compromise increase to $1.4 billion. The issue was dead, but the Defense Department kept trying. It informed the House and Senate Armed Services Committees that it had discovered $266 million of unobligated prior year funds and asked to have this amount excluded from the ceiling. The committees agreed that this would be proper, but on 6 May, the Senate passed a resolution, sponsored by Senator Kennedy, to the effect that any expenditures over $1,126 million in FY 74 would be illegal.

The dispute between the administration and Congress over the FY 74 Vietnam program, clearly won by the latter, was only the preliminary to the main event: the fight for the FY 75 authorization and appropriation.

By imposing rigid controls, the RVNAF managed to survive through the summer. Many of its vehicles were on blocks, its aircraft grounded because of parts and fuel shortages, its radios silent for lack of batteries, and its far-flung outposts suffering from inadequate artillery support. The stream of supplies had dwindled to a trickle, and weeks would pass after the start of the new fiscal year before the pipeline would again be flowing.

Meanwhile, General Murray arrived in Washington at the end of April 1974 to consult with the Defense Department and services on military assistance programs. He followed this visit with a brief, much needed vacation and returned to Vietnam toward the end of May. On 23 May, Admiral Bigley cabled General Murray that the House had passed the Defense Authorization Bill for FY 74 with the familiar ceiling of $1,126 million for MASF, while the Senate Committee was recommending $900 million. The best compromise in committee conference that Defense could expect was a $1 billion ceiling, but the likelihood that this would be trimmed on the Senate floor was great. The Admiral asked General Murray to furnish some impact statements describing the results in Vietnam if the authorized program for FY 75 were $1,126 million, or reduced respectively to $900 million, $750 million, or $600 million. (Msg, Bigley to Murray, 2321187Z May 74, Log 353-74.)

General Murray saw Admiral Bigley's message upon his return from Washington. His staff began working on the reply immediately, and a 30-page message, carefully drafted by General Murray and bearing the unmistakable marks of his incisive rhetoric, was dispatched on 1 June. (Msg, Murray to Bigley, 0111157, June 74, Log #377-74.)

It would seem from half way around the world that enormously effective use could be made of Secretary Schlesinger's comments to the press on 21 May. The most telling argument is the point he made so eloquently that it was we who told the South Vietnamese that we would give them the tools and they would have to finish the job. It was we who undertook a commitment to replace their combat losses on a one-for-one basis. It should be emphasized that all of us hoped in January 1973, at the time of the cease-fire, the other side would really observe it. It should be kept in mind that the GVN losses not only in manpower, about which we can do nothing, but in materiel have not been replaced as we promised. The importance of the above needs to be reemphasized after reading Senator Kennedy's comments during the debate on his amendment to eliminate the $266 million repayment authority. The Senator was extremely careful to try to point out that his proposed amendment would not really cripple the South Vietnamese military effort and implicitly recognized the obligations which the Secretary had pointed out, as recorded above. Therefore, it would seem useful to take the Secretary's comments as the point of departure and to drive home that any further reductions will seriously cripple the South Vietnamese capability to defend themselves and will be a violation of the clear understandings they had from us at the time of the cease-fire.

General Murray then reviewed the current situation and the impact FY 74 funding constraints had had on the RVNAF. "Cuts and economies have mortgaged the future," he told Washington. The entire program was in trouble. Because stock replenishment had been at a virtual standstill for over four months, the stockage of many common supplies was below safety levels. Included in this category were clothing, spare parts, tires, batteries, and M-16 rifle barrels. Despite intensive management of shortages to afford minimum combat support to engaged units, the deadline rate on vehicles, weapons, and communications equipment was bound to increase during the next quarter. In other words, even if the authority to requisition the supplies needed were provided at that moment, the lag in order-to-ship time would prevent immediate recuperation.

When it had first become apparent that the assistance program was in trouble, economies had been made in the usage of motor vehicle and marine fuels. The RVNAF staff had estimated that they could afford to operate about 70 percent of the vehicle and naval fleets. But even this drastic measure was not enough. The reduction in the fuel program permitted support of only 55 percent of South Vietnam's equipment operating at severely curtailed levels.

The quality and responsiveness of the medical service had also suffered. Stocks of supplies, many of which were in the lifesaving category, were seriously depleted, such as blood collection bags, intravenous fluids, antibiotics, and surgical dressings. Meanwhile, hospital admissions of wounded increased from 8,750 per month during the first three months of 1974 to over 10,000 per month by summer and would continue to rise as enemy operations intensified. The onset of the wet monsoon would bring with it the scourge of falciparum malaria in the northern provinces, and the supply of insect repellent for the troops was exhausted. In fact, the total supply picture was bleak. Roughly half the items on stockage lists were not there, and shipments into the depots had fallen off dramatically: from about 24,000 metric tons received in March to less than 8,000 in May.

Other effects of the cut-back in funds were readily apparent. The moratorium imposed on requisitions prevented the timely ordering of essential parts for the engine-rebuild program, and the lack of certain long-lead-time parts would soon stop production lines of truck and jeep engines, as well as power generators. The dependent shelter program was cancelled in its entirety. The ARVN engineers had to adopt less expensive and less durable methods in the program to improve lines of communication, a temporary saving to be offset by increased maintenance costs.

Because of the severe controls placed on ammunition usage, and because ammunition was given top priority for available funds, the stockage of ammunition had remained relatively constant during the last half of the fiscal year. Nevertheless, an NVA attempt to seize and hold the Iron Triangle had imposed new demands on the system. These demands were likely to increase. Roughly 177,000 short tons of ammunition had been on hand in South Vietnam at cease-fire. Including ammunition in transit through April 1974, DAO calculated that only 121,000 short tons would be available by the end of that month. With only $301 million allocated for ammunition purchase in FY 74, it would be impossible to regain the cease-fire ammunition posture. That amount of ammunition, $301 million worth, could be used in less than three months of intensive combat and would disappear in nine months even at the austere rates imposed by JGS.

The adequacy of ammunition stockage had not been foreseen as a problem when the Military Assistance Command, Vietnam, was preparing to turn over the management of U.S. military assistance to DAO, Saigon. The MACV planners expected that the cease-fire would take hold enough to permit cutting ARVN ammunition usage by up to 70 percent in some categories. Further, it was anticipated that by reducing the allowable expenditure rates, the level of combat would drop accordingly, providing more encouragement for a true cease-fire environment to develop. While the U.S. could and did impose ammunition restrictions on the RVNAF through the budgetary process and by establishing "defense expenditure allocations," which amounted to dictating the number of rounds that could be expended per weapon per day, unfortunately no such restriction applied to the NVA. Consequently, as the tempo of combat increased, the ARVN was compelled to exceed the expenditure limits, and the funds allocated to replace the stocks were not sufficient. Furthermore, although the RVNAF exceeded the rates on which the $301 million allocation was based, the ammunition expenditures were far below those of prior years, even though the level of combat in many individual engagements was equivalent to the most intense periods of the 1968 and 1972 offensives.

While ammunition constituted a management problem for the DAO and JGS, the impact of the restrictions in the field was immediate and often decisive. Experienced infantrymen, accustomed to carrying six grenades into battle but now limited to two, responded with less confidence and aggressiveness to orders to advance and were less tenacious in holding threatened positions. Defenders in beleaguered outposts, restricted to two or three mortar or artillery rounds, were not inclined to wait and watch enemy sappers break through the wire and drag their recoilless rifles into firing position after ARVN artillery had fired its meager allocation. Artillery was limited to clearly identified targets, and harassing fires were stopped altogether. While experienced infantrymen and artillerymen could argue the worth or extravagance of such fires placed on trails and suspected assembly areas, they made enemy operations more difficult and hence had some value, however difficult to quantify. Although tactical and long-line communications were in poor condition, the need to economize still pertained. The RVNAF took measures to reduce the comsumption of radio batteries by 25 percent. By combining nets, such as air/ground with command, they reduced the number of radios in operation and even then could plan on operating fewer than 20 days per month. As tactical efficiency suffered, casualties mounted. After noting that 41 percent of the authorized stockage list for tactical communications equipment had been depleted, General Murray reported (Ibid.):

Equipment in the combat divisions is suffering between 30 to 40 percent deadline rate. The divisions are losing communication flexibility and in MR 2 can no longer provide telephone and teletype communications to attached forces such as ranger units that do not possess VHF TO/E assets. The AN/PRC-25 radio operational readiness had decayed to 67 percent. 848 module and other repair parts ASL lines are at zero balance and are stopping the repair production lines for this radio. AN/FGC-25 teletype equipment in the area communications system is suffering from lack of repair parts. ARVN has adjusted to priorities and are reducing tactical divisions to 40 percent of authorized TO/E teletype assets. Equipment will be withdrawn from the divisions and used in the area communications system where the high volume of record traffic is processed and transmitted. Continued depletion of communications parts stocks is creating a catastrophic threat to an already seriously degraded tactical communications posture.

Long-line communications, which the U.S. mission also relied on for its own needs, were in similar difficulty. Even though emergency action had been taken to reprogram FY 74 funds for the long-line system, all communications were expected to decay, and if sufficient funds were not provided in FY 75, a collapse could be predicted.

The funding pinch was felt in the VNAF program as well. Requisitioning of essential "move-shoot-communicate" items for aircraft and supporting equipment had been severely curtailed since January 1974. The result was that one-fifth of the force was grounded for maintenance, a condition bound to worsen before FY 75 funds would have any effect.

The situation with ground combat equipment was similar. For example, in early March, the deadline rate for medium tanks was 25 percent; by mid-May, the lack of repair parts had forced the rate to 35 percent. The availability of armored personnel carriers, the main fighting vehicle of the armored cavalry, was sinking to only one-half of organizational strength. In December 1973, RVNAF's mobility, exemplified by the air movement of the ARVN 23d Division from Kontum and the rapid shift of the 22d Division to cover the gaps, had been crucial in rescuing Quang Duc Province. This mobility had all but vanished with the decline in funding for maintenance requirements and the skyrocketing costs of all supplies, particularly fuel.

Military Assistance, Fiscal Year 1975

Such was the situation facing the RVNAF as Congress began to deliberate the FY 75 military assistance program. A proposal of $1.45 billion had been developed in Saigon in September 1973 based on requirements and prices known at that time. After hearings on the FY 75 Military Procurement Bill, the House Armed Services Committee recommended $1.4 billion for the FY 75 Vietnam MASF Program, but the House on 22 May passed its version of the bill with a $1.126 billion limit.

Although in the ten intervening months much had happened to change priorities, the changes could be managed under a $1.45 billion program, and the critical elements could be done within a $1.126 billion ceiling. General Murray was especially concerned about the need to expand depot repair facilities. Below $1.126 billion, this requirement was out of reach. But the greatest problems were caused by inflation. Ground ammunition was programmed at $400 million; when April 1974 prices were posted, the cost was $500 million. The prices of other common, high-volume supplies had undergone comparable increases. What had appeared to be a generous program during the 1973 planning days had become an austere one.

Another matter of concern was that South Vietnamese Air Force and Navy equipment losses had not been replaced in FY 74 and the U.S. commitment to replace losses on a one-for-one basis had not been fulfilled. Although surpluses existed in some categories at cease-fire and all lost equipment need not have been replaced, the almost complete lack of replacements hindered tactical operations, particularly those of the VNAF. Specifically, as General Murray pointed out, VNAF pilots were taking such extreme measures to reduce losses that their bombing and strafing techniques were ineffective. VNAF had lost 281 aircraft since the cease-fire (including 66 transferred to the USAF) and had received only eight O-1's as replacements. The Navy had lost 58 ships and boats, and none had been replaced. In essence, if the FY 75 program were held to $1,126 million, the minimum operational requirements of the RVNAF could be supported, but one-for-one replacement of losses could not be accomplished, and very little investment in long-term projects was possible. The current restrictions on mobility—only 49 percent of the vehicles would be operated, for example—and the severe controls on ammunition usage would be continued. General Murray concluded his discussion on RVNAF capabilities under the constraints of a $1.126 billion FY 75 program with an unequivocal, prophetic statement: RVNAF would be capable of defending the country against the FY 74 level of enemy activities and of countering country-wide high-points of enemy activity, but not capable of defending against a sustained major offensive. (Ibid., msg. of 1 Jun 74.)

Reductions below the $1,126 million ceiling could only have a disastrous effect on RVNAF capabilities and morale, and correspondingly enhance the enemy's potential. If the ceiling were reduced to $750 million, no investment program, that is, equipment buys, could be supported at all. Critical operational requirements—fuel, ammunition, spare parts, medical and communications supplies—would not be met. The construction program would be eliminated. VNAF flying hours would be further reduced. Training would be slashed severely, as would the maintenance programs of the Army, Navy, and Air Force. The impact on RVNAF capabilities would be that the RVNAF could no longer defend the country against a level of enemy activity approximating that of the past 12 months. A program of $750 million "would cause the GVN to abandon large segments of the country and weaken possibilities and probabilities of a negotiated settlement."

In his concluding paragraph, General Murray summarized the impacts of successively austere support (Ibid.):

In the final analysis, you can roughly equate cuts in support to loss of real estate. As the cutting edge of the RVNAF is blunted and the enemy continues to improve its combat position and logistical base, what will occur is a retreat to the Saigon- Delta area as a redoubt. In a nutshell, we see the decrements as follows: (a.) $1.126 billion level—gradual degradation of equipment base with greatest impact in out-years. Little reserve or flexibility to meet a major enemy offensive in FY 75. (b.) $900 million level—degradation of equipment base that will have significant impact by third or fourth quarter of FY 75. No reserve or flexibility to meet major offensive in FY 75. (c.) $750 million level—equipment losses not supportable. Operations ("O") funds would not support hard-core self-defense requirements. Any chance of having Hanoi see the light and come to conference table would be sharply diminished. If enemy continues current level of military activity, RNVAF could only defend selected areas of country. (d.) $600 million level—write off RVN as bad investment and broken promise. GVN would do well to hang on to Saigon and Delta area. The Vietnamese are a determined people, capable of defending themselves and progressing economically, provided they are given the tools we promised them when we decided to end our own military participation. $1.450 billion will provide the essential elements of a viable defense.

On 11 June, the Senate passed the FY 75 Military Procurement Bill with a $900 million limit on Vietnam MASF. In Senate-House conference the limit was raised to $1 billion, and a bill including that amount was signed by the President on 5 August. But it soon became apparent that the appropriation for Vietnam would be much less. On 23 and 24 September, the House and Senate appropriated only $700 million for Vietnam in the Defense Appropriation Bill for FY 75. The $1 billion ceiling became irrelevant. The $700 million appropriation, furthermore, covered all shipping expenses, certain undelivered FY 73-74 items and commitments, as well as the operational costs of the DAO itself, leaving less than $500 million to be applied to the operational requirements of the RVNAF.

His term of assignment completed, and facing retirement, General Murray left Saigon in August and devoted his final active duty days to squeezing as much out of the $700 million and prior year funds as possible. Meeting with Defense officials and service chiefs, he managed some small successes. But none could reverse the trend of diminishing U.S. support.

Meanwhile, Deputy Commander of USSAG, Maj. Gen. Ira Hunt came over to Saigon from his headquarters in Nakhon Phanom, Thailand, to fill in as Defense Attache until the newly appointed Maj. Gen. Homer Smith could arrive. General Hunt continued the conferences and working sessions between DAO and RVNAF staffs to revise the MASF program within the $700 million appropriation, which at that time was all but certain. The ARVN would get about $410 million, half of what it needed. Army ammunition requirements alone, originally estimated at $400 million, would be $500 at 1974 prices. The VNAF would receive about $160 million, less than 30 percent of its requirement, while the Navy would have to make do with about $9 million.

Draconian measures were applied. Only 55 percent of available transportation could be fueled, and tactical movement required the approval of the corps commander. Bandages and surgical dressings were washed and reused, as were other disposable surgical supplies such as hypodermic syringes and needles, intravenous sets, and rubber gloves. Replacement criteria for combat boots were changed from six to nine months, and the issue of boot socks dropped from three to two pairs per year. Ammunition issues were even more rigidly controlled than before. In the Air Force, squadrons were reduced from 66 to 56; no replacements were ordered for 162 destroyed aircraft; flying hours, contractor support, and supply levels were further reduced; and 224 aircraft were placed in storage, among them all 61 remaining A-1 bombers, all 52 C-7 cargo airplanes, 34 C-47 and C-119 gunships, all 31 0-2 observation airplanes, and 31 UH-1 helicopters. Among other operational reductions, the Navy inactivated 21 of its 44 riverine units. This was hardly the posture for an armed force on the eve of its final battle for survival.

Note on Sources

General Murray's message file was a prime source of information. Ambassador Graham Martin contributed his own message on the subject, and General Murray provided the author a comprehensive review of the entire chapter, adding significant new information and insight.

The author participated in frequent discussions on the subject while in DAO Saigon and referred to his own notes and recollections. The DAO Security and Assistance Division's fact sheets and reports were also essential sources of precise fiscal data.

Newspaper accounts were used to report congressional activity and DAO Saigon Quarterly Assessments were used for information concerning the status of RVNAF during this period.

9

1974, Year of Decision

Critical decisions leading to an end to the third Indochina war were made in Washington and Hanoi in 1974. In Washington, Congress reduced military assistance to South Vietnam to below operating levels, a decision that seriously undermined South Vietnamese combat power and will to continue the struggle. While in Hanoi, taking fresh heart from the political fall of Richard Nixon and waning Congressional support of the war, Communist leaders decided that 1975 would be the year of final victory.

Estimates and Plans

In early October 1973, the DAO, Saigon, suggested that North Vietnam had three courses of action from which it would select the one most likely to provide the earliest achievement of its national goal, the conquest of South Vietnam. The first was political: creating a recognized government within South Vietnam capable of competing in the economic and political struggle. The second a limited military offensive designed to create a military, economic, and political situation beyond the capability of South Vietnam to handle. The third a major military offensive to cause the immediate collapse of South Vietnam's government and armed forces.

The DAO postulated that North Vietnam would base its decision for 1974 primarily on expectations of Soviet and Chinese military and economic support and on an assessment of the probable U.S. reaction to an escalation of the war. Enough was known about external Communist assistance and the size of NVA stockpiles, however, to conclude that logistics would not inhibit a major NVA offensive. On the other hand, little could be said about the reactions of the Soviets or Chinese to a major NVA offensive, nor could anyone estimate with confidence the influence they could or would exert on the North Vietnamese. But the DAO did know that North Vietnam's leadership was cognizant of the decline of U.S. support for South Vietnam and would not be inclined toward caution.

The political option would be indecisive because the VC infrastructure was too weak, South Vietnam too strong, and a reversal would take a long time. The great effort under way by the NVA to improve its offensive capability in the South indicated overwhelmingly the inclination toward a military course of action. The DAO concluded that North Vietnam was not yet ready for a major, decisive offensive—despite heavy infiltration of replacements, some NVA units in the South were still too far understrength—but that as the failures of the political struggle became more evident, the NVA would embark on a phased offensive, to create gradually conditions beyond the capacity of South Vietnam to cope with. While pursuing this military course of action North Vietnam would continue political and economic actions to support it and proceed with the development of the military strength required for a decisive offensive.

In the early spring of 1974, Hanoi's military leaders met to study the resolutions of the Lao Dong Party Central Committee's 21st Plenum. The DAO had scant knowledge of this event at the time, but the strategic concepts that emanated from this council paralleled remarkably the Saigon assessment. In a post bellum account, Senior General Van Tien Dung, the architect of the final offensive, described the situation as viewed from Hanoi (quotes from Foreign Broadcast Information Service, *Daily Report: Asia and Pacific,* vol. IV, no. 110, Supplement 38, 7 Jun 1976):

... the party Central Committee's 21st Plenum held in October 1973 set forth the method of combining the political military and diplomatic struggles and pointed out: The path of the revolution in the south is the path of revolutionary violence. No matter what the situation, we must firmly grasp the opportunity and the strategic offensive line and effect flexible leadership to advance the southern revolution. True revolutionary strength is both an urgent and a basic requirement in the new situation. In March 1974 the Central Military Party Committee went into session to thoroughly study and implement the party Central Committee resolution. The committee asserted: The Vietnamese revolution may develop through various transitional stages, and it can only achieve success by way of violence with the support of political and military forces; if the war resumes on a large scale, a revolutionary war will be waged to win total victory. The southern revolution must firmly grasp the concept of strategic offensive. We must resolutely counterattack and attack the enemy, and we must firmly maintain and develop our active position in all respects.

The conference of the Central Military Party Committee completed its work and presented its plan to the Central Party Committee, which approved it. Orders went out to the military regions, directing training and maintenance preparations in the North and prescribing offensive operations for the expeditionary army in the South. How these operations were conducted, why some succeeded and others failed, is the subject of this and the following chapters. Major events occurred in each

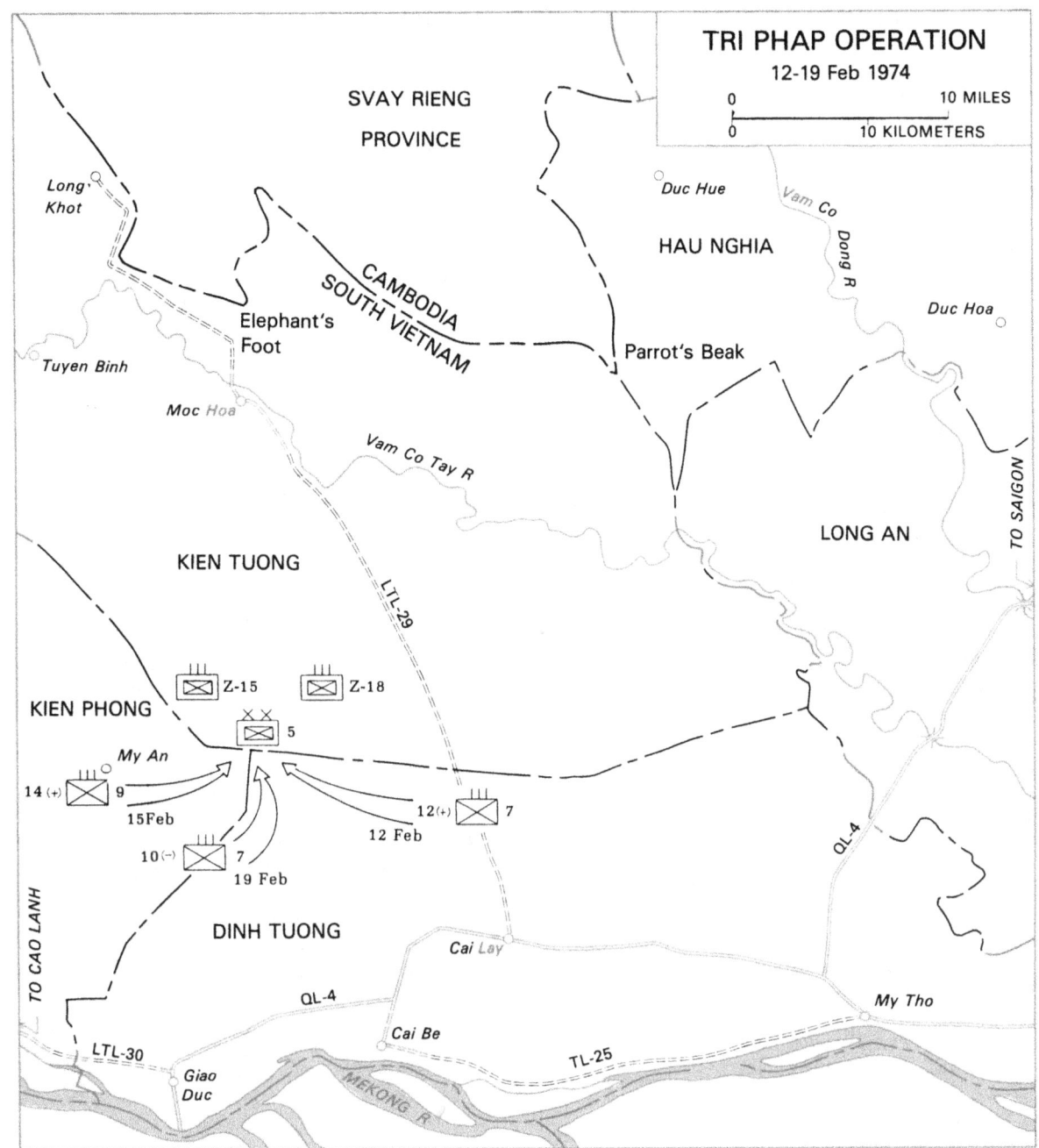

Map 12

military region, and only in the delta of South Vietnam's Military Region 4 and the border areas of Svay Rieng Province, Cambodia, was the RVNAF the clear victor. In Military Region 3, although the ARVN eventually ejected the NVA from the Iron Triangle, this costly success was vastly overshadowed by the critical loss of Phuoc Long Province to the NVA. In the highlands of Military Regions 1 and 2, all remaining outposts fell to NVA attack and the protective screen around Hue and Da Nang continued to decay.

The Tri Phap Campaign

Cambodia's Svay Rieng Province is a 60-mile-long salient, only 16 miles wide at its neck, thrust into the rich delta of Vietnam, ending in what was called the Parrot's Beak 30 miles west of Saigon. Although the Cambodian government maintained a garrison at the province capital, it did so only at the sufferance of the NVA, which controlled the rest of the province and did not consider the hostile Cambodians a threat of any significance. The only threat to the NVA in Svay Rieng came from the RVNAF operating out of the provinces which enclosed the salient on three sides: Tay Ninh, Hau Nghia and Kien Tuong. As far as the South Vietnamese were concerned, Svay Rieng and the sizable enemy forces and bases it contained constituted a serious threat to the security of the three bordering provinces and was the source of infiltration and support of enemy forces throughout the northern delta. Consequently, the RVNAF maintained outposts and operational bases as close as possible to the international frontier to slow the movement of enemy forces and supplies into South Vietnam. (Map 12)

North of Tay Ninh City the RVNAF was at a disadvantage. The forests of northern Tay Ninh Province belonged to the NVA, and the principal port of entry, Lo Go, could be reached only by air strikes. But from Tay Ninh City south to Hau Nghia Province, the RVNAF maintained bases west of the Vam Co Dong River that impeded the free flow of enemy traffic out of Svay Rieng as well as contraband traffic into it. From these bases the South Vietnamese periodically probed into the border region but rarely intruded into Cambodia. During much of the year, the flat, marshy land was under water, but even when the weather was suitable for large expeditions into Cambodia, the RVNAF were restrained for political reasons and by the realization that the forces required to achieve significant gains were rarely available. The RVNAF strategy for the Hau Nghia flank was therefore one of active defense west of the Vam Co Dong.

The situation was quite different on the Kien Tuong side of the salient. Maintaining large forces in central Kien Tuong, principally the Z-18 and Z-15 regiments, the NVA operated major infiltration corridors through the province, anchoring this logistical system on a vast base area around a location called Tri Phap. The South Vietnamese held the province capital of Moc Hoa and a base at Long Khot, both of which were well within 105-mm. howitzer range of NVA artillery in Svay Rieng, but there were great reaches of uncontrolled, unoccupied territory between the Cambodian border and the first major population concentration along National Highway 4 (QL-4) through My Tho. Another important element of the threat was contributed by the NVA 5th Division, which had operated out of Svay Rieng Province in both directions, through Tay Ninh to An Loc and south toward My Tho. In early 1974, the 5th was north of Tay Ninh City, but available for operations into Kien Tuong and Hau Nghia.

Although South Vietnamese forces were not strong enough to contain the NVA in Svay Rieng, they could in Military Region 4 impose limits on the enemy's freedom of movement, make resupply of troops costly and difficult, and inflict high casualties. To do this much, the RVNAF had to hold Long Khot and Moc Hoa, seize the enemy's logistical and operational base around Tri Phap, and protect National Route 4 between Cay Lay and My Tho.

In January 1974, intelligence information became available to Maj. Gen. Nguyen Vinh Nghi, commanding IV Corps and MR 4, indicating that elements of the NVA 5th Division were being ordered to Dinh Tuong Province from Tay Ninh. Later in the month, advance elements of the division were detected in the division's Svay Rieng base.

Two NVA soldiers captured on 27 January told their interrogators that a battalion of the division's 6th Regiment had been sent south to reinforce the understrength NVA Z-18 Regiment in the Tri Phap area. Their testimony, along with that of four recent ralliers and captured documents, also indicated that the Dong Thap 1 Regiment, which traditionally operated in Dinh Tuong, was still badly understrength, though it had recently received 300 NVA replacements following its December 1973 battles, and would also probably receive more replacements from the 6th Regiment, 5th NVA Division. The interrogators also learned that the Z-15 Regiment had just received about 200 replacements from the North but that it was short weapons and ammunition.

Meanwhile, RVNAF outposts, patrols, and air observers detected enemy transportation elements moving past Tuyen Binh on infiltration Route 1A. Some of these were intercepted, and the ARVN captured large quantities of rice and ammunition, as well as an NVA transportation company commander.

Time became important. If the 5th were allowed to occupy the Tri Phap, it would be extremely difficult to dig out, and the threat to Route 4 would become intolerable. The previous year's experience had shown General Nghi that his troops were capable of driving into and probably clearing the Tri Phap of the NVA elements, particularly if he moved fast while the NVA regiments were still reforming and receiving replacements. If he could establish a base of operations at Tri Phap, he could deny a vital logistical complex to the 5th NVA Division, one that it would require for operations in Dinh Tuong.

On 12 February, the 12th Infantry Regiment of the 7th ARVN Division, reinforced with two battalions of the 10th Infantry and two troops of armored cavalry in personnel carriers, attacked through Tri Phap from the east and advanced to the Kien Phong-Dien Tuong Province boundary. Three days later, the 14th Infantry Regiment, 9th ARVN Division, reinforced with one battalion of the 16th Infantry and two troops of armored cavalry, attacked east from My An District town and linked up with the 12th Infantry on the western edge of the Tri Phap. This two-pronged attack was followed on the 19th by an attack by the 10th Infantry Regiment, minus the two battalions attached to the 12th, from Hau My village in northern Cai Be District, north to clear the southern edge of the Tri Phap. Completely enveloped, the enemy in the Tri Phap suffered heavy losses in men, supplies, ammunition, and food. Elements of the Z-15 and Z-18 were identified in the battle, but most NVA casualties were among rear service troops. Another element of the 5th NVA Division, the 6th Battalion, 174th Infantry, was also identified in the heavy fighting around My An on the western edge of the Tri Phap, indicating that earlier intelligence concerning probable deployment of elements of the 5th from Tay Ninh was valid. Enemy casualties were heavy that first week of the Tri Phap campaign; over 500 were killed, and the ARVN captured tons of ammunition and nearly 200 weapons. ARVN casualties were light in comparison.

Fighting flared through most of Kien Tuong and Dinh Tuong Provinces for the rest of February and until the last week of March. The center of action remained in the Tri Phap where the NVA again reinforced, this time with the Dong Thap 1 Regiment which was sent north to join the Z-18. The ARVN kept up the pressure, and in successive weeks killed another 250 enemy, capturing as many weapons. Meanwhile, COSVN directed NVA Military Region 3 (the southern delta command) to launch widespread attacks to take the pressure off Kien Tuong and Dinh Tuong. Replacements, up to 3,000 according to two ARVN soldiers who escaped from captivity in Cambodia, were being readied for assignment to units in Svay Rieng Province.

Unable to counter RVNAF advances on the battlefields, the NVA resorted to an increased terror campaign throughout the delta. On 9 March they fired one 82-mm. mortar shell into the primary school yard at Cai Lay while the children were lined up waiting to enter their classes. Twenty-three children died instantly; 46 others were badly wounded. Far to the south, in Bac Lieu, terrorists tossed a grenade into a religious service killing 9 and wounding 16.

ARVN operations on the My An front, that is, on the western edge of the Tri Phap area, were being supported out of Cao Lanh, with supplies coming up from Giao Duc on interprovincial Route 30. The forces on the eastern edge of the Tri Phap and those fighting north around Moc Hoa were being supported along Interprovincial Route 29 (LTL-29) out of Cai Lay. The ARVN successfully countered NVA attempts to cut these two routes.

The first phase of the Tri Phap campaign slowly wound down during the last part of March. The Dong Thap 1 Regiment picked up 150 replacements, freshly arrived from North Vietnam, and NVA Military Region 2, whose regiments were being so badly abused in the Tri Phap fighting, received 200 replacements who had been previously destined for Military Region 3. Reinforcing success in the last week of March, General Nghi sent the 7th Ranger Group against the NVA Dong Thap 1 Regiment in the Tri Phap, where the Rangers killed over 30 and captured more weapons.

By the end of March, more than 1100 enemy had been killed in the Tri Phap campaign, while the ARVN had about 700 wounded but fewer than 100 killed. Nearly 5,000 tons of rice and paddy were captured, along with over 600 weapons, 8 tons of ammunition, and a large haul of weapon accessories, radios, and other military equipment. Three NVA regiments, the Z-15, Z-18 and Dong Thap 1, had been severely mauled, and the Tri Phap base area was denied to the 5th NVA Division.

Work began immediately on the construction of fortified positions in the Tri Phap, enough to provide for posting an ARVN regiment there. The NVA Z-15 Regiment, meanwhile, was recuperating in southwestern Dinh Tuong Province, attacking ARVN outposts and preparing to return to the Tri Phap. On 26 April two NVA battalions attacked the RF battalion base at the village of Tri Phap. In a complementary attack farther south on the Kien Phong-Dinh Tuong Province boundary, the Dong Thap 1 Regiment struck an RF outpost. Although temporarily successful, the enemy soon faced ARVN's 14th Regiment and a troop of the 2d Armored Cavalry and was routed with heavy casualties. Meanwhile, the 11th Infantry counterattacked in the Tri Phap and restored the lost position. The ARVN, by the first week in May, was therefore in firm control in the Tri Phap, with four RF battalions holding strong positions there. NVA forces in the area were weakened and demoralized, but elsewhere in the delta they kept up their campaign of terror as the slow deterioration of local security continued. Although abductions and assassinations were predominant, the enemy attacked another school. On 4 May, eight rounds of 82-mm. mortar fell on the school at Song Phu, in Vinh Long Province. Six children were killed and 28 wounded.

Elephant's Foot and Angel's Wing

A glance at the map of the Svay Rieng salient shows two minor prominences whose names described their shapes. On the southwest side was the so-called Elephant's Foot, appearing on the verge of crushing Moc Hoa, the capital of Kien Tuong Province. Against the underside of the elephant's leg was the Vietnamese village of Long Khot, less than 1,000 meters from the Svay Rieng border. As the

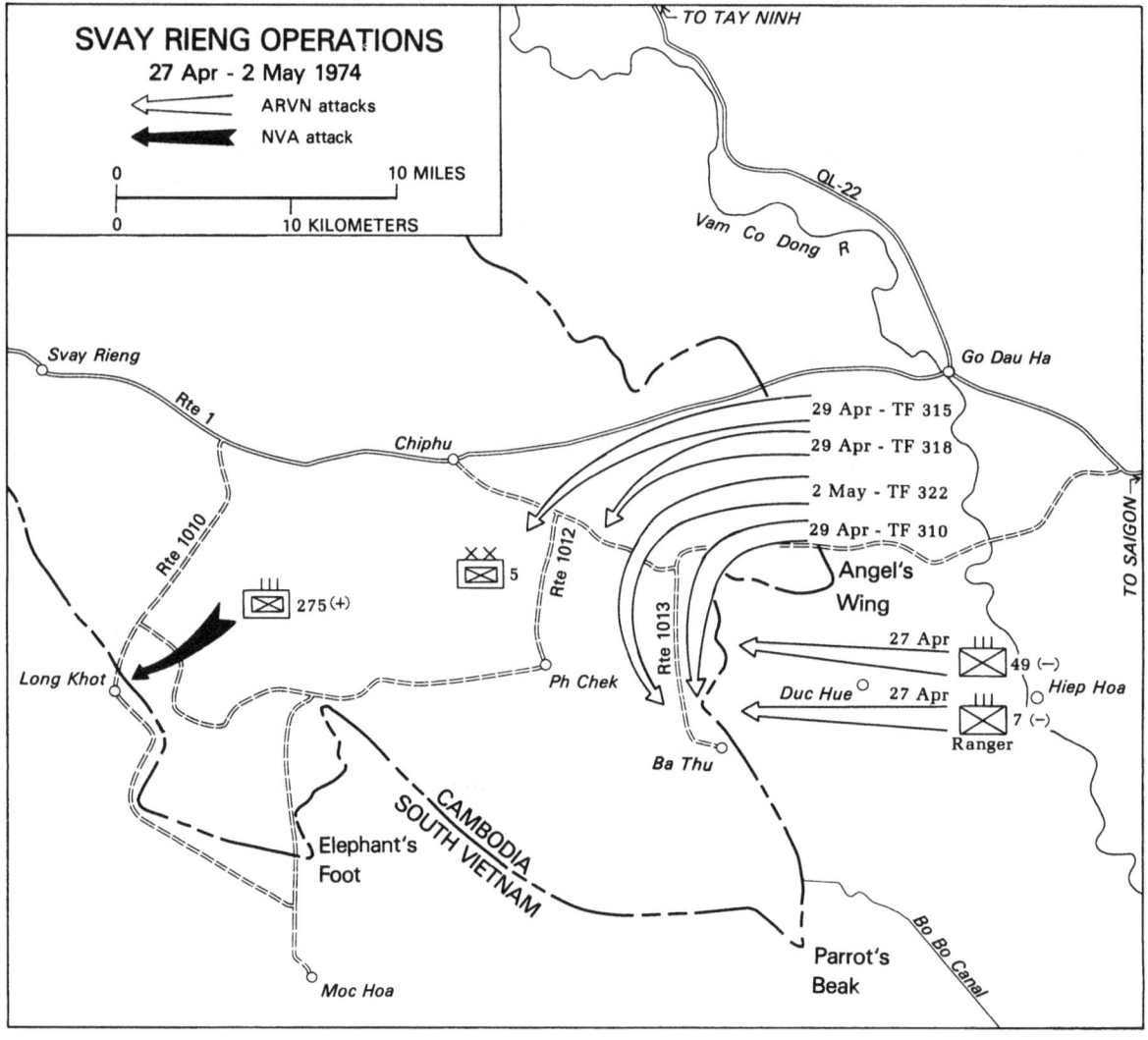

Map 13

RVNAF vigorously pursued the Tri Phap campaign, the NVA increased pressure against RVNAF defenses around the Elephant's Foot.

Opposite the Elephant's Foot, bordering the Vietnamese provinces of Tay Ninh and Hau Nghia, what was known as the Angel's Wing spread toward Go Dau Ha, the port on the Song Vam Co Dong through which passed the main highway between Tay Ninh and Saigon. The southern tip of the Angel's Wing dipped toward an ARVN fire-base at Duc Hue, and the Svay Rieng border only five kilometers away nearly enveloped this exposed position. The Angel's Wing and Duc Hue became the focus of heavy action in the spring and early summer of 1974 as the RVNAF sought to reduce the threat to the Saigon-Tay Ninh line of communication and inflict damage on the NVA 5th Division as it concentrated in southern Svay Rieng. (Map 13)

The NVA 5th Infantry Division was perhaps the most versatile of all Communist divisions; at least it was called upon to perform missions of extreme diversity. In the Nguyen Hue offensive of 1972, it participated in the Binh Long campaign, and after suffering heavy casualties in the jungles and plantations around An Loc, invaded the paddies and swamps of the Mekong Delta. Forced to withdraw, it sent elements to relieve the battered NVA forces in the forests of Quang Duc. In early 1974, it pulled these units back to bases in Tay Ninh and dispatched some battalions again to the delta to try to save disintegrating defenses in the Tri Phap. This mission failed in the face of powerful ARVN attacks, and COSVN ordered the division to assemble forces in southern Svay Rieng. From here, generally centered on Chi Phu, it could direct forces against southern Tay Ninh, Hau Nghia, and Kien Tuong. In early February an advance element of division headquarters began moving toward the Angel's Wing from Tay Ninh, and by mid-March it was established there east of Chi Phu.

Although units of the 6th and 174th Regiments of the 5th Division had fought in the Tri Phap battle, other battalions of these two regiments were in the Angel's Wing along with divisional artillery. South of Duc Hue, the K-7 Sapper Battalion of Long An was ready to strike. On 27 March at 0300 the attack began on the RVNAF base at Duc Hue. Defending against two battalions of the NVA 6th Regiment was the ARVN 83d Ranger Battalion. Across the border in Cambodia NVA 105-mm. artillery fired at the defenders while recoilless rifles and heavy mortars (120-mm.) bombarded the garrison from closer ranges. Although 30 ARVN Rangers died, the NVA infantry assault failed to break the position; the two battalions of the 6th NVA Regiment were forced to wihdraw, leaving 95 dead on the battlefield, together with a large number of weapons.

Under orders to maintain a loose siege of the Duc Hue post, the NVA, assisted by the local sapper battalion, blocked the only land access to the camp and continued the artillery bombardment but abandoned the idea of taking it by storm. On the ARVN side, the 25th Division committed a task force consisting of a battalion of the 46th Infantry, a battalion of the 50th Infantry, and a tank company to break the siege. Fighting raged in the paddies east and north of the camp for several days, and the VNAF provided effective support to the counterattacking infantry, losing an A-1 fighter-bomber and an observation aircraft to SA-7 fire. Meanwhile, the ARVN task force command post was hit by NVA 107-mm. rocket fire and the commander was one of those killed.

As April wore on, the threat of renewed assaults on Duc Hue by the NVA 5th Division remained. The situation was particularly dangerous because the 7th and 9th NVA Divisions were probing aggressively in the eastern part of Military Region 3. Lt. Gen. Pham Quoc Thuan, III Corps Commander, determined that he must reduce the threat to his western flank and the Tay Ninh corridor while he had the opportunity to do so. And if anything was to be done, it would have to be done soon to beat the onset of the southwest monsoon. After the rains started, most of the land around Duc Hue and the Angel's Wing would be under water.

The plan was complicated but workable. General Thuan used 18 of his own maneuver battalions and flew to Can Tho where he coordinated with General Nghi for a supporting attack by 2 IV Corps battalions from the Moc Hoa sector.

The details and timing of the operation were carefully safeguarded, and few, if any, Americans in the U.S. Mission knew anything about it until 27 April when 45 sorties struck targets in Cambodia and known and suspected bases of the 5th NVA Division. These strikes began Phase I, which lasted through the 28th and included infantry sweeps by two RF battalions between the Song Vam Co Dong and the northern shoulder of the Angel's Wing. Meanwhile, the 49th Infantry Regiment, less one battalion, and the 7th Ranger Group, also short one battalion, left assembly areas near Hiep Hoa on the Song Vam Co Dong and advanced westward through the swamplands, past Duc Hue to the Cambodian frontier. To the south, three RF battalions provided security by conducting reconnaissance in northern Long An Province, generally between the Bo Bo Canal and the Song Vam Co Dong.

Another supporting maneuver, which quickly developed into a major operation, was the attack into Svay Rieng Province south of the Elephant's Foot by two battalions from MR 4. The northernmost of the two advanced from the border area north of Moc Hoa and established a blocking position near the local route 1012 that led eastward from an assembly area occupied by the 5th NVA Division. The other battalion crossed midway between the Elephant's Foot and the tip of the Parrot's Beak and established a lodgment on the southeastern edge of the enemy's logistical base and assembly area in Svay Rieng.

While Phase I of the ARVN sweep into Svay Rieng was getting started, the NVA on 28 April struck heavily at Long Khot, an ARVN post and district town at the inside curve of the Elephant's Foot. Whether the attack was pre-planned or reactive was unknown. Regardless, enemy tanks were reported at first by the defenders. Later, aerial observers correctly determined that the vehicles were captured M-113 armored personnel carriers. The defenders held strongly against the NVA's 275th Regiment and 25th Sapper Battalion of the 5th NVA Division. More than 100 sorties were flown on the 28th against NVA positions, weapons, and vehicles in the Svay Rieng area, many of them in support of Long Khot. On this same day, the ARVN at Long Khot captured nine prisoners from the NVA 275th Regiment and four from its supporting artillery, which had been employing 122-mm. guns and U.S. 105-mm. howitzers, as well as AT-3 antitank missiles and SA-7 antiaircraft missiles. Many enemy weapons were salvaged, and 75 enemy soldiers were counted dead on the battlefield.

Not only were the Long Khot defenders tenacious and prepared for the onslaught, but the VNAF proved its worth in close support as over the two days, the 27th and 28th, it flew 188 tactical and logistical sorties in the Svay Rieng Campaign. In a departure from normal practice, the 3d Air Division supporting III Corps in the Svay Rieng campaign, located a forward command post at Cu Chi alongside the III Corps forward command post in order to improve coordination and responsiveness. Combat pilots returned to their bases with encouraging, morale-building reports about enemy troops throwing down their weapons and running when faced with low-level strafing.

By the night of 28 April, 11 ARVN battalions of infantry, RF, and Rangers were conducting screening, blocking, and reconnaissance-in-force operations as a prelude to Phase II of the Svay Rieng sweep. Meanwhile, the VNAF was assaulting enemy troop locations and bases, and Long Khot was fighting off a violent NVA armor, artillery, and sapper-infantry attack.

In Phase II, originally planned by General Thuan to encompass only three days of armored sweeps into the Cambodian bases of the NVA 5th Division, three columns drove west, generally parallel to each other, crossing the frontier west of Go Dau Ha and penetrating as deeply as 15 kilometers into Svay Rieng before wheeling south and southwest into Hau Nghia Province. Making the main effort and the deepest penetration was Task Force 315 with the 15th Armored Cavalry Squadron, the 64th Ranger Battalion, and a company of medium tanks as its striking force. Supported by a composite battery of 105-mm. and 155-mm. artillery this northernmost column crossed the border through the paddies south of Highway 1 and attacked west, turning south short of the swampy ground east of Chiphu, following local route 1012 toward the blocking position held by a IV Corps battalion near Ph Chek. It was screened on its right flank by a mobile RF battalion that advanced along Highway 1 about 12 kilometers inside the international frontier.

Along the center axis, which started about 2,000 meters south of Task Force 315, was Task Force 318, built around the 18th Armored Cavalry Squadron, a Ranger battalion, a tank company, and a howitzer battery. This column drove west for about 10 kilometers before turning inside the sweep south by Task Force 315.

Task Force 310, the only one of the attacking columns without tanks, had a battalion each from the 18th and 25th Infantry Divisions and the 3d Troop, 10th Armored Cavalry. Along with a supporting howitzer battalion it crossed into Svay Rieng just north of the southern tip of the Angel's Wing, along Cambodian Route 1013, and wheeled south inside Task Force 318, generally along the international boundary.

In reserve at Go Dau Ha General Thuan had two companies of medium tanks of the 22d Tank Battalion, a cavalry troop from the 1st Armored Cavalry Squadron, a battalion of infantry from the 18th Division, and a battery of 105-mm. howitzers. Designated Task Force 322, this powerful force was ready to exploit opportunities uncovered by the attacking echelons.

The 3d Armored Brigade controlled operations from Go Dau Ha. Fifty-four UH-1 helicopters mustered for the campaign were effectively used in surprise air assaults into enemy defenses. Secrecy was more rigidly enforced in this campaign than perhaps any operation since the cease-fire, partly because it was important to surprise the 5th NVA Division in garrison, and partly to conceal, for political reasons, an ARVN offensive into Cambodia.

By 29 April, Task Force 315 had penetrated about seven kilometers into Cambodia and, at the cost of only one wounded, had killed nearly 50 enemy and captured one prisoner. To the south, Task Force 318 had experienced similar success, killing nearly 60 and capturing 5 while suffering only 6 wounded. The following morning, the 315th continued the attack, killing 40 more and sustaining light casualties. Meanwhile, the VNAF was pounding the enemy with nearly 200 sorties, accounting for nearly 100 killed, destroying many storage and defensive positions, and knocking out mortar and antiaircraft positions.

As the threat to the 5th NVA Division base in southern Svay Rieng became critical, the NVA was compelled to reduce the pressure at Long Khot and concentrate on attempting to relieve the E-6 and 174th Regiments and logistical installations lying in the path of the ARVN armored thrusts. By the end of April, nearly 300 NVA soldiers had fallen in ground combat, over 100 more had been killed by VNAF air strikes, and 17 prisoners of war were in ARVN hands. On the other hand, the speed, audacity and superior air-ground coordination that characterized the RVNAF attack had kept friendly casualties extremely low: only 21 killed and 64 wounded. In fact, success was so striking that General Thuan elected to extend the operation a few days.

Westward, over in the Elephant's Foot, matters were becoming desperate for the 275th NVA Regiment and its supporting troops. The 7th ARVN Division had moved a forward command post into Moc Hoa and was controlling the operation of two task forces then committed in the Elephant's Foot. One was composed of the 15th Infantry, 9th ARVN Division, and part of the 16th Armored Cavalry Squadron; the other included the 10th Infantry and elements of the 6th Armored Cavalry Squadron. In 12 days of fighting in the border area, these two mobile task forces killed 850 NVA soldiers, captured 31, collected over 100 weapons, and suffered fewer than 300 casualties, including 39 killed.

Making the adjustments required by the situation, particularly the fact that the most lucrative enemy contacts were being made in the southern sweeps of the 318th and 310th Task Forces, General Thuan ordered Task Force 315 withdrawn from its northern axis on 2 May and returned to Go Dau Ha where it reverted to reserve. Meanwhile, Task Force 322 was committed and advanced about four kilometers into the center of the Angel's Wing, and the infantry battalions of the 25th ARVN Division continued their sweep between Duc Hue and Go Dau Ha. By 6 May the land route to Duc Hue Camp was secured and was being improved by ARVN combat engineers, the threat to the vital road junction at Go Dau Ha was substantially reduced, and the ARVN was in complete control of the battlefield. The tank-heavy 322d Task Force turned south and headed for Ba Thu, the long-held NVA base on the border southwest of Duc Hue. On 10 May, the offensive ended, the last ARVN forces began their march homeward. Their sortie had killed nearly 300 NVA soldiers, captured 17, collected 100 weapons, and seriously disrupted the communications and logistics of the 5th NVA Division.

But this was the last major South Vietnamese offensive. The severe constraints on ammunition expenditures, fuel usage, and flying hours permitted no new initiatives. Although the RVNAF could react strongly to local threats within supporting distances of major bases, outlying threats were beyond their capability to cope with. For South Vietnam, a decline had begun to develop early in 1974 and would prove irreversible.

Note on Sources

The DAO Monthly Intelligence Summary and Threat Analyses for the period October 1973 to February 1974 were used as the basis for the first part of this chapter, also Senior General Van Tien Dung's account of the final offensive.

Operational data on the Tri Phap and Cambodian battles came from DAO Saigon fact sheets, reports, and weekly intelligence summaries, as well as from J2/JGS weekly summaries. Gaps in the information were filled in by reference to the author's notes and to reports from offices of the U.S. Embassy, Saigon.

10

Strategic Raids

We have seen how the vigorous RVNAF attack into the Tri Phap in February had thwarted the NVA attempt to sever Saigon from the delta at My Tho and had prevented the NVA 5th Division from establishing a base from which to extend its operations southward into Dinh Tuong, and westward toward Saigon through Long An. Denied this approach, the 5th NVA had concentrated between the Elephant's Foot and the Angel's Wing in Cambodia, threatening the district headquarters at Moc Hoa, but, more seriously, preparing to occupy the narrow strip of marshland between the Svay Rieng border and the Vam Co Dong River, the last real barrier between the Cambodian border and Saigon, only 30 miles away. NVA success would have strangled Tay Ninh Province, since the seizure of Go Dau Ha would end all land and water communications between Saigon and the province capital. The RVNAF had dealt with this threat by the daring armored thrust into Cambodia beginning in late April. Suffering severely, the NVA 5th Division was never again to seriously threaten the South Vietnamese in this sector.

But in spite of these encouraging operations, the North Vietnamese were pressing ahead with what they called their strategic raids campaign against the crucial defensive perimeter of bases north of Saigon. The first to fall was the relatively unimportant outpost of Chi Linh.

Chi Linh

In defense of Saigon, the 5th ARVN Division had its main base at Lai Khe, about 25 miles due north of the capital. This base, in fact, was the last strongly held position with an uninterrupted connection to Saigon. A few miles north, the 5th Division maintained a series of strongpoints, generally in the vicinity of the deserted hamlet of Bau Bang. North of Bau Bang, National Route 13 passed through dense jungle and was blocked by NVA units, usually the 9th NVA Division, the 7th NVA Division, or independent regiments of COSVN. The ARVN maintained a major garrison and artillery firebase at Chon Thanh, near the junction of National Route 13 (QL-13), which continued north to An Loc, and Local Route 13 (LTL-13), curving northeast to the ARVN base at Don Luan, about 25 miles away. About halfway to Don Luan, where Local Route 13 crossed the Song Be, the RVNAF had a small firebase called Chi Linh, manned by the 215th Regional Force Company with a platoon of two 105-mm. howitzers. (Map 14)

The 7th NVA Division attacked Chi Linh in the first week of April, quickly damaging the two howitzers and destroying the ammunition dump. On 5 April the 3d Battalion, 141st Regiment, with the division's 28th Sapper and 22d Artillery Battalion supporting, overran the base. By the 10th, about half of the defenders and 20 dependents had straggled into Don Luan or Chon Thanh. The rest, about 50 men, remained unaccounted for.

With the elimination of Chi Linh, the 7th NVA division enjoyed unimpeded movement along Local Route 13 between Chon Thanh and Don Luan, from north to south along the Song Be corridor, and had reduced the effectiveness of the defenses of Don Luan and Chon Thanh.

Tong Le Chon

Situated alongside the Saigon River on the Tay Ninh-Binh Long border, Tong Le Chon had been under siege since the cease-fire. By March 1974, the situation was becoming desperate for the defending 92d Ranger Battalion. Seriously wounded soldiers could be neither treated nor evacuated. Resupply was by parachute drop only. Morale in the camp was deteriorating under the strain of isolation and constant heavy bombardment. The cost of the continued defense of Tong Le Chon, as a symbol of gallantry, was exceeding its real worth. The human suffering was incalculable, but the expense in flying hours, ammunition, and other logistical support was great. As scarce resources became even more scarce, it was clearly time to reassess priorities and determine how best to end this intolerable situation.

As of 15 March, about 255 officers and men of the 92d were still alive in Tong Le Chon, and five of these were critically wounded. On 20 March Lt. Gen. Pham Quoc Thuan proposed to the Chief of the Joint General Staff, General Cao Van Vien, that one of three methods be selected to relieve the 92d Battalion. First, a division-sized operation could be launched from An Loc to secure a corridor through which the 92d could be withdrawn, replaced, or reinforced. Second, the commander of the NVA siege forces could be enjoined to permit the orderly and safe withdrawal of the 92d, surrendering the

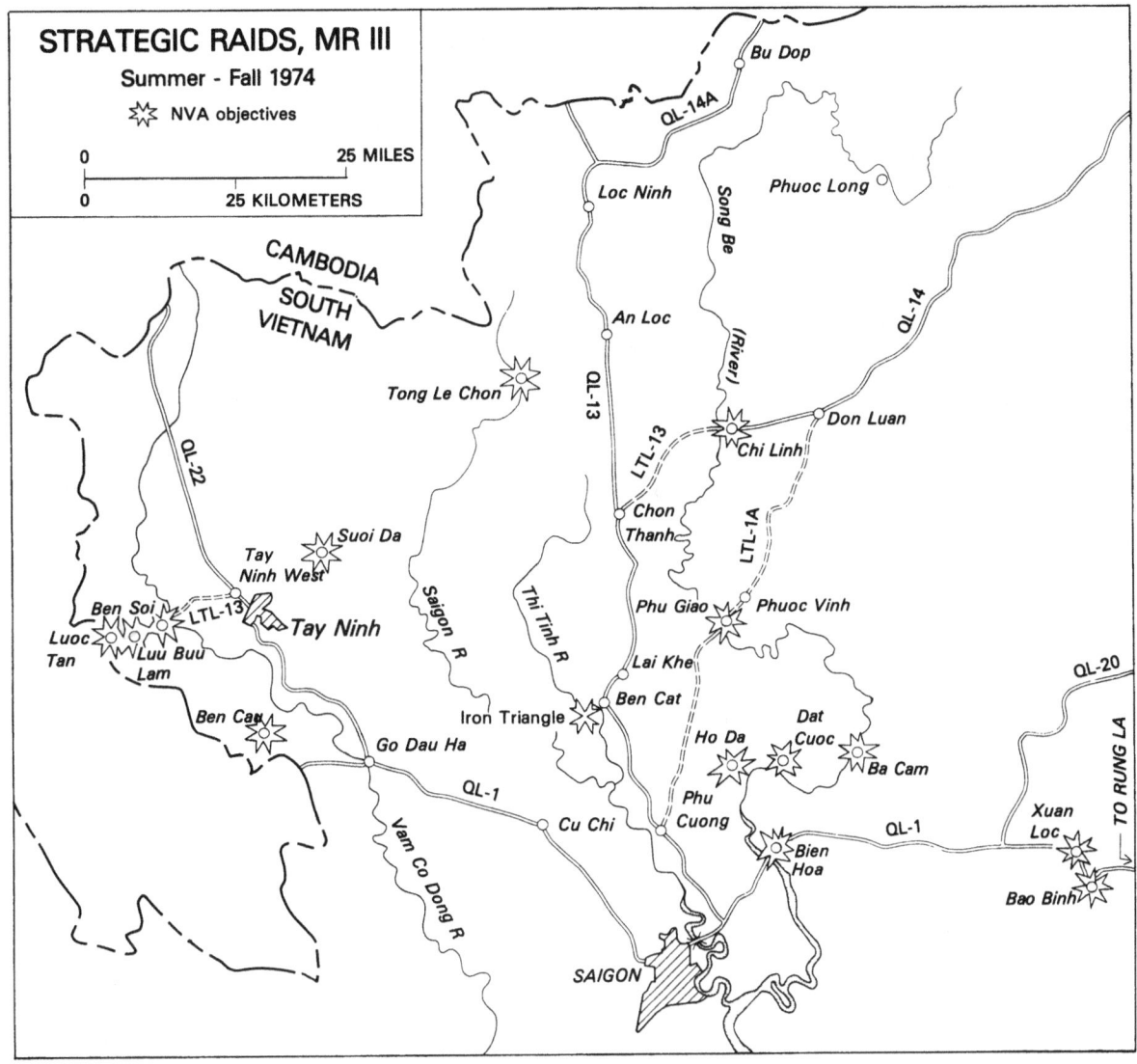

Map 14

camp to the enemy. Third, the 92d Battalion commander could be ordered to plan and execute a withdrawal—by exfiltrating in small groups—bringing out all his men, including the sick and wounded.

General Thuan realized at the outset that only the third plan was even remotely feasible, as General Vien and his staff no doubt understood. How could an ARVN division be expected to punch through from An Loc to Tong Le Chon when repeated efforts to attack even a few miles north of Lai Khe had failed? How could a division be assembled when the road to An Loc was held by the NVA, and even if this obstacle could be overcome, where would a division be found for the mission? The inescapable fact was that all ARVN divisions were heavily committed coping with other threats.

The second option was equally unrealistic, if for different reasons. There could be no "surrender." The political repercussions would be unmanageable for President Thieu, and the precedent could portend future such capitulations, some possibly with less than adequate justification.

Only the third option had any merit, but the decision could not be made at the JGS or at III Corps Headquarters. Matters of this import, even though essentially tactical, had to be settled at the presidential palace.

Meanwhile, as the problem was being studied, the situation at Tong Le Chon was becoming critical. The intensity of the enemy's artillery and mortar attacks increased greatly in the week of 17-24 March. In the Two-Party Joint Military Commission meetings in Saigon, South Vietnam's representative warned the Provisional Revolutionary Government that if the attacks on Tong Le Chon did not cease, the VNAF would launch devastating attacks against enemy bases in Tay Ninh and Binh Long. In fact, the VNAF did fly 30 or more sorties around Lo Go in Tay Ninh and around Tong Le Chon on the 23d. But the NVA bombardments continued. NVA artillery used against Tong Le Chon between 22 and 24 March included 122-mm. rockets, 122-mm. howitzers, 120-mm. mortars, and nearly 1,000 rounds from 82-mm. and 60-mm. mortars. Many of the bunkers and fighting positions were badly damaged. Enemy sappers attempted to break through the defensive wire on the night of 21 and 22 March but were driven off. On the 21st, the commander of the 92d Battalion, Lt. Col. Le Van Ngon (who had been promoted ahead of schedule in recognition of his courageous leadership at Tong Le Chon), sent a message to Colonel Nguyen Thanh Chuan, commander of the 3d Ranger Command at An Loc. Colonel Ngon said, in effect, get us some support or destroy this camp. He asked for more air strikes, although it was already apparent that the VNAF could not materially change the situation. He asked for a ground relief column, but he probably knew as well as did Colonel Chuan that this could not succeed. In emotional desperation, he asked for air strikes on his own camp as the only feasible alternative to surrender, which he said he and his men would never do.

Colonel Chuan relayed this urgent message to General Thuan. General Thuan replied that he had received no response from the JGS to his earlier proposals for evacuation or relief. By this time, the survivors at Tong Le Chon included 254 Rangers, 4 artillerymen, 7 stranded helicopter crewmen, and 12 field laborers. Of this force, 10 were seriously wounded and 40 slightly wounded. Sappers on the nights of the 24, 25, and 26 March penetrated three of seven rings of barbed wire before being forced to withdraw.

The unrelenting bombardment and repeated sapper attacks continued through the month and into April. Still no initiatives or decisions emanated from the presidential palace, III Corps, or 3d Ranger Command to ameliorate the suffering or offer hope to the defenders of Tong Le Chon. While nearly 1,000 rounds of mortar and artillery fire were falling on the base the night of 11 April, Headquarters, III Corps, received a final request from Colonel Ngon: give us authority to abandon the camp. Whether General Thuan conferred with General Vien or President Thieu is not known, but at 2330 that night he ordered Colonel Ngon to defend at all costs.

Shortly after midnight, the defenders of Tong Le Chon reported that sensitive papers were being burned. Later they requested that VNAF stop dropping flares over the camp because they were moving out. Radio contact with the Rangers was broken until 0900 on 12 April, when a radio operator outside the camp responded to a call. By that time the march to An Loc, some 10 miles northeast through the jungle and enemy lines, had started. The ranks of the wounded had swollen by 14 during the night's action, and 35 more were wounded during the withdrawal. All wounded were brought out; those who could not walk were carried. In the firefights during the withdrawal four more Rangers were killed, but even these bodies were carried on to An Loc.

It was a remarkable feat of courage and leadership to bring a group of 277 men, many of whom were wounded, out of an encircled position, and arrive inside friendly lines with 268. In fact, the outstanding success of the operation led many observers, Vietnamese and Americans alike, to suspect that the enemy had somehow collaborated in the withdrawal. Although possible, this is quite unlikely. Not only would the arrangement have had to be approved at a high echelon, but also the North Vietnamese would certainly have exploited the propaganda value of such an event. Furthermore, an eyewitness report on the NVA occupation of the camp strongly refuted such speculation.

According to a NVA participant, following an intensive artillery preparation, a ground attack of infantry and tanks had forced the Rangers to give up the position, but the defenses were so heavily mined that the NVA was unable to get through the barriers until the 13th. The Communists found that all equipment had been destroyed or removed and all wounded had been carried out. Only two Ranger bodies were found, and only one ARVN Ranger was captured. This NVA soldier ended his report with the comment that the attacking NVA infantry had been ordered to block the withdrawal but had disobeyed the order for fear of the RVNAF air and artillery fire, and that the discipline displayed by the ARVN 92d Ranger Battalion was extremely high, much higher than that found in NVA or VC main forces.

Although the record was clear that Colonel Ngon had disobeyed orders by withdrawing, he was not punished, but the battalion was dissolved and its men sequestered from the press. The official South Vietnamese position was that the camp had been overrun in clear violation of the cease-fire, and appropriate protests were made to the ICCS and the Two-Party Joint Military Commission. On 13 April, VNAF flew 19 sorties against what remained of the camp. The last of the survivors entered the An Loc perimeter on 15 April. The 92d ARVN Ranger Battalion had clearly distinguished itself by enduring the longest siege of the war and by conducting a remarkable withdrawal under fire.

With Tong Le Chon obliterated, the NVA had unrestricted use of its important east-west line of communication between Tay Ninh and Binh Long and controlled the Saigon River corridor from its source to Dau Tieng.

Binh Duong

In Binh Duong, the NVA's strategic raids campaign began on 16 May with a coordinated attack by the 7th and 9th NVA Divisions on Phu Giao and Ben Cat. ARVN 25th Division operations in Hau Nghia, Tay Ninh, and Cambodia had, by 10 May, significantly diminished the threat of the NVA 5th Infantry Division to the western approaches to Saigon, but the NVA 7th and 9th Divisions, in the jungles and plantations north of the capital, were in fair fighting form. Replacements had been received, trained, and integrated into the force; supplies had been stockpiled and moved into forward positions; and the divisions had received their orders.

The 7th NVA Division forces that had taken Chi Linh were still responsible for the zone of operations generally on the east side of National Route 13 (QL-13). Their main objective in the imminent campaign was the bridge at Phu Giao, where interprovincial Route 1A (LTL-1A) spanned the Song Be. Their capture of this bridge, and its controlling terrain, would isolate the 5th ARVN Division's regimental base at Phuoc Vinh and provide the forward positions needed for subsequent attacks toward Phu Cuong, the Bing Duong provincial capital, and Bien Hoa with its huge air base and logistical concentrations.

The 9th NVA Division was west of National Route 13, concentrating in the old secret zone, the Long Nguyen, north of the famous Iron Triangle. From here its artillery regularly bombarded the ARVN 5th Division base at Lai Khe, but its objectives in this May campaign were farther south. It would strike into the Iron Triangle, try to sever National Route 13 at the district seat of Ben Cat, and open the Saigon River corridor nearly as far south as Phu Hoa. By accomplishing this latter objective, it could position artillery to reach Tan Son Nhut Air Base and support operations against the ARVN 25th Division at Cu Chi. By cutting National Route 13 at Ben Cat, it would isolate the ARVN base at Lai Khe and, in coordination with the 7th NVA Division, threaten Phu Cuong and eventually Saigon.

A glance at the map shows the strategic location of the Iron Triangle. Bounded on the north by the jungle and overgrown rubber planations of the Long Nguyen, it was enclosed on the west by the Saigon River and on the east by the smaller but unfordable obstacle of the Thi Thinh River. The Thi Thinh joined the Saigon River near Phu Hoa, at the southern apex of the Triangle, 7 miles from Phu Cuong. Phu Cuong itself, the capital of Binh Duong Province, was an important industrial and farming center and contained the ARVN Engineer School. It was linked by a major highway with the large ARVN base at Phu Loi (called Lam Son) and, farther east, with Bien Hoa. Lying as it did in the center of the Saigon River corridor, at the junction of Routes 13 and 1A, and only 10 miles from the outskirts of Saigon, Phu Cuong was vital to the defense of Saigon.

The terrain within the Iron Triangle was flat, almost featureless, and covered by dense brush and undergrowth. The clearings, especially in the northern part, were thick with elephant grass, higher than a man's head. The surface was scarred by countless bomb and shell craters so that vehicular movement off the narrow, rough dirt roads was nearly impossible. Even tracked vehicles had difficulty. A vast network of tunnels and trenches, most of them caved-in and abandoned, laced this ground that had been the scene of battles since the early days of the second Indochina war.

A weak string of three ARVN outposts protected the northern edge of the Triangle, from Rach Bap on the west, close by the Saigon River, along local Route 7 (TL-7B) to An Dien on the Thi Thinh River opposite Ben Cat. Each of these outposts, including Base 82, which was midway between Rach Bap and An Dien, was manned by a company of the 321st RF Battalion. Another country road passed by the Rach Bap outpost: local Route 14 (LTL-14) which generally paralleled the Saigon River from Tri Tam, through Rach Bap, and veered to the southeast through the Triangle, crossing the Thi Thinh River before it joined Highway 13 (QL-13) north of Phu Cuong. The NVA had blown the bridge on Route 14 over the Thi Thinh a few weeks earlier, but the stream could be spanned by pontoon sections. About midway between Rach Bap and the Thi Thinh crossing of Route 14, the ARVN had another small firebase. (Map 15)

Frequent sweeps and some semi-fixed defensive positions north of Cu Chi manned by the ARVN 25th Division and Hau Nghia Regional Forces screened the western flank of the Triangle, but enemy resistance in the Ho Bo woods, opposite Rach Bap, and the formidable obstacle of the Saigon River, as well as a lack of resources, limited the influence that the 25th could exert on the situation within the Triangle.

The ARVN was strong with infantry, armor, and mutually supporting fire bases and outposts in Ben Cat District east of the Thi Thinh boundary of the Triangle, but only one bridge, a weak span, connected the district town and the Triangle hamlet of An Dien.

Such was the situation on the eve of the initiation of the strategic raids campaign in western Binh Duong Province. As mentioned earlier, this was a coordinated attack, with the 9th NVA Division conducting the main effort in the west, while the 7th NVA attacked in the east against ARVN posi-

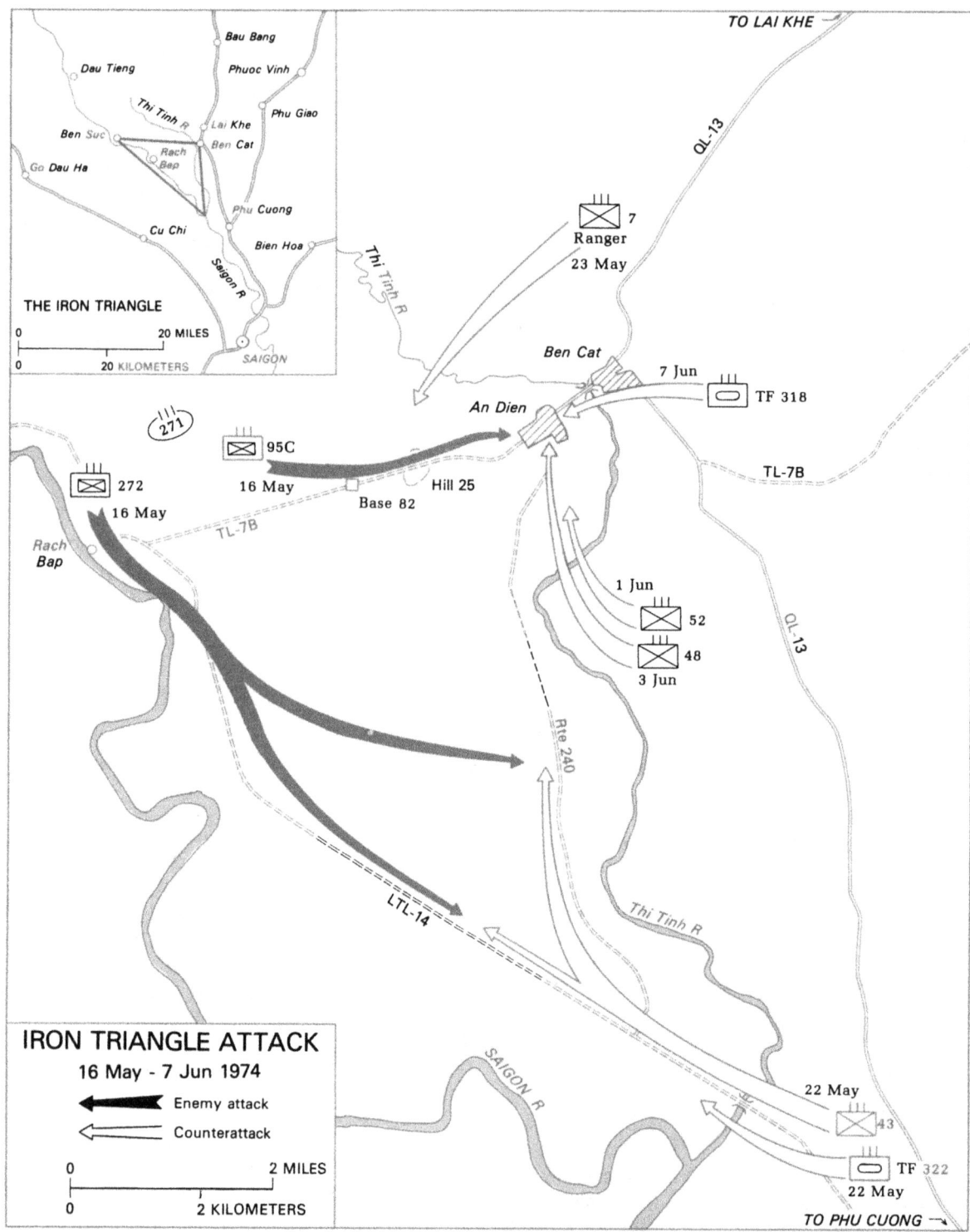

Map 15

tions along Highway 1A near Phu Giao. The distances between the two thrusts were too great, however, to provide for mutual support, and the ARVN III Corps was able to deal with them as separate operations. For these reasons, although they occurred simultaneously and demanded the concurrent attention of the III Corps commander and his staff, they can best be described sequentially, beginning first with the Iron Triangle attack of the 9th NVA Division.

The Iron Triangle Attack

The attack began with heavy artillery, rocket, and mortar concentrations falling on Rach Bap, Base 82, and An Dien on the morning of 16 May. The RF company at Base 82 abandoned its bunkers, many of which had collapsed under the weight of the bombardment, late that afternoon. Rach Bap held out until about 0300 the following morning, its surviving defenders withdrawing in the direction of An Dien. The fighting was fierce in An Dien on the 16th, but by the night of 17 May, NVA forces held the flattened village and its defenses. Remnants of an RF battalion, however, held the western end of the Thi Thinh bridge in a shallow blocking position, while the eastern end, by Ben Cat, was secured by ARVN forces. The enemy dug in around An Dien but was unable to dislodge the RF positions at the bridge.

Two infantry regiments of the 9th NVA Division, with about ten T-54 and PT-76 tanks, were employed against the dispersed 321st RF Battalion. The 272d Regiment overran Rach Bap and continued the attack south into the Triangle along Route 14, while the 95C Regiment attacked Base 82 and An Dien. The 271st Regiment was held in reserve.

The RVNAF at Ben Cat were unable to counterattack the NVA immediately at An Dien because the bridgehead held by the RF was too shallow to protect the crossing of any large forces, but General Thuan quickly began reinforcing Ben Cat. Task Force 318 arrived in Ben Cat District on the afternoon of the 16th and on the 17th began reinforcing the RF holding the bridge and moving against the enemy's blocking positions west of the bridgehead. The weakness of the ARVN bridgehead and the strength of the enemy positions in An Dien, which included antitank guns and tanks, made it impractical to send any armor of the 318th across the An Dien bridge at this time.

Meanwhile, the 322d Task Force moved from Tay Ninh Province to Phu Cuong and was ordered to prepare to attack into the Triangle along Route 14 (LTL-14) in order to oppose the 272d Regiment, which was moving south from Rach Rap.

VNAF aerial observers and photography on 17 May revealed two T-54 tanks inside Base 82, which VNAF fighter-bombers destroyed the next day, and four more in the An Dien base. Initial negative reactions at ARVN III Corps Headquarters to the seemingly hasty, if not unwarranted, withdrawal of the RF companies from their positions softened somewhat when the size and composition of the enemy force was revealed.

Six months would pass before the situation existing before 16 May would be restored along the northern edge of the Iron Triangle. The campaign was never officially divided as such, but major operations fell into four distinct phases. In the first, 16-17 May, the NVA had captured the northern edge of the Triangle and launched a major column into the center of this strategic approach to Phu Cuong. In the second phase, 18 May to 5 June, the ARVN counterattacked and regained control of An Dien. Four months later, on 4 October, ARVN troops concluded the third phase by reoccupying the devastated wasteland that was once Base 82. Finally, on 20 November ARVN infantry re-entered Rach Bap, concluding the last phase of the 1974 Iron Triangle campaign.

An Dien Counterattack

General Thuan greatly underestimated the strength and tenacity with which the 9th NVA Division would defend An Dien, although he had accurate intelligence concerning the size, composition, and location of the enemy. His initial plans for the second phase, which proved unrealistic, called for virtually simultaneous recapture of the three lost bases by about 22 May. Perhaps the remarkable successes his corps troops had in repulsing the NVA 7th Division attacks on the Phu Ciao front had given him this unwarranted over-confidence.

Except for the few ARVN infantry and engineers that were thrown across the Thi Thinh River to reinforce the An Dien bridgehead, the first major ARVN unit to move into the Triangle was a battalion of the 43d Infantry, 18th ARVN Division, which crossed on Route 14 north of Phu Cuong. Shortly reinforced by the rest of the regiment, this element, followed by the 322d Armored Task Force, was to attack Rach Bap and Base 82. Meanwhile, the 318th Task Force would cross the An Dien Bridge, pass through An Dien, and proceed to Base 82. Three Ranger battalions attacking south out of Lai Khe were to strike Base 82 from the north. None of this worked as planned. The 43d Infantry became stalled after advancing only four or five kilometers north. Then, the tracked vehicles of the 322d Task Force found the going extremely slow in the dense brush and cratered terrain. General Thuan, concerned lest this armored force become bogged down and have a bridge blown behind it, ordered its withdrawal. He discovered, meanwhile, that the An Dien bridge had been seriously weakened by enemy artillery (including AT-3 missiles) and would not support the tanks of the 318th Task Force. Under enemy observation and, sporadically, heavy mortar and artillery fire, ARVN combat engineers attempted to repair the bridge. Casualties mounted, and the work progressed very slowly. About the same time, the 7th Ranger Group, with three battalions, moved southwest out of Lai Khe, crossed the Thi Thinh River and advanced on Base 82. The Rangers were immediately opposed in the thick jungle and rubber plantation by the dug-in troops of the NVA 9th Division, and their attack stalled well short of the objective.

While III Corps was experiencing great difficulty getting moving, it was pounding An Dien with heavy artillery fire. The North Vietnamese responded in kind against ARVN batteries and the stalled Ranger and infantry columns and sent sappers into an RF command post just south of Ben Cat, where they destroyed a 105-mm. howitzer and routed most of the small garrison.

The VNAF, meanwhile, gave only limited support. NVA antiaircraft artillery and SA-7 defenses were plentiful in the area, forcing VNAF aircraft to high altitudes. On 24 May, an armored cavalry squadron of the 25th ARVN Division launched a diversionary attack from Go Dau Ha east toward the Boi Loi Woods. General Thuan's purpose was to cause enough of a threat here to prevent the 9th NVA Division from committing its reserve, the 271st Regiment, against either the 318th or the 322d Task Forces. By the 25th, the armored cavalry squadron had passed Suoi Cau without encountering any resistance, and another supporting maneuver began with two battalions of the 50th Infantry, ARVN 25th Division, moving north from Phu Hoa along the west bank of the Saigon River.

On 25 May, General Thuan met with the commander of the 18th ARVN Division, Brig. Gen. Le Minh Dao, and with the commander of the 3d Armored Brigade, Brig. Gen. Tran Quang Khoi, to coordinate the following morning's attack. At that time, the 43d Regiment was about seven kilometers south of An Dien, about to attack north, while the 3d Armored Brigade was preparing to send a cavalry squadron and a Ranger battalion across the An Dien bridge.

Although the enemy's heavy mortar and artillery fire had so weakened the bridge at An Dien that the cavalry could not follow the Rangers, by nightfall the 64th Ranger Battalion was dug in on the eastern edge of An Dien Village. The 43d Regiment was again ordered to resume the attack north, and the 7th Ranger Group, coming down from Lai Khe, was ordered to take Base 82 by night attack on 27 May. Because no progress was made General Thuan on 28 May decided to try a fresh approach. First, he turned the operation over to General Dao, told him to move his 52d Regiment over from Phu Giao, gave him operational command of the 7th Ranger Group, which was still north of Base 82, and attached to Dao's 18th Division a reinforced squadron of the 3d Armored Brigade. Since it would take two days to relieve the 52d Regiment on the Phu Giao front and move it into position at Ben Cat, the new operation was scheduled for 30 May. Delays in the relief and movement forced General Dao to set the date ahead to 1 June.

With the Rangers still holding the shallow bridgehead opposite Ben Cat and the 43d Regiment making slow progress attacking the dug-in 272d NVA Regiment south of An Dien, General Dao sent the 2d Battalion, 52d Regiment, across the Thi Thinh River on an assault bridge south of Ben Cat on 1 June. Once across, it turned north to attack the defenses of the 95C NVA Regiment in An Dien. Meanwhile, the reconnaissance company and an infantry company from the 18th Division crossed the An Dien bridge and advanced toward the village. Casualties on both sides were heavy that day in An Dien as the commander of the ARVN 52d Regiment committed his 1st Battalion behind the 2d. The 9th NVA Division responded by assaulting the ARVN infantry that night with infantry and at least 10 tanks. The two battalions of the 52d held their positions and were reinforced by the 3d Battalion the next afternoon. Meanwhile, ARVN combat engineers were clearing the road past the An Dien bridge. Working at night with flashlights to avoid enemy observation and fire, they removed 38 antitank mines from the route of advance.

Weakened by casualties, the 52d Infantry made very little progress on 2 and 3 June, and the 43d Regiment was still being blocked by the NVA 272d Regiment. General Dao then ordered his 48th Infantry across the Thi Thinh south of Ben Cat, to pass through the 52d and take An Dien. While the NVA artillery continued to pound ARVN positions, two battalions of the 48th crossed into the Iron Triangle on the night of 2–3 June.

The fighting at An Dien was especially fierce on 3 June as the NVA used tanks against ARVN infantry. Armed with light antitank weapons, ARVN infantry knocked out at least four enemy tanks in the final day of the battle. On 4 June, troops of the 18th ARVN Division finally entered An Dien, and on the 5th overran the last position of the NVA's 95C Regiment, which had since been reinforced by elements of the 9th NVA Division's 271st Regiment. On the morning of the 5th, two battalions of the 48th and two of the 52d were holding An Dien, bracing for a counterattack. One Ranger battalion was in a blocking position north of the destroyed village, while another secured the An Dien bridge. The 43d Regiment was still stalled by the NVA's 272d Regiment's defenses south of An Dien. The 7th Ranger Group had not been able to advance toward Base 82 from the north, and a new major ARVN attack would be required to advance past the positions held in and around An Dien.

NVA soldiers captured by the 18th ARVN Division in An Dien told of horrendous losses in the three battalions—the 7th, 8th, and 9th—of the 95C Regiment. Fourteen surviving members of the 9th Battalion were captured when the last strongpoint fell on 5 June. They said that casualties in the 8th and 9th Battalions between 16 May and 4 June were 65 percent, that a company of the 7th Battalion had only one man left, that a company of the 8th Battalion was totally destroyed, and that the 9th Battalion lost two complete companies. These accounts were confirmed by the large number of bodies left on the battlefield and by the quantity of weapons and equipment captured. ARVN losses were substantial, but none of its units were decimated as were those of the 9th NVA Division. Well over 100 ARVN soldiers had been killed in action, and the hospitals held over 200 wounded from An Dien, while 200 more suffered light wounds not requiring evacuation.

The expected NVA counterattack came on the night of 5-6 June as two battalions of the 271st Regiment, 9th NVA Division, supported by up to 14 tanks, attacked from two directions. The ARVN 18th Division held and its infantrymen knocked out 5 tanks and damaged 5 others.

The second phase of the Iron Triangle campaign was over with the recapture of An Dien, and General Thuan was anxious to get the attack moving again toward Base 82 and Rach Bap. Although the An Dien bridge would soon be in condition to carry the tanks of the 318th Task Force—one company of armored personnel carriers had already crossed into An Dien—a knocked-out T-54 tank blocked the narrow road from the bridge into An Dien. Swampy ground on each side prevented bypassing the tank, and it had to be blown off the road with demolitions. ARVN combat engineers were laboring at this task while infantrymen of the 18th Division were holding the perimeter around An Dien.

Base 82

The first of several attempts during the third phase to retake Base 82 began on 7 June 1974 when the 318th Task Force finally brought its tanks across the Thi Thinh River and passed through the 18th Division position in An Dien. While the 52d Infantry of the 18th Division remained in reserve holding the An Dien perimeter, two battalions of the 48th Infantry moved south and west to protect the southern flank of Task Force 318 as it attacked along Route 7 (TL-7B) toward Base 82. To the south, the 43d Regiment maintained contact with the NVA 272d Regiment. Meanwhile, the 9th NVA Division had withdrawn the remnants of the 95C Regiment from action and placed its 271st Regiment at Base 82, where it prepared deep, mutually supporting defensive positions. Clearly indicating its resolve to conduct a determined defense along Route 7 in the Iron Triangle, COSVN sent the 141st Regiment of the 7th NVA Division south from its position along Highway 13, north of Lai Khe, to reinforce the 9th Division north of Base 82. The 9th Division meanwhile began shifting the 272d Regiment north from the southern part of the Iron Triangle to assist in the defense of Base 82 and Rach Bap.

The wet summer monsoon had arrived in Binh Duong Province. Rains and low cloud cover further reduced the effectiveness of VNAF's support of the attack. A dense rubber plantation northwest of Base 82 provided excellent concealment for supporting defensive positions and observation of local Route 7, the only avenue of approach available for ARVN armor. Dense brush covered the southern approaches to the base and concealed more enemy supporting and reserve positions. The only fairly open terrain was on either side of Route 7 where high grass offered no concealment to the ARVN column but reduced the visibility of ARVN tanks and infantry to a few meters. Furthermore, this approach was under the observed fire of the 9th NVA Division's supporting artillery, which included 120-mm. mortars, 122-mm. howitzers, 105-mm. howitzers, and 85-mm. field guns. Infantry mortars, 82-mm. and 61-mm., added to the indirect fire, and, in addition to the B-41 antitank grenade launchers carried in great numbers by the NVA infantry, NVA soldiers were amply equipped with the new Soviet 82-mm. recoilless gun, a superb antiarmor weapon.

By the evening of 8 June, Task Force 318 reached its first objective, Hill 25, about 1,000 meters short of Base 82. There it fought a battalion of the NVA 271st Infantry, killing 30 and capturing 10 while taking light casualties. The prospects seemed bright for recapturing Base 82 by the following day, and General Thuan told General Dao of the 18th ARVN Division that Rach Bap should be taken by 15 June. But on 10 June Task Force 318, advancing very slowly in two columns, one north of Route 7 and one south, was struck by a battalion of the NVA 271st Infantry supported by four tanks and a heavy concentration of mortar, howitzer, and rocket fire. Four of Task Force 318's tanks and one of its personnel carriers were knocked out but personnel losses were light. By nightfall only 200 meters had been gained, the enemy's minefields and 82-mm. recoilless guns having stopped the task force 800 meters short of Base 82.

No progress was made on 11 June, but ARVN artillery and VNAF pounded the base. Antiaircraft fire was intense and kept the VNAF fighter-bombers above their most effective attack altitudes. Meanwhile, General Thuan, determined to get the attack moving again, directed Brig. Gen. Khoi, commander of the 3d Armored Brigade, to assemble the 315th Task Force at Ben Cat and send it across the Thi Thinh to reinforce the attack. The 315th was to move southwest and attack Base 82 from the south, while the 318th continued its frontal assault.

Farther south, another change was taking place. Detecting that all but one of the NVA's 272d Regiment's battalions had moved north toward Route 7, General Dao left only one of his 43d Infantry battalions in the Phu Thu area, placing the balance of the regiment in reserve.

By noon on 12 June, the 315th Task Force had reached a position about 1,600 meters southeast of Base 82. At this point, General Dao changed the original concept of a two-pronged attack from the east and south. As soon as the 315th was ready to attack, he would withdraw the 318th to defend the eastern approaches to Ben Cat that had been weakened by the commitment of the 315th against Base 82.

Thick brush, rough terrain, and accurate enemy artillery fire prevented the 315th from making any gains on 13 June. In fact, as the 318th withdrew from contact, it left positions much closer to the objective than those reached by the 315th.

In another change in plans, General Dao proposed to General Thuan that two battalions each from the 43d and 52d Regiments take over the attack role, while the 315th remained in its defensive perimeter southeast of Base 82. The infantry battalions would move into the rubber plantation and attack from the north. General Thuan agreed and left for JGS headquarters to ask for a new ammunition allocation for the attack. He returned to his headquarters in ill humor, for General Khuyen, the RVNAF Chief of Logistics, was unable to satisfy this request.

By 15 June, the two leading ARVN 43d Infantry battalions, one of which was attempting to swing north of Base 82 from An Dien, had made very little headway against strong resistance and heavy enemy artillery fire. In contacts south of Route 7 on the 17th, prisoners of war were taken from the 272d Regiment, soldiers who had recently arrived in South Vietnam and had been assigned to the 272d for only three days before their capture. ARVN casualties continued to mount, troops were desperately fatigued, artillery support was too severely rationed, and the weather all but eliminated effective air support. On 21 June, General Thuan ordered a halt in the attempt to take Base 82, while a new approach, better supported by artillery fire, could be devised. Consideration was also given to replacing the 18th Division, whose troops had been in heavy combat for a month, with the 5th Division.

Instead of relieving the 18th, General Thuan decided to try his armor again. Holding the infantry in position, he sent the 318th and 322d Task Forces back into the Triangle, one north of Route 7, the other generally along the road. The enemy's antitank defenses, primarily employing the 82-mm. recoilless gun, stopped the attack once again, destroying 13 personnel carriers and 11 M-48 tanks between 27 June and 1 July, even though ARVN artillery and the VNAF supported the attack with 43,000 rounds and 250 sorties. The tired infantrymen of the 43d Regiment tried once again to take Base 82 from the south on 1 July but got nowhere.

On 2 July, General Thuan finally decided to relieve the 18th Division and replace it with the 5th. The armored task forces would be withdrawn for rest and refitting. General Thuan allowed his commanders ten days to complete the relief; he wanted it done gradually and expertly so that constant pressure could be maintained against the enemy. In order not to weaken the 5th Division's defenses north of Lai Khe, elements of the 18th Division's 52d Regiment, which had seen little action, and two battalions of the 25th Division's 50th Infantry were attached to the 5th Division in the Iron Triangle. The relief was accomplished on schedule, and a relative calm settled over the Base 82 battleground.

The 9th NVA Division also made adjustments during the last part of June and the first weeks of July. While the 272d Regiment retained defensive positions in the southern part of the Iron Triangle, the 95C Regiment, refitted and with fresh replacements, returned to the Base 82 area and assumed responsibility for its defense. The third regiment of the 9th NVA Division, the 271st, held defensive positions in the Base 82 area, primarily to the north and northeast. Meanwhile, the 141st Regiment of the 7th NVA Division returned to its normal area of operations north of Lai Khe, and artillery support for the 9th NVA Division was assigned to the 42d NVA Artillery Regiment. The 75th NVA Artillery Regiment moved from the Ben Cat area to support the 7th NVA Division east of Route 13.

The 5th ARVN Division made no determined effort during July or August to alter the status quo. The NVA, however, pulled the 95C Regiment out of Base 82 and replaced it with the 141st Regiment of the 7th NVA Division, in time to meet the next concerted ARVN effort to take Base 82.

By autumn the 8th Infantry, 5th ARVN Division, had been selected to try to plant South Vietnam's red and yellow banner on Base 82, having replaced its sister regiment, the 7th, in the Iron Triangle. Prior to an attack scheduled for 7 September, ARVN reconnaissance patrols had successfully reached the base's perimeter. The 8th Regiment formed a task force around its 1st and 2d Battalions, reinforced by the 5th Division Reconnaissance Company and a small armored troop with three M-41 tanks, three M-48 tanks, and three armored personnel carriers. The 1st Battalion advanced south of Route 7, while the 2d Battalion, with the reconnaissance company and the armored troops, advanced on an axis north of the road. Unopposed and moving quickly the two battalions reached the outer defenses of Base 82 in the early morning of 7

September but could go no further that day. Faced with barbed wire and mines and under fire from the front and flanks, the 8th Infantry dug in. As the rain of enemy shells continued, much of it heavy 120-mm. Soviet mortars, the 8th kept digging and improving fighting positions with logs overhead.

On 8 September, the NVA shelling increased, and at 1600 it began to rain, ending all VNAF aerial observation and air support for the 8th Infantry. As the rain increased, so did the enemy bombardment, 1600 rounds falling in one hour, and the battlefield was obscured in smoke. ARVN infantry could hear the approach of tanks. One column of T-54's came out of the rubber plantation and forest to the north, and another line of six advanced from the south. The three ARVN M-48's withdrew, and at 1800 hours, nearly caught in a double envelopment, the 8th Infantry fell back, first about 300 meters where the leaders attempted to establish a new line, then 300 meters farther back where the troops of the 8th rallied and held on the western slope of Hill 25.

With victory seemingly so close, General Thuan was deeply disappointed by the rout of the 8th Regiment, and his disappointment changed to anger when he learned of the relatively light casualties suffered by the 8th: 6 killed, 29 missing, and 67 wounded. But even if the 8th Infantry leaders on the scene could have held their troops in their exposed positions in front of Base 82, the regiment probably could not have survived the NVA counterattack. In any case, General Thuan ordered an immediate investigation of the circumstances of the 8th Infantry's failure and subsequently dismissed the regimental commander. On 11 September, the 8th Infantry was replaced in the Iron Triangle by the 9th, and the final phase of the fight to retake Base 82 was about to begin.

All three battalions of the 9th Infantry moved into position on the west slope of Hill 25. Combat losses since the start of the NVA offensive in May, combined with the slow flow of the replacements into the regiment, had reduced battalion strength to under 300. Between 12 and 18 September, the 9th concentrated on reconnaissance, planning, and improvement of positions. As the ARVN 9th Regiment prepared for the attack, the NVA was beginning to execute another relief in the Ben Cat battlefield. The 141st Regiment of the 7th NVA Division made preparations to leave the Base 82 area and turn over its defense once again to the 95C Regiment of the 9th NVA Division.

With the 2d Armored Cavalry Squadron protecting the right (north) flank, and two Ranger battalions protecting the left, the 9th ARVN Infantry Regiment began its attack toward Base 82. The two attacking battalions, the 3d Battalion on the right, north of Route 7, and the 2d on the left, crossed the line of departure on Hill 25 on 19 September.

Moving slowly, with excellent reconnaissance and effective artillery support, the ARVN infantrymen methodically eliminated, one by one, the enemy's mutually supporting bunkers that lay in a dense pattern all along the route of advance. Although the NVA infantrymen defended tenaciously and their artillery support was heavy and accurate, they gradually gave ground. On 29 September, the 1st Battalion relieved the weary 3d Battalion, and the relentless attack continued. On 2 October, the 2d Battalion, 46th ARVN Infantry, 25th Division, was committed to reinforce the 2d Battalion of the 9th Infantry. Before midnight on 3 October, as enemy artillery and mortars were still firing heavy barrages, a 12-man assault team from the 1st Battalion, 9th Infantry, attempted to breach the barbed wire and scale the earthen wall. An antipersonnel mine detonated, disclosing the team's position, and heavy fire from the base pinned it down. Very early the next morning, the NVA infantry counterattacked, forcing the withdrawal of the assault team. But it became apparent to the ARVN commander on the ground that victory was within grasp. A 100-round concentration of 155-mm. howitzer fire, which he requested, had the desired effect: enemy resistance and return fire was notably diminished by 1300, and a half hour later NVA infantrymen were seen climbing out of their crumbling fortress and running to the rear. At 1500 on 4 October the 1st Battalion, 9th Regiment, raised South Vietnam's flag over Base 82, ending a bitter four-month struggle and the third phase of the Iron Triangle campaign.

Return to Rach Bap

Calm returned to the Iron Triangle as the remnants of the 95C and 272d NVA Regiments withdrew from Base 82. For three days, even the NVA artillery was silent. Meanwhile, far to the north of the Ben Cat battleground and in the COSVN rear area, a significant event was taking place. Recognizing the need to plan and coordinate the operations of multi-divisional forces, COSVN organized a corps headquarters in the Tay Ninh–Binh Long region and designated it the 301st Corps. This corps would soon direct the combat operations of the 7th and 9th NVA Divisions, separate regiments, and additional formations already en route from North Vietnam.

After the long and costly victory at Base 82, General Thuan decided to rest the tired troops of the 5th ARVN Division and turned his attention to sending his 25th Division to clear out the enemy bases in the Ho Bo area west of the Iron Triangle. The ARVN defenses around An Dien and Base 82 were taken over by Regional Forces and Rangers. For what became the fourth phase of the campaign, III Corps Headquarters worked on plans to resume the attack to retake Rach Bap, the last of the three outposts still remaining in enemy hands. General Thuan also recognized the need to clean the enemy out of the southern part of the Iron Triangle, around Phu Thu, and a plan encompassing Rach Bap, Phu Thu, and the Phu Hoa area west of the Iron Triangle began to take shape. But on 30 October, before the execution of the plan, President Thieu relieved General Thuan of command of Military Region 3 and III Corps and replaced him with Lt. Gen. Du Quoc Dong. Other important command changes took place on the same day. The II Corps Commander, Lt. Gen. Nguyen Van Toan, was replaced by Maj. Gen. Pham Van Phu, and Maj. Gen. Nguyen Khoa Nam became the new commander of IV Corps, in place of Lt. Gen. Nguyen Vinh Nghi. Only I Corps was untouched, where Lt. Gen. Ngo Quang Truong retained command.

General Dong immediately surveyed the situation in the Iron Triangle and reviewed the plan of his predecessor, which as modified became operation Quyet Thang 18/24 (Operation Will to Victory). Battalions from all three divisions of the corps were committed; D-Day was 14 November. The 9th Infantry of the 5th ARVN Division, the victors of Base 82, started from An Dien and marched west, along Route 7, past Base 82 toward Rach Bap. The 48th and 52d Regiments of the 18th Division crossed the Thi Thinh River south of Ben Cat and entered the Iron Triangle and attacked west toward the Saigon River. Elements of the 50th ARVN Infantry, 25th Division, were already in this area. Meanwhile, the 46th ARVN Infantry and one battalion of the 50th moved into the plantations north of Phu Hoa District Town to prevent enemy infiltration across the Saigon River.

Along Route 7, the 9th ARVN Infantry advanced without incident until 19 November when sharp fighting west of Base 82 resulted in over 40 ARVN soldiers wounded. The enemy withdrew leaving 14 dead and many weapons and radios behind. The next morning, Reconnaissance Company, 9th Infantry, entered Rach Bap unopposed. The Iron Triangle campaign was virtually over, although mopping-up operations continued in the south along Route 14 until 24 November. Measured against the costs and violence of the earlier phases of the campaign, this final chapter was anticlimactic. Casualties on both sides were light, and contacts were few and of short duration. The NVA had given up its last foothold in the Iron Triangle with only token resistance in order to replace losses, reorganize, re-equip, and retrain the main forces of the new 301st Corps for the decisive battles to come.

Phu Giao

As mentioned earlier, the NVA 16 May offensive in Binh Duong Province was a two-division attack, with the 9th NVA Division west of Route 13 into the Iron Triangle and the 7th NVA Division east, against Phu Giao District. The principal 7th Division objective was the bridge on Interprovincial Route 1A (LTL-1A) over the Song Be south of the major ARVN 5th Division base at Phuoc Vinh and northeast of the Ben Cat-Iron Triangle battlefield. (See Map 14.)

The 7th NVA Division on 5 April overran the ARVN outpost at Chi Linh. After taking Chi Linh, the division's 141st Infantry Regiment remained in the Chon Thanh area until detached for duty in the Iron Triangle under the 9th NVA Division. Meanwhile, the other two 7th Division regiments were preparing for the May offensive in the jungles around Phu Giao. The 165th NVA Infantry Regiment was west of Route 1A and north of the Song Be; the 209th NVA Infantry Regiment was south of the Song Be, with battalions disposed on both sides of Route 1A. But sometime before 16 May, the 165th crossed the Song Be and moved into attack positions in the Bo La area, south of Phu Giao, and the 209th moved north to positions close to the Song Be bridge. The 7th NVA Division's plan called for the 165th to attack ARVN positions and block Route 1A south of the bridge, while the 209th would seize the bridge and its controlling terrain.

The defense of the Song Be bridge was the responsibility of the 322d RF Battalion, while the 7th and 8th Regiments of the ARVN 5th Division and the 318th Task Force were in position to provide support from the Phuoc Vinh base south to the Bo La area. Based on good intelligence, the 8th ARVN Infantry attacked assembly areas occupied by elements of the 209th NVA Infantry on 15 May. The disruption caused by this attack was probably largely responsible for the poor showing made by two battalions of the 209th which, the following morning, attacked RF outposts around the Song Be bridge. In any event, the troops of the 322d RF Battalion fought off the attack, losing a few positions but maintaining control of the key terrain and the bridge.

Meanwhile, the 165th NVA Infantry Regiment had better success in attacking the Bo La area, managing to hold enough of Route 1A to prevent reinforcements from breaking through to the bridge. But its accomplishment was short-lived. The 5th ARVN Division reacted immediately and sent its 7th Infantry Regiment and the 315th Task Force north to break the block on Route 1A. Casualties on the ARVN side were light, but the NVA lost heavily; the 209th was especially hard hit by ARVN artillery and air strikes in the bridge area. By 23 May, despite reinforcement of the 165th NVA Regiment by a battalion of its sister regiment, the 141st, the ARVN tank and infantry counterattack had cleared the road to the bridge and beyond to Phuoc Vinh. Although the 7th NVA Division maintained its 165th and 209th Regiments in the Phu Giao area for the rest of the summer, the strategic raids campaign in eastern Binh Duong Province was a failure, essentially over a week after it began, and the ARVN successfully countered the sporadic attacks the enemy continued to make along Route 1A in the Phu Giao area.

Bien Hoa

The strategic raids campaign in Bien Hoa Province differed from that in Binh Duong, principally because the main objective, the sprawling air and logistical base at Bien Hoa, was beyond the reach of large NVA formations. But even if a main-force regiment could have penetrated the Bien Hoa defenses, it would most likely have been cut off, surrounded, and destroyed. The attacks in Bien Hoa were therefore stand-off artillery bombardments, sapper raids, and small-scale infantry assaults against outposts.

The first large attack of the summer came on 3 June. From launching sites north of the air base, the NVA artillery launched at least 40 122-mm. Soviet rockets. Most of them struck inside the base, where they did minor damage to runways and destroyed 500 napalm cannisters, but the rest exploded in hamlets surrounding the base, killing and wounding civilians. Surprisingly, no aircraft were damaged. The NVA artillery struck again early on 10 August with 25 rockets. Of these, seven hit the F-5A storage area, slightly damaging a few airplanes. Most of the rest fell on civilian communities causing light casualties. The bombardment continued sporadically throughout the morning and resumed the next day, but no significant casualties or damage resulted.

The 10 August rocketing of Bien Hoa signalled the beginning of the NVA's attack on the outposts along the north bank of the great Dong Nai River in Tan Uyen District north of the air base. Employing primarily the 165th Infantry Regiment, the 7th NVA Division attacked RF-manned outposts intended to prevent the enemy's crossing of the Dong Nai and deny him easy access to areas from which he could launch rockets against Bien Hoa.

The first outpost to fall, Ho Da, west of Tan Uyen District Town, was overrun on the night of 9 August but was recovered by the ARVN 52d Infantry five days later. On the 10th, a battalion of the 165th NVA Infantry captured Dat Cuoc outpost at the big bend in the Dong Nai east of Tan Uyen. The enemy managed to hold on to this outpost until 24 August, when the 346th RF Battalion recaptured it.

East of Dat Cuoc on the river north of Thai Hung village, was the Ba Cam outpost, manned by the 316th RF Battalion. In successive attacks, the 316th was driven out of its defenses by a battalion of the 165th NVA Infantry, heavily supported by artillery. By 13 August, the 316th had withdrawn to Thai Hung, virtually destroyed by NVA and ARVN artillery. By the end of the month, ARVN counterattacks had recovered all lost positions north of the Dong Nai, the enemy having suffered heavy casualties during the brief campaign.

The only other incident of note in the Bien Hoa area during 1974 was the NVA sapper attack on 21 October against the Hoa An bridge over the Dong Nai linking Bien Hoa with Saigon. This bridge, the most important of three across the Dong Nai northeast of Saigon, was 800 meters of reinforced concrete. By floating two rafts loaded with explosive downstream so that the rope that joined them wrapped around a bridge pillar, the water-sappers were able to accomplish their mission even though all of them were killed in the river by ARVN sentries before the explosion, which knocked down two 60-meter spans and rattled the windows in the American Consulate offices at the river's edge. Three days later, ARVN engineers had a one-way Bailey span in place and traffic resumed.

Xuan Loc

General Thuan, commanding III Corps at the time, could not give the crucial battles north of Saigon his undivided attention during the summer of 1974. He was forced to look over his shoulder as the strategic raids campaign spread to the eastern limits of Military Region 3 and threatened to close National Route 1 (QL-1), Saigon's major connection with the central coastal provinces.

About 50 kilometers along Route 1 east of Saigon was Xuan Loc, capital of Long Khanh Province. Set in the midst of vast, lush rubber plantations, Xuan Loc was the eastern terminus of the railroad that once carried passengers and freight up the coast all the way to Hanoi. Xuan Loc was also close to the beginning of Route 20 (QL-20), which joined Route 1 west of the city, and provided Saigon its connection with the mountain resorts and bountiful gardens of Dalat. Adding to the strategic importance of Xuan Loc, Local Route 2 began there and wound south through the plantations into Phuoc Tuy Province, providing an alternate route to the port city of Vung Tau.

The 18th ARVN Division usually kept a regiment at Xuan Loc, frequently operating against the NVA's 33d and 274th Regiments that maintained base areas in the jungles north and south of Route 1. Because of heavy requirements for combat power in Binh Duong and Bien Hoa Provinces, General

Thuan pulled the 18th Division out of Long Khanh in the summer of 1974, leaving the security of that province and its lines of communication to Regional and Popular Forces and creating opportunities for the local VC, supported by the main force NVA regiments, to take the offensive in Long Khanh and Phuoc Tuy Provinces.

Bao Binh and Rung La

The cluster of hamlets called Bao Binh, in the rubber plantations east of Xuan Loc, was the first major objective of Communist forces in the strategic raids campaign in Long Khanh Province. On 24 May, an NVA force of two battalions of the 274th NVA Regiment, a battalion of the 33d NVA Regiment, and an NVA engineer battalion invaded the hamlets, overrunning the local force defenses with ease. Tentative efforts by Regional Force battalions failed to dislodge the enemy, and the NVA still held Bao Binh when General Thuan visited province headquarters on 8 June. General Thuan was not pleased with the district chief's assertion that the clearing of Bao Binh would have to wait until the 18th Division returned to Xuan Loc.

On 11 June, a strong NVA force attacked the Rung La refugee resettlement village and cut Route 1 about 30 kilometers east of Bao Binh. Rung La was one of several villages established in eastern Military Region 3 to provide new homes and farmland for refugees who fled the NVA invasion of Binh Long Province in 1972. People from Loc Ninh and An Loc, after suffering weeks of inactivity in crowded tent camps following their escape from the Communist offensive, were clearing virgin land for farming and harvesting wood from the forests that surrounded new, government-sponsored villages. Some 132,000 refugees were making a fresh beginning in this region, and the struggle would have been difficult enough without frequent harassment from VC and NVA forces. Mortar attacks, minings, kidnapping and murder, all intended to disrupt resettlement efforts, failed, however, to drive the refugees away.

Communist terrorism had been relatively minor until April, when a definite rise in incidents was noted. The frequency of mortar attacks increased, and the Communists became bolder in early June as they exploited the absence of the 18th ARVN Division. On 1 June, they entered the Thai Thien resettlement village and burned 25 houses, warning the people to leave. Returning on 6 June, they burned 50 houses and again warned the villagers to leave. On 11 June they burned 80 houses in Rung La village and closed Route 1 nearby.

Rung La was one of the largest settlements of An Loc refugees, the first of whom began occupying the village in December 1973. By June the population had grown to 18,000. When an NVA road block isolated Rung La from Xuan Loc, up to 10,000 villagers fled eastward into Binh Tuy and Binh Thuan Provinces. The 347th RF Battalion and the 358th RF company of Long Khanh Province were dispatched to break the enemy's hold on Route 1, but both were repelled by heavy mortar fire. An RF battalion from Binh Tuy experienced a similar reception at Rung La. The political and psychological damage, to say nothing of the serious effects on local commerce of cutting the principal north-south artery, was enough to draw the corps commander's attention away from the Iron Triangle and his other serious problems in Military Region 3. General Thuan flew over the roadblock on 13 June and viewed the NVA force and its defenses. He then ordered a task force, assembled at Xuan Loc, to start moving east along Route 1 to clear the road. The force included two battalions of the 5th ARVN Division's 8th Infantry, the 32d Ranger Battalion of the 7th Ranger Group, and a tank company. Making good use of heavy artillery support and air observation, the task force by 15 June cleared two of three enemy positions. When the last position fell on 17 June, and the road was again open, the villagers of Rung La began returning to rebuild their settlement.

Leaving the Ranger battalion and one of the 8th Infantry Regiment's battalions to secure the construction of a new RF base at Rung La, General Thuan ordered the province chief to use the other 8th Infantry Battalion and Long Khanh RF battalions to retake the Bao Binh hamlets still under enemy control. This force, however, proved to be too light for the task. Since heavy demands elsewhere precluded reinforcement, Bao Binh remained in enemy hands.

On 8 July, the NVA again moved against Rung La and succeeded in holding a segment of Route 1 until the 13th. Although these harassments were to continue throughout the year, the enemy was unsuccessful in blocking traffic again.

Bao Binh was a difficult objective. In late July and August, the province chief employed the 7th Ranger Group against the well-established enemy defenses, and the Rangers cleared all but one hamlet before being pulled out to operate around Rung La. But by the end of the year, all of Bao Binh was under South Vietnamese control as Communist units withdrew, probably to receive orders for the final offensive.

Tay Ninh

Because of the beating the 5th NVA Division had taken in the Duc Hue and Long Khot actions during the spring, the strategic raids campaign was slower getting started in Tay Ninh Province. The main attacks were against the ARVN outposts along

Interprovincial Route 13 (LTL-13) west of Tay Ninh City and the Song Vam Co Dong, but supporting and diversionary attacks were conducted against the Ben Cau outpost near the Angel's Wing, the southern edge of Tay Ninh City, and Suoi Da, a hamlet and outpost northeast of Tay Ninh City in the shadow of Nui Ba Den. The NVA also moved 107-mm. rockets in close enough to bombard the city; some of these struck the civilian hospital on the night of 18 August and on the morning of the 19th, wounding 16 patients and killing one.

The NVA's purpose was parallel to the one it had tried to achieve at Duc Hue; to seize the territory between the Cambodian frontier and the Vam Co Dong. The focus of this attack, however, was northwest of Duc Hue.

A string of three outposts guarded the western approach to Tay Ninh City between the Svay Rieng Province border and the Vam Co Dong. Ben Soi post was closest to Tay Ninh City; it was on Local Route 13 on the west bank of the Vam Co Dong. The two forward posts were Luu Buu Lam on Route 13, about halfway to the border, and Luoc Tan, located on seasonally flooded land within sight of Svay Rieng Province, Cambodia. The blow fell simultaneously on the three posts on the morning of 14 August as the 6th Regiment, 5th NVA Division, launched heavy mortar and artillery bombardments into the fortresses. About 1,000 civilians began streaming into Tay Ninh City to escape the onslaught, but some 3,000 were trapped behind the block that the NVA 6th Regiment placed on the road between Luoc Tan and Luu Buu Lam.

The ARVN 312th RF Battalion's 2d Company at Luoc Tan reported absorbing intense shellings in which all of the buildings and three-fourths of the bunkers there had been destroyed. But it held on and beat back successive assaults by tank-supported battalions of the 6th NVA Regiment. As of 15 August, the company commander reported that his men had repaired most of the defensive positions and that very effective artillery and air strikes had knocked out one tank and killed over 300 of the enemy around Luoc Tan. Of the 97 men he had when the attack began, 45 were still able to fight.

East of Luoc Tan, Luu Buu Lam and Ben Soi were quiet after the second day as the NVA concentrated on Luoc Tan and the 25th ARVN Division's 46th Infantry Regiment sent a battalion in to reinforce Luu Buu Lam. To the south, at Ben Cau, two NVA soldiers captured from the 174th NVA Infantry said that their regiment was severely undermanned and its mission was only to test the ARVN reactions to the attack at Ben Cau. The NVA found the reaction to be violent as well as firm.

The staunch defense put up by the company of the 312th RF Battalion at Luoc Tan boosted RF and civilian morale throughout Tay Ninh. Resupply of the little garrison was made by helicopter as the relief column of the 46th ARVN Regiment approached along Route 13. On 20 August, the company commander at Luoc Tan reported driving off a three-pronged infantry assault; the 46th Infantry's battalion was stalled about three kilometers away, where it had been for four days. Fearing an ambush, General Thuan had ordered the battalion to halt its attempt to link up with Luoc Tan. The night of 20 August was the last for the 2d Company, 312th RF Battalion, as a battalion of the 6th NVA Regiment breached the shattered defensive works and captured the garrison. It remained in NVA hands, but the cost was high. The 6th NVA Regiment had to be withdrawn to Cambodia for another refitting and to receive replacements.

This has been an account of the main events that took place around Saigon during the NVA's strategic raids campaign in the summer and fall of 1974. No attempt has been made to cover all combat actions; the purpose has been rather to treat those which changed the map in a significant way, illustrated the relative strengths and weakness of the opposing forces, demonstrated the strategies and tactics adopted by the two sides, and set the stage for the final NVA offensive.

In the deep forests of northern Tay Ninh, Binh Long and Phuoc Long Provinces, COSVN was building a mighty combat capability, stockpiling weapons, ammunition, fuel, and supplies, marshalling and training replacements, building hospitals, improving roads and bridges, while its major fighting forces, the 5th, 7th, and 9th NVA Divisions pressed forward against the ARVN's outer line of defense.

Note on Sources

Principal among the sources of this chapter were the author's notes recording visits to the field, particularly in Binh Duong Province and to III Corps headquarters at Bien Hoa, and meetings with the J2/JGS.

The Weekly Summary published by DAO Saigon Intelligence Branch and by the J2/JGS provided the chronology of events as well as detailed order-of-battle information. Heavy reliance was also placed on the reports of the Consul General, Bien Hoa, and offices of the U.S. Embassy, Saigon. As usual much reliable information was also derived from rallier and prisoner of war interrogation reports and from captured documents.

11

The Highlands to the Hai Van

Just as the COSVN forces in South Vietnam's Military Region 3 were conducting the strategic raids campaign to reduce the defenses around Saigon, so the forces of the B-3 Front and the NVA's Military Region 5 were embarked on their campaign to eliminate the isolated ARVN outposts in the Central Highlands and move into the coastal lowlands of South Vietnam's Military Regions 1 and 2. Heavy fighting lay ahead in the vast region from the high plateau of Darlac to the narrow coastal plain of Quang Nam.

Quang Tin

In the spring of 1974, South Vietnam still had two district seats deep in the highlands of Quang Tin Province but controlled only shallow perimeters around the towns, Tien Phuoc and Hau Duc, and maintained a tenuous hold on the lines of communication into them. The enemy still held Hiep Duc with elements of the 2d NVA Division (reorganized and redesignated from the old 711th NVA Division) and protected the headquarters area of NVA Military Region 5 between Tien Phuoc and Hau Duc.

The population was sparse in the mountain districts of Quang Tin, and its requirements for products from outside the region were relatively small. But after the NVA moved in with large troop units and commerce with the coast became restricted, shortages and hardships grew. The local Communists, striving to recruit a larger following among the villagers, were finding it difficult to provide incentives since the people knew that conditions were better around the South Vietnamese communities of Tien Phuoc and Hau Duc where infrequent but adequate convoys brought rice and other commodities from the province capital, Tam Ky. Part of the Communist strategy thus was to improve NVA lines of communication from southwestern Quang Tin Province to the coast near Tam Ky and to block South Vietnamese access to Tien Phuoc. If the NVA could succeed in these objectives, the mountain population would be impelled to shift to the areas under Communist control. (Map 16)

In 1973 the NVA engineers had improved the channel and constructed docks on the Song Tranh west of Hau Duc, thus providing a secure water route to the NVA base at Hiep Duc. The NVA engineers also widened the road southeast to Tra Bong District in Quang Ngai. The next steps were to gain access to the coast south of Tam Ky and block local Route 533 west from Tam Ky, thus isolating Tien Phuoc.

The first target was the sprawling village of Ky Tra, a minor road junction in the hills west of Chu Lai. Outside the village was an outpost called Nui Ya. On 4 May, after a battalion of NVA infantry overran Nui Ya, the attack quickly shifted to Ky Tra as mortar, rocket, and artillery fire fell on the defending 931st RF Company, two PF platoons, and about 60 People's Self-Defense Force militia. While Ky Tra was under attack, all four ARVN fire support bases within range came under heavy mortar and rocket fire. Contact was lost with the defenders on 5 May as the NVA's 1st Infantry Regiment, 2d Division, occupied Ky Tra. This maneuver placed a major NVA force in position to support attacks against the line of communication to Tien Phuoc and to block overland movement to Hau Duc.

The attack on Ky Tra signalled the eruption of attacks by fire and ground attacks on ARVN bases and outposts throughout Quang Ngai and Quang Tin Provinces. A relief column headed by the 1st Battalion, 4th ARVN Infantry, 2d Division, was stopped by heavy enemy mortar and rocket fire nine kilometers from Ky Tra. A battalion of the 6th Regiment, 2d ARVN Division, also failed to reach Ky Tra. Meanwhile, the 31st Regiment, 2d NVA Division, launched an attack on outposts protecting Tien Phuoc, and one ARVN position, held by the 131st RF Battalion, was lost. The attacks continued on 16 and 17 May, but two RF battalions at Tien Phuoc repelled the 31st NVA Regiment attacks with heavy losses.

The fighting around Ky Tra continued. On 19 May, the 1st NVA Regiment again attacked the 1st Battalion, 4th ARVN Infantry. The understrength ARVN battalion broke and lost nearly 200 weapons and 13 field radios, impossible to replace, in the rout. While the infantry fought in the hills, the NVA pounded the 2d ARVN Division Headquarters at Chu Lai and the city of Tam Ky and its airfield with 122-mm. rockets.

Brig. Gen. Tran Van Nhut, commanding the 2d ARVN Division, sent the 12th Ranger Group, under his operational control, to reinforce Tien Phuoc. Although the NVA 31st Regiment continued to attack, it was unable to break through to Tien Phuoc. In early June, the 12th Ranger Group

The Highlands to the Hai Van

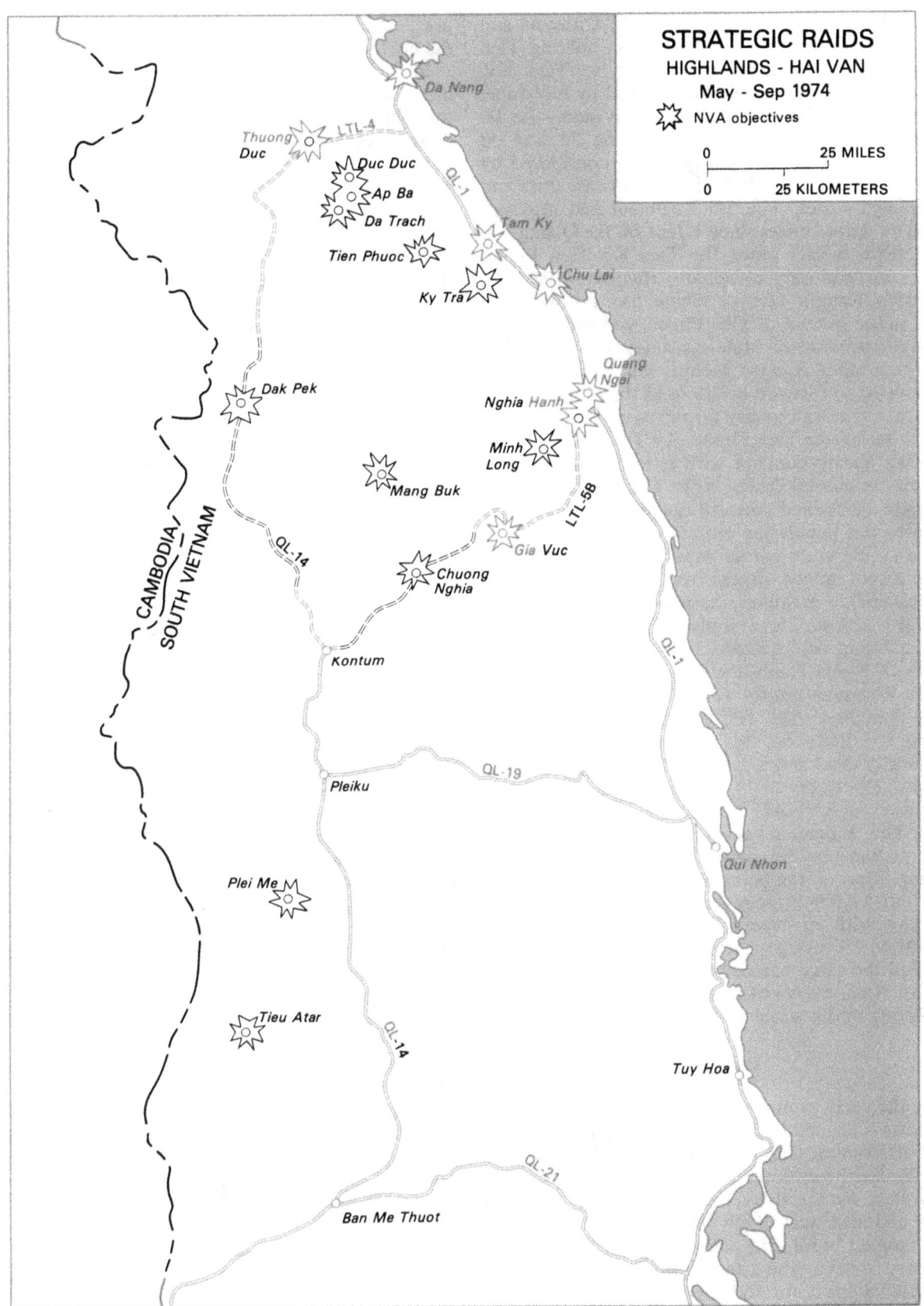

Map 16

was relieved by the 5th Regiment, 2d Division, and the ARVN infantrymen succeeded in holding Tien Phuoc and keeping the road open to Tam Ky. Losses on both sides were heavy, and by mid-June, three battalions of the 2d ARVN Division—the 1st battalion of the 4th Infantry and the 2d and 3d Battalions of the 6th Infantry—were considered by General Nhut to be ineffective due to casualties and equipment losses. The 5th Regiment had also suffered moderate losses since 1 June on the Quang Tin battlefield, mostly along the Tam Ky-Tien Phuoc road, and was only marginally effective. Likewise, the 12th Ranger Group, which had distinguished itself in the defense of Tien Phuoc, was badly understrength because of high casualties. General Nhut had two other Ranger groups, the 11th and 14th, committed to forward positions in the hills and kept his 4th Armored Cavalry Group as division reserve.

All during the Tien Phuoc–Ky Tra battle, General Nhut had to contend with serious threats to the security of coastal Quang Ngai. There the 52d NVA Brigade maintained pressure against lines of communication and population centers, defended largely by RF and PF units whose usual performance under main-force enemy attacks was desultory at best. Occasionally, however, responding to unusually strong leadership, territorials of Quang Ngai turned in a stunning performance. For example, on 5 May south of Nghia Hanh, the 9th Battalion of the 52d NVA Regiment reinforced by the 15th NVA Engineer Battalion, 52d NVA Brigade, attacked the 117th RF Battalion, but the attack was repelled, leaving 21 dead and a number of weapons at the RF defensive position. NVA soldiers in this battle were disguised in RVNAF uniforms, a tactic frequently seen. The increase in enemy attacks during May was not confined to the coast, however. In southwest Quang Ngai, on the boundary of Kontum Province, the 70th ARVN Ranger Battalion engaged in heavy fighting with an enemy force east of Gia Vuc in mid-May. Although these inconclusive struggles typified the early summer of 1974 in Quang Tin and Quang Ngai, events of a more decisive nature were occurring in the western highlands.

Dak Pek

By the early summer of 1974 three totally isolated outposts remained in the mountains north and northeast of Kontum City. Astride Route 14 (QL-14) in the far northwestern tip of Kontum Province was Dak Pek, occupied by the 88th Ranger Battalion with 360 men and 10 PF platoons with about 300. All contact with the camp was by air, and no artillery outside the camp itself was available to provide support for the subsector headquarters or the camp. About 3,200 people, nearly all Montagnards, lived under the protection of Dak Pek outpost, which interfered with enemy logistics along the north-south line of communication.

In fighting near the camp on 27 April, a document was captured indicating that an attack to capture Dak Pek was imminent; in early May, Ranger patrols detected the presence of an enemy regiment near the camp and discovered a cache of 60 105-mm. artillery rounds. Unknown to the Rangers then, the 29th Regiment of the 324B NVA Division had been trucked south from the A Shau Valley of Thua Thien Province. The deployment of the 29th Regiment exemplified the remarkable flexibility and newly developed mobility of the NVA, the latter attributable to its road network and to antiaircraft defenses that prevented effective interdiction. In order to assign the Dak Pek mission to the 29th Regiment, the NVA had to move it secretly 75 miles and place it under the command of B3 Front.

The commander of the 88th Ranger Battalion had sealed orders to be opened in the event Dak Pek were overrun. He was to lead the survivors through the mountains to Mang Buk, some 60 kilometers southeast. It is doubtful that Major Di ever got around to opening the orders; certainly he had no opportunity to execute them.

The Rangers had a series of encounters with NVA patrols beginning on 10 May. Two days later, following artillery, rocket, and mortar bombardments, the NVA attacked the outpost and subsector headquarters. The defenders were able to hold the enemy infantry at bay until the morning of the 16th, when, following an intense concentration of fire support, the 29th NVA Regiment, supported by tanks, closed in on the camp and subsector. Major Di maintained contact with the VNAF, flying over 70 bombing and strafing sorties during the morning and destroying at least one tank in a futile effort to save the camp. Using 37-mm. antiaircraft guns, the enemy reduced the effectiveness of South Vietnamese air support. At noon Major Di's radio fell silent under the rain of enemy fire, over 7,000 rounds of artillery, mortar, and rocket hitting the camp in the 12 hours before capitulation.

Months later, at the end of November, 14 survivors of Dak Pek escaped from NVA work camps in the jungle where they had been held since their capture on 16 May and reported to an ARVN Ranger outpost northeast of Kontum City. They said that Major Di and his executive officer had both been captured along with the survivors, that both had escaped during VNAF air strikes, but that Major Di had been recaptured the following day.

Tieu Atar

Tieu Atar was a frontier post manned by two companies from a battalion of Montagnard RF, stationed north of Ban Me Thuot, the capital of

Darlac Province. Close to the Cambodian border, it interfered in a minor way with the NVA line of communication south of Duc Co. Beginning on 18 May 1974 Communist propaganda teams entered the Montagnard settlement around Camp Tieu Atar, telling the people of an impending attack and urging them to leave. About 1,200 took the warning and began a long trek south.

The attack began on 27 May when the NVA slammed 60 rounds of 82-mm. mortar into the camp. On 30 May, a concentration of 1,000 rounds began to fall on the camp. Radio contact with the 211th RF Battalion was lost when the battalion commander's bunker was destroyed by a direct hit. One to two infantry battalions attacked before noon and overran the camp. Effective VNAF support was not possible because of bad weather and lack of communications. For the NVA, the way was now clear from its major logistical center at Duc Co all the way to Ban Don.

While the enemy was toppling the few remaining ARVN outposts in the remote reaches of the Central Highlands, an NVA offensive of major proportions was taking shape farther north. Its focus was the Quang Nam lowlands.

Quang Nam

Two major rivers entered Quang Nam Province from the south and formed a fertile delta, which, except for a narrow coastal strip on the south, was enclosed by steep mountains rising to 4,000 feet. The Province capital, Da Nang, rested at the northern edge of the delta on the beach of the strikingly beautiful crescent of Da Nang Bay. Da Nang was the most important South Vietnamese city north of Saigon and the site of a major port, a major air base, and the headquarters of I Corps and Military Region 1. National Highway 1 (QL-1) passed through Quang Nam close to the sand dunes along the coast and continued through the Hai Van Pass to Hue in Thua Thien Province. The national railway operated daily trains between Da Nang and Hue on a roadbed, much subjected to Communist harassment and sabotage, that generally paralleled the highway. The delta of Quang Nam had been a contested area before the cease-fire, but by the spring of 1973, the ARVN 3d Infantry Division and the Quang Nam territorials had established control in the flatlands up to the hills of Duc Duc District in the southwest and Thuong Duc District in the west.

Local security in Quang Nam's nine districts— which in the military chain-of-command were subsectors, subordinate to the sector chief who was also the province chief—varied from poor in the mountainous regions to good in the area of Da Nang. Hoa Vang District, the most populous, surrounded Da Nang. Its least secure villages were in the southwest corner of the district, centered on Hoa Hai Village, close to the major line of communication, Route 530, between Da Nang and the forward positions of the 3d ARVN Division in Dai Loc and Duc Duc Districts. That part of Dai Loc District which was south of the Song Vu Gia was for many years a VC stronghold—the Americans who operated there named it the Arizona Territory—but the ARVN had cleared it about the time of the cease-fire. North of the Song Vu Gia, the mountains of Dai Loc, where the ARVN could maintain no continuous presence, offered the Communists access to the lowlands.

The Communists exploited this situation frequently and interdicted from time to time the one road linking Thuong Duc District with the rest of the province. This road, local Route 4 (LTL-4), followed the north bank of the Song Vu Gia, passed through a narrow defile between the hills and the river just west of an ARVN artillery base on Hill 52, and then entered the district town of Thuong Duc. The valley of the Song Vu Gia was only 3,000 meters wide here; steep hills overlooked the district seat of Thuong Duc on the north, west, and south. There were no villages outside the district town itself secure enough for South Vietnamese officials to spend the night, and only three villages in the district had government administration by day. NVA lines of communication from the northwest and southwest reached Thuong Duc via National Route 14, which terminated there, and Route 614, which began in the large NVA logistical complex south of the A Shau Valley and joined Route 4 west of Thuong Duc. This district, therefore, was a key entrance to the Quang Nam lowlands.

Southwest of Dai Loc District was the vast mountain district of Duc Duc. Only in the extreme northeast region of Duc Duc did South Vietnamese officials maintain full-time residence. The area west of the Song Thu Bon, which included part of the Arizona Territory, was insecure and sparsely populated, as were the southern and western reaches of Duc Duc. ARVN influence extended south to the Nong Son coal mines in the narrow canyon of the Song Thu Bon, about 10 kilometers from the district seat. Here at a place called Da Trach, not far north of the major operating base of the 2d NVA Division, the ARVN maintained a garrison with outposts manned by RF units and PF platoons. Duc Duc was the other principal entrance to the Quang Nam lowlands from the NVA-held highlands of Quang Nam and Quang Tin.

The ARVN 3d Infantry Division was responsible for the defense of Quang Nam and that part of Quang Tin lying within the Que Son Valley. In June of 1974, General Hinh, the division commander, had his 57th Infantry Regiment, reinforced by the attached 3d Battalion, 56th Infantry, defending in the

Que Son Valley. His 2d Infantry Regiment was operating in the Go Noi and Duc Duc areas, while the 56th Infantry, minus its 3d Battalion, was in division reserve. The 56th's 1st Battalion was in training, and its third was at Fire Support Base Baldy at the northern entrance of the Que Son Valley. The 14th Ranger Group, which had been under the operational control of the 3d Division in Quang Nam, had been sent south to operate with the 2d ARVN Division to deal with the crisis that developed in Quang Tin. The 14th took along its 79th Ranger Battalion, which had been stationed in Thuong Duc. The 78th Ranger Battalion, which remained in Quang Nam to hold Da Trach, sent one of its companies to Thuong Duc to relieve the 79th.

Observing that matters were pretty well under control in Quang Nam and that the enemy had committed most of his 2d Division in the Quang Tin–Tien Phuoc battlefield, General Thuong, commanding I Corps, sent the 2d Infantry Regiment, 3d Division, into Tien Phuoc to eliminate elements of the 2d NVA Division and local main force units still threatening the district. Named QUANG TRUNG 3/74, the operation included, in addition to the entire 2d Infantry, a troop of the 11th Armored Cavalry, a battalion of 105-mm. howitzers, and a battery each of 155-mm. howitzers and 175-mm. guns. The operation lasted from 2 until 15 July and was a remarkable success. The NVA was forced to withdraw from the Tien Phuoc with heavy losses; 315 of its soldiers were killed, and 150 weapons were captured. Its mission completed, the 2d Infantry began moving back to Quang Nam on 16 July but left its 3d Battalion to assist the territorials of Quang Tin Province with local security. The 1st and 2d Battalions settled into the division base camp at Hoa Khanh in the hills above Da Nang.

Meanwhile, the 79th Ranger Battalion and the 14th Ranger Group Headquarters moved back to Quang Nam Province. The 79th returned to Thuong Duc, relieving the company of the 78th Ranger Battalion, which then moved back to Da Trach. The 12th Ranger Group still had three battalions around Mo Duc in Quang Ngai Province, but rotated one battalion at a time back to Quang Nam for refitting and retraining. Two battalions had completed the cycle by 16 July.

Da Trach and Duc Duc

Da Trach, a battalion-sized camp, was a strong point situated on a prominent hill about 900 feet above the Song Thu Bong south of the subsector headquarters at Duc Duc. It had been quiet at Da Trach and around the outposts manned by one RF company and seven PF platoons. Three of these outposts were in the hills and along the river south of Da Trach, while the others were in the valley of the Khe Le stream—called Antenna Valley by the Americans who operated there before—which flowed into the Song Thu Bon northeast of Da Trach post. Also located in the valley was the 4th Company, 146th RF Battalion, which had its 80-man garrison in the Ap Ba hamlet group, along the road that twisted eastward over the Deo Le Pass to Que Son. Possession of the Khe Le Valley would give the NVA not only another flanking approach to the ARVN defenses in the Que Son Valley but would provide access to the several good trails into Duy Xuyen district, bypassing the defenses in Duc Duc.

The 78th Ranger Battalion at Da Trach, with about 360 men, was scheduled for retraining at the Ranger Training Center, and on 17 July 1974, the 3d Battalion, 56th Infantry, arrived to execute the relief. The infantry battalion pulled in on trucks just before dark. The relief was to take place at noon the next day, but the 78th had withdrawn most of its outposts and was bivouacked for the night in the village. Although unfamiliar with the layout of the camp defenses, the 3d Battalion, with three of its four companies, assumed the responsibility. Also assembled within the defenses were the drivers who had driven the 3d Battalion to Da Trach and who would take the 78th Battalion out the next morning.

The strength of the 3d Battalion, 56th Infantry, was only about 360 men, but its 2d Company was not in the camp; rather, it had set up outposts on two hills along the east bank of the Thu Bon. One rifle platoon was on Cua Tan directly across the river from Da Trach, and the rest of the company was at Khuong Que, to the north.

NVA Military Region 5 was responsible for all of Quang Nam Province to the Kontum boundary. Its campaign plan for the summer and fall of 1974 involved elements of three regular divisions, a separate infantry brigade, and several independent regiments. Objectives ranged from central Quang Nam to southern Quang Ngai. To cope with the tactical and logistical requirements of this offensive, the NVA leadership activated a new headquarters, the 3d Corps. Operational in June, the corps began concentrating resources for the Quang Nam campaign.

The 36th NVA Regiment was formed in the spring of 1974 from replacement groups sent from North Vietnam into the mountains of western Duc Duc District. It was a light regiment, having only two infantry battalions, an antiaircraft machine gun company, light artillery, and administrative support units. On 10 July, a week before the planned relief of the 78th Ranger Battalion at Da Trach, the 36th NVA Regiment moved undetected into assembly areas close to ARVN outposts around Da Trach. Also on the move toward Da Trach were elements of all three regiments of the 2d NVA Division, the

1st, 31st, and 38th, plus the 10th Sapper Battalion, division artillery, and batteries of Military Region 5 artillery.

Shortly after midnight on 18 July, the midsummer night's silence was shattered by NVA artillery, rockets, and mortar rounds exploding on the defenses and outposts of Da Trach. A relatively weak attack by the 2d Battalion, 36th NVA Regiment, on the camp's main defenses was beaten back with heavy losses to the enemy and light casualties to the defenders, but contact with the 2d Company, 3d Battalion, 56th ARVN Infantry, outposts at Khuong Que and Cua Tan was lost before daybreak. By that time, the 4th Company, 146th RF Battalion at Ap Ba had been attacked and overrun, and the survivors were trying to escape through the mountains toward Duc Duc headquarters.

Shelling of the main camp meanwhile had stopped, and the attackers regrouped for another assault. The 2d Battalion, 1st Infantry Regiment, and a battalion of the 31st Infantry Regiment, both of the 2d NVA Division, joined the two battalions of the 36th Regiment for the next attempt. As the reconnaissance platoon and the 4th Company, 3d Battalion, 56th ARVN Infantry, tried to retake a lost outpost south of the camp, they were stopped by intense artillery and automatic weapons fire, which killed the company commander and the battalion commander of the 78th Rangers. The enemy resumed infantry assaults on the camp, and the 3d Battalion commander, who had assumed command of the 78th Rangers as well, reported the situation critical. The camp's radio was knocked out before noon, and all contact was lost with whatever PF outposts remained in action.

Enemy tanks were sighted about 5,000 meters southwest of the camp, and the VNAF began to provide fire support to the defenders. Heavy artillery, rocket, and mortar fire continued, augmented by antiaircraft guns, up to 37-mm., used in direct fire.

Contact was also lost with the 4th Company, 78th Rangers, and the two-gun platoon of 105-mm. howitzers in the camp had been knocked out of action. At mid-afternoon, the five-battalion enemy assault, which by this time included the 10th Sapper Battalion against the northern sector, had carried through the southwest defense line. With all bunkers and fighting positions demolished by a bombardment of more than 5,000 rounds, the survivors of the 3d and 78th Battalions withdrew, and the NVA rounded up civilians in the hamlets and villages; about 7,500 of them would be moved to Communist controlled regions of Duc Duc District.

General Hinh, from his 3d Division Headquarters above Da Nang, reacted quickly to the crisis in Duc Duc District. The subsector headquarters there had also received a heavy bombardment. General Hinh moved a forward division command post to Dai Loc and ordered the 2d Infantry Regiment to deploy immediately to Duc Duc and relieve the defenders at Da Trach. Operation QUANG TRUNG 4/74 had begun.

Only the 3d Battalion, 2d Infantry, was immediately available; the 1st Battalion remained at Fire Support Base Baldy in the Que Son Valley, and the 2d was still in Quang Tin Province. Orders were sent to both battalions to move immediately to Dai Loc, in Quang Nam Province, and the 3d Battalion moved from Da Nang to Hill 55 in northwestern Dien Ban District to protect the deployment of artillery to support Duc Duc.

These deployments ordered, General Hinh saw as his first priority securing the bridge over the Song Thu Bon, north of Duc Duc subsector headquarters and over which all division elements would have to pass en route to the battlefield. He ordered the 1st Battalion, 2d Infantry, just arrived from FSB Baldy, with the 2d Troop, 11th Armored Cavalry, to secure the bridge and had the 3d Battalion, 2d Infantry, on 18 July move to Duc Duc District Town. His staff went to work immediately drafting the tactical plan for QUANG TRUNG 4/74 with the objective of retaking Da Trach. The bridge secured, the 1st Battalion joined the 3d, and both moved south of Duc Duc, prepared to continue on toward Da Trach. By nightfall on the 18th, the 2d Battalion, 2d Infantry, had also moved to Duc Duc District Town, as had a battery of 155-mm. howitzers. Meanwhile, a battery of 175-mm. guns moved into firing positions in the Que Son Valley, within range of Duc Duc. These ARVN artillery positions soon received heavy and accurate counterbattery fire. The commander of the 2d ARVN Infantry, Lt. Col. Vu Ngoc Huong, having assumed tactical command of all ARVN forces in the Duc Duc–Da Trach battlefield, had communications with only two platoons of the original Da Trach defense force by the evening of 18 July.

The NVA resumed its coordinated offensive in Quang Nam in the pre-dawn hours of 19 July. A salvo of 35 122-mm. rockets fell on Da Nang Air Base; damage to VNAF operations was slight, although 16 people died and over 70 were wounded—many of whom were civilians and military dependents. In the morning Duc Duc Subsector received 45 rocket and mortar rounds. NVA 130-mm. guns hit an ARVN 105-mm. battery and the 2d Infantry's command post. Meanwhile, north of Dai Loc on Route 540, the 370th RF Company repulsed a strong enemy attempt to interdict the ARVN line of communication, killing 30 of the attackers and capturing many weapons.

With the enemy's fire erupting in their rear, the 1st and 3d Battalions, 2d ARVN Infantry, advanced south from Duc Duc toward Da Trach and by noon reported securing their initial objectives without opposition. The 1st Battalion was on Ky Vi Mountain, southeast of subsector headquarters, and the 3d Battalion was on Hill 284, past Khuong Que and at the entrance of Khe Le Valley. The 2d Battalion was in reserve. The plan called for the 3d Battalion to continue the attack to Cua Tan Mountain, across the river from Da Trach, and for the 1st Battalion to attack south, first seizing Hill 454 and then descending into the Khe Le Valley at the village of Ap Ba. The feasibility of the plan came into question, however, when the last contact with the Da Trach defenders on 19 July revealed that the command group and two companies of the 78th Rangers were under heavy attack on the hill at Cua Tan.

After seizing Da Trach, the North Vietnamese placed infantry battalions and antiaircraft guns in the hills above the valley, awaiting the arrival of the 2d ARVN Infantry. The VNAF struck hard at these forces on the 18th and 19th and caused heavy casualties, but the NVA could not be dislodged. By the afternoon of 19 July, the 1st Battalion, 2d Infantry, was in contact with elements of the NVA 36th Regiment on Ky Vi Mountain and on Hill 238, to the west. The VNAF flew 18 attack sorties in support, killing 75 enemy infantrymen and destroying a mortar. But the ARVN advance had to be halted. Suspecting a trap in the Khe Le Valley, General Hinh ordered the 2d Infantry to stop and send reconnaissance patrols forward.

Correctly anticipating that the enemy's Quang Nam campaign had only begun and that more forces would be required to deal with it, General Truong on 19 July ordered the 12th Ranger Group to move from Quang Ngai to Quang Nam. The 37th Ranger Battalion, already in Da Nang for rest and retraining, moved to Hieu Duc District on 20 July. That day, the 6th Infantry, 2d ARVN Division, began relieving the other two battalions of the 12th Ranger Group in Duc Pho and Mo Duc in Quang Ngai Province, and the 12th began to move north.

By 22 July, the NVA command at Da Trach apparently discovered that the ARVN 2d Infantry Regiment was not advancing into the trap in the Khe Le Valley. Plans were accordingly changed; the rest of the 1st NVA Regiment was ordered to Da Trach to attack the ARVN 2d Regiment in the hills above Duc Duc, while the 38th Regiment was to move through the hills above the valley toward Go Noi and Dien Ban. On 24 July the 1st NVA Regiment began moving into the attack, and the 38th Regiment started deploying east. General Truong was gathering more forces also. He ordered the 29th and 39th Ranger Battalions, 12th Ranger Group, newly arrived from Quang Ngai Province, to displace west of Go Noi Island, and he directed that the 1st Division in Thua Thien and the 2d Division in Quang Ngai each prepare one regiment for deployment to Quang Nam on 24-hour notice.

On 24 July, the 2d ARVN Infantry established its command post 700 meters north of the first hill south of Duc Duc, Nui Song Su. The 2d Troop, 11th Armored Cavalry, was providing security for the command post. The 2d Battalion was moving past Hill 238 and advancing on Hill 284, which had been vacated by the 3d Battalion under strong enemy pressure. The 3d Battalion had withdrawn to the hill at Nui Duong Coi, above a lake between it and Duc Duc Subsector, where the 1st Battalion was in reserve. The 1st Battalion, 56th Infantry, attached to the 2d Infantry, was protecting the regiment's right flank west of the Song Thu Bon.

The attack of the 1st NVA Regiment met the advancing 2d Battalion, 2d ARVN Infantry, on the slopes of Hill 284. The two leading companies of the 2d Battalion broke under a withering attack. By early afternoon on 24 July, the 1st NVA's attack reached the 3d Battalion on Nui Duong Coi. The battalion held and with good air and artillery support inflicted heavy casualties on the enemy. But the assault continued, the 3d Battalion commander fell wounded, and the battalion began to break. By dusk, both forward battalions of the 2d Infantry were badly scattered and withdrawing toward Duc Duc. The NVA attack reached into the rear area of the 2d Infantry and forced the command post to drop back 1,000 meters. Seeing a disaster for the 2d Infantry in the making, General Hinh had his division reconnaissance company lifted in by helicopter to help defend the command post. Reaching the command post late in the afternoon, the reconnaissance company was soon joined by the 37th Ranger Battalion and two troops of the 11th Armored Cavalry which General Hinh had sent overland to reinforce the beleaguered 2d Infantry.

On the morning of 25 July, while an attempt was being made to regroup the scattered 3d Battalion, General Hinh ordered the 12th Ranger Group to bring its three battalions forward and relieve the 2d Infantry. As this relief was beginning, General Truong had the 1st Division send its 54th Infantry Regiment to Quang Nam for attachment to the 3d Division. Further, he cancelled all unit training in I Corps except for the 137th RF Battalion, soon to complete its training cycle.

The fighting in the hills south of Duc Duc took a heavy toll of the NVA 1st Regiment, and the 2d NVA Division had to withdraw it from action, just as the 3d ARVN Division had to relieve the 2d Infantry. The 38th NVA Regiment was ordered to stop its eastward movement and come to the relief of the 1st Regiment, while elements of the 31st NVA Regiment still around Hau Duc in Quang Tin Province were called forward to the division base at Hiep Duc to prepare to assist the 1st and 38th

Regiments. The NVA plans for the 38th Regiment to move east into Go Noi were upset by the rapid ARVN deployment of the 12th Ranger Group. The battered 1st NVA Regiment was no longer equipped to protect the rear of the 38th or its line of communication against the expected counterattacks of the three Ranger battalions of the 12th Group. Further, the North Vietnamese soon learned of the movement of the 54th ARVN Regiment to Quang Nam, but they could not discover its mission or location. Considering these uncertainties, the NVA command suspended the attack and held its gains, replacing depleted battalions with fresh ones.

General Hinh had reached similar conclusions on 25 July. He declared the counterattack to retake Da Trach at an end; QUANG TRUNG 4/74 was over and QUANG TRUNG 8/74, an interim operation to defend the shallow positions south of Duc Duc Subsector, began. By this time, virtually all of the survivors of Da Trach had made their way back to friendly lines. Sixty-four were from the 3d Battalion, 56th Infantry; 79 from the 78th Ranger Battalion; 59 from the 4th Company, 146 RF Battalion; and 20 from the PF platoons. A few were village officials.

The 54th Infantry, 1st ARVN Division, arrived in Quang Nam on 26 July, put its headquarters at Dien Ban District Town, and immediately went into action. While the 1st Battalion took over a security mission in the Da Nang rocket belt near Hill 55, the 2d and 3d Battalions began clearing the area around Ky Chau Village on Go Noi Island. Both the 2d and 3d met heavy resistance and proceeded westward slowly, engaging an enemy force on 28 July and dispersing it with heavy losses.

Duc Duc and Dai Loc were struck on 25 July and again the next day by enemy rocket and artillery fire, but casualties were light. On 26 July, the Rangers completed their relief of the 2d Infantry and assumed responsibility for the sector. The 21st Ranger Battalion to the east was holding Nui Van Chi, the 37th Ranger Battalion was on Hill 238, just south of Nui Song Su, and the 39th Ranger Battalion was at Duc Duc Subsector in reserve. The shattered 2d Infantry moved west of Dai Loc District Town along Route 4 to protect the division right flank, while its 3d Battalion was being reformed at the division base near Da Nang. Meanwhile, the VNAF was trying its best to blunt the enemy attacks. The 1st Air Division flew 67 attack sorties on the 25th and 57 on the 26th, destroying a tank and several antiaircraft and mortar positions, striking large troop concentrations, and killing about 90 enemy soldiers.

The NVA continued to batter ARVN rear areas. Water-sappers reached the Nam O Bridge on Highway 1 north of Da Nang before dawn on 27 July and dropped one span, but ARVN engineers had the bridge open with a Bailey truss by early afternoon. On 29 July NVA gunners sent 70 122-mm. rockets into the inhabited area around Da Nang Air Base and its ammunition dump. Casualties and damage were light, however.

With the withdrawal of 2d Infantry, QUANG TRUNG 8/74 was declared over on 29 July. QUANG TRUNG 9/74 was to begin on 30 July. The troop list had the 12th Ranger Group in contact south of Duc Duc, the 2d Infantry on the flank west of Dai Loc, the 54th in the Go Noi east of Dai Loc, and the 1st and 2d Battalions of the 56th Infantry in reserve in Dai Loc District Town. The 3d Battalion, 56th Infantry, the battalion destroyed at Da Trach, was being reformed at Da Nang, while the 78th Ranger Battalion was undergoing the same process at the Duc My Ranger Training Center in Khanh Hoa Province.

Thuong Duc

When the 79th Ranger Battalion, 14th Ranger Group, returned from Quang Ngai to Quang Nam in mid-July of 1974 and assumed the defense of the post at Thuong Duc, the westernmost ARVN position in the province, the battle in the hills south of neighboring Duc Duc District Town was under way as NVA Military Region 5 committed all of its 2d Division there and in the Que Son Valley south of Duc Duc. Ranger and PF patrols and outposts around Thuong Duc reported little enemy activity, not unexpectedly since known enemy forces in Quang Nam were heavily engaged. Neither the Thuong Duc garrison nor, for that matter, the G-2 at I Corps Headquarters even suspected that the 29th NVA Regiment was rolling north to Thuong Duc following its mid-May conquest of Dak Pek.

The NVA shelling of Thuong Duc began on 29 July, while a volley of rockets fell on Da Nang Air Base. Infantry assaults on all outposts followed. Communication was quickly broken between Thuong Duc Subsector and three PF outposts. Contact was also lost with two Ranger outposts in the hills west of the town. ARVN artillery on Hill 52, near Dai Loc, gave effective support to the Thuong Duc defense, and enemy casualties were high.

Early on the morning of 30 July, the subsector commander was wounded by the continuing heavy bombardment, but all ground attacks were repulsed. Later that morning VNAF observers saw a convoy of tanks and artillery approaching along Route 4 west of Thuong Duc, and subsequent air strikes halted the column, destroying three tanks. As NVA attacks continued throughout the day, the Rangers of Thuong Duc took their first prisoner of war, and identified the presence of the 29th Regiment on the battlefield. Not apparent at the time, the 29th had been detached from the 324B NVA Division and was operating under NVA Military Region 5.

In an assault on 31 July, NVA infantrymen reached the perimeter wire of Thuong Duc. The Ranger battalion commander asked for artillery fire directly on his command post. With the NVA occupying the high ground above Route 4 east of Thuong Duc, the ARVN 3d Division and I Corps commanders believed that the forces available to them were inadequate to relieve Thuong Duc. To protect his flank, General Hinh had placed the battered 2d Infantry on the road west of Dai Loc, but it was not strong enough to move west along Route 4. More fire support for Thuong Duc was provided, however, when General Hinh moved a platoon of 175-mm. guns to Hieu Duc. Conditions in the Thuong Duc perimeter were serious but not yet critical. Most of the South Vietnamese bunkers and trenches had collapsed under heavy artillery fire, the enemy controlled the airstrip just outside the camp, and casualties were 13 killed and 45 wounded.

Although the intensity of the NVA bombardment dropped off between 31 July and 1 August, Ranger casualties continued to mount. NVA gunners shifted their concentrations to 2d Infantry positions and ARVN artillery batteries near Dai Loc, causing moderate casualties and damaging four howitzers. The Ranger commander at Thuong Duc asked for medical evacuation for his wounded, but the commander of the VNAF 1st Air Division advised that air evacuation would not be attempted until the NVA antiaircraft guns around Thuong Duc had been neutralized. Meanwhile, General Truong ordered one M-48 tank company to move immediately from northern Military Region 1 to Quang Nam for attachment to the 3d Division; he told General Hinh to keep the tank company in reserve and to employ it only in an emergency. General Hinh then formed a task force to attack west from Dai Loc and relieve the Rangers at Thuong Duc. The tank company from Tan My, in Thua Thien Province, arrived in Da Nang in good order on 1 August, and General Hinh's task force, composed of the 2d Infantry and the 11th Armored Cavalry Squadron, prepared for the march to Thuong Duc.

On 2 August, with only light attacks by fire striking the camp, the Ranger battalion resumed patrolling beyond its perimeter. On 4 August Ranger patrols discovered 53 NVA bodies killed by VNAF air strikes in the hills southwest of Thuong Duc, but attempts at air evacuation of ARVN casualties failed when VNAF sorties against six antiaircraft positions south of the camp were unable to silence the guns. The next day, the first indication of another committed NVA regiment was revealed when the 2d Battalion, 2d Infantry, captured a soldier from the 29th NVA Regiment east of Thuong Duc. According to the prisoner, the entire 29th Regiment was positioned in the hills overlooking Route 4 between Hill 52 and Thuong Duc, while a regiment of the NVA 304th Division had been given the mission to seize Thuong Duc. Events proved this interrogation to be accurate. The 2d Battalion had fought all afternoon in the rice paddies and hills north of Route 4. Slowly moving toward Thuong Duc, it was still four kilometers east of the ARVN fire base on Hill 52, which itself was under enemy artillery and infantry attack. By 5 August, the 2d Battalion was still struggling to move forward along the foothills north of Route 4, and the 1st Battalion, 57th ARVN Infantry, reinforcing the 2d Regiment, was stopped by heavy enemy machine gun fire from the hills west of Hill 52.

Back at Thuong Duc, the situation was rapidly becoming critical as ammunition and food supplies were being exhausted. The VNAF attempted a resupply drop on the camp on 5 August, but all eight bundles of food and ammunition fell outside the perimeter. The VNAF tried to destroy bundles that were within reach of the NVA, and one A-37 attack plane was shot down in the attempt.

The next day, while the relief task force was battling its way west against heavy resistance, General Truong, concerned about the critical threat to Da Nang from a large NVA force west of Dai Loc, ordered fresh reinforcements to Quang Nam. Appealing personally to General Vien at the Joint General Staff in Saigon, General Truong succeeded in getting the 1st Airborne Brigade released from the general reserve for deployment to Quang Nam and attachment to General Hinh's 3d Division. The brigade was ordered to reach Da Nang by 11 August with three airborne infantry battalions and one artillery battalion. Additionally, the 3d Airborne Brigade, then deployed in the defense of Hue, was told to prepare for movement to Da Nang. But none of these measures would save Thuong Duc; the NVA overran the small garrison on 7 August.

Thuong Duc had absorbed hundreds of artillery and mortar shells since the attack began, but the bombardment of 7 August was singular in its intensity. Over 1,200 rounds, including many from 130-mm. guns, landed inside the perimeter beginning on the night of 6 August. The first wave of infantrymen was repulsed that night, but the assault at dawn the next day penetrated the defense. At midmorning, the Ranger commander reported that he had started a withdrawal. Soon radio contact was lost. The gallant ordeal of another ARVN Ranger battalion was over. With Dak Pek and Tieu Atar lost in May, speculation at II Corps Headquarters in Pleiku held that Mang Buk would be next.

Mang Buk

Perched on a hill above the Dak Nghe River, about 4,000 feet above sea level, Mang Buk was over 50 kilometers north of Kontum City and about 30 kilometers north of Chuong Nghia (Plateau Gi). A Communist supply route, locally known as A-16, connected Kontum with Quang Ngai and Binh Dinh Provinces and passed south of Mang Buk. The small garrison at Mang Buk, two RF companies and two PF platoons, had no capability to interfere with movement along this route. The subsector commander was under orders to keep one company in the camp and to patrol out to 2,000 meters. His firepower consisted of two 106-mm. recoilless rifles, two 81-mm. mortars, and some machine guns.

Realizing the threat to Mang Buk as well as its vulnerability, the Kontum province chief, Lt. Col. Mai Xuan Hau, ordered the evacuation of civilians from Mang Buk in June 1974. By the time the Communists began their siege on 25 July, all but 800 civilians had left.

Measured against other NVA sieges, the one at Mang Buk was light indeed; only 3,000 rounds hit the camp between 25 July and 4 August, while the subsector claimed 55 enemy killed. Other than 107-mm. rockets, the heaviest projectiles the enemy used were 82-mm. mortars. On 18 August, after a respite, the camp again came under heavy fire. The next day two battalions of the 66th Regiment of the 10th NVA Division, supported by artillery, overran the camp. Without artillery and denied air support by the low cloud cover, the defenders withdrew and headed for Chuong Nghia, the last remaining outpost in Kontum Province. The enemy was not far behind.

Plei Me

When II Corps Headquarters announced on 4 August 1974 that the first phase of the Mang Buk siege was over, the siege of Plei Me began. A well-fortified position about midway between Pleiku City and the fallen outpost of Tieu Atar, Plei Me was defended by the 82d Ranger Battalion, which in April had been ejected from Fire Support Base 711 by an NVA assault. By early August FSB 711, an artillery base north of Plei Me, was back in ARVN hands and able to support the Plei Me defense.

From its base near Duc Co, the 320th NVA Division planned and executed the attack on Plei Me. Reconnaissance and deployments for the attack began in early June as the 48th Infantry Regiment, elements of the 64th Infantry Regiment, and an artillery battalion and an antiaircraft battalion of the 320th moved close to Plei Me. The ARVN II Corps reacted by reinforcing FSB 711 with the 42d Infantry of the 22d ARVN Division and striking enemy assembly areas with air and artillery attacks. The 320th delayed its attack but kept elements of its 48th Regiment near Plei Me. When ARVN II Corps moved the 42d Infantry back to Binh Dinh Province, the NVA B-3 Front saw an opportunity for a long-awaited assault on Plei Me.

The ARVN 82d Ranger Battalion at Plei Me, in addition to its four rifle companies, was reinforced by the 2d Company, 81st Ranger Battalion. The main defense was inside Plei Me Camp itself, with outposts in Chu Ho Hill and Hill 509. When the attack began, the 2d Company was patrolling outside the camp, and only 22 men were able to get back to the camp before the enemy closed off all access. The battalion headquarters was also outside the main defenses when the attack started, but the staff managed to dash in through the main gate before being cut off.

The 320th NVA Division employed at least four infantry battalions from its 9th and 48th Regiments, plus the 26th Independent Regiment of the B-3 Front, and later a battalion of its 64th Regiment, against the 410 men of the ARVN Rangers and the fire bases and relief columns supporting them. Artillery support included at least two 130-mm. guns and three 120-mm. mortars in addition to 85-mm. field guns, 82-mm. mortars, and recoilless rifles. At least 12 heavy antiaircraft machine guns (12.7-mm., equivalent to the U.S. .50-caliber) were in position to fire into the camp and at VNAF aircraft.

Vacating the bunkers bombarded by heavy Soviet mortars firing delay-fused projectiles, ARVN Rangers fought from their spider-web pattern of trenches. Two concentric fences of concertina barbed wire ringed the camp. The outer fence, six rows of concertina laced with mines, enclosed a 25-meter minefield strewn with claymores, trip grenades, and command-detonated 105-mm. howitzer projectiles.

Unlike Dak Pek and Tieu Atar, Plei Me was supported by artillery from outside the area under attack. ARVN batteries of 105-mm. and 155-mm. howitzers at Fire Support Base 711 provided excellent support. Artillery at Phu Nhon helped on the southern and eastern approaches, and 175-mm. guns covered the entire perimeter. The commander of the 82d Ranger Battalion and his deputy called and adjusted all fire missions, restricting radio traffic to themselves because the enemy monitored ARVN tactical nets.

Six days after the attack began, the outpost of Chu Ho fell on 10 August, followed five days later by Hill 509, but the main camp held on. Later, the battalion commander said that the outposts fell because they had run out of food. The main camp would have been defeated too if it had not rained, for there was no resupply of water during the 29-day siege. In any case, on 2 September the NVA 320th Division withdrew from the bloody field of

Plei Me. It had launched 20 ground assaults, fired over 10,000 artillery and mortar rounds, and lost at least 350 soldiers in its attempt to overrun the 82d Ranger Battalion.

Duc Duc and Que Son

On 29 July 1974, when the NVA first attacked Thuong Duc, the ARVN 21st Ranger Battalion on the left flank of the Ranger positions protecting Duc Duc District came under heavy attack. Although they inflicted heavy casualties on the 36th NVA Regiment, the Rangers were forced back about 1,000 meters to the slopes of Nui Duong Coi. The NVA pursued, and fighting continued in the rough terrain in front of Nui Duong Coi for several days. Then on 3 August, the 36th Regiment launched a strong attack. Several Ranger positions collapsed, and the commander of the 12th Ranger Group ordered the 39th Ranger Battalion to assist the 21st. After an all-day battle, the enemy withdrew and the Rangers regained all lost ground. The VNAF contributed greatly to the ARVN success; although Ranger casualties were high—more than 35 killed, 100 wounded, and 25 missing—the NVA left over 200 dead on the field. While the infantry fought in the hills, the NVA artillery slammed 280 rounds of 122-mm. rockets and 100-mm. gunfire into the command post of the 12th Ranger Group. Casualties were light, however. Fatigued and badly depleted, the 12th Ranger Group was relieved by the 54th Infantry, 1st ARVN Division. With its battalions down to 200 men each, the group withdrew to the rear to receive replacements and a much-needed rest. Through August and early September, the ARVN 54th Infantry made major advances even though the NVA reinforced the 36th Regiment with the 1st Infantry.

Other reinforcements were on their way from North Vietnam. The 41st Infantry Regiment with three infantry battalions and a sapper battalion arrived in Thanh My, southwest of Thuong Duc, in mid-August and soon deployed between Thuong Duc and Duc Duc.

While central Quang Nam Province was quaking under the NVA offensive, ARVN forces defending the Que Son Valley also came under heavy attack. The first outpost to fall was a hill southwest of Que Son District Town defended by an RF company and one company of the 57th ARVN Infantry. When contact was lost with the defenders on 31 July, General Truong ordered major changes in I Corps dispositions that inevitably weakened the ARVN hold on contested regions of Quang Ngai Province.

On 1 August, the responsibility for the Que Son Valley was transferred from the 3d ARVN Division, heavily engaged in Thuong Duc and Duc Duc, to the 2d Division. The 57th Infantry, minus a battalion attached to the 2d Infantry in Duc Duc, was attached to the 2d Division in the Que Son Valley, and the 4th Infantry was deployed to the valley from Binh Son District in Quang Ngai Province to be the I Corps reserve south of the Hai Van Pass. To compensate for the 4th Infantry's departure, the 5th Infantry was moved to Binh Son, and the 6th Infantry took over the 5th Infantry's mission in Duc Pho. Only territorials and a few Rangers were left in the threatened Mo Duc District of Quang Ngai.

The 4th Infantry was immediately engaged by two NVA battalions between Fire Support Base Baldy and Que Son. Although no more important positions were lost, fighting continued sporadically for the rest of the year in the Que Son Valley. Da Nang air base was subjected to several rocket attacks during August, but casualties and damage were negligible.

In September, faced with a deteriorating situation north of the Hai Van Pass, General Truong returned troops to the 1st ARVN Division in Thua Thien. Since the 54th Infantry Regiment had pushed the forward defenses of Duc Duc south almost to the Khe Le Valley and the 56th Infantry had partially recovered from punishing summer battles, he ordered the 54th to return to its parent division. General Hinh relieved the 54th with his own division's 56th Infantry. Thus, in early September, the infantrymen of the 56th Regiment returned to the battle-scarred hills of Duc Duc. The 3d Battalion took up positions on the right, on Khuong Que Hill where its 2d Company had fought and lost the first engagement of the enemy's Duc Duc campaign. The 1st Battalion was on the left, on Ky Vi Hill, and the 2d Battalion was in reserve with the regimental headquarters near Duc Duc Subsector.

The 1st NVA Regiment, 2d Division, launched simultaneous, heavily supported assaults on both forward battalions of the 56th Regiment on 4 October. While mortar and artillery fire pounded the 3d Battalion command post, NVA sappers entered the headquarters perimeter and severed communications with the two forward ARVN companies. These companies, under infantry attack from the front, withdrew and were caught in a devastating crossfire from the rear and flanks. The 1st Battalion fared little better; its outposts were also overrun, but casualties were lighter. The NVA coordinated artillery fire with great skill in this assault; a steady rain of shells kept the 56th Regiment's headquarters and the 2d Battalion from reacting while the two forward battalions were being overrun. As soon as he was able, the regimental commander ordered the attached 21st Ranger Battalion back into the line to relieve the shattered 3d Battalion.

The 1st NVA Regiment had accomplished its mission, but casualties were heavy, and it lacked the strength either to pursue or to consolidate its gains. The ARVN defensive line south of Duc Duc remained virtually unchanged, but the 56th Regiment was nearly out of action. Only the 2d Battalion could put more than 300 men in the field, and the 3d Battalion had only 200. General Hinh had to relieve the regiment again with the 12th Ranger Group.

During the summer and fall of 1974, the 3d ARVN Division and attached Rangers had reached exhaustion. By any standards, casualties had been extremely high. More than 4,700 men had been killed, wounded, or were missing in the actions in and around Duc Duc in the three months since the Communist offensive began at Da Trach on 18 July. A disproportionate number were officers and noncommissioned officers for whom no experienced replacements were available.

Hill 1062

The first contingent of the 1st Airborne Brigade was flown into Da Nang on 8 August 1974, the day after the 79th Ranger Battalion was driven out of Thuong Duc. Meanwhile the brigade's heavy equipment was moving up the coast from Saigon on Vietnamese Navy boats. On 11 August General Truong ordered the 3d Airborne Brigade to deploy with three airborne battalions to Da Nang. By 14 August, the brigade headquarters and the 2d, 3d, and 6th Battalions were in Quang Nam, their defensive sectors in Thua Thien having been taken over by the 15th Ranger Group under the operational control of the ARVN 1st Infantry Division. Brig. Gen. Le Quong Luong, commanding the Airborne Division, established his command post at Marble Mountain south of Da Nang. His 2d Brigade remained in Thua Thien attached to the Marine Division.

A steep ridge extended north from the Song Vu Gia and Route 4. The low hills at the southern foot of the ridge had been seized by the 29th NVA Regiment, which had blocked the ARVN task force's relief of the Rangers at Thuong Duc. The highest point on the ridge was about six kilometers north of Route 4 on Hill 1235, but Hill 1062, about 2,000 meters south of Hill 1235, offered the best observation of the road and Dai Loc. Having placed an observation post on Hill 1062, the NVA was delivering accurate artillery fire on ARVN positions in Dai Loc. Consequently, the first mission assigned to the Airborne Division was the capture of Hill 1062 and the ridge south to the road. To deal with the threat developing west of Da Nang, the 3d Airborne Brigade was assigned the secondary mission of blocking the western approaches in Hieu Duc District.

The 8th and 9th Airborne Battalions began the attack and made their first firm contact with elements of the 29th NVA Regiment on 18 August east of Hill 52, the same area in which the 3d ARVN Division Task Force had run into strong resistance. For an entire month, these battalions doggedly pressed forward along the ridge toward Hill 1062. In the meantime, having sustained heavy casualties, the 29th NVA Regiment brought in reinforcements. The NVA 3d Corps ordered the 31st NVA Regiment, 2d Division, to Thuong Duc to relieve the 66th Regiment, 304th NVA Division, so that the 66th could be deployed in support of the 29th, which was steadily giving ground to attacking Airborne troops. Additionally, the 24th Regiment, 304th NVA Division, arrived in the battle area in early September. Finally, on 19 September, the 1st Airborne Brigade reported that it had troopers on Hill 1062.

While the ARVN was taking nearly two weeks to consolidate the controlling terrain along this section of the ridge, the 66th NVA Regiment relieved the severely depleted 29th, and elements of the 24th NVA Regiment joined the fight against the 1st Airborne Brigade. By 2 October, the brigade was in possession of the high ground, and the 2d and 9th Battalions were digging in on the ridge to the south. About 300 enemy soldiers were killed in this phase of the battle on Hill 1062, and seven prisoners of war were taken. All were from the 304th—the Dien Bien Phu Division—one of the first regular units in the Viet Minh formed by General Giap in 1950.

During the weeks that followed, the 1st Airborne Brigade fought off repeated attempts by the 304th NVA Division to retake the ridge. Making skillful use of air and artillery support, the brigade managed to hold on despite the heavily supported assaults of superior numbers. In one incident, when the 24th NVA Infantry was allowed to penetrate the defenses on hills 383 and 126 and advance directly into a killing zone of preplanned artillery fires, nearly 250 of the attacking force was killed.

By mid-October, the 1st Airborne Brigade had also taken heavy casualties, and the four battalions in the hills above Thuong Duc were down to about 500 men each. Estimated enemy losses were over 1,200 killed during the first half of October, and 14 soldiers of the Dien Bien Phu Division were prisoners of war. The NVA, nevertheless, was determined to regain the dominating heights. On 29 October, the reinforced 24th NVA Regiment began another assault on Hill 1062, this time firing large concentrations of tear gas. This assault carried to the highest position on the ridge, forcing an airborne battalion to withdraw. On 1 November, Hill 1062 was again in enemy hands.

Meanwhile in Thua Thien Province, enemy pressure against the lightly held Hue defenses was becoming severe, and General Truong was receiving strongly phrased requests from his elements north of the Hai Van Pass to return at least some of the Airborne Division. General Truong resisted and ordered Brig. Gen. Le Quong Luong of the Airborne to retake Hill 1062. The attack began on 8 November, and three days later ARVN troopers were back on the ridge. They established new defensive positions on the slopes, leaving the furrowed, shattered crest to the dozens of NVA dead who remained there. Although heavy fighting continued in the hills and on the ridge for several more weeks as the Airborne Division expanded its control of critical terrain, the most violent phase of one of the bloodiest battles since the cease-fire was over. The Airborne Division had lost nearly 500 of its soldiers killed since its commitment in Quang Nam Province on 15 August. Nearly 2,000 had been wounded. Enemy casualties were estimated to be about 2,000 killed and 5,000 wounded. Seven of the nine airborne battalions had fought in the three-month campaign, and by mid-November six of these were on Hill 1062. The enemy had observation of the airborne positions from the heights of Hill 1235, but General Luong could not muster enough force to take this peak and still defend what he had. Similarly, the enemy lacked the forces to counterattack in strength.

By the end of 1974, all but two airborne battalions were withdrawn from Hill 1062. The remaining 1st and 7th Battalions kept patrols there and depended on artillery fires to deny the terrain to enemy occupation, but placed their main battle positions near Dong Lam Mountain, about 4 kilometers to the east, and in the ridges above Hill 52.

The rainy season had reached Quang Nam Province in October and provided some respite from the intense and continual combat of summer. Both sides needed this time to recuperate and prepare for the next dry season and, although neither knew it then, the final NVA offensive.

Kontum

While the first phase of the siege of Mang Buc was under way, the rest of Kontum Province was relatively quiet. On 2 August 1974, Brig. Gen. Le Trung Tuong, commanding the 23d ARVN Division and responsibile for the security of the western Central Highlands (Kontum, Pleiku, Darlac and Quang Duc Provinces), moved his main headquarters from Kontum to a more central location in Pleiku. In Kontum he left a forward command post and a sizable force of infantry under the command of his deputy, Colonel Hu The Quang. The troops under Colonel Quang's command included the 45th ARVN Infantry Regiment, defending the northeast approaches to Kontum City and operating in the mountainous jungle between Route 5B (LTL-5B) and Outpost Number 4. About 15 kilometers northeast of Kontum, Outpost Number 4 was lost to an NVA attack during the summer and never recovered by the ARVN. It had provided a base for interdicting an NVA road, called Route 715, which the Communists were constructing from Vo Dinh, northeast of Kontum, toward Binh Dinh. North of Outpost Number 4, Outpost Number 5 served a similar purpose, but it was also lost to the NVA that summer.

Colonel Quang had the 40th ARVN Infantry Regiment, attached from the 22d ARVN Division, securing the northwestern approaches to the city. Two battalions of the 44th ARVN Infantry Regiment were in reserve behind the 40th northwest of Kontum, while the third battalion was retraining in Ban Me Thuot. Three RF battalions manned outposts along the northern and western approaches, while a fourth RF battalion and two Ranger battalions secured the southern reaches of the province and the Chu Pao Pass.

Although Colonel Quang felt that he could defend Kontum City, ARVN formations in the highlands had lost the mobility that had previously enabled II Corps to deploy forces rapidly by air—from small patrols to entire divisions—to meet enemy threats and somewhat nullify the advantages of initiative and surprise. Constraints on fuel and maintenance had all but eliminated air mobility. Long range reconnaissance patrols, formerly moved by helicopter, were now walking to objective areas, their range and ability to remain drastically shortened. Logistical airlift for the entire province was limited to one CH-47 helicopter; consequently, nearly all supply and evacuation was trucked as far as possible, then carried over steep trails to forward positions. Thus, even in good weather, the ARVN could not reinforce or rescue isolated outposts such as Mang Buc.

As Mang Buc was overrun, the NVA B-3 Front conducted attacks along the Kontum defenses that held the meager II Corps reserves in place, denying reinforcements to Mang Buc. Enemy pressure declined after Mang Buc's fall, and the ARVN in Kontum concentrated on the enemy's Route 715, which by mid-September had been extended to within 15 kilometers of the boundary of Binh Dinh and Pleiku Provinces, bypassing the Kontum defenses on the east. The ARVN II Corps sent long range reconnaissance patrols against the road to lay mines and sabotage trucks and roadbuilding equipment, and air strikes were called in. Four 175-mm. guns in Kontum, with fires adjusted by the Province's remaining L-19 observation plane, also interdicted Route 715. Persistent ARVN attacks caused high casualties among the NVA work parties and temporarily stopped further extension of the road.

Chuong Nghia

While II Corps was pounding away at Route 715, the NVA B-3 Front was preparing to attack Chuong Nghia. Aware of an impending attack, II Corps headquarters moved the 254th RF Battalion, operating west of Kontum City, to reinforce the defense of Chuong Nghia. By the end of September 1974 the garrison had 600 men—280 from the 254th, one RF Company, and nine PF platoons. The defense included a ring of outposts as far as six kilometers from the camp, intermediate outposts about three kilometers away, and an inner ring about 1,000 meters out. About 2,000 civilians lived within the camp's perimeter.

The NVA attacked the outposts on 30 September. Two 105-mm. howitzers in Chuong Nghia could not adequately support the widely scattered platoons and companies and one by one, the outposts were overrun. Although the commander of II Corps, General Toan, ordered two 175-mm. guns to move up Route 5B from Kontum to support the defense, the poor condition of the road made the going very slow. As the attacks continued on 1 October, II Corps sent an RF company by air to Chuong Nghia.

By 2 October, five outposts had fallen and the camp was under heavy bombardment. The ARVN 251st RF Battalion was at the Kontum airfield waiting to be flown to Chuong Nghia, but heavy enemy fire on the airstrip prevented the landing. The two 175-mm. guns were not yet in range.

The final assault began on 3 October with heavy artillery concentrations falling on the subsector headquarters and on the command post of the 254th RF Battalion. Volleys of 1,000 rounds were followed by the assault of a battalion of NVA infantry, from the 28th Regiment, against the subsector and 254th RF Battalion. Defensive positions were quickly overrun. Chuong Nghia was lost, and few survived. Although VNAF fighter-bombers were employed against the 28th NVA Regiment and its supporting artillery, the last major outpost in Kontum Province had fallen. Without supporting artillery, the South Vietnamese had no way to hold a small, isolated garrison against a determined, well-supported NVA attack.

Quang Ngai

The demands for reinforcements in Quang Nam Province and in the Que Son Valley had spread the ARVN very thin in Quang Ngai Province, which had been boiling with enemy activity since early summer. The 2d ARVN Division, under Brig. Gen. Tran Van Nhut, had conducted fairly successful pacification and security operations in Quang Ngai, but the vast expanse of territory it had to cover was vulnerable to hit-and-run Communist attacks. Furthermore, a number of ARVN outposts were deep in the hills beyond supporting or quick reinforcing distance.

The principal adversary opposing the ARVN in Quang Ngai was still the 52d NVA Brigade, which had four infantry battalions, a sapper battalion, and supporting artillery. The brigade had its battalions deployed west of National Highway 1 (QL-1), and south of Nghia Hanh District Town in position to threaten the populated areas of Mo Duc and Duc Pho, as well as the mountain district seats at Son Ha, Tra Bong, and Minh Long and the frontier outpost of Gia Vuc in the far western edge of Ba To District. Five other battalions of local sappers and infantry were disposed close to Route 1 from the northern district of Binh Son south to Duc Pho, and one battalion had infiltrated into the Batangan Peninsula east of Binh Son.

Augmenting the 2d ARVN Disivion in Quang Ngai Province were 12 RF battalions and 3 battalions of the 11th Ranger Group. The 68th Ranger Battalion was at Son Ha District Town, over the mountains west of Quang Ngai City; the 69th Ranger Battalion was in Tra Bong, up the Tra Bong River from Binh Son; and the 70th Ranger Battalion was still defending the outpost at Gia Vuc.

Timing operations with the opening of the offensive in Quang Nam Province, the NVA initiated heavy attacks by fire and ground assaults throughout Quang Ngai on the night of 19 July 1974. The following morning, NVA gunners fired at the base at Chu Lai with eight 122-mm. rockets but caused no damage. Attacks continued for five days before the intensity began to fall off.

Meanwhile, the critical situation in Quang Nam impelled General Truong to order Maj. Gen. Le Van Nhut to send his 4th Infantry Regiment to take over defense of the Que Son Valley, relieving the 3d ARVN Division of a responsibility that had distracted General Hinh from the principal threat in central Quang Nam. Heavy NVA attacks flared again on 3 and 4 August in the central district of Nghia Hanh. In the hills south of the district town in the Cong Hoa Valley, the 118th RF Battalion was overrun following a heavy artillery concentration. Two battalions, one RF and the other from the 5th Infantry, were sent to reinforce the 118th, but they arrived too late to rescue the position. General Truong and General Nhut saw the hard-won gains of the summer slipping away. There were no spectacular enemy initiatives: just a gradual erosion of security as one small position after another fell to short, violent enemy assaults. But with so few troops available, South Vietnamese commanders could do little to halt the decline, much less restore the earlier situation.

The first of the district headquarters to fall during the NVA offensive was Minh Long when elements of the 52d NVA Brigade overran the two defending RF Companies on 17 August. Outposts held by the 15 local PF platoons collapsed quickly under the weight of NVA artillery. A platoon of 105-mm. artillery was soon out of action, its howitzers damaged by enemy fire. A three-battalion ARVN relief force failed to make any headway, and NVA trucks were seen hauling ammunition into Minh Long on 23 August.

Three days after the fall of Minh Long, General Nhut asked General Truong for permission to withdraw the 70th Ranger Battalion from Gia Vuc, now completely isolated and exposed to Communist attack. General Nhut also wanted to pull the 68th and 69th Rangers out of Son Ha and Tra Bong because these battalions had poor prospects for survival against heavy NVA firepower. General Truong understood, but he would not agree to abandoning any districts to the Communists without a fight.

Artillery fire on Gia Vuc began on 19 September, followed shortly by ground assaults. Five outposts fell, but the Rangers moved out quickly and retook three of them. But without artillery support or air strikes—the weather was bad—and losing 50 men killed and as many wounded, the 70th Ranger Battalion was unable to hold. The camp fell on 21 September. Only 21 survivors eventually made it back to ARVN lines.

Some help for beleaguered Quang Ngai Province appeared on 1 October when the 4th Infantry, 2d ARVN Infantry Division, returned to Chu Lai from its operations in the Que Son Valley to try to recover the terrain lost to the NVA south of Nghia Hanh District Town. Well entrenched, the Communists had even moved a battery of 37-mm. antiaircraft guns to within four kilometers of the district town, but the guns were soon destroyed by ARVN artillery. The enemy force blocking the 4th Infantry's advance included three battalions of the 52d NVA Brigade. The 4th Infantry took heavy casualties but made no significant gains.

In December, the reconstituted battalions of the 14th Ranger Group from Quang Nam Province reinforced the 6th ARVN Infantry in heavy fighting on the Batangan Peninsula. Casualties were high, but the improvements to local security were slight.

As the year ended in Quang Ngai, the advantage and initiative lay in enemy hands. South Vietnamese territorial forces were understrength and dispirited; the once-effective 2d ARVN Division could field battalions of only 300 men each, and Ranger battalions were sorely fatigued from continual combat.

The NVA's strategic raids campaign in the vast region south of the Hai Van had accomplished three things that placed NVA forces in an excellent position to begin a major offensive. First, although NVA casualties were very high, the campaign had severely depleted the ARVN of experienced leaders and soldiers. Replacements were not well trained or in sufficient numbers to bring battered battalions up to strength. On the other hand, the NVA replacement flow was copious and free from interference. Second, NVA command, staff, logistics, and communications had been thoroughly expanded and proven during this campaign; the new 3d Corps had the valuable experience of a major offensive behind it. Third, the NVA had pushed its holdings to the edge of the narrow coastal plain and was within artillery range of nearly every major South Vietnamese installation and population center. Similar progress, meanwhile, was being made north of the Hai Van Pass.

Note on Sources

The field reporting from the Consul General's Office, Da Nang, was especially copious and usually reliable; these reports formed a large part of the basis of this chapter. Additionally, the author made a number of visits to Military Region 1 and 2 and has referred to his notes. DAO, Saigon, and J2/JGS Weekly Summaries provided most of the information on order-of-battle and combat activity. Most significant in this chapter, however, were the comments and corrections made by Generals Truong and Hinh whose personal recollections provided accurate data and understanding.

12

The Ring Tightens Around Hue

Throughout the early months of 1974, the NVA maintained continual pressure against RVNAF defenses north of the Hai Van Pass and concentrated on the ARVN Airborne Division and 1st Infantry Division positions west and south of Hue. Aware that with three full-strength Marine brigades holding the line in Quang Tri Province an overly agressive campaign would invoke retaliations against its burgeoning logistical complex around Dong Ha, the NVA did little to disturb the balance in the northernmost province. The most serious erosion of ARVN defenses took place during the skirmishes for the high ground south of Phu Bai, the only major airfield serving Hue. There the ARVN 1st Infantry Division was responsible for protecting the airfield, Highway 1 as it passed through the narrow defile in Phu Loc District, and the vital Ta Trach corridor to Hue.

Nui Mo Tau, Nui Bong, and Hill 350

The Hai Van Ridge formed the Thua Thien-Quan Nam Province boundary from the sea to Bach Ma Mountain, which was occupied by the enemy in October 1973. The ridge continued west past Bach Ma until it descended into the valley of the Song Ta Trach at Ruong Ruong, where the NVA had established a forward operating base. Local Route 545 twisted through the mountains north from Ruong Ruong, joining Highway 1 just south of Phu Bai. As it crossed over the western slopes of the Hai Van Ridge, Route 545 passed between two lower hills, Nui Mo Tau on the west, and Nui Bong on the east. Nui Mo Tau and Nui Bong were only about 300 meters and 140 meters high, respectively, but the ARVN positions on them, and on neighboring hills, formed the main outer ring protecting Phu Bai and Hue on the south. Outposts were placed on hills 2,000 to 5,000 meters farther south, including hills as identified by their elevations of 144, 224, 273 and 350 meters. (Map 17)

At first, the corps commander, General Truong, viewed the see-saw contest for the hills south of Nui Mo Tau as hardly more than training exercises and of no lasting tactical or strategic importance. That assessment was supportable so long as the enemy was unable to extend his positions to within range of Phu Bai. Once this extension occurred, protecting Hue's vital air and land links with the south became matter of great urgency.

During inconclusive engagements in the spring of 1974, the ARVN 1st Division managed to hold on to Nui Mo Tau and Nui Bong, losing Hill 144 between the two but regaining it on 7 April. Hills 273 and 350 were lost; then Hill 350 was recaptured by the 3d Battalion, 3d ARVN Infantry, in a night attack on 4 June. By this time, I Corps units were bothered by reductions in artillery ammunition. Tight restrictions had been imposed by General Truong on the number of rounds that could be fired in counterbattery, preparatory, and defensive fires. These conditions impelled the infantry commanders to seek means other than heavy artillery fires to soften objectives before the assault. In recapturing Hill 350, the 3d ARVN Infantry worked around behind the hill and blocked the enemy's access to defenses on the hill. Within a few days, NVA soldiers on the hill were out of food and low on ammunition. When the ARVN commander, monitoring the enemy's tactical radio net, learned this, he ordered the assault. No artillery was used; mortars and grenades provided the only fire support for the ARVN infantrymen. But they took the hill on the first assault even though the NVA defenders fired a heavy concentration of tear gas against them. ARVN casualties were light while the NVA 5th Regiment lost heavily in men and weapons.

Order of Battle

As the 1st ARVN Division pressed southward against the NVA 324B Division's battalions trying to hold hard-won outposts in the hills, another new NVA corps headquarters was organized north of the Hai Van Pass and placed in command of the 304th, 324B, and 325th Divisions. Designated the 2d Corps, it was a companion to the new 1st Corps in Thanh Hoa Province of North Vietnam, the 3d Corps south of the Hai Van, and the 301st Corps near Saigon. In the Thua Thien campaign, the 324B Division eventually assumed control of five regiments: its own 803d and 812th and three independent NVA infantry regiments, the 5th, 6th, and 271st.

In early June 1974, after releasing the 1st Airborne Brigade to the reserve controlled by the Joint General Staff, General Truong made major adjustments in command and deployments north of the Hai Van Pass. The Marine Division was extended to cover about 10 kilometers of Thua Thien Province

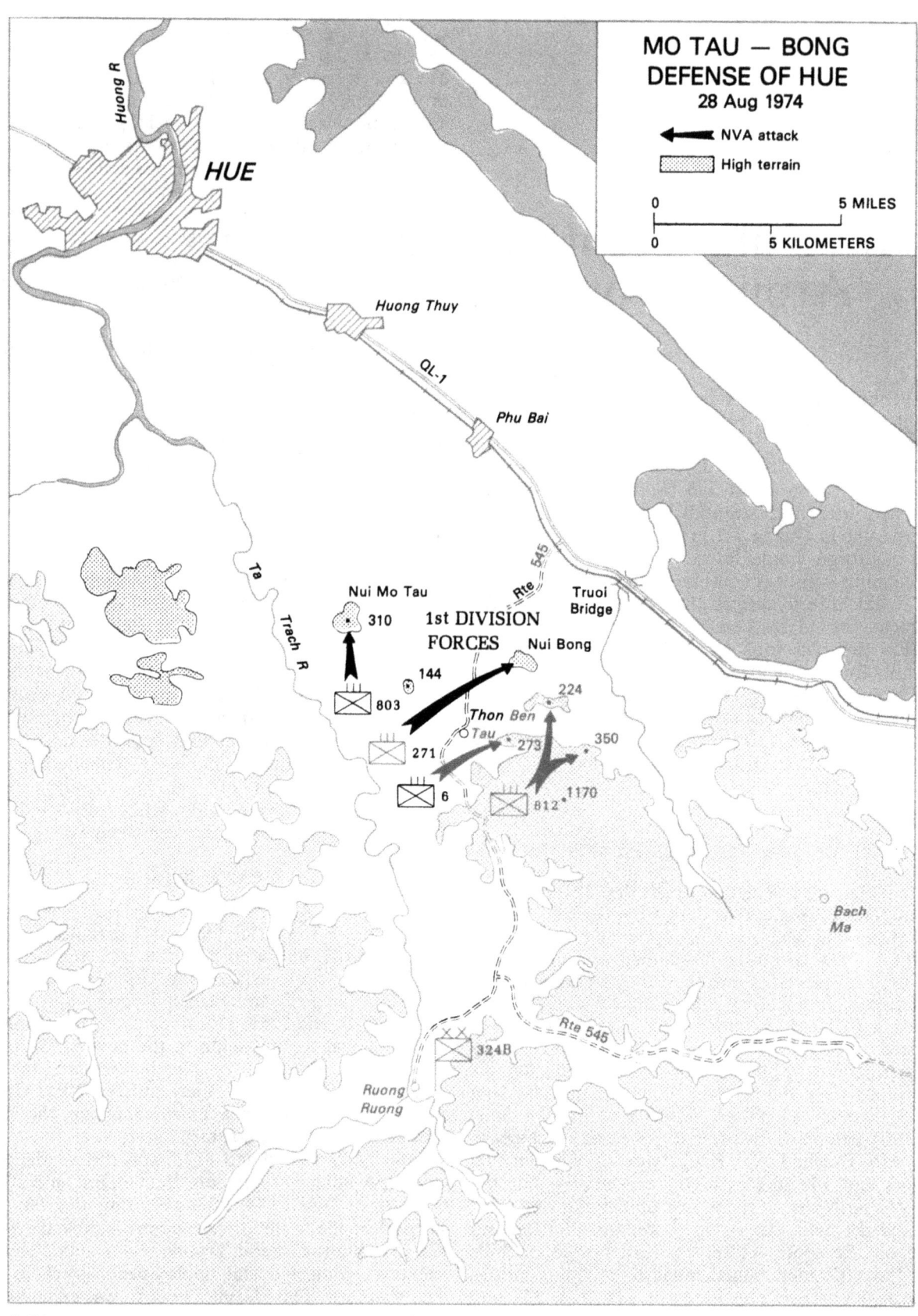

Map 17

and was reinforced with the 15th Ranger Group of three battalions and the 1st Armored Brigade and had operational control of Quang Tri's seven RF battalions. The division commander, Brig. Gen. Bui The Lan, positioned his forces with the 258th Marine Brigade, with one M-48 tank company attached, defending from the sea southwest to about five kilometers east of Quang Tri City. The 369th Marine Brigade held the center sector, Quang Tri City and Highway 1. Southwest of the 369th was the attached 15th Ranger Group along the Thach Han River, and the 147th Marine Brigade was on the left and south of the 15th Rangers. When he had to extend his forces southward to cover the airborne sector, General Lan used a task force of the 1st Armored Brigade, two Marine battalions, and an RF battalion, keeping three tank companies on the approaches to Hue.

The Airborne Division retained the responsibility for the Song Bo approach, placing its two remaining brigades, the 2d and 3d, to the west. The 2d Brigade had two RF battalions and one company of M-41 tanks attached. The 4th NVA Regiment was the principal enemy unit in the 2d Brigade's sector, while the 271st NVA Regiment opposed the 3d Airborne Brigade to the south near Fire Support Base Bastogne.

The four regiments and two attached RF battalions of the 1st ARVN Infantry Division were deployed in a long arc from the Airborne Division's left through the hills to Phu Loc District, with the 54th Infantry Regiment protecting Highway 1 from the Truoi Bridge, just north of Nui Bong, to the Hai Van Pass.

The Railroad

The national railroad paralleled Highway 1 through Thua Thien Province, and daily freight and passenger trains ran between Da Nang and Hue. Since the restoration of traffic in April 1973, passenger trains were heavily used because of low fares and regular service. In January 1974, the railroad carried 128,000 passengers and 1,500 tons of freight along a 100-kilometer run. In mid- May, the Communists increased their efforts to disrupt this service, for although the railroad had negligible economic and military value, it was popular with the people and its operation demonstrated the South Vietnamese government's ability to provide security.

Saboteurs concentrated their attacks along the stretch of rail that ran along the coast from the Lang Co Bridge, the first major bridge north of the Hai Van Pass, and northern Phu Loc District, just south of Phu Bai. More than 40 bridges and numerous defiles were in this section. By mid-June attacks became so frequent that work crews refused to repair track and roadbed without greater protection; one of their work trains was hit by rocket fire near Phu Loc District Town. The enemy placed large stone blocks on the rails, and the workmen, suspecting that they were mined, refused to remove them. Large sections of rail went unrepaired, and the line had to be closed on 22 June.

With territorials providing security for the crews, service on the line was restored on 9 July, only to be closed again the same day when a mine tore up 100 meters of rail. Nevertheless, the line was back in service the following day. In early August, the attack shifted to south of the Hai Van Pass. A large mine planted between the first and second tunnels north of Da Nang destroyed three cars and caused a few civilian casualties.

Interest in riding the railroad naturally began to wane. In August only 4,500 passengers and 180 tons of freight were carried until traffic was again suspended on the 20th. During the eight months of operation in 1974, a locomotive and 15 cars had been destroyed, 3,000 meters of rail had been torn up, and civilian casualties numbered 11 killed and 50 wounded. When he chose to do so the enemy showed that he could close down the railroad.

Naval Engagement Off Quang Tri

While skirmishing for the hills south of Hue occupied the 1st ARVN and 324B NVA Divisions, an event occurred along the Quang Tri coast, demanding the attention of the high commands on both sides. On 20 June 1974, a South Vietnamese Navy patrol sighted a convoy of two steel-hulled landing craft and 30 wooden boats off the South Vietnam coast, south of the mouth of the Cua Viet River. Although there was no clear line of demarcation defining the depth of the NVA's control south of the Cua Viet, these boats were about three kilometers off shore and, by RVNAF reckoning, in South Vietnamese waters. Accordingly, a VNAF helicopter gunship was sent to attack. After a few rounds, the helicopter's guns jammed, and it broke off the attack. Meanwhile, the small convoy changed course and headed north toward the Cua Viet, its original destination; poor navigation had caused it to miss the channel and continue south.

But one of the steel-hulled boats, its master apparently still confused about his location, lumbered on towards Hue, and the forward headquarters of I Corps at Hue ordered its capture. By this time, ARVN units along the coast and Vietnamese Navy elements had been alerted. Eventually, the ARVN 17th Armored Cavalry Squadron, using TOW missiles and tank gunfire, sank the boat off the coast of Thon My Thuy Village, northeast of Hai Lang District Town. The boat's log, recovered along with the bodies of the eight-man crew and part of the cargo (200 cases of Chinese canned pork and 1,000 NVA uniforms), revealed that the vessel belonged to the 102d Boat Company and that there were 10 other boats and 2 barges in the 102d, 7 of which routinely operated between North Vietnam and Dong Ha in the Cua Viet.

The North Vietnamese protested the sinking, claiming that the boat, on a peaceful mission in their waters, was wantonly and illegally destroyed in an act of piracy. The South Vietnamese replied in equally strong terms, charging hostile intrusion by an armed vessel into their territorial waters. Both sides were obviously embarrassed; the North because of the demonstrably poor seamanship of its boat crew; the South because of the uncoordinated action that resulted in the sinking of an enemy boat that could have been easily captured. But the GVN was clearly the winner; it did have the ship's log with its interesting information concerning NVA logistics, and it had a few cases of good canned pork.

An Assist From the Hungarians

While the RVNAF was gaining a modicum of intelligence through the sinking of the enemy boat the NVA was apparently reaping a bountiful harvest of data concerning RVNAF dispositions, defenses, and operations through its connections with the Hungarian delegation on the International Commission of Control and Supervision (ICCS). Strong indications that this was so appeared north of the Hai Van Pass early in 1974, and the case was the subject of a detailed report submitted in June by the National Police of Military Region 1 to police headquarters in Saigon.

The essence of the report was that several members of the Hungarian delegation to the ICCS had been observed since February taking pictures and making notes at RVNAF bases, outposts, bridges, and other sensitive sites and that this activity bore all the earmarks of espionage. The inescapable conclusion was that the information so collected was delivered to the NVA. Because of the diplomatic status accorded ICCS delegations, South Vietnamese authorities could not confiscate anything from the Hungarians but did try to limit their apparent espionage activities. The following elements of the report were considered significant examples of the kind of reconnaissance the Hungarians were engaged in:

February—Lieutenant Colonel Markus, Chief of the Hungarian ICCS group in Quang Tri, together with Lieutenant Gyori and Sergeant Szabo toured Phu Vang and Phu Thu Districts of Thua Thien Province, using maps and a camera to record the RVNAF defensive positions in the area.

March—LTC Markus, with camera and maps, was stopped at an RVNAF checkpoint on a road leading to the forward positions of the 3d Infantry Regiment, 1st ARVN Division. A few days later, LTC Markus and another member of his team drove from Hue to Quang Tri, recording on maps the GVN positions and installations along Highway 1. On the last day of the month, LTC Markus and CPT Gyula Toser were seen photographing all bridges on Highway 1 between Hue and Da Nang.

April—Three Hungarian field-grade officers arrived in Quang Tri from Saigon and, guided by LTC Markus, drove around the ruined city taking pictures of the Marine positions.

May—Hungarian Signal Sergeant Toth and two other members of the Da Nang team drove from Da Nang to the Hai Van Pass, taking pictures of the Nam O Bridge, the Esso gasoline storage area, and RVNAF military installations en route. Later in the month, Major Kovacs, chief of the Hungarian unit at Phu Bai was observed photographing, with a telephoto lens, aircraft landing and departing Phu Bai Airbase. He was also seen using binoculars and recording the locations of the RVNAF defenses around Phu Bai. Also in May, LTC Varkegyi and Lt. Borkely from Saigon toured the Hai Van Pass with Major Kovacs—taking pictures of all RVNAF installations.

June—Another delegation visited from Saigon. Brigadier General Csapo, Colonel Vida and three others were given the tour to the Hai Van Pass by Lieutenant Colonel Horvath (Chief of the Hue unit) and Major Kovacs. Using a map to note the locations, the party took pictures of installations all along the way.

There was probably no direct connection, but during the last week of June enemy sappers got to the fuel storage area at Camp Evans northwest of Hue and the ammunition storage at Phu Bai. About 8,000 gallons of gasoline burned at Camp Evans; 4,600 tons of ammunition blew up at Phu Bai.

Infiltration into the Thua Thien Lowlands

Ever since the flurry of battles following the January 1973 cease-fire subsided, the lowlands of Thua Thien had been considered almost totally free of Communist-controlled hamlets. Unlike the other southerly coastal provinces of Military Region 1, there were no so-called leopard spots of VC enclaves in either Thua Thien or Quang Tri Provinces. In the fall of 1974, however, disturbing evidence began to appear indicating that three small VC fortified areas had been established since June in Phong Dien District north of Hue. This district of Thua Thien was lightly populated, mostly a wasteland of sand dunes and tidal marsh, little of which was suitable for agriculture or even habitation.

One enclave was in the northwestern corner of the district on the edge of Phong Hoa Village. Occupying an area approximately two kilometers square, it was controlled by a body of about 50 VC political cadre and sheltered about 20 political and armed cadre from neighboring Hai Lang District of Quang Tri. During late October, a company from the 33d NVA Sapper Battalion entered the enclave and helped local forces construct bunkers and install antiaircraft machine guns. The company also mined the perimeter with 105-mm. howitzer projectiles and posted signs warning citizens of the minefields. One of these mines blew the tracks off an ARVN armored personnel carrier during an ARVN probe of the area, but a later operation eventually penetrated and cleared the area.

Another enclave, larger but less well defended was in eastern Phong Dien District. Located in Phong Hien Village, it provided a base for a small armed unit that raided other hamlets in the region and attempted to proselyte in nearby refugee resettlements. But these disturbances in rear areas were of minor importance when measured against the expanding conflict in the hills south of Phu Bai.

The Hills of Phu Loc and Nam Hoa

Hills 144, 273, 224, 350, and Nui Bong, and Nui Mo Tau, overlooking the lines of communication through Phu Loc District and providing observation and artillery sites in range of Phu Bai, were generally along the boundary between Phu Loc and Nam Hoa Districts of Thua Thien Province. Having recaptured Hill 350 on 4 June, the ARVN 1st Division continued the attack toward Hill 273. A fresh battalion, the 1st Battalion, 54th Infantry, took the hill on 27 June, incurring light casualties, and by the next day, the 1st ARVN Division controlled all of the important high ground south of Phu Bai.

On 29 June General Truong directed his deputy north of the Hai Van Pass, General Thi, to constitute a regimental reserve for the expected NVA counterattacks against the newly won objectives. General Thi accordingly replaced the 54th Infantry with the 3d Infantry on July, the 54th becoming the corps reserve north of the Hai Van. General Truong had good reason to be concerned. The NVA was preparing for increased and prolonged operations in Thua Thien Province, as revealed by aerial photography of NVA rear areas on 30 June. A 150,000-gallon fuel tank farm, connected to the pipeline through the A Shau Valley, was photographed under construction in far western Quang Nam, only 25 kilometers south of the NVA base in Ruong Ruong. The Ruong Ruong region, also called the Nam Dong Secret Zone, was seen growing in logistic capacity. Local Routes 593 and 545 were shown to be repaired and in use, and a tank park and two new truck parks were discernable.

The 324B NVA Division took a while to get organized for renewed attacks in southern Thua Thien. Its battalions had taken severe beatings, and a period of re-equipping and replanning was necessary. In the meantime, action shifted to the old Airborne Brigade sector in northern Thua Thien where the 6th and 8th Marine Battalions, attached to the 147th Brigade, came under heavy attack. Attacks continued through July, and some Marine outposts, targets for 130-mm. gunfire, had to be given up. No important changes in dispositions took place, however.

Mid-July passed in southern Thua Thien without much activity. But on 25 July, as the 2d Infantry Regiment, 3d ARVN Division, was trying to regroup following a devastating engagement above Duc Duc, General Truong ordered the 54th Infantry, 1st ARVN Division, from Thua Thien to Quang Nam for attachment to the 3d. The 1st Infantry Division, with only three regiments, was left with a 60-kilometer front including Highway 1 and no reserve north of the Hai Van Pass. Since this situation was hazardous, General Troung on 3 August ordered General Thi to reconstitute a reserve using the 15th Ranger Group, at that time attached to the Marine Division on the Thach Han River.

Consequently, on 5 August the 121st RF Battalion replaced the 60th Ranger Battalion on the Quang Tri front. Shortly afterward the 61st and 94th Ranger Battalions pulled out, relieved respectively by the 126th RF Battalion and the 5th Marine Battalion. But events in Quang Nam forced General Truong to change his plans for the 15th Group; because Truong Duc had just fallen, he needed the 3d Airborne Brigade in Quang Nam. So, as soon as the Marines and territorials replaced the battalions of the 15th Group, the relief of the 3d Airborne Brigade began in the Song Bo corridor. But, General Thi was still without a reserve north of the Hai Van Pass, and fresh opportunities for the new NVA 2d Corps appeared in Phu Loc District.

While General Truong was shifting forces to save Quang Nam, the NVA 2d Corps was moving new battalions near Hill 350. First to deploy, in late July, was the 271st Independent Regiment, previously under the control of the 325th Division. In mid-August, the 812th Regiment, 324B Division, began its march from A Luoi in the northern A Shau Valley. Covering the entire 50 kilometers on foot, the regiment arrived undetected on 26 August. On 28 August attacks on ARVN positions in the Nui Mo Tau–Hill 350 area began. Over 600 artillery rounds hit Nui Mo Tau where the 2d Battalion, 3d Infantry, was dug in. The ARVN battalion held the hill against the assault of the NVA infantrymen, but an adjacent position, manned by the 129th RF Battalion, collapsed, and the battalion was scattered. To the east, on Nui Bong and Hills 273 and 350, the other two battalions of the 3d Infantry were bombarded by 1,300 rounds and driven from their positions by the 6th and 812th NVA Regiments. Meanwhile, the 8th Battalion, 812th NVA Regiment, overran Hill 224. Thus, in a few hours, except for Nui Mo Tau, all ARVN accomplishments of the long summer campaign in southern Thua Thien were erased. The 51st Infantry of the 1st ARVN Division was rushed into the line, but the momentum of the NVA attack had already dissipated. The casualties suffered by the 324B NVA Division were high, but it now controlled much of the terrain overlooking the Phu Loc lowlands and Phu Bai.

Heavy fighting throughout the foothills continued into the first week of September with strong NVA attacks against the 3d Battalion, 51st Regiment, and the 1st and 2d Battalions of the 3d Regiment. The 6th and 803d NVA Regiments lost nearly 300 men and over 100 weapons in these attacks, but the 3d ARVN Infantry was no longer combat effective due to casualties and equipment losses.

Immediate reinforcements were needed south of Phu Bai. Accordingly, General Truong ordered the 54th Infantry Regiment back to Thua Thien Province, together with the 37th Ranger Battalion, which had been fighting on the Duc Duc front. General Thi took personal command of the ARVN forces in southern Thua Thien and moved the 7th Airborne Battalion from north of Hue and the 111th RF Battalion, securing the port at Tan My, to Phu Bai. These deployments and the skillful use of artillery concentrations along enemy routes of advance put a temporary damper on NVA initiatives in the foothills.

In an apparent diversion to draw ARVN forces northward away from Phu Loc, the NVA on 21 September strongly attacked the 5th and 8th Marine and the 61st Ranger Battalions holding the Phong Dien sector north of Hue. Although some 6,600 rounds, including hundreds from 130-mm. field guns, and heavy rockets, struck the defenses, the South Vietnamese held firmly against the ground attacks that followed. Over 240 enemy infantrymen from the 325th Division were killed, mostly by ARVN artillery, in front of the 8th Marines, and General Thi made no deployments in response to the attack. The next week, however, renewed assaults by the 803d NVA Regiment carried it to Nui Mo Tau, and by the end of September, the 324B NVA Division had consolidated its control over the high ground south of Phu Bai from Nui Mo Tau east to Nui Bong and Hill 350. The NVA 2d Corps immediately began to exploit this advantage by moving 85-mm. field gun batteries of its 78th Artillery Regiment into position to fire on Phu Bai Air Base, forcing the VNAF to suspend operations at the only major airfield north of Hai Van Pass.

The attack to retake the commanding ground around Phu Bai began on 22 October with a diversionary assault on Hill 224 and Hill 303. The 1st ARVN Infantry Regiment was to follow with the main attack against the 803d NVA Regiment on Nui Mo Tau. Bad weather brought by Typhoon Della reduced air support to nothing, and little progress was made by ARVN infantrymen. Nevertheless, the attack on Nui Mo Tau, with a secondary effort against elements of the 812th NVA Regiment on Nui Bong, began on 26 October. The 54th ARVN Infantry, with the 2d Battalion, 3d Infantry, attached, made slight progress on Nui Mo Tau, and the 3d Battalion, 1st Infantry, met strong resistance near Nui Bong. But the ARVN artillery was taking its toll of the NVA defenders, who were also suffering the effects of cold rains sweeping across the steep, shell-torn slopes. Heavy, accurate artillery fire forced the 6th Battalion, 6th NVA Infantry, to abandon its trenches on Hill 312, east of Hill 350, and the 803d Regiment's trenches, bunkers, and communications were being torn up by the ARVN fire placed on Nui Mo Tau. Toward the end of October, the 803d and 812th NVA Regiments were so depleted that the 2d NVA Corps withdrew them from the battle and assigned the defense of Nui Mo Tau and Nui Bong to the 6th Regiment and 271st Regiment respectively.

As heavy rains continued, movement and fire support became increasingly difficult, and the ARVN offensive in southern Thua Thien Province slowed considerably. Enemy artillery continued to inhibit the use of Phu Bai Air Base, and 1st ARVN Division infantrymen around Nui Bong suffered daily casualties to NVA mortars and field guns. On 24 November, Maj. Gen. Nguyen Van Diem, commanding the 1st Division, secured permission to pull his troops away from Nui Bong and concentrate his forces against Nui Mo Tau.

For a new assault on Nui Mo Tau, General Truong authorized the reinforcement of the 54th Infantry Regiment by the 15th Ranger Group drawn out of the Bo River Valley west of Hue; the 54th would make the main attack. The 54th Infantry commander selected his 3d Battalion to lead, followed by the 2d Battalion and the 60th and 94th Ranger Battalions. When the 3d Battalion had difficulty reaching the attack position, it was replaced on 27 November by the 1st Battalion. Weather was terrible that day, but two Ranger battalions made some progress and established contact with the enemy on the eastern and southeastern slopes of the mountain. On 28 November, with good weather and long-awaited support from the VNAF, the 1st Battalion, 54th Infantry, began moving toward the crest of Nui Mo Tau. On the mountain the enemy was approaching a desperate state; one battalion of the 5th NVA Regiment was moving to reinforce but washouts on Route 545 between Ruong Ruong and Thon Ben Tau south of Nui Mo Tau had all but eliminated resupply.

Despite difficulties, however, the enemy continued to resist strongly on both mountains. On 1 December, Colonel Vo Toan, the highly respected commander of the 1st ARVN Infantry, returned to his regiment from a six-month absence at South Vietnam's Command and General Staff College. His timely arrival was probably responsible for injecting new spirit and more professional leadership into the attack, which had bogged down so close to its objective. But help also arrived for the defenders; the 812th NVA Regiment, refitted and somewhat recovered from its earlier combat, returned to Nui Mo Tau, replacing the badly battered 6th NVA Regiment. Over on Nui Bong, however, the remnants of the 271st NVA Independent Regiment were without help. On 3 December, the 1st Reconnaissance Company and the 1st and 3d Battalions, 1st ARVN Infantry Regiment, were assaulting a dug-in battalion only 50 meters from the crest. But the expected victory slipped from their grasp. Intense fires drove the South Vietnamese back, and although the 1st Infantry retained a foothold on the slopes, it was unable to carry the crest.

The attack by the 54th ARVN Infantry and the 15th Ranger Group had more success. On 10 December, the 1st Battalion of the 54th took one of the twin crests of Nui Mo Tau and captured the other the following day. As bloody skirmishing continued around the mountain for weeks, the NVA executed another relief, replacing the 812th Regiment with the 803d. Although the enemy remained entrenched on Nui Bong, his access to lines of communication and the base in Ruong Ruong were frequently interdicted by the ARVN units operating in his rear. Furthermore, the 78th NVA Artillery Regiment was forced to remove its batteries because resupply past the ARVN position around Nui Mo Tau became too difficult. The VNAF, meanwhile, resumed military traffic into Phu Bai on 13 December.

By making timely and appropriate economy-of-force deployments, often accepting significant risks, General Truong was able to hold the NVA main force at bay around Hue. But the ring was closing on the Imperial City. Reinforced NVA battalions—equipped with new weapons, ranks filling with fresh replacements from the north—were in close contact with ARVN outposts the length of the front. Behind these battalions, new formations of tanks were being assembled and large logistical installations were being constructed, heavily protected by antiaircraft and supplied by newly improved roads. While the situation in the north appeared ominous, one of the most tragic events of the war was unfolding in Phouc Long Province to the south.

Note on Sources

As in the previous chapter, heavy reliance was placed on the reports of the Consul General, Da Nang, and weekly summaries from DAO and J2/JGS. DAO's regional liaison office in Da Nang filed numerous valuable reports during this period, and these were also useful for this chapter. Comments by the I Corps commander, General Truong, were essential to establish the accuracy and completeness of the data.

13

The Last Christmas: Phuoc Long

In his serialized account of the "Great Spring Victory" (translated in the Foreign Broadcast Information Service—FBIS—*Daily Report: Asia and Pacific*, vol. IV, no. 110, Supplement 38, 7 Jun. 1976, pp. 2, 5-6), Senior General Van Tien Dung of the North Vietnamese Army described deliberations of the Central Military Party Committee and the General Staff as they reviewed the events of the summer campaign. He wrote of how, between April and October, from Thua Thien to Saigon, NVA forces had stepped up the offensive actions and had won great victories. The facts were, of course, that the NVA was stalemated at the extremes of this long battlefield—in Thua Thien and around Saigon—but had overrun isolated bases in the Central Highlands and succeeded at great cost in penetrating to the edge of the Quang Nam lowlands. This latter success loomed large in significance to General Dung and NVA planners:

We paid special attention to the outcome of a battle which destroyed the district capital of Thuong Duc in the 5th Region. This was a test of strength with the best of the enemy's forces. We destroyed the enemy forces defending the Thuong Duc district capital subsector. The enemy sent in a whole division of paratroopers to launch repeated and protracted counterattacks in a bid to recapture this position, but we heavily decimated the enemy forces, firmly defending Thuong Duc and forcing the enemy to give up.

However distorted the account, the victory at Thuong Duc and the numerous, more easily won objectives in the highlands demonstrated to the satisfaction of the North Vietnamese high command that the time had arrived for an even bolder strategy. General Dung went on to relate how

the General Staff reported to the Central Military Party Committee that the combat capability of our mobile main force troops was now altogether superior to that of the enemy's mobile regular troops, that the war had reached its final stage and that the balance of forces had changed in our favor.

General Dung believed, and the Military Committee and the General Staff agreed, that the NVA's superiority should be exploited in a new strategy. The NVA would no longer attack only to destroy the RVNAF but would combine this objective with attacks to "liberate" populated areas. It would move out of the jungles and mountains into the lowlands. NVA planners observed that, "the reduction of U.S. aid made it impossible for the puppet troops to carry out their combat plan and build up their forces" and that the South Vietnamese were "forced to fight a poor man's war," their firepower having decreased "by nearly 60 percent because of bomb and ammunition shortages" and their mobility was reduced "by half due to lack of aircraft, vehicles and fuel."

According to General Dung, the conference of the Politburo and the Central Military Committee met in October, considered the General Staff's assessments and recommendation, and unanimously agreed on the following:

1. The puppet troops were militarily, politically and economically weakening every day and our forces were quite stronger than the enemy in the south.
2. The United States was facing mounting difficulties both at home and in the world, and its potential for aiding the puppets was rapidly declining.
3. We had created a chain of mutual support, had strengthened our reserve forces and materiel and were steadily improving our strategic and political systems.
4. The movement to demand peace, improvement of the people's livelihood, democracy, national independence and Thieu's overthrow in various cities was gaining momentum.

Having assessed their own capabilities and those of RVNAF, and having concluded that the time was right for the final offensive, the conferees had to consider how the United States would react. They concluded:

After signing the Paris agreement on Vietnam and withdrawing U.S. troops from Vietnam, the United States had faced even greater difficulties and embarrassment. The internal contradictions within the U.S. administration and among U.S. political parties had intensified. The Watergate scandal had seriously affected the entire United States and precipitated the resignation of an extremely reactionary president—Nixon. The United States faced economic recession, mounting inflation, serious unemployment and an oil crisis. Also, U.S. allies were not on good terms with the United States, and countries who had to depend on the United States also sought to escape U.S. control. U.S. aid to the Saigon puppet administration was decreasing.

Comrade Le Duan drew an important conclusion that became a resolution: Having already withdrawn from the south, the United States could hardly jump back in, and no matter how it might intervene, it would be unable to save the Saigon administration from collapse. Phuoc Long became the battleground for the first test of this assessment.

Phuoc Long—the Setting

The summer and fall of 1974 in South Vietnam's 3d Military Region had been difficult times. Unlike the losses in Military Regions 1 and 2, however, very little terrain of consequence had been given up to the NVA summer offensive. The divisional battles in Binh Duong, Tay Ninh, and Bien Hoa Provinces had produced thousands of casualties, but all positions—except those on the Tay Ninh–Cambodian frontier—were eventually retaken by ARVN troops. The mop-up of the Iron Triangle was not completed until 24 November, the eve of the next phase of the NVA offensive, the most significant step before the ultimate offensive of 1975.

Since Phuoc Long Province was far outside the defenses of Saigon, its importance to South Vietnam was essentially political in that the government could still claim possession of all province capitals. On the other hand, the presence of RVNAF bases deep inside otherwise NVA-controlled territory was anathema to the enemy. Several important COSVN tactical and logistical units and activities were in the Bo Duc–Bu Dop complex of villages and plantations. The COSVN M-26 Armor Command, usually with three of its tank battalions, was based at the Bu Dop airfield only 25 kilometers from the ARVN base at Song Be. The COSVN Engineer Command had a headquarters at Bo Duc and kept three or more battalions working on roads between Loc Ninh and Bu Gia Map to the northeast. Antiaircraft battalions, transportation battalions, training centers, and other rear service organizations contributed to a relatively dense NVA military population, nearly within medium artillery range of Phuoc Binh, the capital of Phuoc Long Province. Additionally, four major NVA infiltration-supply routes traversed Phuoc Long Province from north to south, past RVNAF bases and crossed sections of National Route 14 patrolled by South Vietnamese troops. (See Map 18, also Map 14.)

The summer in Phuoc Long had been relatively uneventful. In August an enemy soldier turned himself in to the Phuoc Long Sector Headquarters and described a recent reconnaissance of RVNAF installations by two NVA patrols. While one patrol had reconnoitered Song Be, the other had concentrated on Duc Phong District. Since no attacks followed, the province chief concluded that the reconnaissance was probably related to infiltration and logistical movements. In any event, the major NVA combat formations in the area were not sufficient to create a serious threat to Phuoc Long, although they could interfere with RVNAF movements on the major routes to Song Be, Highway 14 from Quang Duc and the provincial road between Song Be and Bunard. The 7th NVA Division, however, had for some time permanently blocked Highway 14 between Bunard and Don Luan, causing traffic to the province capital to detour through Quang Duc. Because the 7th NVA Division also cut Route 1A south of Don Luan, that town relied exclusively on helicopter resupply.

NVA interdictions of Highway 14 east of Phuoc Binh–Song Be were often enough to require the RVNAF to mount road-clearing operations each time a major rice and military convoy was scheduled to roll into Phuoc Long. The province required about 500 tons of rice per month, of which only half was produced locally and frequent convoys were necessary. The forces in Phuoc Long kept enough ammunition on hand to last for a week of intensive combat, and these stocks also had to be replenished frequently. Road convoys were supplemented by VNAF C-130s using the airstrip at Song Be.

Anticipating a resupply convoy in early November 1974, the Phuoc Long Sector, commanded by Colonel Nguyen Tan Thanh, started to clear the road. To protect its bases while RF battalions were on the highway, the III Corps, lacking infantry reserves, sent three reconnaissance companies to Phuoc Binh and Song Be, one from each of the three III Corps divisions. Forces at Duc Phong—the 362d RF Battalion, four PF platoons, and a 105-mm. howitzer platoon—and two companies from the 304th RF Battalion from Song Be were committed along Highway 14. In their one brief encounter with the enemy, near the Quang Duc boundary, these forces killed four enemy soldiers from the 201st NVA Regiment of the newly formed 3d NVA division. (This Division, formed in Phuoc Long, was separate from and unrelated to the 3d NVA Division operating in Binh Dinh.) Although the ARVN operation was a success, the presence of an NVA regiment so close to Duc Phong was an ominous sign.

In addition to the 340th and 362d RF Battalions already mentioned, Colonel Thanh also controlled the 341st RF Battalion at Don Luan and the 363d RF Battalion at Bunard. Thirty-four PF Platoons were scattered about the hamlets and military installations around Song Be, while 14 PF platoons defended eight hamlets in the Duc Phong Subsector. South of Song Be at New Bo Duc, where the refugees of Communist-occupied northern Phuoc Long settled, were nine PF platoons; in the eight hamlets and military posts around Don Luan, were a like number. Artillery support was provided by four 155-mm. and 16 105-mm. howitzers, employed in two-gun platoons throughout the sector. The RF battalions were fielding about 340 men each—about 85 precent of full strength—but the PF platoons were seriously understrength.

Diversions

Phuoc Long Province during late November and early December was relatively tanquil, and the attention of the ARVN III Corps commander was divided between his eastern and western flanks. The situation in the northern reaches of his region were of little immediate concern. Outposts around An

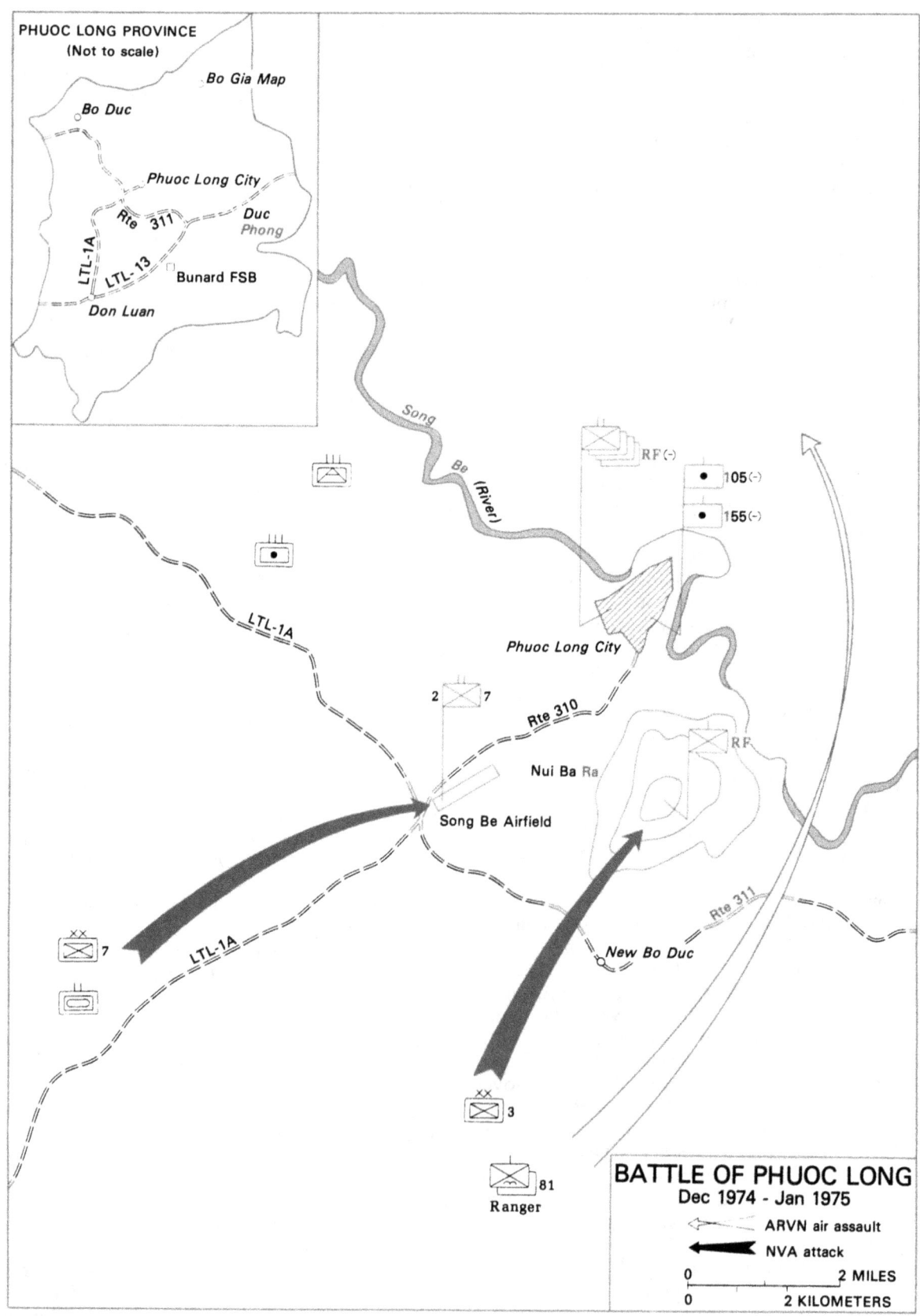

Map 18

Loc in Binh Long Province received sporadic enemy attacks by fire but were not in peril, although resupply was a constant problem due to NVA antiaircraft fire. On 5 December an SA-7 missile shot down a CH-47 helicopter nine kilometers south of An Loc, killing all 15 passengers and crew members.

The major enemy threats appeared in Tay Ninh Province in the west and in Long Khanh and Binh Tuy Province in the east. A skirmish northeast of Xuan Loc at the end of November netted a document revealing enemy plans to attack Gia Ray and eliminate ARVN outposts along Route 333 north into Binh Tuy Province. Supporting attacks in Binh Tuy were to be conducted by the 812th NVA Regiment.

While the threat on the eastern flank was inchoate, heavy combat in Tay Ninh was under way, NVA rockets falling on the province capital and on adjacent military installations. Although an RF company guarding the radio relay station on the summit of Nui Ba Den began receiving attacks of increasing intensity and frequency, the main NVA effort was against hamlets and RF outposts along local Route 13 northeast of Tay Ninh City. The NVA attacked early on 7 December. By noon, forces from the 205th Independent NVA Regiment were in the hamlets, although the RF post at Soui Da held on. The 8th and 9th Battalions, 205th NVA Regiment, were on local Route 13 southwest of Soui Da, and the NVA D-14 and D-16 Tay Ninh Battalions were blocking ARVN relief efforts. Meanwhile, the 7th Battalion, 205th NVA Regiment, in trying to overrun Soui Da, lost over 100 of its soldiers. The ARVN RF battalion defending Soui Da captured two NVA soldiers to confirm the identification of the 205th NVA Regiment in the attack, and one of the RF patrols ambushed and captured a 100-mm. Soviet field gun. The ARVN 46th Infantry, pushing a column up Route 13 from Tay Ninh City, did not fare so well. Ambushed on 12 December about three kilometers short of Soui Da, it suffered heavy casualties.

While heavy combat was taking place around Nui Ba Den, the 80-man RF company at the top fought off repeated assaults. Helicopter resupply and evacuation had become impossible, and although the company commander reported sufficient food and ammunition, water was running very short and several severely wounded men required evacuation.

Binh Tuy–Long Khanh

The RVNAF JGS and the III Corps commander had excellent warning of the impeding NVA attacks in Long Khanh and Binh Tuy Provinces. They knew that the 33d NVA Regiment planned to attack Hoai Duc District in Binh Tuy Province and that the recently formed 812th NVA Regiment, composed of battalions from neighboring Lam Dong, would attack in Tanh Linh District. Furthermore, they rightfully estimated that the 274th NVA Regiment would be involved. A new NVA division headquarters had been created to control the operation. Lacking information on its designation, the RVNAF called this new adversary the MR 7 Division, after the NVA military region in which it operated. Later, it was identified as the 6th NVA Division, and it controlled the three infantry regiments mentioned, plus the usual supporting arms and services found in the regular NVA divisions.

There were no regular ARVN units in Binh Tuy Province when the NVA offensive began. Territorial companies were deployed in the principal villages, and smaller territorial detachments secured bridges and checkpoints along local Routes 333 and 335, Hoai Duc's and Tanh Linh's only usable land routes out of the province. The province's small population was concentrated in the villages along these two roads, which generally followed the meandering course of the Song La Nga. Beginning in the 5,000-foot mountains overlooking the flat, deep forests of Binh Tuy on the northeast quadrant, the Song La Nga flowed through the rice bowl of the province. The two district towns, Tanh Linh on the east and Hoai Duc on the west, each had an airfield. The only other sizable village in the Province was Vo Xu, about midway between the two.

The 812th NVA Regiment attacked at Tanh Linh on 8 December. Supported by the 130th Artillery Battalion, one sapper and three infantry battalions attacked the subsector, the artillery position on the hill above the town, and the villages between Tanh Linh and Vo Xu. By the next day, the NVA Regiment had captured two 155-mm. howitzers at Tanh Linh, occupied the surrounding villages, and held the road between Vo Xu and Tanh Linh.

The ARVN III Corps ordered the 18th Infantry Division, with the 7th Ranger Group attached, from Xuan Loc to reinforce the territorials in Binh Tuy Province. When the 32d Ranger Battalion fell into a well-laid ambush along Route 333 and sustained heavy casualties, it became clear that the 33d NVA Regiment was not going to permit the reinforcement of Binh Tuy to proceed without a fight. Later the 1st and 2d Battalions of the 48th ARVN Infantry, 18th Division, joined the attack along Route 333 and were soon in heavy combat north of Gia Ray. In the days that followed, the 85th Ranger Battalion made it a four-battalion task force pushing up Route 333, but the lead elements—the Rangers— never made it past Gia Huynh, still 16 kilometers south of Hoai Duc. The NVA 33d Regiment was dug in along the road, well supported by mortars and artillery.

On 17 December Duy Can Village, between Vo Xu and Tanh Linh, was overrun by the 812th NVA Regiment, and the few survivors of the 700th RF Company struggled into Tanh Linh. Although outposts still in ARVN hands, as well as Hoai Duc and Tanh Linh, were receiving heavy indirect fire, General Dong, commanding III Corps ordered the 18th Division not try to press forward past Gia Huynh on Route 333. With his Military Region under attack from Tay Ninh to Phuoc Long, he was unwilling to risk having four of his battalions cut off and decimated. Meanwhile, the NVA blew a bridge south of Hoai Duc, occupied Vo Xu, and increased the intensity of its attack on Tanh Linh. Following a 3,000-round bombardment on 23 and 24 December, the NVA launched five successive assaults, finally overrunning the last defenses in Tanh Linh on Christmas. Hoai Duc, meanwhile, was under attack by the 274th Infantry, 6th NVA Division.

After the 274th NVA Regiment had penetrated the local defenses of Hoai Duc and had gained a foothold in the northeastern and southwestern edges of the town, the ARVN 18th Division moved the 1st and 2d Battalions, 43d Infanfry by helicopter west and north of the town respectively, and began pushing the enemy out. While two battalions of the 48th ARVN Infantry held their positions on Route 333 north of Gia Ray, the tired and depleted 7th Ranger Group was withdrawn to Binh Duong Province to rest and refit. Since all available battalions of the 18th Division had been committed, the JGS moved the 4th Ranger Group from Kontum to Long Binh where it was rested and re-equipped and made available to General Dong as a reserve.

Tay Ninh

NVA assaults on Nui Ba Den in Tay Ninh Province continued throughout December 1974, but the tough little ARVN RF Company held on. Meanwhile, by mid-month, an ARVN relief column eventually reached Soui Da and found that the besieging enemy force had withdrawn. VNAF efforts to resupply the troops on the mountain were largely unsuccessful. Helicopters were driven off by heavy fires, and fighter-bombers were forced to excessive altitudes by SA-7 and antiaircraft artillery. One F-5A fighter-bomber was shot down by an SA-7 on 14 December. Finally, without food and water and with nearly all ammunition expended, the 3d Company, 314th RF Battalion, on 6 January picked up its wounded and withdrew down the mountain to friendly lines.

The Last Days of Phuoc Long

The 301st NVA Corps conducted the campaign for Phuoc Long Province, using the newly formed 3d NVA Division, the 7th NVA Division, which had been operating in eastern Binh Duong Province, a tank battalion from COSVN, an artillery and an antiaircraft regiment, and several local-force sapper and infantry units. This was a formidable force to concentrate against four widely dispersed ARVN RF battalions and PF platoons. One by one the isolated garrisons came under attack and were overrun.

The first blow fell on Don Luan on 13 December 1974. Simultaneous assaults on Duc Phong and New Bo Duc Subsectors on 14 December succeeded in overrunning these posts while the defense at Don Luan held. The next to go was the post at Bunard, along with two platoons of 105-mm. howitzers. Enemy casualties were heavy at New Bo Duc, but these were local NVA units, not main force. Still, the NVA artillery damaged both of New Bo Duc's 105-mm. howitzers before Phuoc Long Sector's counterattack retook New Bo Duc on 16 December. Although Phuoc Binh Subsector, near the province headquarters, was also under artillery attack, its positions for the moment appeared strong. Three ARVN reconnaissance companies, which had been deployed there to support the road-clearing operation in November, augmented the defenses of the 340th RF Battalion, and the VNAF flew six 105-mm. howitzers, ammunition, and other supplies into Song Be airfield, carrying out noncombatants and wounded. But the NVA did not permit this to continue. Artillery fire on 21-22 December heavily damaged a C-130 upon landing and destroyed another. The 3d NVA Division, meanwhile, launched another strong attack and took New Bo Duc for the last time.

While the battle raged around Song Be and New Bo Duc, the ARVN 341st RF Battalion continued to beat back successive assaults on its positions at Don Luan. The battalion lost the airstrip on 17 December but counterattacked and took it back again. In the north, however, the only positions still in ARVN hands were the Song Be airstrip, Phuoc Binh, and the crest of Nui Ba Ra overlooking the entire region.

The crisis at Phuoc Long, the strong enemy pressure in Tay Ninh, and the attacks in Binh Tuy presented General Dong with no favorable choices. He had to stop enemy advances toward Tay Ninh and hold Binh Tuy Province. On the other hand, he well knew the political and psychological damage that would follow the loss of Phuoc Long. Having to reinforce the north somehow, he ordered the 5th ARVN Division to send the 2d Battalion, 7th Infantry, by helicopter from Lai Khe to Song Be.

On 23 December, as the 2d Battalion reached Song Be, General Dong told Lt Gen. Dong Van Quang, President Thieu's National Security Adviser, that III Corps needed at least part of the Airborne Division from Military Region 1 to save Phuoc Long. Informed of the request, President Thieu rejected it, stating that the Airborne Division was not available and that it could not be moved in time anyway. General Dong would receive priority on air and logistical support, but he would have to make do with his own troop units.

More grim news reached the JGS and III Corps Headquarters on 26 December. Following a 1,000-round artillery preparation, the NVA 7th Division, assisted by diversionary attacks against ARVN positions in and around Phu Giao, finally overran Don Luan.

Meanwhile, refugees poured into Song Be, and the RVNAF tried to resupply the isolated garrison. Ten attempts were made in early January 1975 to drop supplies, but none of the bundles could be recovered by the defenders. At least 16 enemy tanks had been destroyed in prior attacks, but on 6 January 10 more were seen approaching the city. That day General Dong sent two companies of his best troops into the battle: the 81st Airborne Rangers, whose highly trained volunteers were usually employed in commando operations. Also on 6 January, VNAF RF-5 photography disclosed seven 37-mm. antiaircraft positions around the city. It was only the first week of January and the RF-5 flying-hour allocation for the month had been nearly used up.

Very few infantry joined in the assaults on Song Be. Instead, squads of sappers followed the tanks as they rolled through the streets firing at ARVN positions, the sappers followed, mopping up bypassed positions and establishing strong points. Most of the NVA tanks damaged or destroyed were hit by M-72 LAW and 90-mm. recoilless rifles. Often the ranges were so short that the LAW missiles failed to arm themselves and harmlessly bounced off the tank hulls. Making tank kills even more difficult, the NVA M-26 Armor Group had welded extra armor plating on the sides of the hulls, and the crews kept buttoned up so that grendades could not be dropped through the hatches.

NVA artillery was devastating, particularly after 3 January when the rate of fire increased from about 200 rounds per day to nearly 3,000. Structures, bunkers, and trenches collapsed, and casualties mounted. ARVN artillery was out of action, its guns destroyed by fire from tanks, recoilless rifles, and 130-mm. guns. Finally, on 6 January, the province chief realized that he could no longer influence the battle. With no artillery and shattered communications, under direct fire from four approaching T-54 tanks, and seriously wounded, he and what remained of his staff, withdrew from Song Be. The NVA had captured the first province capital since the cease-fire.

There were some military and civilian survivors from Song Be. Pitiful little bands of Montagnards treked through the jungles to Quang Duc, and VNAF helicopters rescued about 200 men of the Rangers, 7th Infantry, and sector territorials in the days immediately following the collapse. The province chief never made it to safety. His wounds slowed him down and he was not seen again. A few members of the command group eventually reached the ARVN outpost of Bu Binh on Highway 14 in Quang Duc. RVNAF losses were staggering. Over 5,400 officers and men of the 7th Infantry, Airborne Rangers, and territorials were committed; less than 850 survived. Especially costly were the high losses in the Airborne Ranger Battalion—85 troopers survived—and in the 2d Battalion, 7th Infantry, fewer than 200 returned from Phuoc Long. About 3,000 civilians, Montagnards and Vietnamese, out of 30,000 or more, escaped Communist control. The few province, village, and hamlet officials who were captured were summarily executed.

Although it was the time of the dry, northeast monsoon, unseasonably heavy torrents drenched Saigon. As this writer's Vietnamese driver dolefully remarked, even the gods were weeping for Phuoc Long.

Note on Sources

General Dung is quoted from his article as translated by the Foreign Broadcast Information Service.

The principal sources of operational and intelligence information came from the DAO liaison officer in Bien Hoa who had daily contact with III Corps headquarters, primarily with Colonel Le Dat Cong, the G-2. These reports were most complete, reliable, and perceptive.

The author made frequent visits to Bien Hoa, and his notes were also used in this chapter. DAO and J2/JGS weekly and daily reports were important references, as were many reports issued by the U.S. Embassy.

14

On the Second Anniversary of the Cease-Fire

Reaction to the NVA's Winter Campaign

The conquest of Phuoc Long Province was clearly the most blatant breach of the cease-fire agreement thus far. Anticipating its fall, the U.S. Department of State on 3 January 1975 asserted that the offensive "belies Hanoi's claims that it is the United States and South Vietnam who are violating the 1973 Paris truce agreements and standing in the way of peace." The PRG promptly rejected the accusation, and North Vietnam's Communist Party newspaper claimed that the offensive was "a legitimate right of riposte" in defense of the Paris agreements. On 13 January, the State Department released the text of an official protest, dated 11 January, delivered to the non-Vietnamese participants in the International Conference on Vietnam and to members of the International Commission of Control and Supervision:

> The Department of State of the United States of America . . . has the honor to refer to the Agreement on Ending the War and Restoring Peace in Viet-Nam signed at Paris January 27, 1973, and to the Act of the International Conference on Viet-Nam signed at Paris March 2, 1973.
>
> When the Agreement was concluded nearly two years ago, our hope was that it would provide a framework under which the Vietnamese people could make their own political choices and resolve their own problems in an atmosphere of peace. Unfortunately this hope, which was clearly shared by the Republic of Viet-Nam and the South Vietnamese people, has been frustrated by the persistent refusal of the Democratic Republic of Viet-Nam to abide by the agreement's most fundamental provisions. Specifically, in flagrant violation of the Agreement, the North Vietnamese and "Provisional Revolutionary Government" authorities have:
>
> —built up the North Vietnamese main-force army in the South through the illegal infiltration of over 160,000 troops;
> —tripled the strength of their armor in the South by sending in over 400 new vehicles, as well as greatly increased their artillery and antiaircraft weaponry;
> —improved their military logistics system running through Laos, Cambodia and the Demilitarized Zone as well as within South Viet-Nam, and expanded their armament stockpiles;
> —refused to deploy the teams which under the Agreement were to oversee the cease-fire;
> —refused to pay their prescribed share of the expenses of the International Commission of Control and Supervision;
> —failed to honor their commitment to cooperate in resolving the status of American and other personnel missing in action even breaking off all discussions on the matter by refusing for the past several months to meet with U.S. and Republic of Viet-Nam representatives in the Four-Party Joint Military Team;
> —broken off all negotiations with the Republic of Viet-Nam including the political negotiations in Paris and the Two Party Joint Military Commission talks in Saigon answering the Republic of Viet-Nam's repeated calls for unconditional resumption of the negotiations with demands for the over throw of the government as a pre-condition for any renewed talks; and
> —gradually increased their military pressure, over-running several areas, including 11 district towns, which were clearly and unequivocally held by the Republic of Viet-Nam at the time of the cease-fire. The latest and most serious escalation of the fighting began in early December with offensives in the southern half of South Viet-Nam which have brought the level of casualties and destruction back up to what it was before the Agreement. These attacks—which included for the first time since the massive North Vietnamese 1972 offensive the over-running of a province capital (Song Be in Phuoc Long Province)—appear to reflect a decision by Hanoi to seek once again to impose a military solution in Viet-Nam. Coming just before the second anniversary of the Agreement, this dramatically belies Hanoi's claims that it is the United States and the Republic of Viet-Nam who are violating the Agreement and standing in the way of peace.
>
> The United States deplores the Democratic Republic of Viet-Nam's turning from the path of negotiation to that of war, not only because it is a grave violation of a solemn international agreement, but also because of the cruel price it is imposing on the people of South Viet-Nam. The Democratic Republic of Viet-Nam must accept the full consequences of its actions. We are deeply concerned about the threat posed to international peace and security, to the political stability of Southeast Asia, to the progress which has been made in removing Viet-Nam as a major issue of great-power contention, and to the hopes of mankind for the building of structures of peace and the strengthening of mechanisms to avert war. We therefore reiterate our strong support for the Republic of Viet-Nam's call to the Hanoi-"Provisional Revolutionary Government" side to reopen the talks in Paris and Saigon which are mandated by the Agreement. We also urge that the . . . [addressee] call upon the Democratic Republic of Viet-Nam to halt its military offensive and join the Republic of Viet-Nam in re-establishing stability and seeking a political solution.

While the staffers in the State Department were putting together this carefully worded note, the North Vietnamese were claiming that the U.S. was flying reconnaissance over South Vietnam to assist the "Saigon administration to intensify its bombing and landgrabbing operations against the PRG-controlled areas." Defense Department spokesmen defended the appropriateness of U.S. aerial reconnaissance in Indochina in view of the extreme provocation by the North Vietnamese. The photography was of some intelligence value to the South Vietnamese but it was rarely, if ever, useful for targeting. U.S. reconnaissance over Laos was stopped on 4 June 1974, and a good part of the timely, detailed evidence of the flow of men and equipment into the South from North Vietnam terminated at that time.

Significantly, the President made no mention of Vietnam in his State of the Union message delivered to Congress on 15 January. In a press conference on 21 January, he said that he could foresee no circumstances in which the U.S. might actively re-enter the Vietnam War.

North Vietnamese leaders carefully analyzed the U.S. reaction to Phuoc Long, General Van Tien Dung reporting it this way:

> It was obvious that the United States was in this position: Having withdrawn from Vietnam, the United States could hardly return. All the conferees [at the Politburo Conference 18 December to 8 January] analyzed the enemy's weakness which in itself heralded a new opportunity for us. To fully exploit this great opportunity we had to conduct large-scale annihilating battles to destroy and disintegrate the enemy on a large scale. [FBIS *Daily Report: Asia and Pacific* Vol. IV, No. 110, Sup. 38, p. 7.]

The dramatic and conclusive victory in Phuoc Long, and the passivity with which the United States reacted to it, confirmed the earlier North Vietnamese estimates that the time for the decisive blow had arrived. The concepts for the spring offensive were discussed and sharpened during this midwinter conference in Hanoi.

Military Region 1

Following the long struggle over commanding terrain south of Phu Bai, a lull in combat came to northern Military Region 1. The monsoon rains and flooding compelled both sides to limit movement, and the VNAF flew no combat sorties between 17 December and 10 January. General Truong, commanding I Corps, took advantage of the temporary calm to pull the 2d Airborne Brigade out of the line west of Hue, placing it in reserve in Phu Loc District. Although the 147th Marine Brigade assumed responsibility for the sector vacated by the 2d, the defenses west of Hue were dangerously thin. The Marine Division itself pulled two battalions out of forward positions northwest of Hue to constitute a heavier reserve and, further thinning the force, sent one company from each battalion to Saigon. These companies formed a new marine brigade for the JGS reserve. Later in the month, marine positions in Quang Tri were taken over by RF battalions, and three marine battalions were shifted south to Thua Thien Province.

By thinning out the line in northern Thua Thien, General Truong not only built up local reserves and contributed to the JGS reserve, but he also concentrated more combat power in the hills south of Phu Bai. The long campaign there continued through the month, and by 29 January, ARVN 1st Division troops were on all important terrain features: Hills 273, 350, 303, and Nui Bong. The battered forces of the 324th NVA Division withdrew to their base areas southwest of Phu Loc to reorganize and await orders for the next campaign. Meanwhile, security around Phu Bai was such that Air Vietnam, the civil airline, resumed regular flights.

After Tet the uneasy quiet that had settled over the battlefields north of the Hai Van Pass showed signs of being shattered. The 324th NVA Division concentrated south of Hue, giving up its positions in the Song Bo corridor, but even more threatening, the 325th NVA Division was relieved on the My Chanh line by local units and was apparently moving into Thua Thien Province. As if this were not enough to concern South Vietnamese commanders, the 341st NVA Division, having been converted from a territorial and training unit to a line infantry division, crossed the DMZ from Quang Binh Province, North Vietnam.

Southern Military Region 1 was more active. After a clearing operation in the Batangan Peninsula of Quang Ngai Province, four RF battalions and a battalion of the 5th Infantry, 2d ARVN Division, lost their effectiveness, and the remainder of the 2d ARVN Division had to be moved into the Province.

Near the border of Nghia Hanh and Mo Duc Districts a 2d ARVN Division clearing operation met with greater success. In six weeks of combat against the 52d NVA Brigade, the division seized the high ground, and inflicted serious casualties.

In late January, the 3d ARVN Division conducted a successful six-day foray into contested ground in Duy Xuyen and Que Son Districts of Quang Nam, again causing high casualties. In the week after Tet, enemy attacks increased markedly in Duc Duc and Dai Loc Districts of Quang Nam, and the ARVN responded with heavy artillery concentrations and air strikes. All indicators in forward areas pointed to a major offensive as the 304th and 2d NVA Divisions, opposing the 3d ARVN Division and the 3d Airborne Brigade, conducted reconnaissance and moved ammunition and artillery forward.

Military Region 2

Ground activity was light in the Central Highlands of Military Region 2 but heavy in coastal Binh Dinh province where the 22d ARVN Division was seriously hurting the 3d NVA Division at the entrance of the An Lao Valley. These attacks were designed to preempt offensive operations by the 3d NVA Division in northern Binh Dinh.

In early January, the 40th and 42d Infantry Regiments, 22d ARVN Division, held all key hills at the entrance to the An Lao Valley and successfully repelled repeated attempts by the 141st Regiment, 3d NVA Division, to dislodge them. The 141st suffered heavy casualties and soon had to pull back. Attacks against ARVN positions diminished in intensity during February and were limited to artillery. But high casualties alone had not caused the lull; rather, a new mission had been assigned to the 3d NVA Division. The first indications of this reached General Niem, commanding the 22d ARVN Division, in early January when a prisoner of war from the 18th Signal Battalion, 3d NVA Division, disclosed the presence of a 3d Division reconnaissance party along Route 19 in the vicinity of An Khe and Binh Khe.

The Vinh Thanh Valley—sometimes called the Song Con Valley for the river which flowed south through it—ended at Binh Khe where the river turned eastward toward the sea and formed the broad fertile delta above Qui Nhon. The valley, which began in the rugged, forested highlands north of Binh Khe, was the natural avenue of approach for the 3d NVA Division to attack ARVN positions along Route 19. RVNAF reconnaissance had discovered in late February and early March that the NVA had improved and extended a road, up to eight meters wide with underwater bridges, from southern Kontum Province through the Kim Son region of Binh Dinh where it joined interprovincial Route 3A. Branches fed the base areas in the northern Vinh Thanh Valley, and heavy truck traffic was flowing into this critical area. Furthermore, a new NVA artillery regiment, the 68th, was discovered moving guns and ammunition south toward Binh Khe through the valley. It was also about this time that fresh evidence appeared that the 3d NVA had shifted major elements into the Vinh Thanh region.

Fully recognizing the threat to Route 19, General Niem confered with the Binh Dinh province chief on measures to secure the route and protect Pleiku-bound convoys. General Niem had had his 47th Infantry Regiment probing north into the Vinh Thanh Valley since early February, and contacts were becoming frequent and sharp. Meanwhile, the enemy increased pressure against Phu My and Phu Cat Districts along Highway 1 with terrorist attacks in the hamlets and by rocketing Phu Cat air base on 18 February for the first time since mid-1974. The focus of NVA activity had clearly shifted from northern Binh Dinh to the passes on Route 19.

General Phu, Commanding II Corps, was particularly concerned about the threat to his principal line of communication. On 2 March, he directed General Niem to pull the 42d Regiment from positions along Highway 1 and to constitute a mobile reserve to be ready to reinforce the 47th Regiment in the An Khe Pass. The security of Highway 1 was turned over to Binh Dinh territorials.

Despite the clear indications that the enemy was shifting his center of gravity southward, General Niem kept fully half of his division in the north, opposite the An Lao Valley. On 3 March, the 22d ARVN Division command post was near Qui Nhon; the 40th Infantry Regiment was in the Phu Cu Pass on Highway 1, just south of Bong Son, and holding the high ground above and east of Hoai An; the 41st Infantry was in Bong Son, covering the entrance to the An Lao Valley, with one battalion north at Landing Zone English on Highway 1; the 42d Infantry was in reserve in Phu My District, along Highway 1, while the 47th Infantry was on Route 19 with two battalions in the An Khe Pass and its 2d Battalion pushing north in the Vinh Thanh Valley. At this time the 22d Division G-2's estimate of the 3d NVA Division dispositions— which later proved to be accurate in all its essential elements—held that two battalions of the 2d Regiment and one battalion of the 141st Regiment were in the hills just north of Route 19 at the entrance of the Vinh Thanh Valley; the 12th Regiment was on the high ground south of Route 19 in the An Khe Pass, about midway between An Khe and Binh Khe; one battalion of the 2d Regiment was in the base area north of Vinh Thanh; while the other two battalions of the 141st Regiment were securing the An Lao base area in northern Binh Dinh. These were the dispositions in Binh Dinh on the eve of the final offensive.

While ground action in January in Kontum and Pleiku was limited to probes, patrols, and attacks by fire, the VNAF was busy daily striking the surge of truck convoys rolling south along new NVA logistical corridors. In one attack in early January, north of Kontum City, 17 loaded trucks were destroyed, an experience frequently repeated throughout the month and into February. Meanwhile, ARVN Ranger teams conducted several raids against the NVA pipeline. Despite the teams' tactical success, the cuts in the line were only temporary inconveniences. On the other hand, an NVA sapper raid on 9 January in Pleiku destroyed 1,500,000 gallons of assorted fuel, a heavy loss to the RVNAF's already severely strained logistics.

By 10 January, spoiling attacks by the 23d ARVN Ranger Group had reached positions 10 kilometers north of Kontum City along Route 14. The objective, Vo Dinh, however, was beyond reach, as NVA resistance stiffened. Meanwhile, in Pleiku Province, along Route 19 east of Le Trung, an NVA attack overran outposts of the 223d RF Battalion. The ARVN 45th Regiment of the 23d Division counterattacked and within a few days recaptured the original positions.

Recognizing a diminished threat in Quang Duc Province, the 271st NVA Regiment having left to participate in the Phuoc Long campaign, General Phu ordered the 53d Infantry Regiment to terminate operations there and return to the 23d Division's base at Ban Me Thuot in Darlac Province. But more significant deployments were under way in the NVA's B-3 Front. The 968th Infantry Division, which had sent its 9th Infantry Regiment to Pleiku the previous January, moved from southern Laos with its 19th and 39th Regiments into Kontum and

Pleiku. Although the combat effectiveness of the 968th was considered low because it had been relatively idle in the Laos panhandle for the past two years, it replaced the experienced 320th NVA Division in the defense of the Duc Co logistical center, thus permitting the B-3 Front to employ the 320th in offensive operations.

In mid-January the 320th NVA Division was noticed moving south toward Darlac, and a buildup near Ban Me Thuot was detected. On 30 January, air strikes damaged three NVA tanks in a base area north of Ban Me Thuot, and the 53d ARVN Infantry launched an operation into the area, meeting light resistance. General Phu sent the 2d Battalion, 45th Infantry, south from Pleiku to reinforce the security along Route 14 near where the Pleiku, Darlac, and Phu Bon Province boundaries met. On 4 February, near the mountain village of Buon Brieng, the battalion picked up an NVA rallier from the 48th Regiment, 320th NVA Division, who confirmed that the 320th was moving to Darlac. He said that the 320th left Duc Co about 12 January and that reconnaissance parties from both the 10th and 320th Divisions had been in Quang Duc and Darlac Provinces, respectively, in recent days.

In Darlac Province in early February, the ARVN had a forward command post of the 23d Division in Ban Me Thuot, two battalions of the 53d Infantry, one battalion of the 45th Infantry, and six of the seven Regional Force battalions belonging to the province. While the seventh RF battalion was deployed in Kontum Province, the six in Darlac were widely separated and in isolated areas. Two were around Ban Don, northwest of Ban Me Thuot; one was patrolling local Route 1 between Ban Me Thuot and Ban Don; one was in an outpost north of Ban Me Thuot on Route 430; another was securing a resettlement village on National Route 21 close to the Khanh Hoa boundary; while the sixth was south in Lac Thien District.

General Phu responded to the growing threat to Darlac Province by committing the entire 45th Infantry to the Darlac–Phu Bon border area, attempting to find and destroy the elements of the 320th NVA Division. While these operations were going on north of Ban Me Thuot, the enemy in the last two weeks of February ambushed three ARVN convoys on Route 21 east of the capital. On the last day of the month, an ARVN unit ambushed an enemy reconnaissance patrol only 12 kilometers north of Ban Me Thuot, and the G-2 of II Corps, as well as the J2 of the JGS, insisted that a major attack on Ban Me Thuot was imminent.

Heavy fighting, meanwhile, had flared in Kontum and Pleiku Province. For the first time since the 1972 offensive, Kontum City on 28 February, and again on 4 March, received an enemy artillery attack. In western Pleiku, the 44th ARVN Regiment and the 25th Ranger Group came under strong attack in Thanh An District. Sensing that the main enemy attack would be in Kontum and Pleiku, and believing that the fighting at Ban Me Thuot was a deception, General Phu recalled the 45th Regiment from Darlac to Pleiku. He also directed the 23d Division to pull its forward command post out of Ban Me Thuot and return it to Pleiku. Further, on 4 March he ordered General Niem to alert his 42d Infantry Regiment for movement to Pleiku.

These orders issued and deployments completed, General Phu settled back to await the enemy onslaught in Kontum and Pleiku. His principal infantry formations in the highlands were, on 3 March, deployed as follows:

The 23d Division—Headquarters at Ham Rong, 12 kilometers south of Pleiku City.

44th Infantry Regiment—20 to 25 kilometers west of Pleiku City in Thanh An District.

53d Infantry Regiment—Headquarters and 1st and 3d Battalions 20 kilometers north of Ban Me Thuot; 2d Battalion at Dac Song in Quang Duc.

The II Corps Ranger Command—Headquarters at Kontum City.

4th Ranger Group—44th Battalion near Pleiku City in reserve; 42d Battalion at Plei Bau Can (on Route 19 west of Route 14); 43d Battalion attached to the 23d Division at Ham Rong.

6th Ranger Group—35th and 36th Battalions east and northeast of Kontum City; 51st Battalion attached to the 25th Ranger Group in Thanh An.

21st Ranger Group—with its 96th Battalion in the Chu Pao Pass between Kontum and Pleiku; 72d Battalion in reserve in Kontum; 89th Battalion attached to the 6th Ranger Group southeast of Kontum.

22d Ranger Group—95th Battalion in Truong Nghia west of Kontum; 88th Battalion in Ngoc Bay Mountain northwest of Kontum; 62d Battalion in reserve in Kontum.

23d Ranger Group—11th, 22d, and 23d Battalions north of Kontum along Route 14.

24th Ranger Group—63d Battalion at Gia Nghia; 81st Battalion south of Kien Duc; 82d Battalion in Kien Duc, Quang Duc.

25th Ranger Group—67th, 76th, and 90th Battalions in Thanh An, Pleiku.

Military Region 3

In Military Region 3, the 18th ARVN Division's counterattack to drive the NVA out of Hoai Duc District progressed slowly but steadily, amply supported by VNAF air strikes, and the 274th NVA Regiment was forced to give ground as casualties mounted. Meanwhile, leaving a small occupying force in Thanh Linh, the 812th NVA Regiment, battered by air strikes, pulled back into the safety of the deep jungle between Thanh Linh and Hoai Duc. The 33d NVA Regiment, its ranks also depleted during an intense, month-long campaign, still held roadblocks along Route 333 in mid-January but was feeling the pressure of the 18th ARVN Division battalions pushing in both directions along the road. During the last week of January 1975, the RVNAF had the road cleared from Gia Ray to Hoai Duc and by February had reoccupied the village of Vo Xu. The Binh Tuy campaign was over. Losses had been high for both sides, and the remote eastern sector of the province remained in NVA control. The RVNAF still controlled the most populous area of the province and had prevented the NVA 6th Division from permanently closing the provinces two major highways, National Routes 20 and 1, which passed Binh Tuy Province on the north and south.

To forestall any NVA attempt to reassert control in the recovered areas, the new III Corps commander, Lt. Gen. Nguyen Van Toan, ordered the 18th ARVN Division to maintain a sizable force in Binh Tuy, but to prepare for employment elsewhere as the corps reserve. As of mid-February, the 43d Infantry of the 18th Division was along Route 333 between Hoai Duc and Gia Huynh; the 52d Infantry headquarters with its 2d Battalion was at the division base at Xuan Loc while its 1st and 3d Battalions operated in Dinh Quan and Gia Ray, respectively; and the 48th Infantry was in corps reserve at Long Binh in Bien Hoa Province. The famine in available forces in Military Region 3 was such that even the few major elements designated as corps reserve were nearly always engaged. But this did not deter General Toan from attempting to keep the enemy off balance through periodic spoiling attacks into contested areas. One such operation was an attempt in February by the 5th ARVN Division to clear Route 13 from Lai Khe and link up with the RF and Rangers at Chon Thanh. After an auspicious beginning, however, the attack stalled, as all previous efforts had on Route 13, well short of its goal. The enemy was clearly determined to keep Route 13 closed and his own rear area intact; further, the 5th ARVN Division obviously lacked either the offensive power or will to succeed in this ambitious undertaking. (General Toan had been in the wings as Commanding General of the Armor Command since his relief from command of II Corps. Despite alleged participation in corrupt practices, he enjoyed a seemingly well-deserved reputation as a skilled and courageous commander. The fall of Phuoc Long Province sealed the fate of Lieutenant General Du Quoc Dong as III Corps Commander. Military Region 3, with Saigon at its heart, required the services of an experienced, decisive campaigner, and General Toan, no matter how tainted, was the best man available.)

III Corps Rangers and Regional Forces conducted less formidable attacks in northern Bien Hoa Province to prevent NVA rocket artillery batteries from locating within range of the airbase and to disrupt 7th NVA Division operations around Tan Uyen District. These forays met with moderate success but did not permanently affect enemy capabilities.

On 17 January, III Corps launched an operation, using the 25th ARVN Division, to retake Nui Ba Den. While artillery, helicopter gunships, and VNAF fighter-bombers pounded the NVA position, ARVN Ranger patrols searched for enemy artillery positions in the jungles north of the mountain. An airmobile assault was attempted, but NVA antiaircraft artillery and small arms fire were effective in preventing the landing. By 26 January it was apparent that retaking Nui Ba Den was beyond the resources available to III Corps. The 46th ARVN Infantry Regiment, which had moved to the base of the mountain, was withdrawn to Tay Ninh City and the operation was terminated. Aided by the excellent observation that Nui Ba Den afforded, NVA artillery continued to shell Tay Ninh City with heavy rockets and 130-mm. guns until the end of the month when the center of the province capital was virtually deserted.

A lull settled over Tay Ninh Province as the soldiers and civilians of South Vietnam prepared for Tet, which began on 11 February. But although combat declined, the enemy was very actively preparing for a major offensive in Tay Ninh and in adjoining Binh Duong and Hau Nghia Provinces. Elements of three NVA divisions, two separate infantry regiments, and a number of separate battalions, all supported by up to 10 battalions of medium and heavy artillery, moved to positions around Tay Ninh City. The 6th Regiment of the 5th NVA Division and at least three local battalions and a separate regiment, were concentrated to the southwest, ready to cut Routes 1 and 22 at Go Dau Ha. The new 3d Division, fresh from its victory at Phuoc Long, was north of the city, while the veteran 9th Division was around the Michelin Plantation, preparing to assault Tri Tam on the Tay Ninh-Binh Duong boundary. Large convoys of trucks were seen moving supplies and ammunition forward.

Faced by a formidable enemy on his western flank as he assumed command in Military Region 3, General Toan in characteristic fashion set about making decisive changes in dispositions and concepts to deal with the threat. To make the 25th ARVN Division, which covered an immense front from the Cambodian frontier nearly to the western outskirts of Saigon, more mobile, he gave responsibility for all static posts to Tay Ninh Regional Forces. Eight RF battalions and seven separate RF companies were placed along lines of communication and major approaches to the city, while the three regiments of the 25th Division conducted mobile operations in the forward areas. The 46th Infantry was east and southeast of the city; the 49th Infantry was north of the city, with battalions around Nui Ba Den; while the 50th Infantry was near Khiem Hanh, to the southeast. A company of M-41 light tanks and two troops of armored personnel carriers were in reserve near Tay Ninh City, and a reinforced company of the 81st Airborne Rangers conducted deep patrols on Nui Ba Den and into the jungle of War Zone C, north of the mountain. The division commander, Brig. Gen. Ly Tong Ba, like General Toan had a background in armor and was exercising vigorous, personal leadership in the forward areas, urging his troops to patrol more aggressively into the contested area north of the city.

Tet was over and the first days of the Year of the Cat passed into March. In the east of his sector, General Toan watched the 6th and 7th NVA Divisions conducting reconnaissance and preparing for combat in Long Khanh and Bien Hoa. In the center, his 5th Division persisted, without much success, in pushing north out of Bau Bang to link up with the Rangers, who had attacked south from Chon Thanh along Route 13. The situation was becoming tense in western Binh Duong, at Tri Tam and throughout Tay Ninh Province, but General Toan's fresh approach renewed the confidence of the 25th Division and the Tay Ninh territorials. To the southwest, at Tan An in Long An Province, astride Highway 4, the newly organized 4th Marine Brigade was deployed. Inexperienced but seasoned with a few veteran campaigners, this brigade stiffened the defenses of the Long An territorials.

Military Region 4

Consistent with its country-wide program of consolidating independent battalions and regiments into larger formations more suited to sustained conventional combat, the NVA in late 1974 organized the 4th Division in Chuong Thien Province and 8th Division in Kien Tuong and Dinh Tuong Provinces of South Vietnam's Military Region 4.

From 6-26 December 1974 Communist forces in the Mekong Delta had conducted the most widespread and intense attacks thus far in the war. They struck with greatest force in the Elephant's Foot area of Kien Tuong Province, but strong attacks also occurred along lines of communication in Dinh Tuong, Chuong Thien, Ba Xuyen, Vinh Binh, Vinh Long, and An Xuyen Provinces. Casualties on both sides were heavy; the RVNAF had over 500 killed in action, and total casualties, including wounded and missing, exceeded 3,000. On the enemy side, the best estimates placed total losses—killed, captured, and permanently disabled—at over 3,500. Despite the generally effective defense put up by the RVNAF, security in the hamlets and countryside of the southern delta deteriorated as a result of widespread attacks against isolated, lightly defended regions.

Up until the end of January 1975, the new 8th NVA Division had been largely uncommitted—only its Z-15 Regiment in northern Dinh Tuong Province had engaged in significant combat—while the veteran 5th NVA Division attempted to secure Svay Rieng border areas. During a flurry of activity in January, the 5th NVA Division suffered high casualties and gained very little, while the ARVN held on tenaciously to Tri Phap bases against probes and harassing attacks launched by the Z-18 and 24th NVA Regiments of the 8th Division.

During January violence spread throughout the delta in a pre-Tet spasm of NVA attacks on lines of communication, cities, villages and outposts. With regard to the latter, Maj. Gen. Nguyen Khoa Nam, upon assuming command of IV Corps and Military Region 4, continued to reduce the number of indefensible, isolated posts and to consolidate combat power in larger positions. Sixty-three posts in the delta were abandoned under this plan in January, while another 87 were either overrun or evacuated under pressure. Of the latter, ARVN counterattacks regained 24. The heaviest losses were in the far south, in Bac Lieu, where 23 posts were lost and only 4 retaken, and in An Xuyen, where 16 posts fell and only 2 were recovered. Half the posts voluntarily abandoned were also located in these two provinces, while the central provinces of Phong Dien and Sa Dec and the northern border sector of Kien Phong suffered very light damage. Even in the key central province of Chuong Thien, where the three regiments (D-2, 18B, and 95A) of the new 4th NVA Division operated, the ARVN lost very little; of the six posts lost to enemy attack, four were recaptured. As the second anniversary of the cease fire came and went, it was clear that the ARVN soldiers of the delta had won the January round, but at high cost. RVNAF casualties in Military Region 4 were very high.

The enemy also lost heavily, but nowhere were his casualties heavier than in the battle between the 5th NVA Division and the 7th ARVN Division in northern Kien Tuong Province along the Cambodian-Svay Rieng border. By the end of January only two ARVN positions remained in Tuyen Binh District; Long Khot outpost was overrun by elements of the 6th and 174th NVA Regiments using captured M-113 armored personnel carriers. But capturing that outpost was the last significant success the NVA would enjoy in Kien Tuong before the final offensive. Toward the end of February, the 5th NVA Division withdrew the battered 6th Regiment from action and sent it into Cambodia to receive replacements and thereafter to southern Tay Ninh Province. Replacements flowed into the 5th NVA Division in great numbers during the month while the 7th ARVN Division kept up the pressure against the 174th Regiment around Moc Hoa.

Athough the ARVN was successful against NVA main forces in most of the central and northern delta, security in the southern provinces—especially in An Xuyen and Bac Lieu —continued deteriorating. Territorials were not competent to deal with the threat, and not enough regulars were available. To strengthen Military Region 4 territorials, the JGS authorized the corps commander to deactivate 16 RF battalions, 5 RF companies, and 76 PF platoons to fill the ranks of other depleted territorial units.

The Navy in the delta was in similar difficulty. Budgetary limitations had cut the number of operational units from 44 to 21, and the riverine forces could no longer provide adequate security on several major canals.

In mid-February another security problem, one with tragic overtones, arose in the northern delta. The collapse of the forces of the government of Cambodia had caused thousands to seek refuge in Chau Doc Province. More than 7,000 people, including at least 500 military, streamed across the border.

Over on the western edge of the delta, north of Rach Gia District town, ARVN regulars intercepted two NVA battalions moving down Infiltration Corridor 1-C and inflicted heavy casualties; more than 350 were killed and a large quantity of ordnance was captured.

Congressional Visitors

Signs of the coming NVA offensive did not go unobserved. The Defense Attache Office, Saigon, and the American Embassy each reported in their own channels events which presaged the approaching campaign, and both were occupied with furnishing information to Washington to support the supplemental appropriation for Vietnam military assistance requested by the Ford administration. To see first-hand the situation which the White House said justified at least the $300 million requested, several members of Congress and their staff aides journeyed to Vietnam.

The first congressional visitor of the new year was Senator Sam Nunn, a member of the Armed Services Committee. His advance man was Don L. Lynch, a member of the committee staff, who arived in Saigon on 7 January and stayed until the senator's two-day visit was over on 14 January. They were given detailed briefings by the Embassy and DAO and by General Khuyen, Chief of Staff of the JGS and Chief of the Central Logistical Command, who explained the military situation and the problems the RVNAF was facing due to the reduction of American assistance. Senator Nunn returned to the United States convinced, as was Representative Leo J. Ryan, who had visited Vietnam in late December 1974, that military aid reductions had seriously weakened the RVNAF.

President Ford requested an additional appropriation of $522 million for Vietnam and Cambodia on 28 January, $300 million of which would be for Vietnam. Accordingly, the Senate and the House of Representatives put together a joint bipartisan group to fly to Vietnam and return to report on the appropriateness of the administration's request. Two of the Congressmen, Senator Dewey F. Bartlett and Representative Paul N. McCloskey arrived in Saigon on 24 February, three days in advance of the main party, which included Representatives William V. Chappell, Donald N. Fraser, Bella Abzug, John P. Murtha, and John J. Flynt. These visiting Congressmen were accompanied by Mr. Philip C. Habib, Assistant Secretary of State for East Asian and Pacific Affairs; Mr. Eric von Marbod, Deputy Assistant Secretary of Defense; and a dozen staff aides and escorts.

Preoccupied though they were with the critical military situation, the South Vietnamese leaders prepared and presented eye-opening briefings and displays. No doors were closed to the delegation members; they were offered trips to any battlefront they wished to see. Bartlett, Murtha, and McCloskey were interested in extensive field trips. Others, particularly Abzug, wanted to see and talk to "political prisoners." The South Vietnamese arranged for such visits, although what constituted a political prisoner in this desperate, war-torn environment was a subject of no little dispute and misunderstanding.

Congressman Murtha went to Military Region 1 and, with General Truong, visited forward positions by helicopter. Congressmen Bartlett and McCloskey devoted their first two full days to extensive battlefield tours. They went first to IV Corps Headquarters at Can Tho where Representative McCloskey asked to see and was shown the compound for prisoners of war. At Dinh Tuong they visted the command post of the 12th Infantry, 7th Division. From there both Congressmen went to Da Nang and on to the headquarters of the 56th Infantry in Duc Duc, where they were briefed by General Hinh, the 3d Division commander. ARVN artillery was responding to a call for fires from a forward observer during this visit, and General Hinh explained the severe conditions imposed by the fuel and ammunition restrictions. The next day the Congressmen were given a close look at the Binh Dinh battle area, north of Bong Son, by the commander of the 22d ARVN Division. General Niem would have taken them to the crests of the hills his men held, but the road was swept by fire, and enemy shells were falling on these positions.

Back in Saigon, the JGS had prepared a display of captured enemy weapons, ammunition, and equipment, including the most modern weapons and fighting vehicles furnished by the Soviet Union and China. Only a few members of the delegation attended. Before leaving Saigon on 2 March, most of the delegation questioned the NVA and VC delegation at Tan Son Nhut about Americans missing in action.

When they departed, some members left with brief cases bulging with fact sheets prepared by DAO, the JGS, and the American Embassy on subjects they inquired about. DAO fact sheets discussed military data supporting estimates for the coming offensive.

The fact sheet on the NVA strategic reserve pointed out that since the January 1973 cease fire, North Vietnam had rebuilt and increased its strategic reserve from two divisions (the 308th and 308B) to seven, and this list did not include the 968th Division deploying from Laos into the Central Highlands. They had returned the 312th and 320B Divisions to the reserve from Quang Tri Province; brought the 316th back to North Vietnam from northern Laos; reconstituted the 341st Division in the southernmost province of North Vietnam; and converted the 338th Division from a training division. Furthermore, they had created a corps headquarters in Thanh Hoa Province for controlling three or more divisions plus corps armor, artillery, and air defense regiments. These changes were viewed as strong indicators of major offensive intent. The fact sheet also showed that the deployment times of these divisions were greatly shortened from those before the cease fire due to the new highways and the absence of U.S. interdiction. Within 15 days, for example, a division in North Vietnam could be moved to South Vietnam's Military Region 2 and committed to combat.

Another fact sheet discussed how heavy infiltration customarily preceded and continued through major NVA offensives in the south and showed that infiltration was especially large during the first two months of 1975. More than half as many replacements would arrive in South Vietnam during the first three months of 1975 than arrived during all of 1973. Since the cease fire, 200,000 replacements had moved south, a clear sign that an offensive was in the offing.

The greatly increased size and strength of the regular NVA forces in South Vietnam was the subject of a number of fact sheets. One listed the major combat and combat support units that had entered South Vietnam or had been formed there from replacement groups since the cease fire. (It did not mention several divisions formed from independent regiments or new regiments built of previously separate battalions.) Most of them were air defense units. Although the 968th Infantry Division was on the way from Laos only its 9th Regiment (since integrated into the 320th Division) was counted among the two other known infantry regiments then new to the southern battlefield—the 36th and 41st in Quang Nam. Five other new regiments of armor, artillery, and sappers were also listed, along with four new sapper battalions.

Another fact sheet displayed DAO Saigon's estimate of the numerical strength changes that had taken place in NVA forces in South Vietnam since the cease fire. Combat units had gained 58,000 men and now had over 200,000. Combat and administrative support units had added about 30,000, for a new strength of over 100,000. Viet Cong were not included in these estimates. Armor vehicles, mostly tanks, had risen from about 100 to over 700, while the number of medium artillery pieces was over 400, up from about 100. The NVA now had twice as many tanks in South Vietnam (about 700) as did the RVNAF (352).

Papers on construction, lines of communication, supply level, and the pipeline showed that the NVA in the South had built a complex logistical system and had stockpiled enough supplies to support a major offensive for over a year. The NVA had never in the history of the war been in such a favorable logistical condition. Significantly, the RVNAF were, for the first time in the war, in an inferior position.

Besides these fact sheets, the DAO furnished the congressional delegation a paper called "Vietnam Perspective." This explained frequently unperceived influences on the relative power, flexibility, and tactical potential of the opposing armed forces. For example, although the NVA's expeditionary force in South Vietnam was less than half the size of the South's combat force, the enemy made up the difference in troops maintained in secure garrisons in North Vietnam, more than 70,000 of which were available for immediate deployment to South Vietnam. Furthermore, the NVA possessed the frequently decisive advantages of surprise and the ability to mass overwhelming force. The RVNAF, even when they were able to discover the enemy's intent in advance, were often unable to move sufficient reserves to the battle area in time to forestall defeat in detail. The NVA's advantages also accounted for its ability to accomplish its objectives through the expenditure of far less ammunition than the defenders. Through careful reconnaissance, registration, and siting of batteries in concealed locations, the attacker concentrated heavy fires on small targets, while the defender had to search great areas, cover many avenues of approach and suspected enemy positions, and use much larger amounts of ammunition in the defense. The requirements for defense of populated areas, thousands of bridges, and hundreds of miles of highway left the RVNAF with few forces available to use in deep or prolonged offensive operations.

Rounding out the set of documents furnished the delegation, the DAO presented its January 1975 threat assessment. Some pertinent paragraphs are quoted:

16. In early 1974, COSVN Resolution 12, based on resolution 21 of the Lao Dong Party which was adopted during the 21st Plenum of the Lao Dong Party in Hanoi, emerged as the basic Communist guidance relating to the South. Resolution 12 reiterated previous emphasis on strengthening revolutionary forces, stressing that, if the Communists remained strong, the GVN would be forced to implement the Paris Agreement. COSVN 12 thus reflected a somewhat conservative outlook which emphasized building Communist strength, rather than exercising it on the battlefield.

17. In August 1974 [President Nixon resigned on August 9], however, the Communists adopted a strategy envisioning a largescale offensive to defeat GVN pacification and bring about new negotiations. It called for an intense military campaign beginning in December 1974 and lasting until mid-1975. In defeating pacification, the Communist forces were to fulfill certain requirements (kill one third of the GVN's MF, RF and PF; neutralize one-half of the PSDF; and cut key LOC's) in order to accomplish certain missions: (1) liberate the bulk of the countryside; (2) increase the population in the Communist areas; (3) obtain rice; and (4) upgrade contested areas.

18. The 1974-1975 dry season campaign began dramatically in December with major attacks throughout MR-3 and MR-4, with the most visible result being the GVN loss of Phuoc Long Province. Major combat has since declined in those areas, but is expected to resume. In MR-1 and MR-2, the bulk of available intelligence indicates that major combat will soon be forthcoming. The campaign, thus, is expected to assume countrywide proportions and a number of indicators point to the introduction of strategic reserve divisions from NVN.

19. Thus, Communist strategy since the ceasefire has evolved from a rather cautious approach in the early stages, involving testing of the Paris Agreement and building up of rear areas, to one based primarily on battlefield victories to exploit the perceived weaknesses of the GVN. The COSVN resolution for 1975 heralds a return to major offensive activity as the primary means of advancing the Communist revolution to a successful conclusion. . . .

46. If reported plans are executed, the Communists will be crossing the threshold between the outpost war and an attempt to deal critical blows to RVNAF and the GVN. In the near term, the Communists will probably experience continued success, to include overrunning of some district towns; however, increased Communist losses may prove prohibitive in the long run.

47. In conclusion, despite the lack of clarity concerning a number of key indicators as regards both specific intent and timing, we anticipate a significant upsurge in combat in northern SVN, as poor weather gradually abates in late February and March, and a resumption of major attacks in MR-3, once Communists preparations are complete. The war in the Delta is expected to remain at the recent intensified levels and to reflect increasingly ambitious Communist attacks on populated areas.

The Congressional delegation's jet left Tan Son Nhut airport on 2 March. As if having waited for the delegation to depart, the NVA launched the final offensive two mornings later with attacks that severed Highway 19 between the highlands and the coast.

Note on Sources

Newspaper accounts were used for the reactions and statements of officials in the United States.

Generals Truong and Vien read this chapter and contributed valuable comments and corrections.

The final DAO Quarterly Assessment provided information concerning the visitors of early 1975, and DAO fact sheets were used to describe the prevailing situation. The January Monthly Intelligence Summary and Threat Analysis was also useful.

Finally, the author accompanied Representative McCloskey on his field trips and attended most of the briefings conducted for the congressional visitors. The author's notes and recollections were referred to in relating the events surrounding this visit.

15

The Central Highlands, March 1975

Senior General Van Tien Dung was the principal architect of North Vietnam's final offensive against South Vietnam. In his account of "The Great Spring Victory" he described the planning of the offensive (FBIS *Daily Report: Asia and Pacific,* Vol. IV, No. 110, Sup. 38, pp. 6–10):

... during the 20 days of the conference the Political Bureau's assessment of the situation and its discussions were influenced increasingly by the obvious week-by-week achievement of major strategic objectives.... While the Political Bureau was meeting, great news came from the south: the main force units in eastern Nam Bo [roughly conterminous with South Vietnam's Military Region 3], in cooperation with the provincial forces, had attacked and liberated Phuoc Binh City and all of Phuoc Long Province.

On 8 January 1975, two days after the Phuoc Long victory, Comrade Le Duan concluded the discussions.... The situation is now clear to everybody. We are now determined to fulfill the 2-year plan....

Le Duan went on: Striking a strategic blow in 1975, Nam Bo will have to create an interrelated and interdependent position throughout the region, bring military pressure closer to Saigon, annihilate as many enemy main-force units as possible and create conditions for localities to deploy forces when opportunities arise.

In the Mekong delta region military pressure must be brought closer to My Tho. We have agreed that this year the attack on the Central Highlands will begin. He pointed to a map behind him and said: Attacks must be unleashed toward Ban Me Thuot and Tuy Hoa. The Fifth Region will have to form a liberated area from Binh Dinh Province northward, and the Tri-Thien forces will have to control an area from Hue to Da Nang.

While we discussed the 1975 strategic combat plan, another very important question was raised: Where to establish the main battlefield?

After considering the RVNAF strength, mobility and deployments, the relative strategic value of each major region, and the strength and mobility of the NVA, "the conferees unanimously approved the General Staff's draft plan which chose the Central Highlands as the main battlefield in the large-scale, widespread 1975 offensive."

According to General Dung, North Vietnamese leaders did not expect total victory in 1975. The major, country-wide offensive they were planning for early 1975 was to prepare the way for a "general offensive" that would finish the task in 1976. Nevertheless, they anticipated the possibility of "opportunities" to "liberate" South Vietnam "early or late in 1975."

General Dung reported that on 9 January, one day after the conference adjourned, the Central Military Party Committee convened to prepare military plans to support the conference resolution. It was here that Ban Me Thuot was selected as the first objective and main effort of the Central Highlands campaign.

The conference had just started when Comrade Le Duc Tho arrived unannounced. He opened the door, entered and joined us in the conference. Later on we knew that the Political Bureau was somewhat troubled because the idea of an attack on Ban Me Thuot had not been clearly outlined in the combat plan; therefore, it sent Comrade Tho to join us and present his idea that such an attack was essential. He said enthusiastically: "We must definitely raise the problem of liberating Ban Me Thuot and Duc Lap. It would be absurd if with almost five divisions in the Central Highlands we could not attack Ban Me Thuot." Comrade Vo Nguyen Giap, secretary of the Central Military Party Committee, concluded the conference by establishing the areas and targets of the offensive, the objectives of the campaign and the orders for deploying and using forces. He also suggested the fighting methods that should be applied, greatly stressing the principle of force, secrecy and surprise, and advised that it was necessary to deceive the enemy into concentration on defending areas north of the Central Highlands.

The Central Highlands campaign was code-named "Campaign 275." At that time on the Central Highlands front, Comrade Vu Lang, the front commander, left for the Ban Me Thuot area with some cadres to assess the situation. At the request of comrades Le Duan and Le Duc Tho, the Political Bureau sent me to the Central Highlands battlefield as a representative of the Political Bureau, the Central Military Party Committee and the High Command to take field command.... I told Comrade Tran Van Tra following the Political Bureau conference: "This time I will fight in the Central Highlands until the rainy season. Then I will go to Nam Bo to join you in studying the battlefield situation and making preparations for military activities in the 1975–76 dry season."... At this time in the Central Highlands we had the 320th, 10th and 968th divisions—divisions that had gained much combat experience on the Central Highlands battlefield. Toward the end of December 1974 the High Command decided to dispatch the 316th Division to this front.

Isolating the Battlefield

To capture Ban Me Thuot, NVA leadership in the B-3 Front—now personified in General Van Tien Dung—counted on surprise and overwhelming force. The element of surprise was to be enhanced by strong diversionary attacks in Kontum and Pleiku Provinces; once achieved, the advantage of mass, or the concentration of force, was to be prolonged by preventing the RVNAF from reinforcing Ban Me Thuot. The diversionary and supporting attacks began while the three NVA divisions that would take part in the Darlac-Quang Duc Campaign—the 10th, 316th, and 320—were still converging on their initial objectives areas.

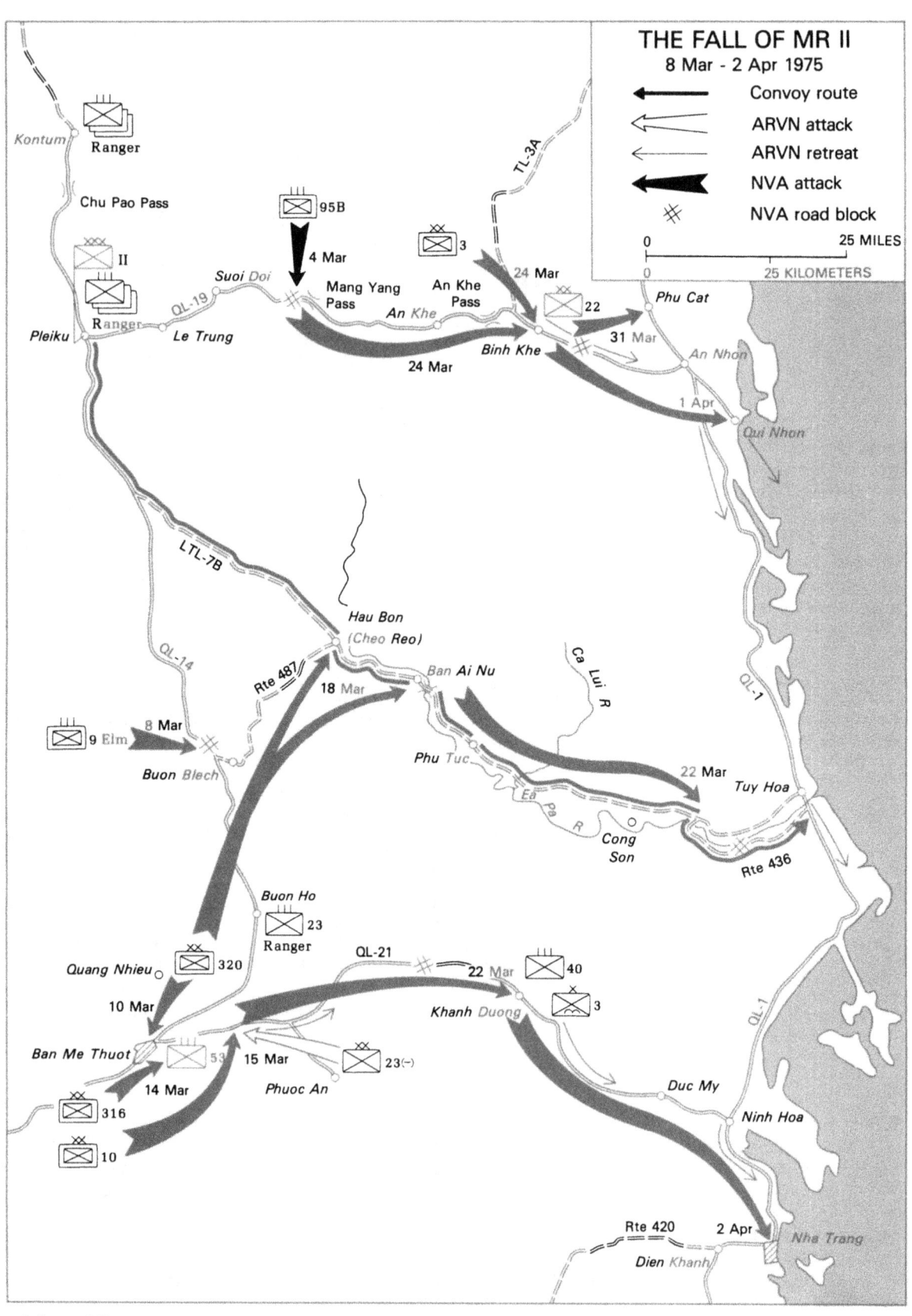

Map 19

The opening guns of Campaign 275 sounded along Route 19 (QL-19), the lifeline to the highlands, in the early morning of 4 March. Simultaneous attacks closed the highway from the Mang Yang Pass in Pleiku Province to Binh Dinh Province. Enemy sappers blew Bridge 12 southeast of Binh Khe, in Binh Dinh, and infantry struck ARVN territorials on the high ground overwatching the An Khe Pass and the RF unit at the Route 3A (TL-3A) junction. Soon an artillery position supporting the 2d Battalion, 47th Infantry, north of Binh Khe was overrun. A strong attack by the 12th Regiment, 3d NVA Division, near the An Khe airfield was repulsed, while Phu Cat air base received a rocket attack and sustained light damage. (Map 19)

While Binh Dinh territorials and the 47th ARVN Regiment struggled to hold their positions against the withering NVA artillery, infantry, and sapper assaults, South Vietnam forces in Pleiku Province came under heavy rocket, mortar, and recoilless rifle fire along Route 19 from Le Trung, 15 kilometers east of Pleiku City, to the narrow defiles of the Mang Yang Pass. Fire Support Bases 92 (east of Le Trung), 93 (near Soui Doi), and 94 (north of Hill 3045), all came under bombardment, while a number of their outposts were overrun. Two bridges and a large culvert between FSBs 93 and 94 were destroyed by enemy sappers. General Phu, the II Corps commander, reacted by sending two battalions of the 4th Ranger Group to join elements of the 2d Armored Cavalry Brigade, then clearing parts of Route 19, to proceed as far as FSB 95 in Binh Dinh Province, just east of the Mang Yang Pass. But before the operation could get under way, Base 94 was overrun. Meanwhile, NVA rockets hit Pleiku air base; although the field remained operational, the maintenance area sustained heavy damage.

While the attacks along Route 19 were viewed by General Phu as strong indicators that the NVA main effort would be against Pleiku, the Communists also interdicted Route 21 (QL-21), the other major road to the highlands, which connected coastal Khanh Hoa Province with Ban Me Thuot. Sappers blew two bridges between the Darlac boundary and Khanh Duong in Khanh Hoa Province, and NVA infantry overran an ARVN territorial outpost close to the provincial boundary. The only two available roads to the highlands were closed; the battlefield of the Central Highlands had been isolated in 24 hours of concentrated assaults.

At II Corps headquarters, South Vietnamese officers debated where the enemy's main effort would take place. Colonel Trinh Tieu, the G-2, insisted that Ban Me Thuot would be the principal objective, with intermediate and supporting objectives at Buon Ho and Duc Lap. Based on indications that elements of the 10th and 320th Division had shifted south or had at least conducted reconnaissance in Quang Duc and Darlac Provinces, he told his commander that the attacks in Kontum, Pleiku, and on Route 19 were diversionary, designed primarily to hold the major RVNAF strength in place in Binh Dinh, Kontum, and Pleiku. General Phu nevertheless, believed Pleiku to be the main NVA objective. His reasoning was based on the weight of the current enemy attacks by fire against the 44th ARVN Infantry in Thanh An District of Pleiku and against the Rangers north of Kontum. Having only two regiments protecting the western approaches to Pleiku, he would not weaken this front to reinforce Ban Me Thuot where nothing significant had yet taken place.

Darlac and Quang Duc

Local Route 487 twisted through the forested highlands of southwestern Phu Bon Province between Cheo Reo, the capital, and Buon Blech, where it joined National Route 14 (QL-14) about 60 kilometers north of Ban Me Thuot. At this junction, also the district seat of Thuan Man in Phu Bon Province, the NVA on 8 March, struck the first direct blow of Campaign 275. Elements of the 9th Regiment, 320th NVA Division, attacked the subsector headquarters and the 23d Reconnaissance Company forcing a withdrawal. Meanwhile, the 45th ARVN Regiment on Route 14 near Thuan Man reported contact with enemy infantry. The fighting continued through the day, but Route 14 was permanently blocked by the 9th Regiment, 320th NVA Division.

On 9 March, the 10th NVA Division launched simultaneous attacks throughout Quang Duc Province. The assault against the Rangers at Kien Duc was repulsed, and the Quang Duc territorials at Duc Lap also held their positions. But south of Duc Lap, at the Dak Song crossroads, heavy artillery bombardment and infantry assaults drove the 2d Battalion, 53d ARVN Infantry Regiment, from its defenses. By noon it was overrun.

General Phu was now convinced that Darlac was the main battlefield and his forces there needed immediate reinforcement. He asked the JGS for an additional Ranger group but was turned down; the JGS had few reserves, and threats to Saigon and Tay Ninh were mounting. Failing to acquire additional combat power from outside the region, General Phu pulled the 72d and 96th Ranger Battalions, 21st Ranger Group, from the Chu Pao Pass and Kontum and flew them to Buon Ho; once there they boarded trucks for the 35-kilometer ride to Ban Me Thuot. He also ordered the 45th Reconnaissance Company at Ban Don to return to Ban Me Thuot.

According to General Dung's account, at 0200 Hanoi time on the morning of 10 March, the offensive on Ban Me Thuot was heralded by the fire from sapper units directed against the Hoa Binh [Phung Duc] and city airfields. Long-range artillery began destroying military targets in the city. From a point 40 kilometers from Ban Me Thuot, our tank unit started their engines, knocked down trees which had been cut halfway in advance, headed for Ban Me Thuot. On the Xre Poc [Krong] River, modern ferryboats were rapidly assembled, while tanks, armored vehicles, antiaircraft guns, and antitank guns formed queues to cross on the ferries. The mountains and forests of the Central Highlands were shaken by a fire storm.

In the early morning of 10 March 1975 heavy rockets and artillery fire fell on Ban Me Thuot, and mortar fire struck the airfield at Phung Duc to the east. The bombardment was followed by infantry and sapper assaults against the ammunition dump on local Route 1 west of the city; the 2d Company, 225th RF Battalion on Hill 559 northwest of the city, and the subsector headquarters at Phung Duc airfield. All attacks were repulsed, and enemy losses were heavy. Just before four that morning, the 3d Battalion, 53d ARVN Infantry, came under heavy attack at the airfield, and NVA tanks were sighted northwest of the city.

Meanwhile, attacks in Quang Duc Province continued as the 259th RF Battalion fought off enemy infantry on Route 12 between Dak Song and Duc Lap and the Rangers held their ground in Kien Duc and Gia Nghia. On 15 March the beleaguered defenders of Kien Duc, however, were finally overrun.

In Binh Dinh Province, General Niem, commanding the 22d Division, reinforced his 42d Infantry Regiment in Binh Khe District with the headquarters and two battalions of the 41st Infantry, but Route 19 was still cut at Le Trung and Binh Khe. Attacking Rangers were stalled at Bridge 31 between Fire Support Bases 93 and 94 in Pleiku Province. Although a heavy rocket attack on the airfield at Pleiku on 10 March closed down operations for several hours, Route 14 between Kontum and Pleiku remained open. A steady stream of traffic surged south through the Chu Pao Pass as the population of Kontum fled the daily rocketing of their city and the imminent threat of Communist invasion. The lines at the Air Vietnam terminal at Kontum flowed out into the streets as residents sought to buy tickets to Pleiku and points south. Highway 14 was closed on 10 March in southern Pleiku by enemy attacks on territorial outposts in the mountains close to the Darlac boundary.

By mid-morning on 10 March, major elements of the 320th NVA Division had penetrated Ban Me Thuot. The heaviest fighting was in the southern sector near the province chief's residence, the sector headquarters, and the 23d Division command post. Five enemy tanks were destroyed or disabled near the command post, but one of the VNAF bombs intended for NVA armor demolished the sector headquarters, cutting off all communications. Two more tanks were destroyed near the city's airfield. The small ARVN garrison there fought back repeated NVA assaults and held on to the control tower, but General Phu's effort to fly two RF battalions from Ban Don to Ban Me Thuot was thwarted by heavy enemy small arms and automatic weapons fire. Both battalions were therefore diverted to Buon Ho, which also came under mortar attack on 10 March. Fighting at the airfield destroyed eight aircraft of the 6th Air Division, a CH-47, one 0-1, and six UH-1s. Four of the seven UH-1s belonging to the 2d Air Division were destroyed on the ground, but air crews managed to fly out three damaged helicopters under heavy fire. The sector ammunition storage site southwest of the city was overrun; 10,000 rounds of 105-mm ammunition were destroyed, and two 105-mm. howitzers were lost.

At the Phung Duc airfield, the 3d Battalion, 53d Infantry took two prisoners who identified the attackers as the 25th Independent Regiment and the 401st Sapper Battalion. Meanwhile, in Ban Me Thuot, the NVA was also taking prisoners. Two members of the ICCS, one Iranian and one Indonesian, had taken refuge with the only American official in Darlac, Paul Struharic, the Consul General's provincial representative. Eight other foreign civilians, missionaries, and their families were with Struharic when NVA soldiers broke into his house and seized them all. Although they were imprisoned in Duc Co, all were eventually released.

By the night of 10 March the NVA had a firm hold on the center of Ban Me Thuot, while the principal remaining ARVN infantry, cavalry, and territorials held positions east, west and south of the city. The 2d Company, 225th RF Battalion, remained on Hill 559, and the 4th Company, 242d RF Battalion still held the main ammunition dump. In a coffee plantation west of Ban Me Thuot, most of the 1st Battalion, 53d Infantry, and Headquarters and 3d Troop, 8th Armored Cavalry, defended their perimeter. The 4th Company, 243d RF Battalion, was dug in on Hill 491 to the south. Small units of the 53d Regiment and territorials were still fighting in the city, but the heaviest combat was at the Phung Duc airfield. There, the forward command post of the 23d ARVN Division fought along with the headquarters of its 53d Infantry, and the 3d Troop, 8th Armored Cavalry. Survivors of the sector headquarters were with some Ranger units west of the airfield.

Very heavy fighting continued on 11 March. ARVN defenders estimated 400 enemy killed, 50 weapons captured, and 13 tanks destroyed, and the 53d Infantry at the airfield reported that the NVA was using flame-throwers in the assault. Isolated pockets of resistance fought on, even though the province chief, Col. Nguyen Cong Luat, was captured.

In Pleiku, the 4th Ranger Group gained no ground on Route 19 in heavy fighting near Bridge 23 and Fire Support Base 93 as the 95B NVA Regiment counterattacked vigorously on 11-12 March. Fighting was widespread but light in the rest of Pleiku. The environs of the city were mortared, the II Corps headquarters sustained minor damage from a rocket attack, and three A-37 light bombers were destroyed along with fuel storage and a parts warehouse at Pleiku Air Base by 122-mm. rockets.

The disastrous turn of events in Military Region 2 led to the turning point in the long and bitter war, compelling President Thieu to make a decision regarding the conduct of the defense which would create chaos for the RVNAF and opportunities for the enemy. Regarding the northern part of the country as expendable in order to preserve the security of Military Regions 3 and 4, he thought it essential to retake Ban Me Thuot, even though Kontum and Pleiku might have to be sacrificed. He wished to convey this new concept to General Phu in Pleiku, but because of the hazards of such a meeting in that war-torn province, he was persuaded by his staff to meet the II Corps commander in Cam Ranh, south of Nha Trang, on 14 March.

On 12 March, General Phu announced that all organized resistance inside Ban Me Thuot had ceased. The 21st Ranger Group was assembling the survivors of its two committed battalions near the Phung Duc airfield, and the 45th ARVN Infantry Regiment was moving by helicopters to Phuoc An District on Route 21, east of Ban Me Thuot. The next day, as the 320th NVA Division consolidated its gains in Ban Me Thuot, the battle for Phung Duc continued. Recognizing the critical situation in the highlands, the JGS decided to send the 7th Ranger Group, its last available reserve, from Saigon to replace the 44th Infantry Regiment west of Pleiku, releasing the 44th to join the counterattack in Darlac.

The situation in Darlac continued to deteriorate. Quang Nhieu Village in the plantations north of Ban Me Thuot was overrun as was Buon Ho Village on Route 14. The South Vietnamese gave up Ban Don and withdrew remaining RF units. The planned relief of the 44th Infantry west of Pleiku had to be aborted after one battalion and the regimental headquarters were moved because the required airlift could not be marshalled to complete it.

On 14 March, General Phu had assembled in Phuoc An a task force under the command of Brig. Gen. Le Trung Tuong, commanding general of the 23d ARVN Division. In the task force were the 45th Infantry Regiment, one battalion and the headquarters of the 44th Infantry, and one battalion of the 21st Ranger Group. The plan was to attack west astride Route 21 to link up with the tenacious defenders at the Phung Duc airfield: the 3d Battalion, 53d Infantry, which had been there through four days of continuous fighting; the survivors of the 1st Battalion. 53d Infantry, who had withdrawn from west of the city; and the survivors of the 72d and 96th Battalions, 21st Ranger Group.

The counterattack was to be supported logistically from Nha Trang. Another task force of five RF battalions from Khanh Hoa Province was ordered to clear the route between Nha Trang and Khanh Duong.

On 14 March, General Phu flew to Cam Ranh for his fateful meeting with the President. With General Vien, Lt Gen. Dang Van Quang, and Prime Minister Khiem present, President Thieu outlined his concept. General Phu's role would be to retake Ban Me Thuot, using the troops he still had in Kontum and Pleiku Province, and the 22d Division from Binh Dinh Province. With Route 19 cut in Pleiku and Binh Dinh, and no way to use Routes 14 and 21 through Darlac, General Phu had only interprovincial Route 7B (LTL-7B) available to recover his Kontum-Pleiku forces, assemble them in Khanh Hoa Province, and fight back along Route 21 into Ban Me Thuot. Although many hazards were discussed, this approach was accepted by the President, and General Phu flew back to his headquarters to set the withdrawal in motion. (American officials had no knowledge of the decision.)

That night, 14 March, NVA sappers penetrated the Pleiku ammunition storage area and blew up 1,400 rounds of 105-mm. howitzer shells. The deployments to Darlac had greatly weakened security in Pleiku, and General Phu had already ordered the evacuation of all nonessential military personnel and dependents from Kontum and Pleiku. Colonel Giao, the acting commander of the 6th Air Division at Pleiku, directed the evacuation from Pleiku Air Base. Brig. Gen. Tran Van Cam, the deputy commander for operations, II Corps, was left in command of forces in Pleiku Province. Colonel Pham Duy Tat, commander of II Corps Rangers, remained in Kontum Province in charge of territorials and three Ranger groups, the 6th, 22d, and 23d. General Phu moved his command post to II Corps Rear at Nha Trang and, surprisingly, replaced the captured Darlac Province Chief with Col. Trinh Tieu, his own G-2, whose correct estimate of the NVA offensive he had so tragically rejected. He made one other significant announcement to his staff before he left Pleiku: Colonel Tat was promoted to brigadier general and would command the evacuation of Kontum and Pleiku down Route 7B to the coast at Tuy Hoa. Upon the insistence of General Phu, Tat's promotion was approved by President Thieu at the Cam Ranh meeting.

As the 23d Division's counterattack from Phuoc An began on 15 March, the 53d Infantry's situation at the airfield was grim. ARVN soldiers had withstood nearly continuous artillery and mortar bombardment and had beaten back successive assaults by the 25th NVA Regiment. But the 316th NVA Division, recently moved with great secrecy from North Vietnam, was poised to attack the battered 53d Infantry and Rangers east of Ban Me Thuot.

To block the 23d Division's counterattack from Phuoc An, General Dung ordered the 10th NVA Division up from Quang Duc. The 10th met the advancing 45th ARVN Infantry and stopped it at the Ea Nhiae River, ten kilometers short of its planned link-up with the 53d. The 2d Battalion, 45th Regiment, was shattered in this fierce engagement, and the ARVN counterattack became a withdrawal. The division commander, Brig. Gen. Tuong, was slightly wounded as his helicopter received fire on 10 March. He had himself evacuated and command reverted to the senior colonel in the task force, Colonel Duc.

Behind the withdrawing survivors of the 23d Division, territorials from Khanh Hoa were meeting stiff resistance at Khanh Duong. Fighting for the high ground overlooking the road to Nha Trang, they captured some enemy soldiers from the 25th Independent Regiment, which had apparently slipped around the 23d Division at Phuoc An after failing to dislodge the 53d Infantry at the Phung Duc airfield.

The renewed NVA offensive in Dalac Province, led by the 10th Division along Route 21, pushed the 23d Division task force eastward, first back to Phuoc An, then through Chu Kuk near the Khanh Hoa boundary. Finally, the 23d Division command post reached Khanh Duong and settled there to recover the remnants of its battalions as they straggled in. Without resupply, the survivors of the 3d Battalion, 53d Infantry, on 18 March gave up the airfield and began a tortuous withdrawal eastward. On 21 March, what remained of the 23d ARVN Division was flown to the relative security of Cam Ranh. By this time, the exodus from Pleiku was well under way. The enemy still held high ground in and around Khanh Duong on Route 21, although the 2d and 3d Battalions of the 40th Regiment, 22d ARVN Division, had been moved from Binh Dinh Province to reinforce the attack. The 3d Airborne Brigade, pulled out of Quang Nam Province on presidential orders to become a reserve in Saigon, was taken off its ships in Nha Trang and rushed to Khanh Duong to halt the pursuing 10th NVA Division. Obviously, the immediate tasks facing II Corps were to regroup its battered forces, complete the evacuation from the highlands, and stop the NVA advance on Route 21 at Khanh Duong. The counteroffensive to recapture Ban Me Thuot would have to wait.

Exodus from the Highlands

The evacuation of South Vietnamese forces from the highland provinces began in great secrecy; General Phu hoped that surprise would make it possible to reach Tuy Hoa before the enemy could discover and react to the movement. Accordingly, only a few staff officers and commanders were told of the plan in advance; the chiefs of the affected provinces, Kontum, Pleiku, and Phu Bon, found out about it when they saw ARVN units moving. The operation was prepared only in outline; detailed orders were never drafted or issued. Not foreseeing the inevitable mass civilian exodus that would accompany the military column as soon as the population discovered what was going on, General Phu made no preparations to control the crowds which became entangled in combat formations, impeding their movement and ability to deploy and fight.

The only road available, Route 7B, was a track southeast of Cheo Reo, overgrown with brush, with fords in disrepair and an important bridge out. Aware of the road's condition, General Phu put the 20th Engineer Group in the vanguard. A few military vehicles began the journey to Phu Bon on 15 March, but the main body was scheduled to move over a four-day period, beginning on the 16th. Two hundred to 250 trucks were to move in each echelon, and each echelon would be protected by a company of M-48 tanks of the 21st Tank Battalion. The Ranger Battalions of the five groups still in Kontum and Pleiku Provinces, together with one tank company, would be the rear guard, to depart Pleiku on 19 March. Logistical units with ammunition and fuel trucks and some of the corps artillery were assigned to the first echelon, followed by more logistical and artillery units on 17 March. The II Corps staff, military police, and the balance of the 44th Infantry would move the next day. Territorial units were supposed to provide security along the route, an unrealistic mission since the province chiefs were not issued orders.

According to the best recollections of those involved in the operation—records are scarce, general, and sometimes erroneous—ARVN military units in the withdrawal included the following: one battalion, 44th Infantry / six Ranger Groups (eighteen battalions): the 4th (just arived from JGS reserve, Saigon), 7th, and 25th Groups in Pleiku; the 6th, 22d, and 23d in Kontum / 21st Tank Battalion / two battalions, 155-mm. howitzer / one battalion, 175-mm. gun (self-propelled) / 20th Engineer Group (three combat battalions, one float bridge company, and one fixed bridge company) / 231st Direct Support Group.

Additionally, there were about 20,000 tons of Army and Air Force ammunition in the supply points, a 45-day stock of fuels, and 60 days of rations, Some UH-1 helicopters and four CH-47 helicopters were sent up from Military Region 4 to reinforce the 2d Air Division. C-130 transports flew civilian and military dependents out of Pleiku on 16 March, but an enemy rocket attack closed the airfield that evening.

The orders for the military evacuation were issued on 16 March; the 6th Ranger Group, defending the northeast sector above Kontum City, had withdrawn to Pleiku City the day before. The 22d and 23d Ranger Groups from north and northwest of Kontum pulled back to Pleiku the next day. Observing the withdrawal, the Kontum province chief joined the stream of traffic flowing south and was killed in an ambush in the Chu Pao Pass. At this time, the small force of the 44th Infantry and the 7th and 25th Ranger Groups were still defending west of Pleiku, and part of the 25th was under heavy attack at Thanh An. General Tat, now in command of the withdrawing troops, moved his command post to Cheo Reo. Altering the plan slightly, he took with him, in addition to the engineers, one of his Ranger groups. This was a prudent modification, since the territorials were not prepared to secure the capital, the road, or the engineer work site. That afternoon, 16 March, Cheo Reo was struck by enemy rockets in the first attack against the town since the NVA offensive began. The withdrawal had been discovered although this rocket attack was probably carried out coincidentally by local forces.

In discussing the final offensive, General Dung describes receiving the first report on 16 March—apparently the source was a communications intercept—that II Corps Headquarters had moved its forward command post to Nha Trang. Later that day, an NVA observation post reported a long column of trucks running south toward Phu Bon. Dung warned the 95B Regiment on Route 19, the 320th Division north of Ban Me Thuot on Route 14, and the 10th Division on Route 21, that the RVNAF was making a major deployment and all should be especially vigilant. Earlier he had asked about the condition of Route 7B and was told that it could not support military traffic past Cheo Reo. With the large ARVN convoy moving into Cheo Reo, Dung was no longer satisfied with this response. Disturbed to learn that the road was apparently usable and that the 320th Division had not moved to block the column, he berated the division commander for laxity and ordered him to attack the withdrawing column without further delay.

Except for the rocket attack on 16 March, the NVA did not interfere with the column in Phu Bon and along the road to Cheo Reo until 18 March. But because II Corps engineers had not yet completed a pontoon bridge across the Ea Pa River beyond Cheo Reo, several convoys were jammed in that town and along the road to the southeast. Late on 18 March, the 320th Division struck at Cheo Reo with artillery, mortars, and infantry. Military and civilian casualties were heavy and wounded still lay unattended on the streets the next morning. Aerial photography taken on the morning of the 19th showed artillery fire still falling in the city and hundreds of vehicles, many of them damaged or destroyed, abandoned along the road and in the streets of Cheo Reo.

The convoy pressed on, fighting as it struggled south. At mid-morning on 19 March, the leading element was at the Con River, eight kilometers east of Cung Son and about two-thirds of the distance from Cheo Reo to its destination, Tuy Hao. But the ragged column stretched back to Cheo Reo where refugees still streamed through the death-littered streets. At a ford over the Ca Lui River, 25 kilometers northwest of Cong Son, a number of heavy vehicles became mired. A VNAF air strike contributed to the carnage and confusion by mistakenly attacking a Ranger battalion and decimating it. By this time, little military order or discipline remained. General Tat no longer had control of the withdrawing forces, and the tank battalion commander was walking, no longer able to command his tanks although at least 10 M-48s were still operational. As the head of the column reached the broad Song Ba, about 10 kilometers east of Cong Son, it found that Route 7B had been so heavily mined by Koreans who had operated in the area that it was impractical to clear the route. Instead, the engineers were ordered to bridge the Song Ba and divert the column to local Route 436, which followed the south bank of the river to Tuy Hoa. Anticipating this movement, the enemy set up five road-blocks along Route 436 in a two-kilometer stretch east of the Song Ba crossing, stopping the movement of bridge sections from Tuy Hoa to the crossing. The 206th RF battalion, one of the best territorial units, was therefore ordered to attack through the roadblocks from the east, while the 34th Ranger Battalion, with 16 M-113 personnel carriers, would attack from the west after fording the Song Ba.

On 20 March, heavy trucks and tanks tore up the ford on the Song Ba so badly that pierced-steel-planking had to be placed on the bottom. This was delivered by the CH-47's, which also began flying in bridge sections to the site about 1,500 meters downstream from the ford.

On 21 March, the column was concentrated around the ford and bridge sites east of Cong Son, but the Ranger rear guard was badly split back at Cheo Reo. The 6th, 7th, and 22d Groups had most of their battalions past the Ca Lui crossing, but the 4th, 23d, and 25th were trapped behind the 320th NVA Division, advancing on Cong Son. On 22 March, elements of the 64th Regiment, 320th NVA Division, attacked blocking positions established by the 6th Ranger Group west of Cong Son, and ARVN engineers completed the bridge over the Song Ba. In a rush to cross, the bridge was overloaded and a section collapsed. But the engineers quickly repaired the span, and many vehicles cleared the north bank of the river that day and night, only to face enemy blocking positions along Route 436 in My Thanh Tay Village.

While the 35th and 51st Ranger Battalions fought as a rear guard in a narrow defile about seven kilometers northwest of Cong Son, the 34th Rangers continued the attack east on Route 436 to clear the roadblocks. By this time, the 6th Ranger Group battalions were the only cohesive fighting units in the column, 3 of 18 battalions that began the long march through the Phu Bon gauntlet.

The 35th and 51st Rangers repulsed a strong attack by the 64th NVA Regiment on the night of 23 March, killing 50 and taking 15 weapons. These two battalions had mustered a force of 15 M-41 light tanks, 8 M-48 medium tanks, 11 105-mm. howitzers, and 2 155-mm. howitzers. Two CH-47s kept the Rangers supplied with rations and ammunition as they fell back through Cong Son. Reinforced by two tank companies, the 320th NVA Division pushed into Cong Son behind the withdrawing 6th Ranger Group late on 24 March.

Meanwhile, the 34th Battalion continued the attack against the blocking positions disposed in My Thanh Tay Village. Even though bad weather prevented air support, the Rangers reduced position after position. By 25 March they had broken the last position and led the shattered column into Tuy Hoa. Now hardly more than a company in strength, the 34th Battalion then turned around to guard the western approaches to Tuy Hoa.

Eventually, about 60,000 refugees from the highlands straggled into Nha Trang, but at least 100,000 remained stranded in western Phu Yen Province without food, water, or medical assistance. One of the most poorly executed withdrawals in the war, and certainly the most tragic, had ended. The 320th NVA Division continued its inexorable march to the sea and by 31 March had Tuy Hoa under fire.

16

The Final Offensive in the North

The Offensive North of Binh Dinh

Campaign 275 in the Central Highlands was the main effort in a country-wide offensive coordinated by the North Vietnamese high command with considerable precision. Coincident with the start of the Ban Me Thuot campaign on 8 March, the NVA attacked the three northern provinces of South Vietnam's Military Region 1, Quang Tri, Thua Thien, and Quang Nam. In Quang Tin strong attacks did not begin until two days later. In Quang Ngai, the enemy's offensive was delayed, apparently by an aggressive RVNAF clearing operation, QUYET THANH A-1-75 in Nghia Hanh District. The 4th Infantry Regiment, 2d ARVN Division, was involved in sharp fighting there on 6 and 7 March, and enemy casualties were substantial.

Initially, the strongest attack in Quang Tri Province struck territorial outposts and strong points in the foothills and the hamlets of the coastal lowlands. The 110th ARVN RF Battalion held its ground in the southwest sector of the province against a strong NVA infantry assault; moderate casualties were sustained by both sides. By 8 March, NVA and local VC were in control of seven hamlets in Hai Lang District and in southern Quang Tri and northern Thua Thien, and refugees streamed southward, until nearly the entire population of Quang Tri Province, as many as 100,000, travelled the road to Hue.

With tanks and armored personnel carriers, an ARVN task force composed of the 8th Airborne Battalion, the 112th and 120th RF Battalions, and the 921st RF Company, succeeded in driving the enemy from nearly all populated areas by afternoon on 9 March. Communist casualties were heavy and ARVN losses few in this opening phase.

The North Vietnamese infiltrated and attacked villages in the coastal lowlands of Thua Thien, as they had in Quang Tri, and vigorously assaulted RVNAF regulars protecting the approaches to Hue.

Southeast of Hue regiments of the NVA 324B Division began the Thua Thien campaign attacking along an eight kilometer sector in the early morning of 8 March. Supported by intense artillery concentrations, enemy infantry swarmed over the surrounding hills. The 2d Battalion, 1st ARVN Infantry Regiment, held on Hill 121, but the 1st Battalion, 1st Infantry, was shattered and driven from Hill 224. The 2d Battalion, 54th Infantry, was initially forced to give ground but recovered its positions on Hill 144 on 9 March. The Reconnaissance Company of the 1st ARVN Division was forced from Hill 50 southwest of Nui Bong.

Brig. Gen. Nguyen Van Diem, commanding the 1st ARVN Division, reacted by dispatching the 15th Ranger Group with the 61st and 94th Ranger Battalions to reinforce the line and recover lost positions. The 61st was ambushed en route, sustained moderate losses, but recovered to join the 94th in a counterattack on 10 March. The next day, the first firm evidence (a prisoner of war) appeared that the 325th NVA Division had moved south and was in position to join the attack in Phu Loc District.

At least 20 tanks accompanied the NVA assault in the Song Bo corridor where the Marine Division had its 147th Brigade of five battalions—the 3d, 4th, 5th, and 7th Marines and the 130th RF Battalion. The attacks continued for two days and one marine position was lost but the 4th Marine Battalion recovered it on 11 March. In two days of heavy fighting, with moderate marine casualties, the 147th Brigade killed more than 200 enemy, destroyed two tanks and damaged seven, and captured many weapons.

Just as the attacks in the forward areas were stronger in Thua Thien than in Quang Tri, so were the invasions into the populated lowlands. A battalion of the 6th NVA Regiment infiltrated through Phu Loc, and two of its companies seized 12 fishing boats, which ferried them across Dam Cau Hai Bay to Vinh Loc District. There they attacked Vinh Hien Village on the southern tip of the island and swept north to attack Vinh Giang. Some of the battalion pushed into Phu Thu District east of Hue. The 8th Airborne Battalion, reinforced with two companies of the 1st Battalion, 54th Infantry, and a troop of armored cavalry, moved against the enemy battalion and badly mauled and dispersed it. On 16 March a unit of the 54th ARVN Infantry ambushed a remnant of the battalion south of Hue, killing the battalion commander, his staff, and 20 men. Five prisoners taken by the 54th Infantry said that the population gave them no support, and only 33 men, mostly wounded, remained alive in their battalion.

Other intrusions into the lowlands were made in Quang Dien and Phong Dien Districts northwest of

Hue. Infiltrating NVA Troops, mostly from the 4th Independent Regiment, were also quickly eliminated by South Vietnamese counterattacks.

South of the Hai Van Pass, NVA sappers penetrated Da Nang on 8 March and fired rocket grenades into subsubsector offices of Hoa Vang District. A heavy rocket attack on Da Nang Air Base on 11 March destroyed a new F-5E fighter-bomber. Meanwhile, artillery-supported infantry assaults were launched against ARVN 3d Infantry Division, Airborne Division, and territorial positions from Dai Loc to Que Son. Nearly all NVA assaults were repelled with heavy enemy losses, but sappers were able to get through and blow the main bridge on Route 540 north of Dai Loc.

The situation in Quang Tin Province was more serious. Long-expected NVA blows against the hill districts of Tien Phuoc and Hau Duc finally fell on 10 March. Two battalions of the 31st NVA Regiment, 2d Division, attacked Tien Phuoc from the north and west, while elements of the 1st NVA Regiment struck from the south and southeast. In Hau Duc, another battalion of the 31st NVA Regiment, with supporting local forces, overran the 102d RF Battalion. Refugees from both districts began streaming into Tam Ky, the province capital, which itself was hit by NVA 122-mm. rockets on 11 March. The major RVNAF base at Chu Lai also received a rocket bombardment.

Remnants of the 116th and 134th RF Battalions, decimated in Tien Phuoc, also straggled eastward toward Tam Ky. The 135th RF Battalion left its positions on Ban Quan Mountain east of Tien Phuoc and withdrew toward Tam Ky, but left four howitzers to the enemy. The 3d Battalion, 5th ARVN Infantry, with the 115th RF Battalion, counterattacked at My Mountain, the last important high ground on Route 533 between Tam Ky and Tien Phuoc, and regained the position, only to be driven off again by intense artillery fire.

General Nhut, commanding the 2d ARVN Division, organized a relief column to push out from Tam Ky and protect the withdrawal of the territorials and civilians from Tien Phuoc. The enemy, however, held the high ground overlooking the column's approach, including a prominent hill called Nui Ngoc. On 11 March the RVNAF column, composed of the 37th and 39th Ranger Battalions and the 1st Battalion, 5th Infantry, 2d ARVN Division, stalled short of Nui Ngoc.

On 12 March, General Nhut sent the 5th Infantry Regiment from Quang Ngai Province and deployed it west of Tam Ky. Its three battalions were in depth along Route 533, the forward elements just east of My Mountain. Two RF battalions, the 115th and 135th, were north of the 5th Infantry, between Route 533 and the Ranger task force below Nui Ngoc. The 21st Ranger Battalion was behind the 135th RF, west of Tam Ky. Thus, General Nhut had nine battalions west of Tam Ky, as a strong enemy was about to continue the attack toward that city. Furthermore, Tam Ky was now within range of the enemy's light artillery.

Meanwhile, in Da Nang, General Truong was facing an even more serious problem. On 12 March, he received the JGS order to pull the Airborne Division out of the line and start it moving to Saigon. The deployment was to begin on 17 March. General Truong immediately called General Vien to protest the decision but learned that President Thieu had personally directed the deployment so that the Airborne Division could participate in the offensive to retake Ban Me Thuot. General Vien told General Truong that, if possible, two battalions of the new 468th Marine Brigade and a Ranger group would be sent North to replace the Airborne Division.

To adjust to the loss of the Airborne Division, General Truong decided to pull the Marine Division out of Quang Tri and northern Thua Thien Provinces and shift it south to cover Phu Loc District and Da Nang. The 14th Ranger Group would move north to relieve the marines on 13 March. Only one marine brigade, the one in Phu Loc, would remain north of the Hai Van Pass. General Nhut would be ordered to pull one regiment out of the Quyet Thang operation in Nghia Hanh to reinforce the defense of Tam Ky. This order effectively cancelled the successful ARVN offensive in central Quang Ngai. Furthermore, General Nhut was told to defend Tam Ky at about the positions his forward battalions then occupied, such defense in effect ending the operation to return to Tien Phuoc. I Corps was to defend Hue and Da Nang, even if it had to give up Quang Tri, Quang Tin, and Quang Ngai Province. General Truong and General Thi agreed, however, that their ability to hold Hue after the Marine Division moved south was questionable indeed.

General Truong flew to Saigon on 13 March to participate in a secret meeting with President Thieu, Prime Minister Khiem, and General Vien during which Truong was told about the evacuation from the highlands and ordered to prepare a plan for the eventual evacuation of Military Region 1. He also was permitted to delay the first airborne brigade's departure to 18 March and the rest of the division until 31 March. The President's reasoning was that Da Nang was most important but that the rest of the region could be sacrificed. He would send the 468th Marine Brigade north to help defend Da Nang as soon as the Airborne Division arrived in Saigon. This division was vital to the defense of Military Regions 3 and 4, without which the Republic could no longer survive.

More disquieting news reached General Truong after his meeting with President Thieu. NVA attacks in southwestern Quang Tri Province had overrun two RF strongpoints on the western flank of the My Chanh Line. Farther south, in the Song Bo corridor, the 4th and 5th Marine Battalions fought off strong attacks in the 147th Marine Brigade's sector. In the 1st ARVN Division's sector, two battalions of the 3d Infantry were forced from the Fire Support Base Bastogne area but regained most of their positions in a counterattack the following day. Heavy fighting continued southwest of Tam Ky. RF positions were crumbling, and NVA tanks were sighted approaching from east of Tien Phuoc. The 3d Battalion, 5th Infantry, and the 37th Ranger Battalion were both locked in close combat and in danger of being overrun.

On 14 March, General Truong met with General Thi, commanding I Corps troops in Quang Tri and Thua Thien Provinces, and General Lan, the Marine Division commander, to explain his concept for the final defense of Da Nang. He would pull all combat forces into Quang Nam and defend Da Nang with the 1st, 3d, and Marine Divisions on line and the 2d Division in reserve. But this deployment would be approached gradually as divisional troops were relieved in Quang Tri and Thua Thien Provinces and terrain in the southern part of the region was abandoned. General Truong ordered the immediate evacuation of all military units, including the 68th Ranger Battalion at Song Ha and the 69th Ranger Battalion at Tra Bong, and all civilians in both areas who wanted to leave.

On 15 March, the 14th Ranger Group was to begin the relief of the 369th Marine Brigade in Quang Tri Province. While one marine brigade would remain in the Song Bo Valley for the defense of Hue, the 369th Marine Brigade would deploy to Dai Loc District in Quang Nam Province, and relieve the 3d Airborne Brigade for movement to Saigon. Generals Truong and Thi anticipated a mass civilian exodus from Quang Tri as soon as the people saw that the marines were leaving, and he directed his staff to prepare plans to assist the refugees.

Meanwhile, General Truong ordered General Nhut of the 2nd Division to keep his 6th Infantry Regiment south of Nghia Hanh town to protect Quang Ngai City. The NVA attacked strongly throughout Quang Ngai on 14 and 15 March, overrunning outposts all around the province capital. Quang Ngai territorials, never strong, had been weakened further by the departure of the 5th ARVN Regiment for Quang Tin Province and the shift of most of the 4th ARVN Regiment to 2d Division reserve in Chu Lai. Only two regular battalions, the 70th Ranger and the 3d Battalion of the 4th Infantry, remained south of Mo Duc; only three RF battalions between Mo Duc and the Binh Dinh boundary. In the northern sectors, on the night of 15-16 March, an NVA attack destroyed five PF platoons north of Binh Son and closed Route 1 to the Quang Tin boundary.

In Quang Tin, the NVA attacked north of Tam Ky close to National Route 1 and overran an RF company north of the city on 15 March. When the NVA also struck west of Tam Ky, the 5th ARVN Infantry Regiment and the 12th Ranger Group fell back and the 37th Ranger Battalion was routed.

While a collapse was imminent in the region's two southern provinces, the shifting of units in Quang Tri Province was proceeding on schedule. The 14th Ranger Group established its command post at Hai Lang and sent its 77th, 78th, and 79th Ranger Battalions forward to replace the 369th Marine Brigade, which began moving south to relieve the Airborne Division in Quang Nam. As the Marines left, they took the courage and morale of the territorials and civilians of Quang Tri with them, even though the last pockets of enemy infiltrators in the lowlands had been eliminated by 16 March.

While this relief was going on, a rallier from the 101st Regiment, 325th NVA Division, was being interrogated in Phu Loc. His testimony confirmed the presence of the entire 325th Division in southern Thua Thien Province, supported by the 85-mm. and 130-mm. guns of the 84th Artillery Regiment. At least two infantry regiments, the 18th and the 101st, were within easy striking distance of Phu Loc as of 15 March.

The 258th Marine Brigade pulled out of Quang Tri to relieve the Airborne brigade in southern Thua Thien on 17 March. The Marine Division command post was set up at Marble Mountain Airfield on the beach east of Da Nang on 18 March while the 2d Airborne Brigade moved to the Da Nang docks for shipment to Saigon.

To support the defense of Da Nang, General Truong ordered the 175-mm. gun batteries north of the Hai Van Pass to begin moving to Da Nang along with a company of M-48 tanks. These deployments, ordered on 18 March, would leave two companies of M-48 tanks of the 20th Tank Squadron in Thua Thien. The next day, NVA tanks attacked across the cease-fire line in Quang Tri.

The evacuation of Son Ha and Tra Bong got under way on 16 March as two CH-47 helicopters began lifting out civilians. The military—the 68th Ranger Battalion, 17 RF platoons, and over 400 PSDF soldiers—were flown to Son Tinh, north of Quang Ngai City. Many of the 12,000 residents of Tra Bong began moving along the road to Binh Son, protected by the 69th Rangers. Also in the column were a battery of territorial artillery, an RF company, 22 PF platoons and 600 PSDF militia. As the 25-kilometer trek began, the NVA attacked outposts north of Binh Son and severed Route 1 between that town and Chu Lai. NVA artillery shelled Binh Son causing light civilian casualties while enemy infantry wiped out several outposts south in Son Tinh District. Meanwhile, General Nhut moved the 2d Battalion, 6th Infantry, from Nghia Hanh to the western edge of Quang Ngai City.

North of the Hai Van Pass, in Phu Loc District of Thua Thien Province, the 15th Ranger Group continued to restore ARVN control in the Nui Bong sector on 17-18 March. General Thi moved two M-48 tank companies of the 20th Squadron from north of Hue to south of the city.

On 18 March, Prime Minister Khiem flew to Da Nang. Drastic measures to adjust the country's defenses to conform to the new national strategy were under way in the highlands. The great, tragic exodus from Pleiku and Kontum had started, but calamitous events were rapidly overtaking the strategy. The goal was to hold a truncated Vietnam with its northern frontier anchored at Ban Me Thuot, but to do that required salvaging the nation's military strength now under savage attack from Phu Bon to Quang Tri. Tri Tam had fallen north of Saigon, and the NVA offensive was gathering momentum in Tay Ninh, Long Khanh, and Binh Tuy Provinces. I Corps had already given up one of its strongest divisions, the Airborne, to bolster the defense of Saigon, and Prime Minister Khiem's mission was to assess the impact of its loss, discuss the rapidly changing situation with General Truong, and advise President Thieu on what part of Military Region I could be defended with the forces available.

The Prime Minister made it clear to General Truong that no additional troops would be sent to his corps; the promised new marine brigade would remain in the defense of the capital. He told General Truong that the 3d Airborne Brigade had been diverted at Nha Trang and sent to block the NVA advance at Khanh Duong; the rest of the division would proceed to Saigon. He also promised to send a staff to Da Nang, representing all interested ministries, to assist in handling the monumental refugee problems that were developing in the region.

While in Da Nang, Prime Minister Khiem listened to briefings by the five province chiefs and the mayor of Da Nang. The mayor told him that civilian morale was very low, that many families had already gone to Saigon, and that the lack of support by the United States at this critical time was deeply felt by the people. The Quang Nam Province chief, Colonel Pham Van Chung, told him that morale among his troops was still good, but the people were very worried about the departure of the Airborne Division. The reports from Quang Ngai and Quang Tin, by Colonels Dao Mong Xuan and Le Van Ngoc, were grim; the territorials had all but given up, and were deserting in large numbers. Units were below half strength. The Quang Tri province chief, Colonel Do Ky, gave a similar report; almost all civilians had left the province, morale was low and the territorials could not be expected to offer serious resistance to an attack now that the stiffening presence of the marines had been removed. Colonel Nguyen Huu Due of Thua Thien, unduly optimistic, said that although people were beginning to leave Hue in large numbers his territorials were in good spirits and would fight.

The Prime Minister left for Saigon, and the next day General Truong returned the visit. He was directed to stop the evacuation of Hue and to defend enclaves at Hue, Da Nang, Chu Lai, and Quang Ngai City. He could, when forced, surrender Chu Lai and Quang Ngai, but he was to defend Hue and Da Nang at all costs.

When General Truong returned to his headquarters on 20 March, he turned around the displacing 175-mm. batteries moving to Da Nang and stopped the evacuation of ammunition from Hue. The Imperial City would be defended despite the fact that enemy artillery had, on 19 March, already struck inside the Citadel and Highway 1 was clogged with the southbound traffic of thousands of refugees.

The contracted organization for the defense of Hue, under the command of General Thi, was divided between the deputy commander of the Marine Division, Col. Tri, who was responsible north of Hue, and the 1st Division commander, Brig. Gen. Nguyen Van Diem, south of the city. Colonel Tri's outposts were just inside the Thua Thien-Quang Tri boundary, nearly 30 kilometers northwest of Hue. Here, under the direct command of the 14th Ranger Group, were the 77th Ranger Battalion, seven RF battalions, and a troop of armored personnel carriers of the 17th Armored Cavalry Squadron. The four marine battalions of the 147th Brigade were in the vital Bo Corridor, within light artillery range of the Citadel, while the 78th and 79th Ranger Battalions were on outposts 10 kilometers west of the marines. South of the marines, on the high ground at Fire Support Base Lion—also called Nui Gio—was the 51st Infantry, 1st Division, with two of its battalions.

General Diem's responsibility began southwest of his 51st Infantry, which was attached to Colonel Tri's command. The 3d ARVN Infantry Regiment, with two battalions, held the high ground around Fire Support Base Birmingham, above the Song Huu Trach, south of Hue. East of the 3d Infantry, the 54th Infantry with two of its battalions defended the Mo Tau sector, while the reinforced 1st Infantry Regiment extended the line southeast to the Nui Bong area. The 1st Infantry had, in addition to its own three battalions, one battalion of the 51st Infantry, a company of M-48 tanks, and a troop of armored personnel carriers. The 15th Ranger

Group, with its three battalions and one battalion of the 3d Infantry, dug in on the hills above Highway 1 west of Phu Loc District Town. The 258th Marine Brigade, with two battalions, was also near Phu Loc Town, while the 914th RF Group of three battalions guarded the Hai Van Pass.

Shortly after General Truong returned from Saigon on 20 March he learned that the situation in northern Quang Tin, which had been bleak on 16 March when the enemy pounded Thang Binh District Town with artillery and overran outposts southwest of the village, now looked better. Two battalions of the 3d ARVN Division, sent from Quang Nam Province, joined two RF battalions in a counterattack causing high enemy casualties in tough fighting east of Thang Binh.

The prospects in Tam Ky, however, were not so favorable, despite the efforts of the 2d ARVN Division to concentrate forces there for its defense. The city was struck by heavy rocket fire on 21 March. On that day, the 4th Infantry Regiment moved its command post to Tam Ky from Quang Ngai, the 1st Battalion, 6th Infantry, moved in from Binh Son District, and the 916th RF Group headquarters moved down from Thang Binh with the 135th RF Battalion.

The situation in Quang Ngai Province was becoming desperate although elements of the 4th ARVN Infantry succeeded in opening Highway 1 in Binh Son District. But west of Binh Son, the NVA struck the long column of refugees and military fleeing from Tra Bong; the 69th Rangers were ambushed and dispersed. The NVA attack south of Duc Pho cut Highway 1, isolating Sa Huynh and the two battalions defending it, the 70th Ranger and 137th RF Battalions. The next day, General Truong gave General Nhut authority to consolidate his forces anyway he could to preserve combat strength.

After NVA tanks and infantry had crossed the cease-fire line in Quang Tri Province on 19 March, they rolled steadily south against the disintegrating resistance of the territorials until they reached the My Chanh Line at the boundary of Thua Thien Province. Here the advance halted while the attackers waited for the next phase to begin. It started west and south of Hue early on the morning of 21 March when the lead battalions of the 324B and 325th NVA Divisions, together with the independent Tri-Thien Regiment, with heavy artillery support, assaulted RVNAF positions from the Bo Corridor to Phu Loc. Heavy artillery fire fell on Hue.

The My Chanh line was quiet, and the attacks against the Marines in the Bo Valley were repulsed with heavy enemy losses. But the Phu Loc sector, taking the brunt of the attack by the 324B and 325th Divisions, began to crumble early. In the area of the 1st ARVN Infantry, the 18th NVA Regiment, 325th Division, supported by the 98th Artillery Regiment, took Hill 350 and drove on to assault Nui Bong. Although the mountain changed hands three times that afternoon, the 2d Battalion, 1st ARVN Infantry, controlled it on 22 March. Other formations of the 325th, notably the 101st Regiment, forced the 60th Ranger Battalion, 15th Group, from Hill 500 west of Phu Loc, and supporting artillery interdicted Highway 1. A stream of refugees began piling up along the road northwest of Phu Loc. By evening, however, one lane was opened for traffic to Da Nang.

To the west, in the hills around Mo Tau, the 271st Independent Regiment and the 29th Regiment of the 304th Division, both operating under the 324th Division, attacked the 54th ARVN Infantry and were repelled. A prisoner from the 271st said that casualties in his regiment were very heavy, that the 9th Battalion was nearly destroyed.

NVA attacks continued all along the Thua Thien front on 22 March. An ARVN counterattack to recapture Hill 224, a key position in the Mo Tau sector, failed. The population of Hue had declined to only 50,000, and the Hai Van Pass was clogged with desperate people trying to escape. Da Nang was inundated by a tragic flood of humanity. City police on 21 March estimated more than 100,000 refugees, and they were still coming. The ministerial delegation promised by Prime Minister Khiem finally arrived on the 22d, but it could offer little help since there was not enough rice to be bought on the Da Nang market.

The official count of refugees in Da Nang, based upon police registrations, was 121,000 by nightfall on 23 March. The unofficial estimate by the U.S. Consul General was 400,000. All the necessities of life were missing or rapidly disappearing: food, sanitation, housing, and medical care. On 24 March, the government began moving refugees south on every available boat and ship. Thousands made it, but many more did not. Fortunately, NVA attacks in Quang Nam Province were largely blunted by the 3d ARVN Division and territorial troops; security, although relative, was better in Da Nang than anywhere else in Military Region 1.

Southwest of Tam Ky in Quang Tin Province, the 2d Battalion, 5th ARVN Regiment, had been in heavy combat since 12 March. Starting the campaign with 350 men, the battalion on 22 March was down to only 130, after heavy casualties and many desertions. General Nhut replaced it with the 2d Battalion, 4th Infantry, committing the 4th Infantry Regiment southwest of Tam Ky together with two battalions of the 5th Regiment and a company of tanks and sending the 1st Battalion, 6th Regiment, from Tam Ky to assist in the defense of Chu Lai. The 12th Ranger Group remained on Tam Ky's northwest perimeter.

The final NVA assault on Tam Ky began on 24 March. Sappers breached the perimeter and by mid-morning were in the center of the city, blowing up the power plant. Artillery fire was intense all along the line and by noon tanks and infantry broke through an RF battalion and the 3d Battalion, 5th Infantry. That afternoon the city was lost, and General Truong ordered General Nhut to pull his forces out of Tam Ky and assemble them for the defense of Chu Lai. By this time, however, General Nhut no longer had enough control of the situation or of his units to comply fully with these orders. He managed to get the headquarters and one battalion of the 4th Infantry, plus some scattered fragments of other 4th Regiment units, moving toward Chu Lai that evening. Two battalions of the 5th Regiment, scattered in the assault also, were assembling for the march south. Units on the northwest perimeter including the dispersed 12th Ranger Group and the staff of the deputy commander, 2d Division, were forced to withdraw north toward Quang Nam, making it to Fire Support Base Baldy just inside the Quang Nam boundary on Route 1.

General Truong also ordered the evacuation of all forces in Quang Ngai Province; they were also to assemble for the defense of Chu Lai. The feasibility of this task was strained by NVA sappers who blew an important bridge on Highway 1 between Quang Ngai and Chu Lai.

Meanwhile, north of the Hai Van Pass, territorials on the My Chanh Line withdrew without orders on 23 March. The front in the Nui Bong-Truoi River sector stabilized, however, and ARVN engineers blew the bridge on Highway 1 east of Loc Son to prevent NVA tanks from advancing toward Hue from Phu Loc. On 24 March, after receiving the report of the collapse of the My Chanh line, General Truong met with his commanders—General Thi, Maj. Gen. Lan, Maj. Gen. Hoang Van Lac, (deputy commander of Military Region 1), and 1st Air Division commander, Brig. Gen. Nguyen Duc Khanh.

The 913th RF Group had started the unauthorized withdrawal from the My Chanh, and the territorials refused to stop at the next delaying position near Phong Dien District Town. The 913th's pullout caused some panic among other forces, and a general rout developed. I Corps officers attempted to rally the troops at the Bo River. The mass desertion was not motivated by fear of the enemy but by the soldiers' overwhelming concern for the safety of their families in Hue.

General Lac reported that Da Nang was close to panic also, with more than 300,000 refugees jamming the streets. Air Vietnam had scheduled all the special flights it could, but its bookings were solid through June.

At 1800 on 24 March, General Truong ordered General Thi to begin the evacuation of all troops defending Hue. All forces north and west of Hue would assemble at Tan My, the port of Hue northeast of the city, cross the narrow channel to Phu Thuan and march southwest down Vinh Loc Island. Crossing the mouth of Dam Cau Hai Bay on a pontoon bridge to be constructed by ARVN engineers and moving along the beach to Highway 1, they would cross over the Hai Van Pass and on to Da Nang. No trucks, tanks, or guns could make this march; all would have to be disabled or destroyed. The 1st ARVN Division would protect the column by blocking in Phu Thu District.

By the time these orders were issued, what was left of the population of Hue was streaming toward Tan My to take any available boat or ship out of Thua Thien Province. I Corps Forward, commanded by General Thi, established its command post in Tan My, together with the command posts of the Marine Division and the 147th Marine Brigade. The 7th Marine Battalion deployed there to secure the port and the command posts. The 1st Division withdrew from the Troui-Nui Bong sector. The 15th Ranger Group, which had held the Troui River for the 1st Division, pulled back to Phu Bai with heavy casualties. The 54th Infantry Regiment withdrew from the Mo Tau sector to Camp Eagle, southeast of Hue near Highway 1. The 3d ARVN Infantry withdrew from its forward positions on the Son Hue Trach and assembled in Nam Hoa, south of Hue. The 51st Infantry pulled back and located just west of the city while the division headquarters and the 1st Infantry, which had suffered moderate casualties in the Nui Bong sector, were around Hue.

Just as the withdrawal was well under way, General Truong was visited by a delegation of officers from the JGS, carrying orders to release the Marine Division immediately for the defense of Saigon. Pointing out that he could not defend Da Nang without the marines, General Truong objected. The JGS suggested giving up Chu Lai and sending the 2d Division to Da Nang. General Truong issued the order to the 2d Division but still insisted that Da Nang could not be held without the Marine Division; by the time he recovered what was left of the 1st and 2d Divisions, neither would be combat effective.

The sealift from Chu Lai would begin after dark on 25 March on LSTs (landing ship tank) en route from Saigon. Boats committed to the withdrawal of forces in Thua Thien Province would also assist at Chu Lai. While the shipping converged on Chu Lai, the battered 6th Infantry, 2d ARVN Division, was fighting its way toward Chu Lai from Quang Ngai. The Quang Ngai province chief and his staff, unable to break through the NVA units on the road to Chu Lai, went by boat to Ly Son Island.

As an embattled column of soldiers and refugees struggled north on Highway 1 north of Quang Ngai

City, dead and wounded littered the road, a scene reminiscent of the carnage on the same highway in Quang Tri during the 1972 offensive. Once the sealift from Chu Lai began, panic took over as soldiers fought for places on the first boats. Sufficient order was restored, however, to move about 7,000 soldiers up to Da Nang. The remnants of the 4th Infantry and the almost nonexistent 6th Infantry were regrouped on Ly Son Island while the 12th Ranger Group, down to only 500 men, and the few remaining soldiers of the 5th Infantry, were assembled near Da Nang.

The situation in Da Nang on 26 March was approaching chaos, but the 3d ARVN Division still held in Dai Loc and Duc Duc Districts against mounting pressure. Early that morning, 14 NVA heavy rockets struck a refugee camp on the edge of Da Nang Air base killing and wounding many civilians, mostly women and children. Morale in the 3d ARVN Division was plummeting, and distraught soldiers deserted to save their families in Da Nang. Population control was almost totally absent in the city; more than 2,000,000 people were in the streets trying to gather their families and escape. Police desertions mounted, and those who remained found it nearly impossible to function while bands of armed soldiers, beyond the control of military police, roamed the streets. There were even some instances of shooting between soldiers and police.

The withdrawal from Thua Thien Province began in a rather orderly fashion. The 258th Marine Brigade linked up with the 914th RF Group on Vinh Loc Island to cross the narrow channel over to Loc Tri in Phu Loc District. But the bridge to be installed by ARVN engineers never got there; engineer boats were evidently commandeered by other military units attempting to escape. The withdrawing forces crossed anyway, using local fishing boats. General Truong flew over the column making its way down the long stretch of Vinh Loc Island and noted that the only apparent disciplined, cohesive units were marines. The rest was a mob.

Delayed by heavy seas on 25 March the 147th Marine Brigade left Tan My the next day for Da Nang. Also on 26 March, the marine battalion of the 258th Brigade holding the Phu Gia Pass—a short, twisting defile about 15 kilometers east of Phu Loc District Town—came under attack. With the enemy approaching the Hai Van Pass from the north and Vietnamese Navy boats breaking down faster than they could be repaired, General Truong stopped the sea movement of forces and equipment from Hue. Further, because he had been unable to reinforce Da Nang with adequate strength from the 2d ARVN Infantry Division, he elected to concentrate the recoverable elements of the Marine Division at Da Nang.

On the afternoon of the 27 March, VNAF pilots destroyed four enemy tanks attacking near Fire Support Base Baldy. Although the NVA broke off the attack, and the 3d Division battalions held their positions, it was apparent that the 3d Division would not be able to contain NVA attacks in the outlying districts of Quang Nam. General Truong therefore ordered a withdrawal to a shorter line within artillery range of the center of Da Nang. Attempts to hold that line failed as large numbers of 3d Division soldiers deserted to save their families. With defeat imminent, General Truong shipped all organized forces, mostly marines, out of Da Nang toward Saigon. Then he and most of his staff left; some of them, General Truong included, had to swim through the surf to the rescuing fleet of boats. Da Nang, the last enclave of South Vietnam presence in Military Region 1, belonged to the NVA by nightfall on 30 March.

Binh Dinh

While the furious battle raged in Darlac Province, and three NVA divisions attacked the out-gunned and out-manned 23d ARVN Division, the 22d ARVN Division, under Brig. Gen. Phan Dinh Niem, continued to fight in Binh Dinh Province. Although the 22d was unable to break the hold of the 3d NVA Division on terrain controlling Highway 19 through the An Khe Pass, ARVN soldiers and artillery and VNAF air strikes inflicted heavy losses on the enemy. In the early days of the engagement, General Niem expected the high casualties would sooner or later cause the 3d Division to withdraw. He did not, however, anticipate the precipitous turn of events in the rest of Military Region 2, which, in effect, made futile the gallant performance of his division in Binh Dinh.

The initial onslaught of the 3d NVA Division at the An Khe Pass and against Binh Khe succeeded in driving ARVN defenders, primarily territorials, from positions overlooking the pass and guarding the bridges. In some cases territorials withdrew without putting up much resistance. By the time General Niem had enough battalions in position to counterattack, the enemy had exploited his early gains and had major elements of all three regiments of the 3d NVA Division—the 2d, 12th, and 141st—plus sappers, artillery, and supporting local units, concentrated at the mouth of the Vinh Thanh Valley, between the An Khe Pass and Binh Khe. (See Map 19.)

On 10 March, as the 320th NVA Division entered Ban Me Thuot, General Niem had three of his four regiments committed between An Nhon, where Highway 19 leaves Highway 1, and the eastern end of the Anh Khe Pass. The 1st and 2d Battalions, 47th Infantry, at the eastern entrance of the An Khe Pass, fought off repeated attempts by battalions of the 2d and 141st NVA Regiments to drive them from the field. On 11 March the 3d Battalion, 47th

Infantry, was airlifted to Binh Khe District Town, completing the deployment of this regiment. The 927th RF Group still held positions inside the pass but could not control the road. Its 209th RF Battalion was overrun on 11 March, and its 218th RF Battalion, with its companies spread thinly through the pass, was extremely vulnerable.

The 42d ARVN Infantry, with its command post in Binh Khe, was attacking west along Highway 19 to attempt a link-up with the two beleaguered battalions of the 47th. The 41st ARVN Infantry, having moved from Bong Son on 8 and 9 March, to An Son on Highway 19, was to secure the line of communication west toward Binh Khe and to protect Phu Cat Air base.

The fourth regiment of the 22d ARVN Division, the 40th, remained in northern Binh Dinh Province, holding the entrance of the An Lao Valley and guarding the Phu Ku Pass on Route 506 north of Phu My.

By 11 March, the 1st and 2d Battalions of the 2d NVA Regiment had been badly hurt by ARVN artillery and VNAF air strikes. The 7th Battalion, 141st NVA Regiment, had been driven across the confluence of the Con and Dong Pho Rivers with two of its companies virtually annihilated. The 3d Battalion, 2d Regiment, and the 5th Battalion, 12th Regiment, were also hit hard. But truckloads of ammunition and replacements kept rolling down the Vinh Thanh Valley and the dead and wounded made the return trip to the NVA base areas north of Vinh Thanh.

On 13 March, a representative of the Defense Attache Office visited forward positions of the 22d ARVN Division. His report reflected the general confidence and optimism in General Niem's command. Heavy attacks of five NVA battalions against the 1st and 2d Battalions, 47th Infantry, had been repulsed, though four successive commanders of the 2d Battalion had been killed in action since 4 March. Now commanded by a captain, the battalion was down to half strength and was withdrawn to the division base camp for refitting. Without its 2d Battalion, the 47th Infantry was to attack the enemy in the eastern portal of the An Khe Pass, and link up with the RF still in the pass. The 927th RF Group, under the operational control of the 47th Infantry, had its command post west of the pass at An Khe and companies of its understrength battalions, the 209th, 217th, and 218th, on outposts through the pass. When the command post of the 218th RF Batttalion and one of its companies were overrun on 12 March, the 47th Infantry appeared unlikely to break through to the pass in time to find any RF positions intact. The 218th reorganized, and maintained some positions at the west end of the pass, but on 17 March it was again under attack by the 5th Battalion, 12th NVA Regiment.

The fighting was intense between the eastern end of the pass and Binh Khe during the period between 15 and 17 March. The 42d ARVN Infantry was attempting to dislodge three battalions of the 3d NVA Division which were occupying the high ground near the eastern end of the pass. Despite killing nearly 500 enemy in two days, the 42d made no real progress. Its commander was wounded twice but remained on duty. Meanwhile, the 41st ARVN Infantry moved up to south of Binh Khe District Town.

General Niem withdrew the two remaining battalions of the 47th Infantry and sent them to northern Binh Dinh Province to relieve the 2d and 3d Battalions, 40th Infantry, which General Phu had ordered to Khang Duong in Khanh Hoa Province. After the 2d Battalion, 47th Infantry, finished refitting at the division base camp, he planned to send it north to replace the 1st Battalion, 40th Infantry, which would then become division reserve.

With only two regiments available and no reserve, General Niem decided on 17 March he could not open the An Khe Pass and ordered his battalions to hold in place. Although several thousand civilians and several hundred territorial troops at An Khe were cut off from Qui Nhon, there was no longer any compelling military reason to pursue the attack. The exodus from the highlands was already under way along the jungle track called Route 7B.

By 19 March, the NVA controlled the pass westward nearly to the outskirts of An Khe. By 22 March, the 5th Battalion, 12th NVA Regiment, was inside An Khe; all ARVN resistance there ended, and over 5,000 people were struggling south over rural roads and trails, trying to escape to Qui Nhon. On 24 March, the 42d ARVN Infantry pulled back along Route 19, east of Binh Khe, and the 41st Infantry assumed the defense of Binh Khe.

That same day, the long-expected NVA assault on Binh Khe began, and the 41st and 42d ARVN Regiments were cut off. The 3d NVA Division then pushed its 141st and 12th Regiments (except for the 5th Battalion still at An Khe) eastward toward Phu Cat. Meanwhile, the B3 Front's 95B Regiment, having marched east from Pleiku along Route 19, joined the 2d NVA Regiment for the continuation of the attack on the 42d ARVN Infantry east of Binh Khe.

But the 41st and 42d ARVN Regiments did not wait for the reinforced attack. Instead, on 27 March, they broke out and attacked eastward toward Qui Nhon, taking with them over 400 territorials rescued by helicopter the day before from the An Khe area. As the 41st and 42d Regiments dug in for the defense of Qui Nhon, orders arrived from Saigon to evacuate what remained of the 22d Division. Military Region 2 was virtually lost.

As NVA attacked Phu Cat Air base on 31 March, the VNAF flew out about 32 aircraft, leaving about 58, mostly disabled or destroyed, on the ground. On 1-2 April, about 7,000 troops of the 22d Division and Binh Dinh territorials boarded Vietnamese Navy craft at Qui Nhon and sailed for Vung Tau. Enemy tanks and infantry were in the streets of Qui Nhon.

Khanh Hoa—the End in MR 2

The 23d ARVN Division counterattack from Phuoc An had been decisively defeated when General Dung committed his 10th Division, up from Quang Duc. Survivors of the 23d Rangers, territorials, and civilians who escaped from Darlac streamed eastward across the plateau along Route 21. The military men were assembled at Khanh Duong, the last district on the high plain before the highway twisted down through the Deo Cao (M'Drak) Pass to the coastal hills and lowlands of Khanh Hoa Province. (See Map 19.)

The Deo Cao Pass was the obvious place for a defensive stand to protect Nha Trang, the site of the headquarters of Military Region 2, II Corps, the headquarters of the Navy's Second Coastal Zone, and 2d Air Division. Nha Trang also held the ARVN Noncommissioned Officer Academy, and Lam Son, a major national training center, was nearby. North of Nha Trang, Route 21 joined National Route 1 at Ninh Hoa. West of Ninh Hoa, midway between the ocean and the hills of Khanh Duong District, was the large training center of Duc My, site of the Ranger Training Center and the ARVN Artillery School. Thus, with its military concentration and population, the Nha Trang-Ninh Hoa area was the last vital enclave in Military Region 2. Without it, a return to the highlands was virtually impossible. If it could be held, NVA divisions could be prevented from rolling down Highway 1 to Saigon.

Most of the survivors from Darlac were moved on past Khanh Duong by road and helicopter, the Rangers to Duc My for regrouping, the 23d Division soldiers to Cam Ranh and Lam Son. A forward headquarters of the 23d Division was established at Khanh Duong to command the forces assigned to defend the pass: the 3d Airborne Brigade, pulled from its ships at Nha Trang after being dispatched for Saigon from Quang Nam, and the headquarters and two battalions of the 40th Infantry, 22d Division, from Binh Dinh Province.

The 10th NVA Division took up the pursuit after Phuoc An and closed rapidly on Khanh Duong. The 40th ARVN Infantry pushed west of the town to meet the advancing 10th NVA Division. The 3d Airborne Brigade dug in on the high ground in the pass, behind the 40th Infantry. On 22 March, the leading battalions of the 10th NVA Division, with tanks supporting, blasted into Khanh Duong and the two battalions of the 40th ARVN Infantry were forced to withdraw through the 3d Airborne Brigade.

A network of logging roads traversed the dense, steep forests of western Khanh Hoa Province. If blocked by the 3d Airborne in the pass on Route 21, the NVA could send a large force south, bypassing the Airborne, and approach Nha Trang from the west through Dien Khanh District. To guard against this threat, the 40th was withdrawn to Duc My, then sent south to eastern Dien Khanh to prepare positions generally astride local Route 420, which led due east into Dien Khanh and on into Nha Trang. The 40th was reinforced with one RF battalion and supported by one 155-mm. and two 105-mm. howitzers.

Long range reconnaissance patrols were sent into the forest south of Khanh Duong to try to detect any significant enemy force moving south toward Dien Khanh. Nothing of any size was detected, although some ominous signs of recent heavy traffic were reported.

In the Deo Cao Pass, with forward positions at Chu Kroa Mountain, a prominent peak over 3100 feet, the 3d Airborne Brigade dug in to await the 10th NVA Division, whose 28th Infantry Regiment and tanks were already in Khanh Duong. A local RF battalion was in the pass south of the Airborne Brigade. The 34th Ranger Battalion, 7th Ranger Group, which had fought its way through the gauntlet of fire on Route 7B, was protecting the northern approach to Ninh Hoa at the Deo Ca Pass.

With the Airborne still holding on Route 21, General Phu announced on 29 March new command responsibilities in what was left of his military region. General Niem, commanding the 22d Division, was responsible for Binh Dinh and Phu Yen Provinces. Qui Nhon, the last enclave in Binh Dinh, fell on 2 April. He controlled for a brief period the 96th Battalion, 21st Group, which had fought at Ban Me Thuot and regrouped to fight again at Tuy Thoa in Phu Yen Province.

The mountain provinces of Tuyen Duc and Lam Dong Districts were the responsibility of Maj. Gen. Lam Quang Tho, commandant of the Military Academy, Vietnam's West Point, at Dalat. In addition to the territorials, General Tho had some of the survivors of the 24th Ranger Group who had marched through the mountains after the fall of Quang Duc.

Brig. Gen. Le Van Than, the Deputy Commanding General of Military Region 2, was sent to Cam Ranh. He would defend the Cam Ranh Special Sector, Ninh Thuan and Binh Thuan Provinces. He was also to re-form the 23d Infantry Division out of the 4,900 troops mustered at Cam Ranh.

The most critical mission, the defense of Khanh Koa Province, fell to Brig. Gen. Tran Van Cam, in command the 3d Airborne Brigade, the 40th Infantry, the 34th Ranger Battalion, and territorials. But before General Cam could move from Phu Yen Province, where he was controlling the eastern end of the exodus on Route 7B, the 10th NVA Division attacked the 3d Airborne in the Deo Cao Pass on 30 March. Supported by the 40th Artillery Regiment and with two company of tanks attached, elements of the 28th and 66th Regiments the next day surrounded the 5th Airborne Battalion, at that time reduced by casualties to 20 percent strength.

The 3d Airborne Brigade was deployed in depth from Chu Kroa Mountain south for about 15 kilometers along the high ground over the highway. Heavy enemy fire knocked out 5 of 14 armored personnel carriers supporting the brigade, and the three 105-mm. howitzer batteries in the force had to move to the rear, setting up near Buon Ea Thi where, unfortunately, they were beyond supporting range of the forward Airborne positions. The collapse of the Airborne defense proceeded very rapidly afterwards. At Buon Ea Thi elements of the 10th NVA Division outflanked Airborne positions along the road and struck the 6th Airborne Battalion. Although the troopers knocked out three T-54 tanks, they could not hold. With the brigade split at Buon Ea Thi, a rapid withdrawal was imperative to conserve what was left of the decimated force.

The 3d Airborne Brigade, less than one fourth of its soldiers still in ranks, marched back through Duc My and Ninh Hoa and stopped in a narrow defile where National Route 1 edged along the beach below Hon Son Mountain, just north of Nha Trang.

The 10th NVA Division was close behind. On 1 April, NVA tanks rolled through Duc My and Ninh Hoa and headed for Nha Trang. The American Consul General and his staff left Nha Trang by air for Saigon, the II Corps staff drove south to Phan Rang, the defeated remnants of the Airborne, Rangers, territorials, and 40th Infantry followed. The VNAF evacuated Nha Trang Air Base at 1500 and all flyable aircraft were flown out. On 2 April, NVA tanks entered the city.

The momentum of the NVA advance was such that a defense at Cam Ranh was no longer feasible. Recognizing this, the JGS authorized the immediate evacuation of all that remained of II Corps through that port, and by 2 April, the evacuation was in full swing.

17

The Last Act in the South

Tri Tam and Tay Ninh

The 1975 Communist offensive was coordinated country-wide. The NVA troops of COSVN struck their first major blow of the campaign at Tri Tam, the district seat of Dau Tieng District at the southwestern edge of the Michelin Plantation. West of Tri Tam, across the Saigon River, local Route 239 passed through another large plantation, Ben Cui, before it joined local Route 26 (LTL-26), which ran northwest into Tay Ninh City and southeast to the ARVN forward base at Khiem Hanh. All traffic to Tri Tam had to pass over Routes 26 and 239, and by outposts manned by Tay Ninh territorials. Tri Tam was defended by three RF Battalions and nine PF platoons. III Corps had anticipated the attack on Tri Tam—major elements of the 9th NVA Division had been observed concentrating north of the town—so the province chief reinforced the garrison with two additional RF companies on 10 March. (Map 20)

The attack on Tri Tam began at 0600 on 11 March with an intense artillery and mortar bombardment, followed by an assault by T-54 tanks and infantry. But the success of the attack was assured by the earlier severing of the line of communication; at 0330, NVA infantry and tanks overran an RF outpost on Route 239 about 10 kilometers west of Tri Tam.

The province chief reacted by sending two RF battalions east along Route 239 toward Ben Cui, but they were stopped by heavy fire short of the lost outpost. NVA tanks were already in the Ben Cui Plantation. Meanwhile, as the day wore on in embattled Tri Tam, the territorial defenders held on, destroying two T-54s in the town. The main attack was coming from the east, and the ARVN soldiers blew the bridge on Route 239 east of the town. Fighting raged through the night, and as dawn broke on 12 March, ARVN territorials still held Tri Tam. The 95C and 272d NVA Regiments, and at least a company of tanks, supported by a regiment of artillery, continued the attack that day and eliminated the last resistance in Tri Tam.

Meanwhile, the ARVN III Corps commander had dispatched another relief column toward Tri Tam. Task Force 318, composed of tanks and armored personnel carriers from the 3d Armored Brigade, with the 33d Ranger Battalion attached, was stopped by heavy B-40 and 130-mm. gunfire before it could reach Tri Tam. Three officers, including a company commander, were among the heavy casualties in initial fighting near Ben Cui.

With Tri Tam in its possession, the NVA now controlled the Saigon River corridor from its beginning, near Tong Le Chon, to the ARVN outpost at Rach Bap in the Iron Triangle. The ARVN base at Kheim Hanh was now within easy range of NVA artillery. Khiem Hanh's principal mission was to prevent major enemy units from closing on Routes 22 or 1 (QL-22 and QL-1) near the critical river port and road junction at Go Dau Ha. Tri Tam was thus the first important objective in a campaign to isolate Tay Ninh Province from Saigon. On the eve of the assault on Tri Tam three main force Tay Ninh NVA battalions, the D-14, D-16, and D-18, with support from the 101st NVA Regiment and the 75th Artillery Division closed Highway 22 between Go Dau Ha and Tay Ninh City. The 75th Artillery Division had five regiments operating in Tay Ninh for this campaign, and the 377th NVA Antiaircraft Artillery Division had about 15 antiaircraft battalions, some providing direct support for infantry.

While the NVA Tay Ninh battalions blocked Highway 22 north of Go Dau Ha, the 6th and 174th Regiments, 5th NVA Division, attacked out of Cambodia and struck the ARVN base at Ben Cau, northwest of Go Dau Ha between the international boundary and the Song Vam Co Dong. Initial assaults were repulsed, and two PT-76 tanks were destroyed. When two large concentrations of tanks were sighted west of Go Dau Ha on 12 March, fighter-bombers destroyed eight and damaged nine, losing three aircraft in the engagement. Ben Cau, however, fell on 14 March as defending territorials pulled back toward Go Dau Ha.

Ben Cau was only one of eight outposts west of the Song Vam Co Dong that came under heavy attack on 12 March. Most of them held out until the night of 13 March, but nearly all were in enemy hands by the next day.

General Toan, commanding III Corps, reacted to the crisis developing at Go Dau Ha by reinforcing at Khiem Hanh and along Routes 1 and 22. He deployed the 3d Armored Brigade, with its three battalions, reinforced by the 64th and 92d Ranger Battalions (from Tan Uyen District, Bien Hoa) and the 48th Infantry, 18th Division, reinforced with armored personnel carriers (from Corps reserve in Long Binh, Bien Hoa) to Khiem Hanh and Go Dau

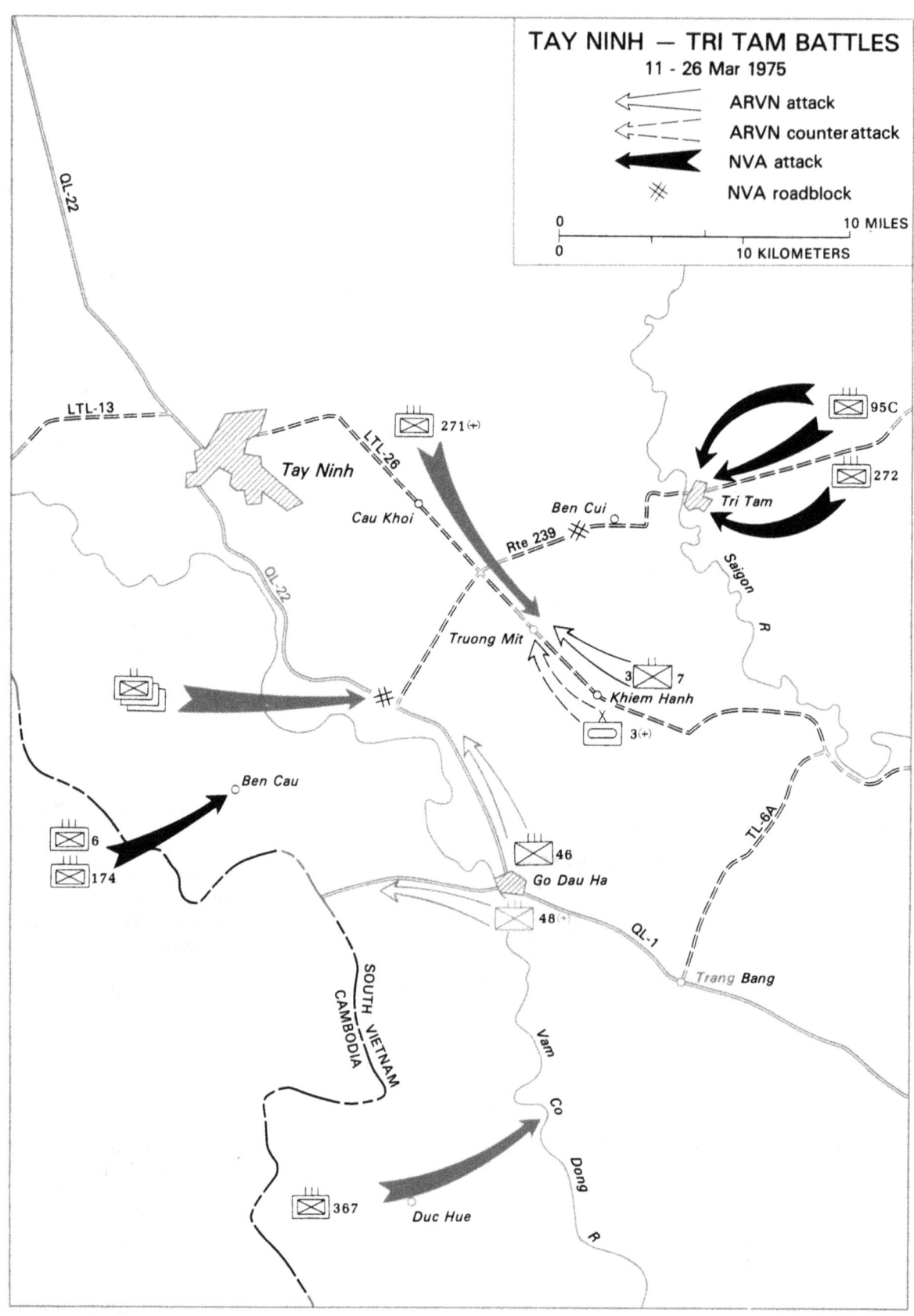

Map 20

Ha. He also pulled the 3d Battalion, 7th Infantry, from the 5th Division at Lai Khe and sent it to reinforce Khiem Hanh.

While a battalion of the 48th ARVN Infantry attacked west out of Go Dau Ha to clear Route 1 to the Cambodian frontier, the 46th Infantry attacked north along Route 22 to help territorials clear the road to Tay Ninh against heavy resistance and intense artillery fire. Antiaircraft fire was so heavy in the area that General Toan was unable to land his helicopter at Go Dau Ha on 13 March. Route 22 between Go Dau Ha and Tay Ninh remained closed.

Long An

Connecting Saigon with the delta of Military Region 4, Route 4, even more critical than Route 22, was also threatened by the widespread offensive in Military Region 3. This highway passed through the rich, densely populated rice lands and pineapple farms of Long An Province on the boundary between the two military regions. Long An territorials were among the best troops in the country, and they gave a good account of themselves in initial fighting with local main-force battalions in early March, although suffering high casualties. Recognizing the need to keep Highway 4 open, the JGS had given General Toan two battalions of Marines, the 14th and 16th, which comprised the new 4th Brigade, to stiffen the defense in Long An. The Marines and RF operated well together and secured Long An throughout March.

The Eastern Front

While General Toan was committing more than half of his corps to the western flank, an NVA offensive erupted in the east and center. Available ARVN forces were inadequate to cope with the widespread attacks. Since the enclaves at An Loc and Chon Thanh in Binh Long were of no further military or political value, the ARVN battalions could be withdrawn and used to bolster the hard-pressed defenses throughout the region. Furthermore, a new enemy division was discovered near Chon Thanh—the 341st from just above the 17th parallel. To save the Rangers and territorials in An Loc and Chon Thanh, General Toan began an evacuation on 18 March. Among the first to be moved were 12 105-mm. howitzers, while 5 of the 155-mm. howitzers had to be destroyed because the VNAF did not have heavy-lift helicopters to move them. But despite the appearance of the 341st NVA Division and a new regiment—the 273d Infantry from North Vietnam's 4th Military Region—the most critical threat developed not in the center but on the eastern flank.

Just before the NVA attacked, the 18th ARVN Division was spread out. The 1st Battalion, 43d Infantry, was securing Route 20 north of Xuan Loc, the capital of Long Khanh Province. The Regiment's 2d Battalion was south of Dinh Quan, and the 3d Battalion was in Hoai Duc District Town in Binh Tuy Province. The 52d Infantry, minus its 3d Battalion on Route 1 between Bien Hoa and Xuan Loc, was in Xuan Loc with elements operating northwest of the town. The 48th Infantry was still attached to the 25th Division in Tay Ninh Province.

The NVA forces of Nambo began the Long Khanh–Binh Tuy campaign with strong attacks against ARVN positions on the two principal lines of communication in the region, Highways 1 and 20 (QL-1 and QL-20), striking outposts, towns, bridges, and culverts north and east of Xuan Loc. On 17 March, the 209th Infantry Regiment and the 210th Artillery Regiment, 7th NVA Division, opened what was to become one of the bloodiest, hardest fought battles of the war, the battle for Xuan Loc. The 209th struck first at Dinh Quan, north of Xuan Loc, and at the La Nga bridge, west of Dinh Quan. Eight tanks supported the initial assault on Dinh Quan, and NVA artillery fire destroyed four 155-mm. howitzers supporting the territorials. Anticipating the attack, General Dao, commanding the 18th ARVN Division, had reinforced the La Nga bridge the day before, but the intense fire forced a withdrawal from the bridge. After repeated assaults, the 209th NVA Infantry penetrated Dinh Quan, and the 2d Battalion, 43d Infantry, as well as the RF battalion were forced to withdraw with heavy losses on 18 March. (Map 21)

The day before, the 3d Battalion, 43d Infantry, killed 10 enemy in heavy fighting northwest of Hoai Duc. At the same time another outpost of Xuan Loc District, Ong Don, defended by an RF company and an artillery platoon, came under artillery and infantry attack. The NVA assault was repulsed with heavy losses on both sides, and another RF company, sent to reinforce, ran into strong resistance on Highway 1 west of Ong Don. North of Ong Don, Gia Ray on Route 333 was under attack by the 274th Infantry Regiment, 6th NVA Division. The 18th ARVN Division headquarters therefore realized that two NVA divisions, the 6th and the 7th, were committed in Long Khanh. While the battle raged at Gia Ray, another post on Highway 1 west of Ong Don came under attack. Meanwhile, a bridge and a culvert on Highway 1 on each side of the Route 332 junction were blown up by NVA sappers. Thus, all ARVN forces east of Route 332 were isolated from Xuan Loc by formidable obstacles and enemy road blocks.

North from Xuan Loc, on Route 20, hamlets along the road were occupied in varying degrees by enemy soldiers, and the territorial outpost far to the

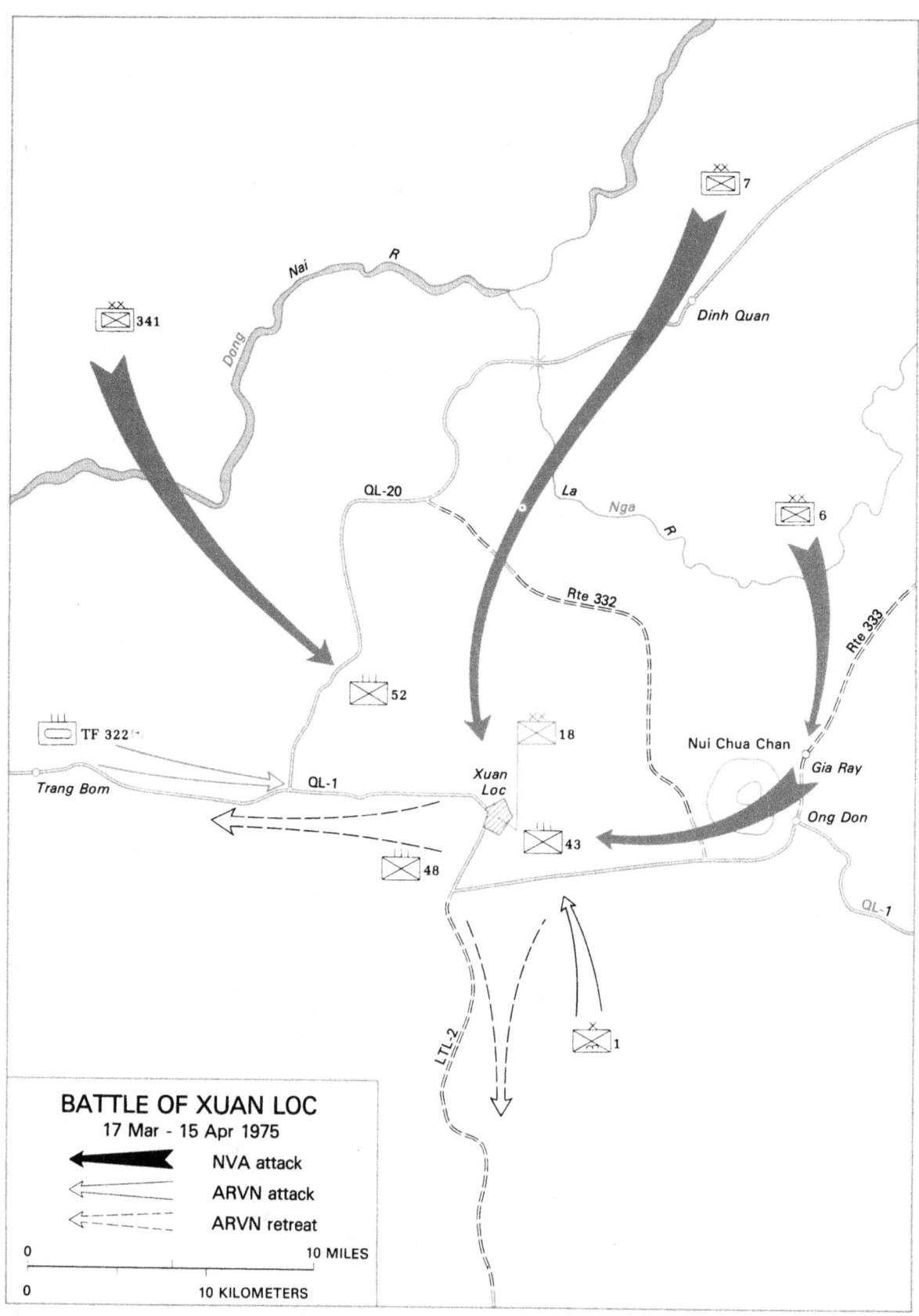

northeast near the Lam Dong boundary was overrun. General Dao decided to counterattack up Route 20 with his 52d Infantry, minus one battalion but reinforced with the 5th Armored Cavalry Squadron from Tay Ninh Province. The regiment was ordered to clear the road as far as Dinh Quan. But the attack quickly stalled as it met heavy resistance well short of its objective.

Evidences of increasing heavy NVA commitments in Long Khanh flowed into III Corps headquarters in Bien Hoa. The 141st Regiment, 7th NVA Division, had apparently participated in the attack on Dinh Quan. Hoai Duc was overrun by the 812th Regiment, 6th NVA Division, while that division's other two regiments, the 33d and 274th, seized Gia Ray. The ARVN outpost on the conical peak of Chua Chan, standing 2200 feet above Xuan Loc and providing excellent observation, also fell to 6th NVA Division forces and Xuan Loc itself began to receive artillery fire, including 105-mm. General Toan responded to the burgeoning threat on his eastern flank first by sending the 5th Armored Cavalry Squadron and then one battalion of the 48th Infantry from Tay Ninh to Long Khanh.

Tay Ninh

The rest of the 48th Infantry was still heavily engaged near Go Dau Ha. The 3d Battalion made contact with an NVA Company west of the Song Vam Co Dong on 17 March, killed 36, and captured a number of weapons. Meanwhile, on Route LTL-26 east of Tay Ninh City, an outpost at Cau Khoi, manned by the 351st RF Battalion, was overrun. (See Map 20.)

The outer defenses of Tay Ninh and Hau Nghia began to crumble rapidly after the fall of Cau Khoi. Following an intense bombardment by 105-mm. howitzers and 120-mm. mortars, the 367th Sapper Regiment, 5th NVA Division, seized Duc Hue on 21 March, advancing enemy-held positions to the Vam Co Dong southwest of the critical village of Trang Bang on Route 1. If the NVA could take Trang Bang, Go Dau Ha and all of Tay Ninh would be isolated.

North of the airfield at Tay Ninh was the main outpost on local Route 13. The NVA struck here on 22 March, and the defenders withdrew to an alternate position, Mo Cong II, to the south. The attack continued on the 23d, and Mo Cong II was lost, compressing the perimeter north of Tay Ninh to less than 10 kilometers deep.

The eastern prong of the NVA offensive in Tay Ninh was still pressing against the vital position at Khiem Hanh. Just north of Go Dau Ha, Khiem Hanh was an essential strongpoint preventing the enemy from reaching Route 1 from the north and seizing Go Dau Ha and Trang Bang. From Trang Bang, Route 1 provided a high-speed approach through the 25th ARVN Division base at Cu Chi and on to Tan Son Nhut and Saigon. On 23 March, ARVN soldiers and tanks made contact with NVA forces near Truong Mit, northwest of Khiem Hanh. The enemy had advanced through Cau Khoi on Route 26. A major battle developed on the 24th and casualties were very heavy on both sides. The 3d Battalion, 7th ARVN Infantry, 5th Division, attached to the 25th Division, lost over 400 men killed, wounded, and missing, and the attacking 271st Regiment, 9th NVA Division, left nearly 200 dead. The artillery, tank, and automatic weapons fire was intense; the 271st was supported by a battalion of 37-mm. antiaircraft weapons used as field artillery, as well as by the 42d Artillery Regiment with its 85-mm. and 122-mm. guns. The decimated battalion of the 7th Infantry was withdrawn from combat and sent to the regimental base at Phu Giao in Binh Duong Province. As a precaution against being flanked by a strong attack down the Saigon River corridor, General Toan sent the 2d Battalion, 7th Infantry, to reinforce Rach Bap, the western anchor of the Iron Triangle.

Then General Toan asked the Chief of the JGS, General Vien, for an Airborne brigade to use in a counterattack at Truong Mit. General Vien refused the request; he could not agree to further dissipating the small general reserve while General Toan still had a few uncommitted units. Therefore, on 25 and 26 March, the hard-fighting 3d Armored Brigade, together with elements of the 25th ARVN Division, attacked the 271st NVA Regiment at Truong Mit and succeeded in reoccupying the position. Losses were again heavy on both sides. General Toan then reinforced the defense by sending the headquarters and two battalions of the 48th Infantry, 18th Division, to Khiem Hanh.

Binh Long

The planned ARVN withdrawal from its two enclaves in Binh Long Province was still under way when the 9th and 341st NVA Divisions attacked at Chon Thanh on 24 March. A battalion of T-54 tanks accompanied the assault, and in the first day's action seven of these were destroyed by the VNAF and the defending 31st and 32d Ranger Groups. The Chon Thanh position held firm, and the evacuation from An Loc continued without interruption. On the 26th, the 341st NVA Division attacked again, apparently trying to retrieve disabled tanks, but was repulsed again. By 27 March the withdrawal from An Loc was complete, and the 31st and 32d Ranger Groups still held Chon Thanh. The 341st NVA Division, reinforced with the 273d Independent Regiment from North Vietnam, got set for yet another assault on the strongpoint. Following a

3,000-round bombardment by 105-mm. and 155-mm. howitzers and 120-mm. mortars, a regimental-sized force supported by an understrength tank battalion attacked Chon Thanh on 31 March. Again the determined Rangers drove back the attackers, destroying 11 more tanks. But it was clear that if the fighting strength of the two Ranger groups was to be preserved to fight again, they would have to pull out of Chon Thanh. Accordingly, on 1 April the VNAF saturated the assembly areas and bivouacs occupied by the badly mauled 341st Division with 52 sorties; under the cover of this attack, the 32d Ranger Group was airlifted out of Chon Thanh and set down in another hot spot, Khiem Hanh in Tay Ninh Province. That night, three battalions of the 31st Rangers and the one remaining RF battalion began a withdrawal to Bau Bang and Lai Khe, taking artillery and light tanks with them.

The northern defenses of Saigon were now about 14 kilometers north of the 5th Division base at Lai Khe, but this was not really a significant change since the fire base at Chon Thanh had long been isolated by strong NVA blocking positions on Highway 13 around Bau Long. Nevertheless, the arc of main force NVA divisions was pressing ever closer to the heart of the nation, and the vital lines of communications to the outer defenses were either severed or dangerously threatened.

Washington

As the ring of Communist divisions tightened around Military Region 3, the flow of military assistance to Vietnam was slowed by events in Washington. Members of a House caucus on 12 March voted 189 to 49 in favor of a resolution opposing more military aid for either Cambodia or Vietnam before the end of the fiscal year. The next day, 13 March, the House Foreign Affairs Committee rejected a compromise proposal that would have provided some additional aid.

The Ford administration pressed ahead with efforts to convince Congress that additional assistance was essential to the survival of Vietnam and that the Congressional approach to this issue was the cause of the Vietnamese decision to withdraw from the highlands.

Although the decline of U.S. support was the crucial factor in the overall disaster in Vietnam, the proximate cause of the highlands debacle was the failure of the corps commander to accept an intelligence estimate and to fight the battle of Ban Me Thuot with forces available. Then, when he followed this critical mistake with two others—inadequate planning and execution of the counterattack from Phuoc An and a horribly mismanaged withdrawal down Route 7B—he started the entire nation on a downhill slide that not even the valor of thousands of loyal officers and soldiers could reverse.

The Defense and State Departments were receiving reasonably accurate daily reports from the DAO and Embassy in Saigon, but most journalists in Vietnam were having difficulty discovering what was really happening on the battlefield, and it has been argued that military assistance could not have stemmed South Vietnam's decline because the South Vietnamese lacked the will to fight. As in every war, some units performed poorly under attack, but the growing certainty that defeat was imminent, now that the United States had cut back military assistance, was at the root of the decline in combat efficiency. Yet there were countless instances of great tenacity in defense and awesome valor in combat, even in the face of overwhelming enemy firepower and numbers.

As the end of March approached, reports from Saigon told Washington that a crisis was rapidly approaching. Blocked by Congress from providing relief in the form of additional assistance, President Ford dispatched General Frederick C. Weyand, U.S. Army Chief of Staff and the last senior American commander in Vietnam, to Saigon to make a personal assessment of the situation. General Weyand arrived on 27 March. He met with Ambassador Martin and Maj. Gen. Homer D. Smith, Jr., the Defense Attache, as well as with President Thieu and General Vien. He also met privately with the author on two occasions before his departure to brief President Ford on 3 April. In these two meetings, the author stressed the point that although a decision to renew the U.S. commitment to Vietnam was essential to its survival, it was already too late for this alone. A U.S. military effort was required and, as a minimum, would have to include U.S. airpower against NVA formations, bases, and lines of communication in South Vietnam. The author followed his discussions with General Weyand with a written summary of his assessment on 31 March, quoted in its entirety:

1. SUMMARY.

a. The GVN has a new strategy. It calls for defending from Khanh Hoa south and what remains of GVN MR's 3 and 4 (see map). This strategy might have held the promise of success

(1) if GVN forces in MR's 1 and 2 could have been extracted more or less intact for employment in the south;

(2) if the enemy forces committed, or to be committed, against the new, truncated South Vietnam were not in the process of being heavily reinforced and

(3) if the U.S. commitment to the defense of South Vietnam were expressed in the form of immediate deliveries of essential equipment, ammunition and supplies; followed by assurances that this support would be continued for as long as the North's aggression makes it necessary.

b. With regard to factor (1), above, of all the major formations in MR's 1 and 2, only the 22d Division stands a chance to be extracted intact (as of now, a slim chance).

c. With regard to factor (2), the enemy *has* reinforced in GVN MR 3. Reinforcement continues and the potential for more is very real.

d. Factor (3) has not been decided, but defeat is all but certain within 90 days without it. Because of factors (1) and (2), material and political support may no longer be enough to provide a successful defense. Only the application of U.S. strategic airpower in South Vietnam can give this any degree of probability.

2. RVNAF CAPABILITY TO REGROUP.

a. Assuming necessary equipment is available and that the 22d ARVN Division is able to disengage from Binh Dinh, the following can be ready for redeployment in 20 to 40 days:

(1) The 22d Division (4 regiments). (now questionable)
(2) A three-brigade Marine Division.
(3) One other division.
(4) Three to four Ranger groups.
(5) Seven direct support and two general support artillery battalions.
(6) Four armored cavalry squadrons.

b. One and probably two additional divisions should be ready for deployment in about 120 days.

c. Although the three existing ARVN divisions in MR 4 have been fairly aggressive, they are seriously understrength. Upgrading the divisions by reassigning territorial forces is underway. Territorial forces themselves, the key to Delta security, must continue to be upgraded.

d. Summary: Success in the above regroupments would provide ARVN with 13 divisions (or division equivalents of ARVN/Rangers/VNMC) within 40 days; an additional two divisions in four months.

3. ENEMY STRENGTH AVAILABLE FOR MR 3 AND 4 OPERATIONS.

We believe that the 341st NVA Division has arrived, that the 320 B Division is currently enroute to MR 3 and that two other divisions currently deployed in the south or from the NVN reserve will also move to MR 3 in the next one to three months. The movement of units to MR 3 will allow the use of infiltrators to rebuild units and the allocation of significantly larger numbers of infiltrators of GVN MR 4. Because of difficulties in terrain and supply, we do not believe that a new NVA division will try to move into MR 4.

4. NEAR TERM PROJECTION.

a. If the Communists allow the GVN six to eight weeks before initiating major attacks in MR 3, the GVN possibly could organize a successful defense. The principal battle area will probably be Tay Ninh Province where the Communists have a three-division equivalent of infantry/sappers plus 20 artillery battalions and three armor battalions. They might deploy one of the newly arriving divisions to the Tay Ninh area.

b. Opposing are two ARVN division equivalents, plus territorials. Probably another four or five ARVN regimental equivalents would be moved to this front, but regiments of the 5th and 18th ARVN Divisions now in Tay Ninh would return to their normal AO's. Thus, in Tay Ninh (with overlap in Hau Nghia) the GVN would probably deploy a total of seven or eight infantry regiments, supported by an armor brigade. An airborne brigade could be reserve. The GVN's ability to withstand and neutralize expected heavy artillery and AAA fire will be key factors.

c. In central MR 3, the Communist threat may have temporarily lessened (since the 7th and 9th Divisions are deployed to eastern and western MR 3 respectively) but the 341st Division and another division will probably be committed to strike southward in southern Binh Duong Province. These forces would be supported by about eight battalions of artillery and several tank battalions. The three regiments of the 5th ARVN Division would probably require support by at least another regiment and an airborne brigade. ARVN could probably withstand a two-division attack although they would probably abandon Phu Giao.

d. In eastern MR 3, elements of the 6th and 7th NVA Divisions, possibly reinforced by another division, will probably continue attacks to overrun Xuan Loc and establish a lodgment north of Bien Hoa. ARVN has only the 18th Division in this area. To meet this threat and also to open routes 1 and 20 will probably require another ARVN division equivalent. The GVN must also protect the water routes to Saigon and the key LOC's from the Delta.

e. The movement of either the 7th or 9th ARVN Division out of the northern Delta would result in Route 4 being closed, and the departure of the 21st Division would endanger Can Tho and open up the southern Delta to nearly unlimited Communist gains.

f. The fighting will be very heavy with high GVN losses which will have to be replaced immediately. The GVN will have trouble matching Communist 130-mm. artillery and VNAF effectiveness will be limited by Communist AA weapons. The last two reconstituted divisions will have to be ready for commitment by early summer. If heavy rains occur early this year, Communist elements in the Parrot's Beak will probably have to withdraw from forward positions. This would allow the GVN time to regroup and refit units in Tay Ninh and Kien Tuong Provinces.

5. CONCLUSION.

It is possible that with abundant resupply and a great deal of luck, the GVN could conduct a successful defense of what remains of MR's 3 and 4. It is extremely doubtful that it could withstand an offensive involving the commitment of three additional Communist divisions in MR 3 without U.S. strategic air support in SVN. With defeat in MR 3 tantamount to defeat of the GVN, South Vietnam would be almost certain to fall within three to six months (or sooner)

By this time agencies in Washington were equally gloomy. A DIA assessment of 3 April gave south Vietnam only 30 Days.

Meanwhile, a misconception was spreading in Washington that the current reverses in Vietnam did not involve much combat. In his news conference of 2 April, Secretary of Defense Schlesinger spoke of "relatively little major fighting." He repeated this view on "Face the Nation" on 6 April: "It is plain that the great offensive is a phrase that probably should be in quotation marks. What we have had here is a partial collapse of South Vietnamese Forces, so that there has been very little major fighting since the battle of Ban Me Thuot, and that was an exception in itself."

General Smith could not let that impression stand and sent a message to CINCPAC and a number of addressees in Washington attempting to correct the record:

On the contrary, there was heavy fighting all along the coastal plain and in the foothills from south of Phu Bai to Khanh Duong in Khanh Hoa Province.

In the hills south of Phu Bai, the 1st ARVN Div repelled numerous heavy two-divisional attacks and even gained some lost positions before it finally was ordered to withdraw because its northern flank was exposed.

In Phu Loc District just north of Hai Van Pass on QL-1, an overpowering attack by up to two regiments of the enemy's 325th Div forced outnumbered ARVN defenders back from their positions and severed the line of communications.

These attacks could not be described as "little fighting."

In the An Khe/Binh Khe region along QL-19 in Binh Dinh Prov, the ARVN 22d Div defended strongly with great perserverence against determined and heavy NVA attacks. Outflanked, outgunned, and eventually cut off, the 22d fought its way back to the beaches and was eventually evacuated. This was a long and heavy battle.

Likewise along QL-21, the ARVN fight at Khanh Duong was a battle of major proportions. The NVA 10th Div employed three and possibly four infantry regiments to overcome the ARVN Defenses. The ARVN 3d Airborne Bde was reduced to only 600 men by the time it was able to fight its way out of encirclement and regroup intact near Phan Rang.

Respectfully recommend that you suggest to the Chairman that he acquaint the Secretary with these facts so that an accurate representation of what has occurred might be presented to the American people. There is a "great offensive" underway.

Meanwhile the bloody struggle continued as the GVN assembled its few forces recovered from the defeated regions, reorganized and redeployed for the final stand.

Reorganization and Redeployment

The stiff ARVN resistance and strong local counterattacks in Tay Ninh, Binh Duong, Binh Long, and Long Khanh Provinces caused the NVA to pull back and regroup. Meanwhile, a relative calm settled over the battlefields during the first week of April, and the ARVN exploited the opportunity to reorganize shattered units arriving from the north and redeploy forces to meet the certain resumption of the NVA attacks.

On 1 April, General Toan commanding III Corps, returned the headquarters and two battalions of the 48th Infantry to their parent division, the 18th, from Tay Ninh Province. The regiment moved to the Xuan Loc area but sent its 2d Battalion down to Ham Tan on the coast of Binh Tuy Province to secure the city and port while large numbers of refugees poured into the province from the north. About 500 troops, survivors of the 2d ARVN Division, were among those arriving from Military Region 1. When reorganized and reequipped, they would take over the security mission in Ham Tan.

The 52d ARVN Infantry, 18th Division, meanwhile was pressing forward on Route 20 south of Dinh Quan and in sharp fighting on 1 April killed over 50 NVA troops. The other regiment of the 18th was fighting east along Route 1, near Xuan Loc and in contact with a major enemy force.

General Toan also returned the battalions of the 7th Infantry fighting on Highway 1 near Go Dau Ha to their division at Lai Khe. This left the defense of Tay Ninh Province and its line of communication to the 25th ARVN Division, elements of the 3d Armored Brigade, Rangers, and territorials.

Shocked by the necessity to withdraw the RVNAF from the northern military regions, intensely preoccupied with the fierce battles raging within sight and sound of the nation's capital, unable to obtain reliable information concerning the status of withdrawing and decimated units, and further concerned with enormous personal and family tragedies that permeated all their thoughts, the officers of the Joint General Staff neglected until very late—and until prodded into action by the Defense Attache Office—the planning required for reorganizing and reequipping shattered units whose members were pouring into the southern ports.

Colonel Edward Pelosky, Chief of the Army Division, DAO, took the lead in encouraging the Central Logistics Command to develop the plan. On 27 March, General Khuyen, the Chief of Central Logistics Command, as well as the Chief of Staff of the JGS, approved a plan setting forth a schedule for the reconstitution of units from Military Regions 1 and 2 and including the requirements for replacement vehicles, weapons, and all types of equipment and supplies. Unfortunately, General Khuyen had been unable to secure from the personnel, plans, and operations sections of the JGS information concerning personnel strengths and unit dispositions, and the plan was therefore not only incomplete but unworkable. Data concerning units available for reconstitution and information on the numbers and locations of officers, noncommissioned officers, and soldiers for these units were therefore not even considered. The unreality of the plan was aggravated by the fact that it was predicated on the availability of funds in a supplemental appropriation and the significant absence of a clear, fully coordinated statement of priorities. But despite these shortcomings, planning and reorganization went ahead, and the Army Division of the DAO reprogrammed unused funds and called forward as much supplies and equipment as could be realistically obtained under the severe funding limits and reasonably employed upon arrival.

By 29 March no contributions to the plan had been received from the J-1, J-3, or J-5 although the Operations and Plans Division, DAO, made another appeal for full JGS participation. Again, although these other staff sections were not represented, joint South Vietnamese–American planning continued, the U.S. side being represented by the DAO, and the South Vietnam side being represented by only RVNAF logisticians from the Central Logistics Command. The revised plan was approved by General Khuyen on 1 April and published as a JGS document, signed by General Vien, on 5 April. By this time, the JGS had become fully involved, and the plan included an activation schedule that dealt with the availability of units, personnel, and equipment as well as an obvious, although unstated, concept for deployment after reconstitution.

By 2 April, the survivors of the Marine Division were disembarking at Vung Tau. Under the leadership of their commander, Maj. Gen. Bui The Lan, they were moved into the 4th Battalion's camp there for processing and reorganization. In all, of the 12,000 Marines who had been deployed in Military Region 1, about 4,000 were at Vung Tau. The equipment for a reorganized division was on hand in the Saigon–Long Binh area, but moving it to Vung Tau would be difficult. A more serious problem was the shortage of infantry leaders; 5 Marine battalion commanders and 40 company commanders had been killed in action during March and April. Nevertheless, the division rapidly took shape. One brigade of three rifle battalions and one artillery battalion was ready to receive equipment in three days. Ten days later, an additional similar brigade was formed.

Meanwhile, on 1 April the evacuation of Nha Trang came to an end when NVA troops moved in to occupy the harbor. But the evacuation of Cam Ranh Bay continued. Farther south, Phan Rang Air Base came under increasing enemy pressure, and its evacuation began, although the VNAF's 6th Air Division continued limited operations from the field. A forward command post of III Corps was established at Phan Rang under Lt. Gen. Nghi and on 7 April the 2d Airborne Brigade was flown into Phan Rang. On 9 April, the brigade moved to Du Long, north of Phan Rang on Highway 1, to block the 10th NVA Division, moving south from Cam Ranh in the face of intensive air strikes by the VNAF. Meanwhile, Phan Thiet, the town and air base southwest of Phan Rang in Binh Thuan Province, was under attack. Binh Thuan territorials fought extremely well, but they could not hold for long against large NVA formations approaching through the hills from the north. Highway 1 would be cut in Binh Thuan and Phan Rang isolated. Phan Thiet on 12 April came under heavy attack, and its three RF battalions and 20 PF platoons were overwhelmed at the end of a determined defense.

As of 11 April, about 40,000 troops from Military Regions 1 and 2 had reported to training camps or had been reassigned to units in Military Region 3. The 2d ARVN Division, which had been assembled at Ham Tan, had grown to 3,600, including two RF battalions assigned to it from Gia Dinh Province. Its reconstituted 4th Infantry Regiment was sent to Phan Rang, relieving the 2d Airborne Brigade, but the balance of the division would have four light battalions when the outfitting was complete. Regrettably, the 4th Infantry was destroyed for the second and final time in the defense of Phan Rang.

The 3d Division on 11 April had about 1,100 men at Ba Ria, Phuoc Tuy, and would be assigned another 1,000 soon, but it was short all types of weapons and equipment. The 1st Division was also at Ba Ria but with only two officers and 40 men. Near Ba Ria, at Long Hai, was the 23d Division with about 1,000 men and 20 rifles.

The 22d ARVN Division, whose tough resistance in Binh Dinh was one of the most remarkable feats of determination, courage, and leadership of the war, was in better shape than other divisions. At the Van Kiep National Training center at Vung Tau, the 22d had about 4,600 men, one-third of whom were territorials from Military Region 2. It was short of all categories of equipment, however; although it had enough artillerymen to man three battalions, it had no howitzers. Nevertheless, sparsely equipped and barely organized, it was ordered to deploy to Long An Province on 12 April.

A critical battle was shaping up in Long An as the 5th NVA Division, moving down from Svay Rieng Province in Cambodia, launched a strong attack near Tan An with its 275th Regiment on 9 April. The Long An territorials fought well and were reinforced from IV Corps by the 12th Infantry, 7th ARVN Division. Against light losses, the 2d Battalion, 12th Infantry, killed over 100 members of the 275th NVA Regiment, forcing its commander to ask for reinforcement. The next day, the NVA attacked the Can Dot airfield in Tan An and, after closing Highway 4, were driven off with heavy losses by Long An territorials. In two subsequent days of heavy fighting, the three Long An battalions, the 301st, 322d, and 330th, accounted for over 120 enemy killed and 2 captured. Meanwhile, the 12th ARVN Regiment, fighting two regiments of the 5th NVA Division, killed over 350 and captured 16. Into this combat the JGS sent the reconstituted 22d Division, the first battalion arriving on 12 April and two more following later. To provide unity of command against the 5th NVA Division, the JGS adjusted the boundary between III and IV Corps, giving the Tan An battle area to IV Corps.

The NVA kept the pressure on Bien Hoa and Tay Ninh Provinces, primarily with frequent heavy attacks by fire during the first two weeks of April. Rockets hit Bien Hoa Air Base and the military training center and schools at Bear Cat, while Tay Ninh was struck repeatedly by 105-mm. and 155-mm. artillery as well as rockets. The ARVN clung to Khiem Hanh, maintaining control of Trang Bang and Cu Chi, but skirmishes with enemy forces were frequent. Meanwhile, the final major battle of the war was taking shape at Xuan Loc.

Xuan Loc

The South Vietnamese fought splendidly at Xuan Loc, but the NVA high command used the battle as a "meat grinder," sacrificing its own units to destroy irreplaceable ARVN forces. Meanwhile I Corps could slip to the west and set the stage for an assault on Saigon.

After the first NVA attempt to seize Xuan Loc had been soundly repulsed, the 341st NVA Division on 9 April began a second assault on the town, defended by the 18th ARVN Division. Infantry and tanks were preceded by an artillery bombardment of about 4,000 rounds, one of the heaviest in the war. With tanks firing down the streets, hand-to-hand fighting developed in a fierce battle that lasted until dusk. By that time, the 43d ARVN Infantry had driven most of the shattered enemy force from the town, and the 52d ARVN Infantry base on Route 20 was still in friendly hands. The enemy resumed the attack the next day, this time committing the 165th Regiment of the 7th NVA Division along with regiments of the 6th and 341st NVA Divisions. Again the attack failed. (See Map 21.)

West of Xuan Loc, between Trang Bom and the intersection of Highways 1 and 20, the ARVN 322d Task Force and 1st Airborne Brigade (two battalions) were trying to force their way east against stiff resistance.

The NVA attacked the rear base of the 52d ARVN Infantry on Route 20, the 43d Infantry in the Xuan Loc, and the 82d Ranger Battalion on 11 April, the third day of the battle. At that time, the battalion of the 48th Infantry securing Ham Tan went back to Xuan Loc, and the 1st Airborne Brigade moved in closer to the town. Task Force 322 was making very slow progress opening the road from Trang Bom to Xuan Loc, and General Toan ordered Task Force 315 from Cu Chi to reinforce.

On the 12th, battalions of the 52d ARVN Infantry were still in heavy fighting north of Xuan Loc, but the town, although demolished, was still held by the 43d ARVN Infantry. NVA losses to that point were probably in excess of 800 killed, 5 captured, 300 weapons captured, and 11 T-54 tanks destroyed. ARVN casualties had been moderate. Most of the 43d ARVN Regiment was holding east of the town; the 48th was southwest; the 1st Airborne Brigade was south but moving north toward the 82d Ranger Battalion; and the 322 Task Force was on Route 1 west of the Route 20 junction, attacking toward Xuan Loc.

With the situation apparently temporarily stabilized, General Smith thought it appropriate to inform Hawaii and Washington that the RVNAF was putting up a determined and so far successful battle for Xuan Loc. He sent a message on "The Battle of Long Khanh" to the Chairman of the Joint Chiefs of Staff, General George S. Brown, on 13 April 1975:

1. We have a victory in the making. In the battle for Long Khanh RVNAF has shown unmistakably its determination, its will and its courage to fight even though the odds are heavily weighted against them. Although the battle may have passed only through Phase 1, we can say without question that RVNAF has won round one.

2. This battle for control of the vital road junction of QL-1 and QL-20 and the province capital at Xuan Loc began on 9 April with a 3,000 round concentration of artillery, rocket and mortar fire. Outnumbered GVN forces were driven from the city and from the many villages and hamlets along QL-20. ARVN quickly counterattacked and by nightfall on the first day of the battle had driven most of the enemy from Xuan Loc, although NVA troops still occupied many hamlets and villages.

3. As the battle progressed, it became clear that the enemy was determined to destroy the defenders and occupy this eastern gateway to Bien Hoa at all costs. By the third day of the battle, elements of three NVA divisions were committed.

4. This morning, the beginning of the fifth day of the battle, ARVN still holds its positions. It has reinforced and now has all regiments of the 18th Div, the 1st Airborne Bde, two Ranger Bns, three RF Bns and two armored task forces in the battle area. ARVN means to stay. VNAF has provided continuous outstanding close support. Enemy losses have been staggering. Even after adjusting for possible double-counting, enemy killed and left on the battlefield exceed 1200. The equivalent of a tank Bn has been wiped out; nearly 30 tanks. Over 200 weapons have been captured including a 37 gun, ten mortars, several recoiless guns and 25 B-40 grenade launchers.

5. The valor and aggressiveness of GVN troops, especially the Long Khanh Regional Forces, is certainly indicative that these soldiers, adequately equipped and properly led, are, man-for-man, vastly superior to their adversaries. The battle for Xuan Loc appears to settle for the time being the question "will ARVN fight."

The message made well the point that the South Vietnamese in Long Khanh were indeed fighting to the death for their country. It was a great cooperative effort between the ARVN and the VNAF that enabled the 18th Division, the 1st Airborne Brigade, and the Rangers to hold on. Two resupply missions were flown into the besieged town; on 12 April, CH-47 helicopters brought in 93 tons of artillery ammunition and followed with 100 tons the next day. Meanwhile, the VNAF reactivated some A1-E fighter-bombers and used a modified C-130 transport to drop 15,000-pound bombs (flown in by the U.S. Air Force) on enemy positions. These airplanes, flying against intense antiaircraft fire, took a heavy toll of the NVA divisions around Xuan Loc.

The NVA assault resumed on 13 April. By this time, seven of the nine regiments of the 6th, 7th, and 341st Divisions had been committed to the Long Khanh battle. The attack began at 0450 against the headquarters and 1st Battalion, 43d ARVN Infantry, and lasted until 0930. When the enemy withdrew, he left 235 dead and about 30 weapons on the field. The attack picked up again at noon and lasted until 1500, but the 43d, with heavy VNAF support held.

Meanwhile, the 1st Airborne Brigade continued to attack north toward Xuan Loc, and Task Force 322, now reinforced by the 315th and 316th Task Forces, struck from the west. VNAF observers had discovered two batteries of 130-mm. guns northeast of Xuan Loc and took them under attack.

The NVA continued sending additional forces into Military Region 3. The I Corps from Thanh Hoa Province in North Vietnam set up its headquarters in Phuoc Long along with the 312th, 320B, 325th, and 338th Divisions. The 312th stayed with corps headquarters in Phuoc Long, but the 320B and 325th moved to Long Khanh where the 325th entered the battle on 15 April. The 10th and 304th Divisions were also on the march toward Saigon from Military Region 2. Aerial photography revealed a major concentration of antiaircraft artillery, including radar-controlled 85-mm. and 37-mm. guns around Don Luan, as well as SA-2 missile tranporters and equipment on Route 14 south of Quang Duc.

The JGS and the ARVN III Corps bolstered the inner defenses of Saigon while the battle continued on the vital eastern approaches at Xuan Loc. General Ba, commanding the 25th ARVN Division, put a forward command post with his 50th Infantry Regiment at Go Dau Ha. In Tay Ninh City he had the 49th Infantry and the headquarters and one battalion of the 46th Infantry. The balance of the 46th was on Route 22 between Tay Ninh City and Go Dau Ha. (Map 22)

The inner defenses of Saigon were manned by territorials and a few regular formations, some of which had been recently reconstituted. Three Ranger groups were on the western approaches. The new 8th Ranger Group had its 1,600-man force near Phu Lam on the edge of Saigon where Route 4 enters the city from the Mekong Delta. Southwest of Phu Lam on Route 4 near Binh Chanh was the 6th Ranger Group, recently reorganized with about 2,600 men. North of the city was the newly organized 9th Ranger Group with about 1,900 men protecting Hoc Mon District only five kilometers north of Tan Son Nhut Air Base. Each group had four 105-mm. howitzers but little fire-direction equipment, and all were short of radios and machine guns. The Rangers and territorials in Hoc Mon intercepted a 100-man NVA group on 14 April, capturing five soldiers from the 115th Sapper Regiment, 27th Sapper Division, and killing 11 others. The sappers were accompanying a special group of terrorists and propagandists whose mission was to start uprisings in Go Vap near Tan Son Nhut. Liberation radio had been calling for popular uprisings since 11 April, but these appeals, like all others in past offensives, were ignored by the population.

The eastern and southeastern approaches to Saigon were anchored at Long Binh by a brigade of marines. The exhausted 18th ARVN Division was falling back from Xuan Loc through Trang Bom toward Bien Hoa City by 15 April, and Long Binh would soon become the front line on the east.

On the west, although Long An territorials and the 12th ARVN Infantry were still holding at Tan An, NVA artillery moved in close enough to Saigon to blast Phu Lam with 122-mm. rockets on 18 April. A large ARVN radio transmitter site was located near the Route 4 road junction at Phu Lam. Two barracks housing the troops and their dependents were demolished. This attack, only seven kilometers south of the Tan Son Nhut runways and the offices of the Defense Attache, emphasized the serious threat to the city. The enemy attack plan called for severing Route 4 near Binh Chanh. Here they would prevent the 7th and 9th ARVN Divisions from moving up Route 4 to assist in the defense of the city, and from Binh Chanh sappers and terrorist teams would infiltrate through Phu Lam to Tan Son Nhut and Saigon.

In Long An Province, the 5th NVA Division persisted in heavy attacks along the old Military Region 3 and 4 boundary, but by 15 April was forced to pull back to the northwest. The 12th ARVN Infantry had inflicted heavy losses on the 6th and 275th NVA Regiments near Tan An. By this time, small, ill-equipped battalions of the reconstituted 41st and 42d Regiments, 22d ARVN Division, had been deployed in Ben Luc and Tan An. But the NVA force was growing rapidly. Elements of five NVA divisions were now in Long An and southwestern Hau Nghia: the 3d, 5th, 8th, and 9th Infantry Divisions and the 27th Sapper Division. Additionally, the 262d Antiaircraft Regiment and the 71st Antiaircraft Brigade had batteries near the Long An-Hau Nghia boundary.

Far to the east and north of the capital, the final battles for Ninh Thuan and Binh Thuan Provinces were being fought. Major attacks by the 3d NVA Division, down from its successes in Binh Dinh Province, began on 14 April against the reconstituted battalions of the 2d ARVN Division, the 31st Ranger Group and the territorials. The attacks were repulsed on the 14th and 15th, but the defenders were finally overwhelmed on 16 April and Phan Rang was lost. The last of the 6th Air Division abandoned the airfield with the remaining flyable airplanes, leaving four AC-119s and two A-37s to the enemy.

Binh Thuan Province held out for two additional days, but Phan Thiet fell on 18 April. Some of the best territorial troops in the country had put up one of the most determined and aggressive defenses of the war.

Xuan Loc was 100 kilometers west of Phan Thiet and it was here that the final decisive battle was still being fought. After a week of the toughest, continuous combat experienced since the offensive began, the 18th ARVN Division had to give ground and fight its way back toward Bien Hoa. The armored task forces on Route 1 had to pull back also; half of their equipment had been destroyed, and the 6th NVA Division was moving north of Route 1 toward Trang Bom. NVA 130-mm. gun batteries were seen in the jungles north of Route 1, also moving toward Bien Hoa and on 15 and 16 April the air base was hit, first by 122-mm. rockets, then by 122-mm. gunfire. The runway had to be closed for awhile on the 15th due to small craters and debris, but the guns on the 16th were more accurate

Vietnam from Cease-Fire to Capitulation

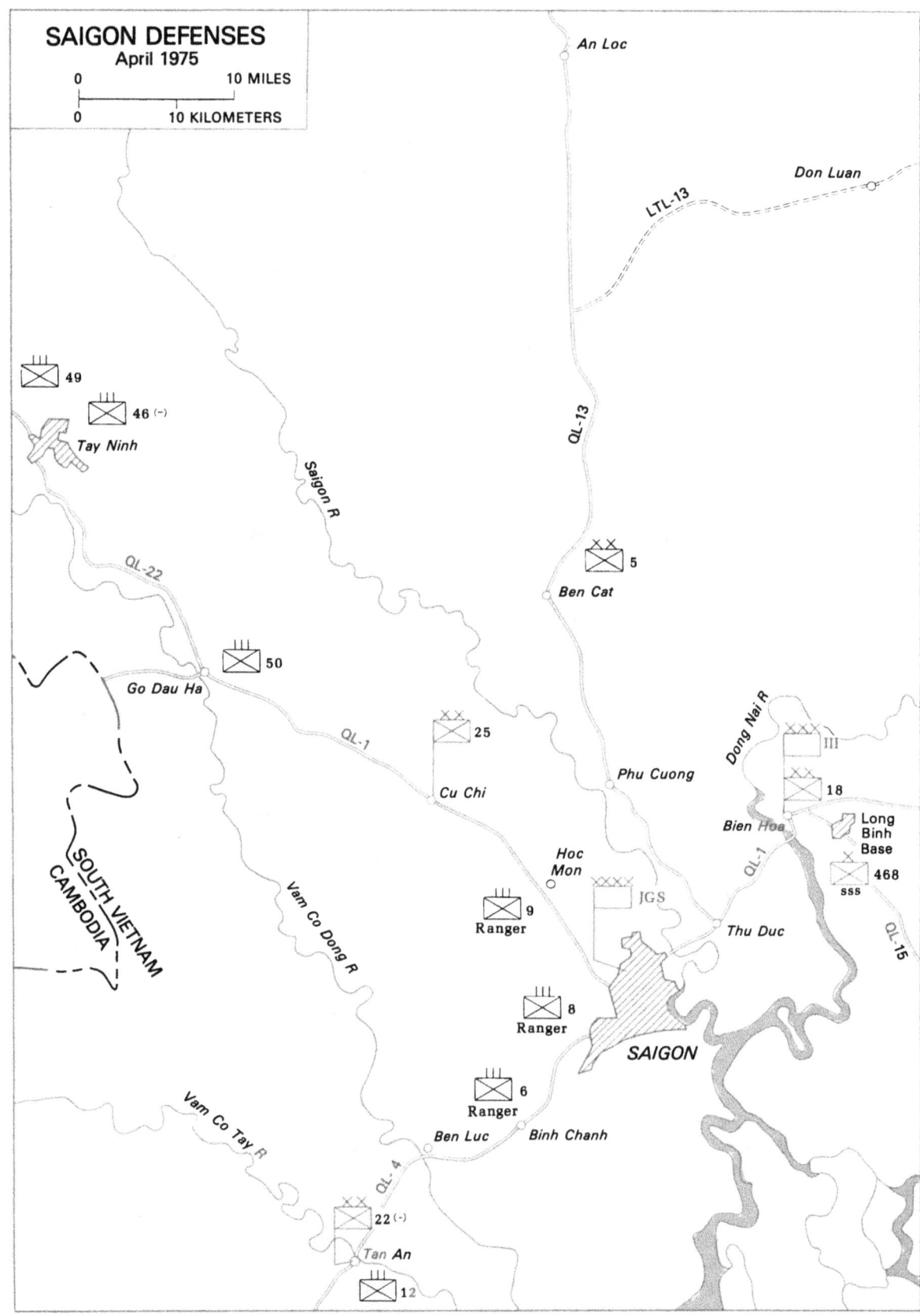

Map 22

than the rockets and damaged 6 F-5s and 14 A-37s. Sappers penetrated the base on the night of the 15th and blew up part of the ammunition storage area. That night also marked the end of the organized defense of Xuan Loc following a furious assault on ARVN positions at the junction of Routes 1 and 20. An artillery bombardment of 1,000 rounds fell on the headquarters and 3d Battalion, 52d ARVN Infantry, an artillery battalion, and elements of the 5th Armored Cavalry Squadron. Four 155-mm. and eight 105-mm. howitzers were destroyed, and the NVA infantry and tank attack forced the battered ARVN force back along Route 1. A general withdrawal began and continued until 20 April, by which time no organized ARVN forces existed east of Trang Bom. Meanwhile, the 1st Airborne Brigade, frustrated in its attack toward Xuan Loc, withdrew through the plantations and jungles toward Ba Ria in Phuoc Tuy Province, where it would defend until South Vietnam capitulated.

The Last Week

An uneasy quiet settled over the battlefields between 20 and 26 April while the enemy made plans, conducted reconnaissance, and issued orders for the final drive. Sixteen NVA divisions were now in Military Region 3 and poised for a three-pronged attack on Saigon.

The Defense Attache Office at Tan Son Nhut had established an evacuation control center on 1 April and had started sending nonessential American civilian employees home on 4 April. On the 20th it began a full-scale evacuation of its personnel, dependents, and Vietnamese civilian employees.

Clinging to the hope that the North Vietnamese might stop the offensive and negotiate a settlement providing for some South Vietnamese representation, President Thieu resigned from office on 21 April. But the removal of this long-trumpeted obstacle to reconciliation of North and South had no discernable effect. The North's successes on the battlefields and the absence of any prospect of U.S. support had left no basis for negotiation. The South no longer had anything to bargain with.

Preparations complete, the NVA resumed the attack on 26 April, with Bien Hoa the focus east of Saigon. The town and air base received heavy artillery fire, and the NVA divisions on Route 1 began moving toward Bien Hoa. South of Long Binh, Route 15 was interdicted, isolating Vung Tau, and Ba Ria fell to the NVA. DAO plans for large-scale evacuation though Vung Tau were abandoned.

The NVA in Long An and Hau Nghia Provinces renewed attempts to dislodge the stuborn ARVN defenses in the west.

On 27 April, Vice President Tran Van Huong, who had succeeded President Thieu, having failed in trying to form a government with which the Communists would negotiate, was succeeded by Duong Van "Big" Minh. But this move was as irrelevant as had been Thieu's resignation.

Early in the evening of the 28th, a flight of A-37s, piloted by VNAF pilots forced into enemy service, bombed Tan Son Nhut Air Base. A number of aircraft were destroyed on the ground, but the field remained operational. The blow was more damaging psychologically than materially, although most Saigonese thought it was an attempted coup d'etat rather than an enemy action. It was the first time airpower had been used against the South and it signalled the beginning of the end.

On 29 April a heavy bombardment of Tan Son Nhut began. Rockets and artillery hit aircraft storage areas and runways, and rockets landed in the DAO compound. Cu Chi was under attack, and NVA sappers and infantry were in Go Vap, just north of Tan Son Nhut. It was clearly the time for the few remaining Americans to leave.

By dawn on 30 April the American evacuation was complete. That morning Duong Van Mính surrendered the country to the North Vietnamese Army.

Note on Sources, Chapters 15–17

General Van Tien Dung's articles on the final offensive set the stage for the action in these chapters. The factual record of the combat actions and order of battle was derived from multiple sources. Principal among them were the following: reports of DAO Regional Liaison Officers in the field, particularly those in Military Regions 1, 2, and 3 who visited units in combat, as well as senior commanders and staff officers; reports of the Consul Generals, particularly those at Da Nang and Nha Trang; reports of offices of the U.S. Embassy, Saigon; notes and recollections of the author, who visited each military region and had conversations with senior commanders and staff officers; DAO fact sheets and assessments prepared for General Weyand, and the author's notes and recollections of meetings with General Weyand.

The Weekly Intelligence Summaries published by DAO and J2/JGS were also used, as were the final DAO Quarterly Assessment and the report of Army Division, DAO.

Generals Vien and Truong read and commented on the deployments, plans, and combat described, and American newspaper accounts were used for statements of U.S. officials concerning the final offensive.

Most of the data on the April reconstitution was derived from the "Army Division Final Report," Vol IX: "Reconstitution of Forces," Defense Attache Office, Saigon, 18 June 1975 (compiled by the

Residual USDAO Saigon Office, Fort Shafter, Hawaii).

Finally, the most important single check on the accuracy of the account of this final offensive was contributed by Colonel Hoang Ngoc Lung, J2/JGS, who corrected several misconceptions and provided invaluable perspectives.

18

Was Defeat Inevitable?

What happened in the last two years of the struggle in Vietnam cannot really be understood in isolation from the many years of war that preceded the final period. Considerable treatment was therefore given to events immediately preceding the Paris agreement, to the balance of forces in the South, to the dispositions of forces following the Communist 1972 offensive, and to the cease-fire landgrab battles. Although measurements of power were not attempted, for the nature of ground combat does not lend itself to such analysis, it was clear that a temporary stalemate had been reached. The South was strong defensively and growing stronger with its newfound confidence, stability, and steadily improving combat efficiency, all brought about largely by the success of the Vietnamization program.

On the other hand, North Vietnam's expeditionary force, although no longer supported by an effective southern guerrilla force and badly battered by the battles of 1972, embarked on an intensive program of reorganization, modernization, and logistical buildup without interference from the United States or South Vietnam. The United States had withdrawn its forces from South Vietnam and that country lacked the military strength to attack the enemy's rear logistical areas and new lines of communications.

Generalizations about the character of the struggle in Vietnam inevitably fail many tests for validity and often lead to less rather than more understanding. That is why so much detail has been included in this account. One generalization, however, seems clear. During the last two years of the war, the South adopted an aggressive defense that strengthened its influence and improved security in the populated regions of the country. Seriously concerned about that success, the Communists responded with plans and operations specifically directed to "defeat pacification."

Although the antipacification plan was a failure, the NVA eliminated step by step isolated government outposts, most of which interfered in some degree with the Communist plan for developing sparsely populated regions and securing the expanded and modernized logistical system supporting the rapidly growing expeditionary force in the South. So, despite some notable Southern gains, as in the Seven Mountains of Chau Duc and the Tri Phap, and in Svay Rieng Province of Cambodia, the South's defenses around major population centers eventually became the forward line of contact.

As outposts fell, the armed forces of South Vietnam benefited in that there were fewer demands placed upon strained logistical and tactical resources. On the other hand, the resources thus freed were insufficient to build up significant reserves. The compression of South Vietnam defenses around the population centers also meant that the advantages of the NVA multiplied. Its heavy artillery came within range of final objectives, its logistical system was able to expand without effective observation or interference, and strategic options increased. It enjoyed the decisive advantage of the ability to mass, with considerable surprise, overwhelming combat power against strategic objective areas. This, essentially, is what happened at Ban Me Thuot.

Yet the outcome could have been different. Unit for unit and man for man, the combat forces of South Vietnam repeatedly proved themselves superior to their adversaries. Missing, however, were inspired civil and military leadership at the highest levels and unflagging American moral and material support. The required leadership was certainly available in the South Vietnamese armed forces, but it was not allowed to surface and take charge in enough situations. The United States might conceivably have responded consistently and more generously had the South Vietnamese been able to demonstrate conclusively the validity of their cause through beneficent and self-sacrificing leadership at the top. But convincing reforms were needed in South Vietnam long before the cease-fire of January 1973 in order to have reversed the momentum of decreasing American support.

Lest the impression be left that the civil and military leadership in North Vietnam was morally superior to that of the South or that the citizens of North Vietnam enjoyed greater freedoms, one need only look at the events that have transpired in the South since May 1975. Even in embattled South Vietnam, the citizenry largely went about its private affairs without interruption or governmental interference, and the rule of law was preserved. But what was missing was a national leader of great stature and strength who was committed to personal sacrifice, willing to get tough with inept or corrupt subordinates, and able to rally the support he would need to stay in office. Such a man did not emerge. But even without strong leadership, substantial

American support for an indefinite period would have made the difference. Given more time, a new generation of younger South Vietnam leaders probably could have produced the leadership to institute the internal reforms so badly needed.

www.ingramcontent.com/pod-product-compliance
Lightning Source LLC
Chambersburg PA
CBHW080544170426
43195CB00016B/2675